OXFORD ENGLISH DRAMA

General Editor: MICHAEL CORDNER

Associate General Editors: PETER HOLLAND · MARTIN WIGGINS

THE NEW WOMAN
AND OTHER EMANCIPATED WOMAN PLAYS

THE 'Woman Question' was the recurrent, the obsessive, subject of late nineteenth- and early twentieth-century drama. This volume contains four of the most interesting examples, three of which appear for the first time in a modern edition. Between them these plays demonstrate the marked shift that took place both in arguments about female emancipation and in the kind of plays that were performed on the English stage of the period. All four dramatists include 'New Woman' characters but whereas these women are variously satirized and problematized in the work of Sidney Grundy and Arthur Wing Pinero, in their Society Plays of the 1890s, only a decade later they are heroized in the plays of Elizabeth Robins and St John Hankin, two of the most stimulating writers of the Edwardian 'New Drama'.

JEAN CHOTHIA is a Lecturer in the English Faculty of Cambridge University and is a Fellow of Selwyn College. Her publications include *Forging a Language: A Study of the Plays of Eugene O'Neill* (1979), *Directors in Perspective: André Antoine* (1991), and *English Drama of the Early Modern Period: 1890–1940* (1996).

MICHAEL CORDNER is Reader in the Department of English and Related Literature at the University of York. He has edited editions of George Farquhar's *The Beaux' Stratagem*, the *Complete Plays* of Sir George Etherege, and *Four Comedies* of Sir John Vanbrugh. His editions include *Four Restoration Marriage Comedies* and he is completing a book on *The Comedy of Marriage 1660–1737*.

PETER HOLLAND is Professor of Shakespeare Studies at the Shakespeare Institute, University of Birmingham.

MARTIN WIGGINS is a Fellow of the Shakespeare Institute in English at the University of Birmingham.

OXFORD ENGLISH DRAMA

J. M. Barrie
Peter Pan and Other Plays

Aphra Behn
The Rover and Other Plays

George Farquhar
The Recruiting Officer and Other Plays

John Ford
'Tis Pity She's a Whore and Other Plays

Ben Jonson
The Alchemist and Other Plays

Christopher Marlowe
Doctor Faustus and Other Plays

John Marston
The Malcontent and Other Plays

Thomas Middleton
*A Mad World, My Masters and
Other Plays*

Arthur Wing Pinero
Trelawny of the 'Wells' and Other Plays

Richard Brinsley Sheridan
*The School for Scandal and
Other Plays*

J. M. Synge
*The Playboy of the Western World and
Other Plays*

John Webster
*The Duchess of Malfi and
Other Plays*

Oscar Wilde
*The Importance of Being Earnest and
Other Plays*

William Wycherley
The Country Wife and Other Plays

Court Masques
ed. David Lindley

Four Jacobean Sex Tragedies
ed. Martin Wiggins

Four Restoration Marriage Comedies
ed. Michael Cordner

Four Revenge Tragedies
ed. Katharine Maus

*The Lights o' London and
Other Plays*
ed. Michael R. Booth

*The New Woman and
Other Emancipated Woman Plays*
ed. Jean Chothia

Trilby and Other Plays
Four Plays for Victorian Star Actors
ed. George Taylor

OXFORD WORLD'S CLASSICS

===

The New Woman

and Other Emancipated Woman Plays

SIDNEY GRUNDY
The New Woman

ARTHUR WING PINERO
The Notorious Mrs Ebbsmith

ELIZABETH ROBINS
Votes for Women!

ST JOHN HANKIN
The Last of the De Mullins

===

Edited with an Introduction and Notes by
JEAN CHOTHIA

Oxford   New York
OXFORD UNIVERSITY PRESS

Oxford University Press, Great Clarendon Street, Oxford OX2 6DP

Oxford New York
Athens Auckland Bangkok Bogota Bombay Buenos Aires
Calcutta Cape Town Dar es Salaam Delhi Florence Hong Kong
Istanbul Karachi Kuala Lumpur Madras Madrid Melbourne
Mexico City Nairobi Paris Singapore Taipei Tokyo Toronto Warsaw

and associated companies
in Berlin Ibadan

Oxford is a trade mark of Oxford University Press

British Library Cataloguing in Publication Data

Data available

Library of Congress Cataloging in Publication Data
The new woman and other emancipated woman plays / edited by Jean Chothia.
(Oxford world's classics)
Includes bibliographical references (p.   ).
Contents: The new woman / Sidney Grundy—The notorious
Mrs Ebbsmith / Arthur Wing Pinero—Votes for women! / Elizabeth Robins—
The last of the De Mullins / St John Hankin.
1. Women—Suffrage—Great Britain—Drama.   2. Suffragists—Great Britain—Drama.
3. Feminism—Great Britain—Drama.   4. Women—Great Britain—Drama.
5. English drama—20th century. 6. English drama—19th century. I. Chothia, Jean.
II. Series: Oxford's world's classics (Oxford University Press)
PR1259.S93N48   1998   822'.8080352042—dc21   97-31284

ISBN 0-19-282427-9

3 5 7 9 10 8 6 4 2

Typeset by Jayvee, Trivandrum, India
Printed in Great Britain by
Cox & Wyman Ltd, Reading, Berkshire

12622709

CONTENTS

v

ACKNOWLEDGEMENTS

I WOULD like to thank the staff of the Manuscripts Department of the British Library and, for assistance with particular notes, Lucy Chothia, Nicholas Cranfield, Mary Doran, Heather Glen, Elsie Duncan-Jones, Chris Greenwood, Nigel Leask, John Ray, and Manuela Tecusan. I am grateful to Michael Cordner for meticulous commentary on text and notes, and to Jane Kingsley-Smith for checking the text.

I am grateful to Mabel Smith and the Trustees of Backsettown for their kind permission to include Elizabeth Robins's *Votes for Women!* in this edition.

This edition is for Sue Spencer, Tamsin Palmer, and Penny Wilson.

J.C.

INTRODUCTION

HOWEVER Ibsen himself may have represented *A Doll's House* (1879) or *Hedda Gabler* (1890), his English contemporaries saw them as works about emancipated women. First produced in England in 1889 and 1891 respectively, and vehemently attacked by conservative critics, they figured in popular imagination as depraved works. Elizabeth Robins was accused by Clement Scott, the leading theatre critic of the day, of having 'glorified an unwomanly woman' in her performance as Hedda.[1] Denunciations in the press linked characters and members of their audiences together as 'desexed . . . the unwomanly, the unsexed females, the whole army of unprepossessing cranks in petticoats . . . educated and muck ferreting dogs . . . effeminate men and male women.'[2]

The association of female emancipation and distorted sexuality was recurrent in the late nineteenth century. Efforts of women towards education and social or economic emancipation were often taken as denials of 'natural' gender roles even by writers otherwise considered advanced. Strindberg, whose *Miss Julie* (1888) was much too shockingly explicit to permit performance on the English stage, makes it clear in the preface to his play that Julie was an example of the emancipated woman, the man-woman, feared by much contemporary medical science and figured in such seemingly advanced works as Kraft-Ebbing's *Psychopathia Sexualis* (1889). Patrick Geddes and J. Arthur Thomson in *The Evolution of Sex* (1889) described men as naturally *katabolic*, active, energetic, variable, and women as *anabolic*, passive, sluggish, and stable, while Havelock Ellis in *Man and Woman* (1894) claimed that biology confirmed man's role as initiating and creative, woman's as nurturing and supportive.

Questions and opinions about female emancipation—rights to education, to earning and retaining one's own income, the ability to make decisions, and, increasingly, the right to participate in democracy by means of the vote—were of pressing interest in the 1890s. They were so because women, albeit mightily slowly, were progressing towards emancipation. In 1894 they gained the right to vote in local government elections. Notable campaigners, such as Annie Besant, were emerging into public life and women such as Beatrice Webb and Charlotte Payne Townsend were prominent in the recently founded Fabian Society.

[1] *Illustrated London News*, 25 Apr. 1891.
[2] Quoted by William Archer, *Pall Mall Gazette*, 8 Apr. 1891.

Somewhat more than 25 per cent of the female population was employed. Although most jobs open to them were menial, the type-writer and the development of large department stores had extended the options. In Lancashire, the cotton industry was relatively stable and well paid. Women who had had access to education, numbers of girls' schools having been established from the 1860s onwards, were increasingly entering the professions, notably teaching and medicine. There were women students in almost all the faculties of English universities and as many as one-third of those graduating from London University were women. Although, notoriously, the vote to enable women to proceed to degrees in Cambridge failed in 1897, they were allowed to attend lectures and to take the examination. After Agnata Ramsay had become the only candidate to reach the first class standard in the Cambridge Classics Tripos in 1887 and, even more startlingly, Philippa Fawcett was placed above the top man in Part I of the Maths Tripos in 1890, the educational success of women students was newsworthy.

Following the introduction of sympathetically represented emancipated woman characters in Sarah Grand's novel *The Heavenly Twins* and George Egerton's *Keynotes* in 1893, came a flood of fictional investigations with such works as Mona Caird's *Daughters of Danaus*, Annie Holdsworth's *Joanna Trail, Spinster*, and Ella Hepworth Dixon's *Story of a Modern Woman* in 1894, and emancipated women also made their appearance among the characters of more established male novelists, George Gissing's *The Odd Women* (1893) and Thomas Hardy's *Jude the Obscure* (1895). The term, 'the new woman', which seems to have been introduced by Grand in 1894,[3] soon became ubiquitous, partly through the efforts of male satirists who were quick to respond to all this activity. Throughout the 1890s, *Punch* both reflected and considerably shaped the habit of addressing female emancipation and educational success as subjects for glorious mirth, while, in September 1894, *The Idler* ran an Advanced Woman number with advice on how to court such creatures and invited eight women of different persuasions to comment on the species. Although much of the humour might seem feeble now, its omnipresence suggests that it answered a need.

Emancipated women had already begun to figure on the stage, usually in comic form. Arthur Wing Pinero's *The Weaker Sex* (1888) and *The Amazons* (1893) make sport with the notion of girls seeking emancipation or being educated as boys. The heroine of W. S. Gilbert's comic opera *Utopia Limited* (1893) is Girton-educated Princess Zara, returned

[3] Sarah Grand, 'The New Aspect of the Woman Question', *North American Review*, 158 (Mar. 1894), 271.

home to reform her father's kingdom (curiously, it was always Girton in comedy, Newnham not really figuring until the more serious representations of the Edwardian period). The pace quickened and the stereotyping hardened with the success of Sidney Grundy's *The New Woman*, which opened on 1 September 1894 and featured a whole set of caricatured proponents of female emancipation: writers of medical tomes, feminist novels, and tracts on marriage. The subplot of Henry Arthur Jones's *The Case of Rebellious Susan*, which appeared later in the autumn of the same year, concerns Elaine, who is described in the stage directions as 'a raw, assertive, modern young lady'. Neurotic and shrill, she is, moreover, accompanied like Grundy's feminists by a parody aesthete, a man of mincing speech and effete manner. Elaine's declaration that she and her like will correct nature draws a much repeated statement from the play's *raisonneur*, Sir Richard Kato:

By changing your sex? Is that what you ladies want? You are evidently dissatisfied with being a woman. You cannot wish to be anything so brutal and disgusting as a man and unfortunately there is no neuter sex in the human species. (Act 3)[4]

Oscar Wilde, not surprisingly wanting to play too, gives new woman traits to both his heroines in *The Importance of Being Earnest* (1895), and Bernard Shaw, having flexed his muscles by introducing the formidably emancipated Julia and setting Act 2 of *The Philanderer* (1893) in 'The Ibsen Club', took the representation a stage further in *Mrs Warren's Profession* later in 1893. With her strong handshake, cigar smoking, and extreme rationalism, Vivie Warren, the co-protagonist, who, being lazy, has settled for *second* place in the Cambridge Maths Tripos, is the type writ large, although her independence and self-sufficiency are clearly offered for admiration by Shaw and the humour is with rather than against her. She remained unknown to the theatre-going world of the 1890s, however, since, although published in 1898, the play, refused a licence, was not performed until 1902, when the Stage Society circumvented the ban by mounting a private performance for its own members in what was known as a 'closed-house' production.

The four plays in this collection all figure emancipated women as central characters. Grundy satirizes them, suggesting that all they really need is the love of a strong man. Pinero, more ambivalent, gives his leading character a certain strength and principle but, to the disappointment of his leading actress, Mrs Patrick Campbell, drives her to penitent retreat to a country vicarage. In contrast with this, only a decade later,

---

[4] Reprinted in Russell Jackson (ed.), *Plays of Henry Arthur Jones* (Cambridge, 1982), 153.

Elizabeth Robins and St John Hankin, like other Stage Society and Court Theatre writers of the Edwardian 'New Drama', heroize their emancipated woman characters. Women characters in three of the plays are 'platform-' or 'public-women', who proselytize for the female cause. Grundy's are writers. Pinero's audience learns that Agnes Ebbsmith, described by one character as having 'Trafalgar Squared' him, gained notoriety speaking in meeting-halls and at Speaker's Corner, while Robins presents Vida Levering in action, in Trafalgar Square itself, quelling a rowdy meeting with a heartfelt speech in support of women's suffrage. Hankin's Janet De Mullin, although neither a speaker nor writer for the cause, is its representative in her life as single mother and successful business woman. The shift from reported to enacted event, from notoriety to fame, reflects the shift in approach to female emancipation that occurred between 1890s West End Drama and the Edwardian Drama as represented here. It also demonstrates the marked change in the English theatre brought about by the creation of such independent organizations as the Stage Society and the Barker–Vedrenne company which had reduced the commercial pressures on new drama. Robins's play, moreover, was the trigger of a new dramatic mode—the suffrage drama—that surged into existence after 1907 and stimulated numbers of women to write for the theatre.

The account of female sexuality had changed radically in the space of a decade. Although one play is a comedy, the other a serious drama, the emancipated women in both the 1890s plays reprinted here are represented as deeply confused, predatory, aspiring to a relationship of the spirit but vulnerable to the needs of the flesh and driven by the desire for male protection. The heroines of the two Edwardian plays, by contrast, like Shaw's Ann Whitefield (*Man and Superman*, 1905), the title roles of his *Major Barbara* (1905) and of Elizabeth Baker's *Edith* (1912), and the courageous young women who take a stand against the old ways in Granville Barker's plays, are nothing if not self-possessed.

The woman question addressed most consistently in 1890s theatre centred on errant sexuality: women engaged in or tempted by sexual activity outside marriage or the attempt of a fallen woman to 'get back' into society. *Mrs Warren's Profession* excoriated the sentimentalities of current stage representations of the buying and selling of sex, as exemplified by Dumas *fils*'s *La Dame aux camélias* (1852), and the titillation of stage representations of the 'double standard', which demonstrated its inevitability even while encouraging audiences to weep over it, as exemplified in the other overwhelmingly popular production of the early 1890s, Pinero's *The Second Mrs Tanqueray* (1893), in which

Mrs Campbell had made her name. Despite their evident differences of tone, female transgression is a central theme of both of the 1890s plays included here; but, after the turn of the century, at least in the advanced drama, it was no longer the pressing issue. In so far as the woman-with-a-past theme surfaces, as it does in both the Edwardian plays included here, it is demonstrably unimportant, except in distinguishing the attitudes and assumptions of the protagonist from a more conservative older generation. Attention focuses instead on women's social and economic role, the quality of male–female relationships and choices about marriage, particularly for women who were educated or had financial independence.

The New Woman

Sidney Grundy's *The New Woman* ostensibly offers itself as a Society Drama and has clearly responded to the interest generated by *The Second Mrs Tanqueray* and the Ibsen productions as well as the current heated discussion of female emancipation, but it draws shamelessly on the conventions of old-fashioned Victorian Comedy. Grundy had, indeed, gone into print in 1891 to argue against the 'new school of philosophers', the 'modern theorists' who

contend that the drama ought to be the study of human nature on the stage, the analysis of character pure and simple—no 'plot', there is none in nature—no 'situations', they are artificial—no 'pictures', they are childish—no 'points', they are theatrical. They do not want a story; an episode is sufficient.[5]

The 'pictures' to which Grundy refers were the tableaux into which actors would freeze to emphasize an emotional climax, usually at the end of an act or scene; 'points' entailed the use of vocal emphasis or a judiciously placed pause to underscore significant lines of dialogue and alert the audience to cruces in the plot—both were common performance conventions of mid-Victorian theatre.

Grundy's output was huge. He was one of the more successful West End dramatists, and author of innumerable farces and melodramas adapted from the French; but very few of his plays—with the exception of *A Pair of Spectacles* (1890), which became a vehicle for John Hare—were much revived after their first production. It was, however, a rare season that included no play by him. They were all but guaranteed to make the profitable minimum of a six-week run. *The New Woman*,

---

[5] Sidney Grundy, 'The Science of the Drama', *New Review*, 5: 26 (July 1895), 89.

which was one of the great successes of 1894, allows fascinating insight into the popular response to contemporary ideas. Female education, interest in art, questions about the sexual double standard are all held up for mirth, and, as Clement Scott put it, 'the audience tingled to the fun and were exhilarated by it'.[6]

The play is a telling example of the regular fare of the London theatre in the 1890s, its hybrid nature being one of its most interesting features. Grundy draws on the patterns and language of melodrama—his *desiderata* of 'plot', 'situation', 'pictures', and 'points' all being well in evidence. He uses the curtain line in a classically melodramatic way. Margery's declaration that she will obey closes Act 1; the thud as she falls to the ground having overheard Gerald's declaration to Mrs Sylvester and his cry of 'Margery!' as he pulls back the curtain to reveal her inert form end Act 2; the third act culminates in the rival and parallel declarations of love of Mrs Sylvester and Margery, while the final curtain closes on the declaration of belief in the future of the womanly woman reconciled with the now confidently masculine man. The language in each of these sequences is notably melodramatic, as it is whenever characters express emotion. So Gerald's speech expressing his regret for the Margery he has betrayed in Act 3 exhibits such characteristics of melodramatic style as the use of parallel syntactical structures; the repetition of Margery's name to punctuate the speech; the frequent repetition of the guilty first person pronoun ('it is I who ... I who ... I see ... I feel ... I ask ...'); the use of rising inflections to end each clause, and recourse to rhetorical questions ('How much did Margery give up for me? ... What do all these things matter? What is a man worth who sets such things above a love like hers?')

Older dramatic forms are evident, too, in the sequences of antiemancipation humour and the flirtations that accompany it. If the problem plays of Pinero and Jones hold firm to the new fourth wall convention, Grundy repeatedly breaks it, for all he apes the themes and settings of Society Drama. His self-conscious theatricality includes recourse to soliloquy to reveal a character's state of mind, the use of asides to point the action or invite audience complicity, the introduction of choric speech and concerted action, evident in such stage directions as '*all shiver*', and duologues which, conducted with increasing fervour, are really comic turns interrupting the progress of the plot.

The satiric energy of the play is located in Grundy's representation of the clutch of feminists, Victoria Vivash, Enid Bethune, and Dr Bevan,

---

[6] *Illustrated London News*, 8 Sept. 1894, 296.

particularly when the formidable dowager, Lady Caroline, is pitted against them. They might be thought of as modern humours figures: once set before the audience, each will respond in an exaggerated and predictable way. Grundy's comedy often works by such simple reversals of normally accepted gender roles as Enid's cry, 'A man in distress! I must help him'; by verbal twists of the 'Nothing can stop it', 'No, it stops at nothing' type; by the kind of parody, that has Victoria, in her fervour for equal rights, declare that women must 'reek with infamy' too, or by the use of farcical action to expose the essential femininity of the feminists as when, Colonel Cazenove having crept off-stage in Act 3, Enid and Dr Bevan are left sighing languorously at one another.

Cazenove functions as the *raisonneur*, the right-thinking figure who guides audience response in the well-made Society Drama, although he tends rather to broad innuendo than the witty sophistication found in the *raisonneurs* of Wilde, Pinero, or Henry Arthur Jones. The sexual suggestiveness and nudging humour that inform this play are characteristic of much contemporary comedy. Bernard Shaw, for one, was incensed that such works were tolerated while serious plays were subjected to the interference of the Examiner of Plays. Indeed, this anomaly fuelled the battle against censorship which was engaged with increasing intensity in the years between 1890 and the First World War.

Shaw identified this and comparably satiric plays as reactions to the shock of *A Doll's House*, commenting that 'it is not possible to put the new woman seriously on the stage in her relation to modern society without stirring up, both on the stage and in the auditorium, the struggle to keep her in her old place'.[7] But it is worth noting that Clement Scott, for all his notorious hostility to Ibsen's drama, suggested that the auditorium might be ready for something stronger than Grundy was offering. Finding the unsympathetic representation of Mrs Sylvester to be the play's one flaw, he argued that 'if we are to discuss the "New Woman" let her be fairly discussed. Mrs Sylvester might have been a true as well as a new woman and thus shown us the earnest side of the movement in contrast to the ridiculous side of it.'[8] These observations by Scott on Agnes Sylvester may well have pointed Pinero to his representation of Agnes Ebbsmith the following year.

---

[7] Bernard Shaw, introduction to William Archer, *The Theatrical World of 1894* (1895), p. xxvi.

[8] *Illustrated London News*, 8 Sept. 1894, 296.

The Notorious Mrs Ebbsmith

Having made his name in farce and romantic comedy, Pinero turned to Society Drama in the 1890s, thereby consolidating his position as the leading dramatist of his day. Unlike Grundy and Henry Arthur Jones, who were hostile to Ibsen's writing from the outset and became increasingly embittered as they saw their work becoming passé, Pinero was interested in Ibsen from the time of the Achurch–Charrington *Doll's House* in 1889 and was consistently supportive of such initiatives as Grein's Independent Theatre, Barker's Court seasons and schemes for a National Theatre, and even the Actresses' Franchise League, being among those who sent a telegram of support at its foundation in December 1908. Pinero's well-made Society Dramas seemed to many of his contemporaries to offer the English answer to Ibsen. Although he endured the fiercest of critical assaults from Bernard Shaw, who saw him as a rival to his own dramatic initiative, he was heralded as a major dramatist by William Archer, the leader of the new generation of drama critics.

The Notorious Mrs Ebbsmith was something of a landmark in 'English Ibsenism' and accordingly offended some sensibilities. The *Quarterly Review* critic complained that it 'exacted a story so revolting as to double the arguments against the play' and was offended by the conception of Agnes, 'the cold theorist, the blue stocking misbehaved, Girton astray'.[9] A more serious play than Grundy's, it presented the type of the new woman much more sympathetically, although, in the end, it is hard not to agree with Shaw that it lacked the courage of the convictions it seemed to espouse in the first two acts. The difficulty, as both Shaw and Archer immediately perceived, as well as the originality of the play, lies in the representation of Agnes, the new woman, although both admitted that Mrs Campbell's remarkable performance and tendency to play against the role in the later scenes disguised this. By comparison, Clement Scott praised the play unreservedly for its originality as well as its depth.

The play is concerned, as is *The Second Mrs Tanqueray*, with a socially inappropriate union, but Pinero breaks new ground by proposing as his heroine a freethinker who despises the allure of femininity and, unlike Paula Tanqueray or Wilde's Mrs Erlynne in *Lady Windermere's Fan* (1892), has no longing to embrace social convention. In differentiating Agnes from the conventional woman-with-a-past, Pinero suggests a theoretical as well as an emotional basis for her affair with Lucas. She is a 'new woman' intent on forming a 'free union'. The plot bears strong

[9] Oct. 1895, 422–7.

resemblance to that of Gissing's *The Odd Women*. Like Pinero's play, Gissing's novel, published two years earlier, includes the decision of a couple to live together in free union and a heroine, Rhoda, who eventually leaves her man, crushed by her recognition that, whereas she loves him, he lusts after her. Although in the early scenes Pinero attempts to flesh out the representation of the new woman, the needs of the plot, and probably his own fundamental attitudes, prevent him from sustaining this. While evidently more positive in approach than Grundy or Jones, he draws as they do on the stereotype in creating the Agnes of the first two acts. Thereafter, the typology becomes confused. Agnes must serve too many different purposes. New woman, fallen woman, and penitent succeed each other as, panicked by the prospective loss of Lucas, she has recourse to sexual seductiveness to attach him to her.

Even in the first two acts conflicting ideas inform the characterization. Although Pinero has picked up on the common association of the new woman with frigidity, the Cazenove view that 'what they really want is a husband' lurks near. The need to make Agnes sympathetic leads Pinero to angel-in-the-house womanhood, whose devotion and nursing skills have saved Lucas's life. So she must be sweet-voiced and gentle despite her history of shrillness in the public arena. She is self-sacrificing although she has a clear-sighted recognition of Lucas's failings. The audience *hears* of her writing and public speaking, but it *sees* her arranging flowers, threading her needle, worrying about Lucas's medicine. Her revolutionary-socialist-atheist background and alcoholic mother have inexplicably left her 'devout as any girl in a parsonage' before her marriage. The marriage having proved abusive, she has adopted her father's viewpoint, becoming both atheist and socialist, but crumbles when presented with a bible. As the action develops, she is shown to be well able to parry St Olpherts's sallies and notably clearer and firmer in her ideas than Lucas, but must renounce these for a country parsonage when the baser side of Society is revealed to her. For all the courage of Pinero's attempt to create a more characterful heroine, it is not easy to gainsay William Archer's comment that 'her spiritual history does not hang together. It is not probably constructed or possibly expressed'.[10]

The idiom in which Agnes describes her socialism is at once a significant marker of the improbability and a strong reflector of contemporary assumptions. The account she gives of her father's and, indeed, her own ideas is that of an outsider—her heterodoxy is expressed in the language

---

[10] *The World*, 20 Mar. 1895.

and from the point of view of orthodoxy. For all that, Pinero's originality in attempting to draw such a character sympathetically is evident in
Mrs Campbell's memory of being 'fired and inspired' by the role. She
found Agnes wholly believable in the first three acts and pointed out that
'she was a new and daring type, the woman agitator, the pessimist with
original independent ideas—in revolt against sham morals'.[11] Agnes's
thrusting of the bible into the fire at the end of Act 3 and the fevered
grasping of it back again thrilled the first audiences, despite the fact that
the sensationalism of that moment and the penitential conclusion are
sequences from sentimental melodrama, at odds with the challenging
situation Pinero seemed to be developing in the opening scenes of the
play.

Pinero is notably innovative in pursuing further the implications of
contemporary Society Drama. If the free-union liaison, the bible burning, and Mrs Campbell's transformation from glamorous actress to
plain new woman and then to siren again, thrilled contemporary audiences, the clarity of the family's cynical proposition for preserving the
socially respectable façade that would sustain Lucas's career was disconcerting. Pinero's real subject, it seems to me, is less female emancipation than social hypocrisy and the mismatch of male and female
sexuality, a harsher version of his concerns in his two earlier Society
Plays, *The Profligate* (1889) and *The Second Mrs Tanqueray* (1893). The
central couple in the former, a debauched man and a puritanical woman,
are finally reconciled, the man having, in a revision demanded by John
Hare, resisted the further sin of suicide. The puritan in the later play,
the step-daughter, learns generosity only after Paula Tanqueray's suicide. Many contemporary Society Plays conclude with reluctant acceptance of society's sexual double standard, but few make their audience
face the implications as directly as *The Notorious Mrs Ebbsmith*, which
does so partly because Pinero denies his audience a suicide to weep over
or a sentimental reconciliation.

The characterization of Lucas Cleeve, which has a consistency that of
Agnes lacks, is crucial in establishing the bleak tone of the play. Whereas
Grundy has hardly introduced the suggestion of his hero's feminization
before disclaiming it, Pinero presses home the idea of the neurasthenic
male, making Lucas notably less sympathetic as the play proceeds.
Characterized in the stage directions as having 'ambition without
patience, self-esteem without confidence', the facile nature of his enthu-
siasms and egocentricity are increasingly apparent. The audience is led

[11] *My Life and Some Letters* (1922), 98.

to perceive his self-deceptions, his failure of responsibility in a marriage abandoned after only three years, his failure to keep faith with Agnes's ideas, his snivelling dependence on being admired, and, most distasteful of all, his willingness to acquiesce in the scheme to set Agnes up covertly as his mistress. The felt shallowness of the hero contributes to the play's account of the moral and sexual barrenness of Society as currently organized.

All the marriages mentioned in the play are dismal if not abusive; the only child to result from any of them has died in infancy. Male sexuality shows as invariably egocentric and rapacious, female as shrinking or frigid. Agnes, the object of her first husband's appalling lust as Gertrude was of hers, need only appear in a sexually suggestive dress to fire Lucas's baser passions, and Pinero's audience is left in no more doubt that this is knowingly done by Agnes, than Ibsen's is that the tarantella Nora dances in *A Doll's House* is a conscious strategy to distract Helmer by inflaming his passion. Indeed, the sell-out of the ending, which puts Agnes literally into a parsonage and implies that she will find sustenance in religion, looks like an attempt on Pinero's part to retreat from the moral bleakness and offer a sop of conventional comfort.

Shaw applauded Mrs Campbell for playing against the grain of the writing in the last two acts. Archer, more sympathetic to Pinero's notion of a woman having 'an hour', took issue with Mrs Campbell's way of wearing the glamorous dress as if it were a hair-shirt and of playing Act 3 in a state of deep hostility, complaining that 'the actress seemed to feel only the irony in Agnes's thoughts, not the genuine underlying joy. There was nothing but bitterness in her realisation that her "one woman's hour" had come.'[12]

Votes for Women!

If in the 1890s most representations of emancipated women were satirical or pitying, the situation shifted remarkably with the coming of the Edwardian New Drama. The heroines of the two remaining plays in this edition do not accept the obedience, selfless suffering, or penitent retirement of the 1890s characters. Joy does not lie in finding true love or erotic mutuality but in finding the confidence to be oneself and to stand alone. Indeed, Vida Levering in *Votes for Women!* takes almost exactly the role Agnes Ebbsmith had projected for herself, although her theme as orator is not the horror of marriage but the demand for female suffrage.

Robins's play, originally called 'The Friend of Women', was

---

[12] Shaw, *Saturday Review*, 16 Mar. 1895; Archer, *The World*, 27 Mar. 1895.

commissioned by Gertrude Kingston; but when the militant nature of the piece led her to hesitate it was taken over and directed by Granville Barker, who suggested using *Votes for Women!*, the words blazoned across the banner in the Trafalgar Square scene, as the play's title. Barker's confidence was repaid. Initially scheduled for eight matinées, the play's success demanded an extension and eleven evening performances before the close of the 1906–7 Court Theatre Season cut its life short. There was input from Henry James who, asked to comment on an early draft, provided some fifty pages of close-written notes; from Shaw, who advised tightening the play, compressing the first two acts into what became the first act and emphasizing the relationship between Vida's past and the suffrage theme; and particularly from Barker, who cut the play and shaped the crowd activity in Act 2.[13]

To many contemporaries in the 1890s, Elizabeth Robins, who incidentally had surrendered the role of Paula Tanqueray when Mrs Campbell became available, was the actress most closely identified with feminism through her productions of and performances in the plays of Ibsen. Arriving in England from America in 1888, following the suicide of her husband and fellow-actor, George Parks, Robins, who had toured with James O'Neill's company in the mid-1880s, gained work first as an understudy, including a six-month stint on Pinero's *The Profligate*, before making an impact as Hedda Gabler in her co-production with Marion Lea in April 1891, followed by the role of Claire de Cintré in Henry James's dramatization of his novel, *The American*. She subsequently became closely identified with Ibsenism, acting in revivals of *A Doll's House*, playing Hilda Wangel in her own production of *The Master Builder*, Rebecca West in *Rosmersholm*, Agnes in a staged reading of the fourth act of *Brand*, first Rita then Asta in *Little Eyolf*, and Ella Rentheim in *John Gabriel Borkman*. She was also praised for her performance as the working-class heroine, Jean Creyke, who smothers her badly deformed child, in the Independent Theatre's production of *Alan's Wife* (1893), although the play itself, which Robins had written anonymously with Florence Bell, was decried as offensive by the critics and denied a licence for public performance. In the latter part of the 1890s she withdrew from acting and, with the exception of the play reprinted here, published not drama but prose fiction, which she wrote under the pseudonym C. E. Raimond.

[13] James's notes are in the Robins Collection, Fales Library, New York University. For information about the contributions of Shaw and of Barker, see Sheila Stowell, *A Stage of their Own* (Manchester, 1992), 16, and Dennis Kennedy, *Granville Barker and the Dream of Theatre* (Cambridge, 1985), 57–8.

Although *Votes for Women!* was a force behind the foundation the following year of the Actresses' Franchise League and Robins became the first President of the Women Writers' Suffrage League, she came much later to suffrage activity than might have been expected of the first English Hedda Gabler. Her conversion, which seems to have been similar to that of Jean Dunbarton in the play, happened by her own account, in 1906, when on a 'certain memorable afternoon in Trafalgar Square', she 'first heard women talking politics in public' and 'a new chapter was begun for [her] in the lesson of faith in the capacities of women'.[14] She joined the Women's Social and Political Union shortly afterwards, giving her first suffrage speech in Autumn 1906. Something of the immediacy and excitement of this is captured in the play which she began later the same year and in the fact that she chose to share her royalties with the two main suffrage societies. Thereafter, she spoke and, particularly, *wrote* frequent letters and articles on the suffrage issue, knew the Pankhursts well, and remained a committee member until 1912.

The play draws on Robins's experience of suffragism, but also of the world of political house parties into which she had entrance through her close relationship with Florence, wife of the Liberal MP, Sir Hugh Bell, friend of Sir Edward Gray, and co-author with Robins of *Alan's Wife*. Mrs Pankhurst, indeed, saw Robins as a useful intermediary with parliamentary political circles.[15] The house party guests in Robins's play and the speakers at the suffrage meeting are closely modelled on people she had met in these two very different spheres.

The play attracted a full and enthusiastic audience of suffrage supporters but was attacked as old-fashioned by some commentators, notably Max Beerbohm, for its conventional Society setting in Acts 1 and 3, its re-working of the erring-woman plot, and its use of melodramatic tricks—the *Tanqueray*-like convergence of ex-lover and new fiancée and the dropped handkerchief that reveals a previous affair.[16] Robins does indeed use the plot and many of the devices of woman-with-a-past drama, but comparison with even the most advanced versions of it makes clear how fully she subverts the convention. The feminist here, unlike Elaine Shrimpton or Vivie Warren, is elegant and at ease in the polite drawing room, well able to hold her own against male prejudice; and, equally importantly, Robins includes other strong-minded women characters with a range of opinions and willingness to

[14] Elizabeth Robins, *Way Stations* (New York, 1913), 40.

[15] For fuller information on Robins's relationship with the Pankhursts and the suffrage movement, see Angela V. John, *Elizabeth Robins: Staging a Life* (1995).

[16] Max Beerbohm, *Around Theatres* (1924), 284.

express them. Unlike Agnes Ebbsmith, neither Vida Levering nor any of the other women becomes shrill in political argument. Male smugness can be disconcerted. The ingenue—the Ellean Tanqueray figure—far from shunning the more experienced woman, is drawn to her, eager to learn, and the wronged woman, far from using her charms to attach a man, or fearing that their fading will be her doom, finds the idea of a proposal from her former lover absurd.

Even Max Beerbohm acknowledged the excitement and originality of Act 2—the suffrage meeting in Trafalgar Square. The Act begins mid-meeting. The play's characters are brought in as needed and the act culminates in Vida's speech and Jean's reaction to it, but the emphasis is primarily on the conduct of the public meeting, the suffrage speeches themselves, and the interaction between platform and crowd. *The Sketch* called it 'the finest stage crowd that has been seen for years, not excepting the particularly good ones in Mr Tree's production of *Julius Caesar*', and the *Observer* critic claimed that 'Mr Tree's *Julius Caesar* crowd is quite eclipsed and M. Antoine at his best could not have done better'.[17] The variousness of the cries from the crowd, the humour ranging from the sharp to the inane, and the characterizing labels—'A Shabby Art Student', 'A Beery Fellow of Fifty'—suggest something of the texture and impression of verisimilitude achieved in performance. The same arrangement, of crowd facing upstage to speakers who address both audience and stage crowd from their raised platform, was used in Barker's 1909 production of *Strife* by Galsworthy, whose *Silver Box* had run in the evening alongside the matinees of Robins's play.

Barker introduced the question of abortion into his own play, *Waste*, which he was writing while working on *Votes for Women!*, but he reversed the situation. The man in *Waste* opposes termination and both he and the woman involved die, while the man in Robins's play has all but forgotten the incident and the woman survives, having coped with and grown through the terrible experience. That the Censor banned *Waste*, having licensed Robins's play, was the cause of much comment at the time and has roused curiosity since. It is possible that the Examiner of Plays was more concerned about the indictment of political life than the sexual and criminal activity in Barker's play[18], but it could also be that, since the termination in *Votes for Women!* occurred in the distant past rather than in the course of the action, as in *Waste*, and was the cause of deep regret to the woman involved, the Examiner was prepared to let

---

[17] *The Sketch*, 15 May 1907, 131; *The Observer*, quoted Kennedy, 61.

[18] Ian Clarke's suggestion in *Edwardian Drama* (1989), 82–3.

it pass, or even, since abortion is never directly named, that he missed it altogether but was alerted to his oversight by the time the application for Barker's play arrived.

As Barker's introduction of an abortion theme and Galsworthy's of a political meeting suggest, plays by women writers, and Robins's play in particular, had an impact on the leading male New Dramatists, some of it very direct. Her subversion of the stock situations of the Society Drama or the well-made play also gave a lead to subsequent dramatists. Following Vida Levering's rejection of marriage came a spate of plays including Hankin's *The Last of the De Mullins*, whose independent heroines choose to reject their suitors. These culminated in the gloriously insouciant logic of Fanny Hawthorn's claim to female sexual equality in Stanley Houghton's comedy, *Hindle Wakes* (1912): 'You're a man and I was your little fancy. Well, I'm a woman, and you were my little fancy. You wouldn't prevent a woman enjoying herself as well as a man, if she takes it into her head?' (Act 3).[19]

Described by Robins as 'A Tract in Three Acts', *Votes for Women!* knowingly proselytized for the suffrage cause and, doing so, provided a model for subsequent suffrage plays, many of which were cast in the simplest didactic form—conversion narratives in which the female protagonist, like Jean Dunbarton, is won to the cause, or reconciliation narratives, in which the male protagonist agrees to support the cause, like, although usually more wholeheartedly than, Geoffrey Stonor. Hundreds of such feminist and suffrage plays, pageants, and sketches were performed in halls and at open air meetings in the course of the next six years, among them Gertrude Jennings's *A Woman's Influence*, Cicely Hamilton and Christopher St John's comedy *How the Vote Was Won*, and Joan Dugdale's *10, Clowning Street*.[20] Shaw's farce, *Press Cuttings*, was written for the London Women's Suffrage Society in 1909, and Inez Bensusan's *The Apple* was staged at the Court Theatre in the same year.

In such Society Plays as Jones's *The Masqueraders* (1894), female characters renounced sexual happiness 'for the sake of the child', but, with the exception of the painful *Alan's Wife*, maternal feelings were scarcely encountered in the drama of the 1890s. In *Votes for Women!* Vida grieves the loss of the aborted infant, whom she refers to as 'my child'; and, although she will herself stay single and active in the fight, she predicts that the greater preoccupation of a child will soon remove

[19] There is no recent reprint of the play, but it can be found in Sidgwick and Jackson, *Plays for Today*, i (1925).

[20] For further information, see, particularly, Viv Gardner's introduction to her edition of *Plays of the Actresses' Franchise League* (Nottingham, 1985).

Jean from action. The theme of maternal commitment and the over-whelming importance of motherhood is reiterated in subsequent plays by women. Although Maggie, the heroine of Elizabeth Baker's *Chains*, is appalled, it is with the announcement of forthcoming motherhood that her sister Lily holds her husband. Githa Sowerby's Mary, in *Rutherford and Son* (1912), abandons her husband and prepares to endure the privations of her father-in-law's house for what she takes to be the future good of her child. As she says, 'he's what matters now—and we've got to live decently for him'. This reflects a widespread concern with maternal feeling and mothering in the Edwardian period.

The Last of the De Mullins

If the use and subversion of the devices of the well-made play are characteristic of Robins's presentation of an early twentieth-century emancipated woman, St John Hankin's *The Last of the De Mullins* is remarkable for the convergence in it of recurrent New Drama themes. The title signals the most obvious of these, the House in decay and in need of the creative energy of iconoclastic youth; but, unlike other plays that concerned themselves with Natural Selection—for instance, Strindberg's *Miss Julie* or Barker's *The Marrying of Ann Leete* (1902) or *The Voysey Inheritance* (1905)—his treatment is essentially comic, with something of the same relationship to the New Drama that Grundy's *The New Woman* has to Society Drama, although its humour is considerably more waspish than Grundy's. Like Grundy's, his comic characters are types—the tyrannical father, the timid mother, the jealous conventional sibling, the formidable dowager; and they had appeared, albeit in different social situations, in Hankin's two earlier plays, *The Return of the Prodigal* (1905) and *The Charity that Began at Home* (1906).

Hankin is an enigmatic figure and not only because he drowned himself at Llandrindod Wells in Wales in 1909. Drama critic of *The Times* in the late 1890s and a seasoned writer for *Punch*, he was developing a respect for the advanced drama and particularly the work of Bernard Shaw, even while parodying these in *Mr Punch's Dramatic Sequels*, published between June 1898 and December 1903, and in 1902 he joined the management committee of the Stage Society. Unlike most of his New Drama colleagues, moreover, he was an enthusiast for Chekhov and attacked Archer for not making more effort to promote the work of the Russian who remained essentially unperformed in England until after the First World War.

What, in effect, we have in *The Last of the De Mullins*, whose heroine, like Vida, rejects a proposal from the father of her child, is a shift of emphasis from woman as wife to woman as mother. Hankin shares the Edwardian women writers' attention to maternal feeling. He shares Shaw's sense of the life force, the biological imperative underlying human activity and relationship, and, as his emphasis on the contrast between the enfeebled De Mullin and the robust health of his illegitimate grandson makes clear, he is alert to contemporary attention to Darwinian ideas of the survival of the fittest. Unlike Robins, however, who has Vida tell Stonor that before long 'little arms' will fetter Jean, and that not mothers but single and childless women must be the fighters, Hankin makes his heroine a single working mother dependent on no man. Janet De Mullin impresses on her sister the importance of maternity. Having used a man to enable her to attain this state, her primary relationship is evidently with her child.

Whereas Robins is silent as to how Vida Levering made her way from poverty to well-dressed guest in the country house party world, Hankin, like Elizabeth Baker, Cecily Hamilton, and the other women writers who succeeded Robins, stresses the role of work in enabling female emancipation. It is income from work, even when poorly paid, that grants independence, although intelligent use of small legacies also comes in surprisingly frequently in such writing, as it does here. Whereas the characters in plays by women are primarily conscious of the limitations imposed by a low income, there is a tendency in the sympathetic men's plays (and Hankin is no exception to this) for the emphasis to be on the woman's rejoicing in the self-sufficiency work allows: the typist in J. M. Barrie's *The Twelve Pound Look* (1910), for example, is envied by the wife kept in luxury and idleness by her husband. Although Hankin's audience does not see Janet De Mullin in her hat shop, it learns of the pleasure she gains from it and is asked to appreciate the status as well as the effort it entails.

Conflict between the generations is another of the recurrent themes of the New Drama that is given a boost by Hankin's plays. *The Last of the De Mullins* could well have been entitled *The Return of the Prodigal*, like the play that drew attention to Hankin as a dramatist when it was staged at the Court Theatre two years earlier. This time, as compared with the disreputable, self-centred free spirit of Hankin's 1905 play, the supposed black sheep is a strong-minded woman, and old money and land rather than the new riches of manufacturing sustain the family to whom she returns. In each case, lively young people repudiate the values and conventions by which their parents, and particularly their domineering fathers, live. Related to this generational strife is the frustration of the spinster whose life chances and opportunities to marry are limited by class or economic restraints. The Huxtable daughters in *The Madras House*, Georgiana in Hamilton's *Just to Get Married* (1910), Rutherford's daughter in *Rutherford and Son* might each say with Violet in Hankin's *The Return of the Prodigal*: 'the great people won't marry me and I mustn't marry the little people'. The comic focus makes Hester's role less poignant if just as desperate in *The Last of the De Mullins*.

The social comedy is Shavian. Janet's manner and commonsensical undercutting of others' shock work to disarm the offence the audience might feel at her situation. It is not easy to resist her teasing self-labelling as 'an abandoned woman' or her amusement at others' embarrassments and insinuations, as when Mrs Heriot hopes a ring at the doorbell does not signal a visitor who might observe the disgraceful prodigal or when Monty, her former lover, expresses sympathy with the shop's reluctance to employ a woman in her condition. 'Monty, don't be vain' is her response to his sentimental suggestion that she remained unmarried for love of him, and his 'You don't mind, do you—about my asking you to go, I mean?' in Act 2 wins the reply, 'Not in the least' as, demonstrating how little she minds, she sits to wait for satisfaction of her curiosity in the arrival of the new fiancée. Snobbery and self-deception are constant targets for Hankin's humour, whether in the form of a declining squirearchy that cannot entertain the idea of one daughter's involvement in trade or a curate as marriage partner for the other, or in the form of an aristocracy that dresses well on credit it does not honour and so associates French fashion with glamour that plain Miss Hicks must masquerade under the name of Madame Claude.

Neither of the men in these Edwardian plays are bounders, nor are they as self-serving as Lucas Cleeve, although each retains something of Cleeve's weakness and egocentricity. Stonor has the self-serving politician's adaptability in the face of pressure. Monty, in keeping with the lighter tone of Hankin's play, seems to have lost Janet through carelessness and clearly still admires her. His idiom makes it evident to the audience how unsuited this callow youth is to the sophisticated Janet. Like Vida, Janet has power because she does not hanker for the rewards society conventionally offers to an attractive woman. Whereas Agnes Ebbsmith despised the erotic element of dressing glamorously even while using it to capture Lucas, Janet, like Vida, regards being well-dressed as a normal feature of her emancipated status. It signifies power and self-respect, not sexual allure or subordination.

The production history of each of these plays is short. *The Last of the De Mullins*, produced by the Stage Society in 1908, ran briefly. After revivals in the immediate pre- and post-First World War period by the Birmingham Repertory Company among others, the play disappeared, its author having slipped from theatrical consciousness, until one of Sam Walters's inspired revivals at the Orange Tree at Richmond of *The Return of the Prodigal* in 1993 redirected attention to Hankin's small cache of plays. Grundy's *The New Woman*, having been one of the successes of the 1894–5 season, appears not to have been revived or republished, a common situation even for very successful plays in the period. *The Notorious Mrs Ebbsmith* ran to excellent houses, with all the top price seats sold and a packer employed to cram the audience into the pit for the fifty-eight performances for which Mrs Patrick Campbell was contracted to play, although audiences dwindled through the next twenty-eight performances after the star surrendered the lead role. Having leased the Royalty Theatre from February 1900 to November 1901, Mrs Campbell reprised her role as Agnes in February 1901. The play was revived again in 1923 with a completely new cast. After the production of *Votes for Women!* Robins reworked the play as a novel, *The Convert*, published in October 1907, the play itself being produced in New York and in Rome in 1909. A benefit matinée was staged in London in 1912 to raise money for the Women Writers' Suffrage League; but, after the outbreak of the First World War, it was forgotten until retrieved through the investigations of a succession of feminist critics.[21]

The four plays allow insight into the political and theatrical contexts of their time and into the very real shifts in perception between the 1890s and the Edwardian period. Each has its own dramatic vitality and, in very different ways, each would repay revival in the theatre.

[21] See e.g. Julie Holledge, *Innocent Flowers* (1981); Dale Spender and Carole Hayman (eds.), '*How the Vote was Won*' and Other Suffragette Plays (1985).

NOTE ON THE TEXTS

THE texts printed here are, with a few minor emendations, those of the
first published edition of each play. Each has been compared with the
Licensing Copy, which was submitted to the Examiner of Plays immediately before the first performance of the play. Some cutting of the
stage directions and dialogue of the Licensing Copy is evident in each of
the published texts. Where such cuts took the form of simple excisions,
occasioning no alteration of the surrounding text, they have been
restored in square brackets within the text of each of the plays. Changes
between the Licensing Copy and the first-published version, and cuts
whose restoration would necessitate alteration to the copy-text, are
recorded in the notes.

The New Woman was published shortly after the play opened in 1894,
by the Chiswick Press, a small private press that had previously prepared the Licensing Copy. There is no more recent edition of the play.
The traditional method of coding stage directions was retained un-
modified in the published version of the play, and changes between the
two texts are negligible. Details of the one exception, a short sequence at
the end of Act 3, are included in the notes. Technical annotations used
by Grundy include R = Right, L = Left, RC = Right of Centre, RUE
= Right Upstage Entrance, etc., and all positions are from the perspective of the actor standing on-stage and facing the audience so 'up' or
'upstage' means 'away from the audience'.

The Notorious Mrs Ebbsmith was published by Heinemann in 1895.
Pinero was one of the pioneers of play publication, following the establishing of international copyright protection at the beginning of the
1890s. Since he rewrote his stage directions to make them more accessible to the reader, it would be perverse to return to the technical directions of the Licensing Copy. These are considerably more extensive,
however, so are included, again in square brackets, where they offer specific help in envisaging performance practice. Pinero told William
Archer that the play 'suffered no mutilation at the Chamberlain's Office'
but that he had himself 'made a few cuts in rehearsal'.[1] These, where
evident, are recorded in the notes.

[1] To Archer (16 Mar. 1895), J. P. Wearing, *The Collected Letters of Sir Arthur Wing
Pinero* (Minneapolis, 1974), 166.

Pinero's practice of modifying his stage directions for publication was continued by Bernard Shaw and had become the habitual practice of dramatists by the time the other two plays included here were published. When he prepared *The Last of the De Mullins* for publication (A. C. Fitfield, 1909), shortly after its first production, Hankin expanded his stage directions to provide a fuller narrative for the reader. These changes are retained here and are discussed only when the tone of the action is altered by them. The dialogue itself is essentially unchanged between the two versions, but some of the play's most interesting passages, which sharpen the relationships between characters, appeared as handwritten additions to the Licensing Copy, and these are registered in the notes.

More significant changes occur in Elizabeth Robins's *Votes for Women!* which was not published until two years after the first performance (Mills and Boon, 1909). Most notably, two of the characters' names are changed between performance and publication and the ending is rearranged and considerably expanded in the published version. The Licensing Copy ending is included here as an Appendix, immediately following the main text. The published version, again, includes sequences which originally appeared as handwritten additions to the Licensing Copy. These, too, are indicated in the notes; presumably made during rehearsal, they usually introduce a more colloquial texture to the dialogue and considerably extend the role of the crowd in Act 2.

Throughout this volume, characters' names have been expanded from the abbreviations commonly used as speech prefixes, and some words, hyphenated in the first editions, now conform to modern practice. The lay-out of the stage directions has been emended in accordance with the series conventions.

SELECT BIBLIOGRAPHY

Place of publication is London unless otherwise stated.

This is the first modern edition of *The New Woman*, *The Notorious Mrs Ebbsmith*, and *The Last of the De Mullins*. Of Grundy's other plays the only one in an at all recent edition is the Hare vehicle, *A Pair of Spectacles*, included in George Rowell (ed.), *Nineteenth Century Plays* (1953). *The Notorious Mrs Ebbsmith* was included in Clayton Hamilton (ed.), *The Social Plays of Sir Arthur Wing Pinero*, 4 vols. (1917–22), but not in such recent collections as George Rowell (ed.), *Plays by A. W. Pinero* (Cambridge, 1986) and J. S. Bratton (ed.), *Trelawny of the 'Wells' and Other Plays* (Oxford, 1995). Hankin's play was reissued in 1923 with an introduction by John Drinkwater, in the three-volume *Dramatic Works of St John Hankin*. Hankin's *Punch* articles were also reissued as *Dramatic Sequels, 1898–1903* (1926). *Votes for Women!* had its first modern reprinting in Dale Spender and Carole Hayman (eds.), *'How the Vote was Won' and Other Suffragette Plays* (1985). The novel Robins developed from the play, *The Convert*, had already been reprinted with a useful introduction by Jane Marcus (1980). *Alan's Wife*, by Robins and Florence Bell, is reprinted in L. Fitzsimmons and Viv Gardner (eds.), *New Woman Plays* (1991), and a selection of other suffragette plays is to be found in Viv Gardner (ed.), *Sketches from the Actresses' Franchise League* (Nottingham, 1985).

Contemporary judgements on the works included in this edition are well worth consulting. The most telling commentaries on Pinero and Grundy in the 1890s are those of Clement Scott, the influential critic at the *Daily Telegraph*, of A. B. Walkley in *The Star* and collected in *Drama and Life* (1908), and of William Archer, whose criticism for *The World* is the basis for the series published as *The Theatrical World of 1893; 1894* etc. (1894, 1895 etc.). Desmond McCarthy's *The Court Theatre* (1907) is an important early study. Trenchant, and most evidently formative of subsequent opinion, are the analyses by Bernard Shaw collected in *Our Theatres in the Nineties* (1932), while Max Beerbohm offers sharp insights in *Around Theatres* (1924) and *Last Theatres* (1971).

Notable among contemporary accounts, memoirs, and letters are: J. P. Wearing (ed.), *The Collected Letters of Arthur Wing Pinero* (Minneapolis, 1974); Mrs Patrick Campbell, *My Life and Some Letters* (1922);

Christopher St John (ed.), *Ellen Terry and Bernard Shaw: A Correspondence* (1931); Sylvia Pankhurst, *The Suffragette Movement* (1931, repr. 1977); Cicely Hamilton, *Marriage as a Trade* (1909) and *Life Errant* (1935); and Hannah Mitchell, *The Hard Way Up* (1968). Elizabeth Robins provides insights into the theatre of the time and her own part in it in *Ibsen and the Actress* (1928) and *Theatre and Friendship* (1932), in which she reprints Henry James's letters to her and to Florence Bell, while in *Way Stations* (New York, 1913) she gives her account of the suffrage movement.

Although his work is discussed briefly in general studies of nineteenth-century drama, there is, so far as I have discovered, no critical study devoted to Grundy's writing. Hankin's fate is much the same, except for Jan Macdonald's invaluable chapter-length study in *The 'New Drama' 1900–1914* (1986), which also provides a succinct and cogent account of the context; but there is a biography by William H. Phillips, *St John Hankin: Edwardian Mephistopheles* (1979). On Pinero, see Penny Griffin, *A. W. Pinero and H. A. Jones* (1991) and John Dawick, *Pinero, a Theatrical Life* (Niwot, Colo., 1993). Having been long out of print, her work all-but forgotten, Elizabeth Robins has attracted much attention in recent years. Angela V. John's recent biography, *Elizabeth Robins: Staging a Life* (1995), is notable for its sympathetic but clear-sighted account of her life and work. Robins also figures in Peter Whitebrook's *William Archer* (1993), as do Pinero and Hankin more briefly. Attention is paid to the work of all four dramatists in Jean Chothia, *English Drama of the Early Modern Period, 1890–1940* (1996).

Among recent works discussing the new woman and her literary and theatrical representation are Viv Gardner and S. Rutherford (eds.), *The New Woman and her Sisters* (1992), which has a particularly useful introductory chapter; Sheila Stowell, *A Stage of their Own* (Manchester, 1992), which includes a chapter-length study of Elizabeth Robins; and two articles, Linda Dowling, 'The Decadent and the New Woman in the 1890s', *Nineteenth Century Fiction*, 33: 4 (Mar. 1979), 434–53 and Catherine Wiley, 'The Matter with Manners: The New Woman and the Problem Play', in J. Redmond (ed.), *Women in Theatre* (Cambridge, 1989), 109–21. For insight into the 1890s context, see John Stokes, *In the Nineties* (Hemel Hempstead, 1989) and Elaine Showalter, *Sexual Anarchy* (1991). Ian Clarke's *Edwardian Drama* (1989) offers a penetrating study of the context in which Hankin and Robins worked, and James Woodfield, *English Theatre in Transition, 1881–1914* (Beckenham, 1984) provides a substantial study of the whole period. Joel Kaplan and Sheila

Stowell, *Theatre and Fashion* (Cambridge, 1994), demonstrates the significance of costume in the drama of the period while offering interesting insights into the representation of the woman question. Julie Holledge, *Innocent Flowers* (1981), was one of the first to draw attention to women's contribution to Edwardian drama.

A CHRONOLOGY OF AUTHORS' PUBLICATIONS

Selective listing of plays by Grundy and Pinero; complete listing of plays by Robins and Hankin; selective listing of other writings.

Sidney Grundy (1848–1914)

1872   *A Little Change* (Haymarket).

1883   *The Glass of Fashion* (with G. R. Sims).

1885   *The Silver Shield* (Strand).

1890   *A Pair of Spectacles* (Garrick).

1893   *Sowing the Wind* (Comedy).

1894   *A Bunch of Violets* (Haymarket).
       The New Woman (Comedy).

1895   *Slaves of the Ring* (Garrick).

1902   *Frocks and Frills* (Haymarket).

1914   *The Play of the Future by a Playwright of the Past* (tract).

Arthur Wing Pinero (1855–1934)

1877   *£200 a Year* (Globe Theatre. First produced play—a curtain raiser).

1885   *The Magistrate* (Court).

1887   *Dandy Dick* (Court, establishes Pinero's reputation as a dramatist).

1888   *Sweet Lavender* (Terry's).

1889   *The Weaker Sex* (Court).
       The Profligate (Garrick).

1893   *The Second Mrs Tanqueray* (St James's).

1895   *The Notorious Mrs Ebbsmith* (Garrick).

1898   *Trelawny of the 'Wells'* (Court).

1906   *His House in Order* (St James's).

Elizabeth Robins (1862–1952)

1893   *Alan's Wife* (with Florence Bell, Independent Theatre).

1894   *George Mandeville's Husband* (novel, under name C. E. Raimond).

1895   'The Mirkwood' (with William Archer, not produced or published).

1898   *The Open Question* (C. E. Raimond novel).

1900   'Benvenuto Cellini' (with William Archer, not produced or published).

1904   *The Magnetic North* (novel, under own name).

1907   *Votes for Women!* (Court Theatre, published 1909).

       The Convert (development of the play as a novel).

1913   *Way Stations* (suffrage writings).

1924   *Ancilla's Share: An Indictment of Sex Antagonism* (anonymously).

1928   *Ibsen and the Actress* (essay/memoir).

1940   *Both Sides of the Curtain* (memoirs).

St John Hankin (1869–1909)

1901   *Dramatic Sequels* (first published in *Punch*).

1903   *The Two Mr Wetherbys* (Stage Society).

1905   *The Return of the Prodigal* (Court).

       The Three Daughters of M Dupont (translation of Brieux, Stage Society).

1906   *The Charity That Began at Home* (Court).

1907   *The Cassilis Engagement* (Stage Society).

1908   *The Last of the De Mullins* (Stage Society, Haymarket).

       The Burglar Who Failed.

       The Constant Lover (One Act).

       Thompson (unfinished).

A CHRONOLOGY OF NEW WOMAN PLAYS

AND RELATED EVENTS

The plays are listed by date of first English production.

1867   Mill's proposal to substitute 'person' for 'man' in the Representation of the People Bill fails.

1872   Girls' Public Day School Trust founded.

1881   Women allowed to take degree examinations in Cambridge.

1884   Fabian Society founded.

        Married Women's Property Act.

1889   Women's Trade Union League formed.

        Henrik Ibsen, *A Doll's House* (produced Achurch [Nora] and Charrington).

1891   Appeal Court rules that a man has no legal right to kidnap his wife.

        Women (two) appointed to the Factory Inspectorate for the first time.

        Henrik Ibsen, *Hedda Gabler* (produced Robins [Hedda] and Marion Lea).

1893   Married women's property rights affirmed.

        W. S. Gilbert, *Utopia Limited* (Savoy).

        Bernard Shaw, *The Philanderer* (written, not produced).

        A. W. Pinero, *The Second Mrs Tanqueray* (St James's).

1894   Women gain right to vote in local government elections.

        Sidney Grundy, *The New Woman* (Comedy).

        Henry Arthur Jones, *The Case of Rebellious Susan* (Criterion).

        John Todhunter, *A Comedy of Sighs* (Vaudeville).

1895   'Richard Henry' (Henry Chase Newton and Richard Butler), *The Newest Woman*.

        A. W. Pinero, *The Notorious Mrs Ebbsmith* (Garrick).

1897   National Union of Women's Suffrage Societies formed (NUWSS).

1902   Granville Barker, *The Marrying of Ann Leete* (Stage Society).

        Bernard Shaw, *Mrs Warren's Profession* (Closed House; wr. 1893, licensed 1925).

1903   Women's Social and Political Union founded (WSPU).

1905   Bernard Shaw, *Major Barbara* (Court); *Man and Superman* (Court).

Granville Barker, *The Voysey Inheritance* (Court).

St John Hankin, *The Return of the Prodigal* (Court).

1907   NUWSS March (Feb.).

Elizabeth Robins, *Votes for Women!* (Court).

1908   Women Writers' Suffrage League founded (WWSL).

Actresses' Franchise League founded (AFL).

NUWSS March (June).

Cicely Hamilton, *Diana of Dobson's* (Kingsway, Lena Ashwell Season).

St John Hankin, *The Last of the De Mullins* (Haymarket, Stage Society).

1909   First hunger strikes by imprisoned suffragettes.

Elizabeth Baker, *Chains* (Court; Duke of York's, 1910).

Cicely Hamilton and Christopher St John, *How the Vote Was Won* (Royalty).

Cicely Hamilton, *A Pageant of Great Women* (Scala).

Bernard Shaw, *Press Cuttings* (Gaiety, Manchester).

1910   Granville Barker, *The Madras House* (Duke of York's).

J. M. Barrie, *The Twelve Pound Look* (Duke of York's).

1911   Women's Coronation Procession (June); 40,000 participants.

Edy Craig founds Pioneer Players with feminist agenda.

Anon [Shaw], *Fanny's First Play* (Little Theatre).

Margaret Nevinson, *In the Workhouse* (Kingsway, Pioneer Players).

1912–13 Suffrage Campaign at peak of activity.

Stanley Houghton, *Hindle Wakes* (Aldwych, Manchester Repertory Company).

Githa Sowerby, *Rutherford and Son* (Court; Little Theatre; Vaudeville).

1918   Limited female suffrage granted.

1928   Universal adult suffrage in Britain.

THE NEW WOMAN
An Original Comedy,
in Four Acts

BY

SIDNEY GRUNDY

THE NEW WOMAN

*The play was first staged at the Comedy Theatre,° London,
on 1 September 1894 with the following cast*

Gerald Cazenove	*Mr Fred Terry*°
Colonel Cazenove	*Mr Cyril Maude*°
Captain Sylvester	*Mr J. G. Grahame*
James Armstrong	*Mr William Wyes*
Percy Pettigrew	*Mr Stuart Champion*
Wells	*Mr J. Byron*
Servant	*Mr Mules Brown*
Margery	*Miss Winifred Emery*°
Lady Wargrave	*Miss Rose Leclerq*°
Mrs Sylvester	*Miss Alma Murray*°
Miss Enid Bethune	*Miss Ethel Norton*
Miss Victoria Vivash	*Miss Gertrude Warden*°
Dr Mary Bevan	*Miss Irene Rickards*

Act 1 Gerald Cazenove's Chambers   (Mr Walter Johnstone)°
Act 2 Study at Gerald Cazenove's   (Mr Walter Hann)°
Act 3 Drawing Room at Lady Wargrave's   (Mr Walter Hann)
Act 4 An Orchard at Mapledurham   (Mr Walter Hann)

2

1

SCENE *Gerald Cazenove's Chambers. A sitting-room, somewhat effeminately decorated. The furniture of the boudoir type, several antimacassars and a profusion of photographs and flowers.° The main entrance, R at the back, in the flat.° Doors, R and L, window, L of flat.*

A knock is heard off, as curtain rises. Enter Wells, L, crosses stage and opens door in flat. Enter Colonel Cazenove and Sylvester

COLONEL Is my nephew at home?

WELLS No, Colonel; but I expect him every moment.

COLONEL Very well; I'll wait. (*Exit Wells, door in flat*) Bah! What a stench of flowers!° (*Opens window and throws out a bunch of lilies standing on the table below*) Sit down, Sylvester—if you can find a chair to carry twelve stone.   5

SYLVESTER Really, I feel a sort of trespasser.

COLONEL Sit down.

SYLVESTER (*sits*) I don't know Cazenove very well—

COLONEL I'm much in the same case. Since he came up to town, I've   10 only called upon him once before. By Jove, it was enough. Such a set as I met here!

SYLVESTER I understood that he was up the river.

COLONEL Came back yesterday. Hope it's done him good. After all, he's my nephew, and I mean to knock the nonsense out of him.   15

SYLVESTER Colonel, you're very proud of him; and you have every reason to be. From all I hear, few men have won more distinction at Oxford.°

COLONEL (*pleased*) Proud of him? My dear Sylvester, that boy has more brains in his little finger than I have—gout. He takes after his   20 aunt Caroline. You remember Caroline?

SYLVESTER Oh, I remember Lady Wargrave well.

COLONEL Wonderful woman, sir—a heart of gold—and a head— phew! Gerald takes after her. At Oxford, he carried everything before him.   25

SYLVESTER (*laughing*) And now these women carry him behind them!

COLONEL But he's a Cazenove! He'll come right side up. We Cazenoves always do. We may go under every now and then, but we come up again! It's in the blood.

3

SYLVESTER According to my wife—and Agnes is a clever woman in her   30
way—

COLONEL Don't know her.

SYLVESTER His cultivated spirit and magnetic intellect are one of the
brightest hopes for the social progress of our time—(*laughs*) whatever that may mean!   35

COLONEL Does it mean anything? That is the sort of jargon Gerald was
full of, when I saw him last. But he'll get over it. Intellectual measles.
Oxford's a fine place, but no mental drainage.

SYLVESTER I can form no opinion. I hadn't the advantage of a university training.   40

COLONEL I had. I was rusticated.° We Cazenoves always were—till
Gerald's time. But he'll redeem himself. We Cazenoves have always
been men, except one. That's my sister, Caroline; and, by Jove, she's
the next best thing—a woman.

Rising, in his enthusiasm—the antimacassar slips on to the seat

SYLVESTER A real woman.°   45

COLONEL Caroline's a heart of gold—

SYLVESTER Yes, so you said.

COLONEL Did I? I beg your pardon. (*Sits on the antimacassar, instantly
springs up, and flings it into a corner. Points to that covering Sylvester's
chair*) Throw that thing away!

SYLVESTER All right. I'm used to 'em. We grow 'em at our house.   50
(*Looks round*) I might be sitting in my wife's boudoir! Same furniture, same flowers, same photographs—hallo, that's rather a pretty
woman over there! (*Crosses*)

COLONEL A pretty woman, where? (*Crosses*) No, not my style!

SYLVESTER Ha! ha!   55

COLONEL What are you laughing at?

SYLVESTER My wife! I didn't recognize her. (*Goes about examining
photographs*)

COLONEL Ten thousand pardons! I had no idea—

SYLVESTER Bless me, my wife again!

COLONEL (*looking*) That's better. That's much better.   60

SYLVESTER It's an older photograph. Agnes was quite a woman when I
married her, but she grows more and more ethereal.° Philosophy
doesn't seem very nourishing.

COLONEL She's a philosopher?

SYLVESTER Haven't you read her book? *Aspirations after a Higher*   65
Morality.

COLONEL The old morality's high enough for me.

SYLVESTER I've tried to read it, but I didn't succeed. However, I've cut
the leaves° and dropped cigar ash on the final chapter. Why, here she
is again!   70

COLONEL *Three* photographs? And you're not jealous?

SYLVESTER My dear Colonel, who am I to be jealous?

COLONEL Her husband, aren't you?

SYLVESTER Yes, I am Mrs Sylvester's husband. I belong to my wife,
but my wife doesn't belong to me. She is the property of the public.   75
Directly I saw her photograph in a shop-window I realised the situation. People tell me I've a wife to be proud of; but they're wrong.
Mrs Sylvester is not my wife; I am her husband.

COLONEL (*taking up a book*) This is what comes of educating women.
We have created a Frankenstein.° '*Man, the Betrayer—A Study of*   80
the Sexes—by Enid Bethune'.

SYLVESTER Oh, I know her. She comes to our house.

COLONEL And has a man betrayed her?

SYLVESTER Never. Not likely to.

COLONEL That's what's the matter, perhaps?   85

SYLVESTER Her theory is, that boys ought to be girls, and young men
should be maids. (*Colonel throws down the book*) That's how she'd
equalize the sexes.

COLONEL Pshaw! (*Takes up another book*) '*Ye Foolish Virgins!—A
Remonstrance*—by Victoria Vivash'.   90

SYLVESTER Another soul! She's also for equality. Her theory is, that
girls should be boys, and maids should be young men. Goes in for
latchkeys° and that sort of thing.

COLONEL (*throws down the book*) Bah! (*Takes up a third*) '*Naked and
Unashamed—A Few Plain Facts and Figures*—by Mary Bevan,   95
M.D.' Who on earth's she?

SYLVESTER One of the plain figures. *She* comes to our house, too.

COLONEL (*reads*) '*The Physiology of the Sexes*'! Oh, this eternal babble
of the sexes! (*Throws book down*) Why can't a woman be content to
be a woman? What does she want to make a beastly man of herself   100
for?

SYLVESTER But my wife isn't a woman.

COLONEL None of them are, my boy. A woman, who *is* a woman,
doesn't want to be anything else. These people are a sex of their own,
Sylvester. They have invented a new gender. And to think my   105
nephew's one of them!°

> *Strides up and down, seizes another antimacassar and flings it
> into another corner*

5

SYLVESTER Oh, he's young. Don't despair!

COLONEL I don't despair! Do you suppose this folly can continue? Do you imagine that these puffed-up women will not soon burst of their own vanity? Then, the reaction! then will come *our* turn! Mark my words, Sylvester, there'll be a boom in men! (*Rubbing his hands*)

> *Enter Gerald, door in flat*

GERALD Good afternoon. I'm sorry to have kept you waiting. (*Shakes hands with Colonel*)

COLONEL Here you are, at last.

GERALD (*shaking hands with Sylvester*) How's Mrs Sylvester?

SYLVESTER I was just going to ask you. You see more of her than I do.

GERALD We are collaborating.

COLONEL In the Higher Morality?

SYLVESTER How are you getting on?

GERALD Oh, we are only on the threshold. I finished the first chapter about daybreak.

COLONEL That's how you waste the precious hours of night? Gad, sir, when I was your age—

GERALD That was thirty years ago. Things have changed since then.

COLONEL And they haven't improved.

GERALD That is a question.

COLONEL Oh, everything's a question nowadays! Nothing is sacred to a young man fresh from Oxford. Existence is a problem to be investigated; in my youth, it was a life to be lived; and, I thank Heaven, I lived it. Ah, the nights *I* had!°

SYLVESTER Would it be impertinent to inquire upon what subject my wife is engaged?

GERALD Our subject is the Ethics of Marriage.

SYLVESTER Of my marriage?

GERALD Of marriage in the abstract.

COLONEL As if people married for ethics! There is no such thing, sir. There are no ethics in marriage.

GERALD That is the conclusion at which we have arrived.

COLONEL You are only on the threshold, and yet you have arrived at a conclusion?

GERALD So much is obvious. It is a conclusion to which literature and the higher culture inevitably tend. The awakened conscience of woman is already alive to it.

COLONEL Conscience of woman! What are you talking about? I've known a good many women in my time, and they hadn't a conscience

6

THE NEW WOMAN   I.I

amongst 'em! There's only one thing can awaken the conscience of 145
woman, and that is being found out.

GERALD I am speaking of innocent women.

COLONEL I never met one.

GERALD Yet—

COLONEL Tut, tut, sir; read your Bible. Who was it had the first bite at 150
the apple? And she's been nibbling at it ever since!

GERALD Well, well, uncle, you don't often come to see me; so we won't
argue. Can I prevail on you to stay to tea?

COLONEL To stay to *what*, sir?

GERALD Tea. At five o'clock, I have a few friends coming. Mrs Syl- 155
vester—(*Sylvester puts down photograph and turns*)—Miss Bethune—Miss Vivash—

SYLVESTER And Dr Mary Bevan?

GERALD Yes, I expect Miss Bevan.

COLONEL 'Naked and Unashamed'? 160

GERALD They may bring Percy with them.

COLONEL Percy?

GERALD Percy Pettigrew.°

COLONEL A man? An actual man? A bull amongst that china?

SYLVESTER Well, hardly! 165

COLONEL You know him, Sylvester?

SYLVESTER They bring him to our house.

GERALD Nobody has done more for the Advancement of Woman.

SYLVESTER By making a public exhibition of the Decay of Man.

GERALD Sylvester, you're a Philistine. I won't ask you to stay. 170

SYLVESTER Man the Betrayer might be dangerous, amongst such foolish virgins.

COLONEL The danger would be all the other way. I am not sorry *I* shall
have protection. My sister, Caroline, will be here at five.

GERALD Aunt Caroline! (*A little nervously*)° 175

COLONEL I came to announce her visit.

SYLVESTER Lady Wargrave has returned to England?

COLONEL After ten years' absence. She has been travelling for her
health, which was never too robust; and since Sir Oriel's death, she
has been more or less a wanderer. 180

GERALD I knew she had arrived, but I postponed presenting myself till
I was summoned. My aunt has the kindest of hearts—

COLONEL A heart of gold, sir.

GERALD And a pocket too. Nobody knows that better than I do. Since
my parents' death, she has been father and mother, as well as aunt, to 185

me. But there was always something about aunt that made one keep one's distance.

COLONEL (*in a milder voice than he has yet used*) And there is still, Gerald.

GERALD Then I'm glad I've kept mine.   190

COLONEL You acted very wisely; I happen to know she wished her arrival kept secret and to descend upon you like a *dea ex machinâ*.° Caroline always had a sense of dramatic effect. But how the deuce did you know of her return?

GERALD Oh, very simply. Margery told me.   195

COLONEL Margery!

GERALD Aunt wrote to summon her to resume her duties.

COLONEL But Margery's at Mapledurham.° Caroline was stopping with some friends in Paris, and Margery was sent on to her father's.

GERALD Six weeks ago.   200

COLONEL Why, you know all about it.

GERALD Yes, I was staying there when she arrived. I have been rusticating for the last six weeks. It's so much easier to write in the fresh air.

SYLVESTER You have been writing down at Mapledurham?   205

GERALD That's what I went for.

COLONEL For six weeks?

GERALD Six weeks.

COLONEL And you have only finished the first chapter?

GERALD It's so difficult to write in the fresh air. One wants to go out and   210
enjoy oneself. And then old Armstrong's such a jolly old boy.

SYLVESTER Armstrong, of Mapledurham? The farmer? Oh, I know him well. I go there for the fishing.

COLONEL Then, do you know Margery?

SYLVESTER Margery? No.   215

GERALD How that girl sculls!°

COLONEL Oh, Margery was rowing?

GERALD Do you know, uncle, she can almost beat me?

COLONEL But what an arm she has!

GERALD And when she feathers°——(*Pantomime*°)   220

COLONEL Ah! When she feathers——(*Double pantomime*)

GERALD What a voice, too!

COLONEL Hasn't she!

GERALD So musical! When she sings out, 'Lock, ho!'

COLONEL (*imitating*) 'Lock, ho!'   225

GERALD No, not a bit like that—more silvery!

8

COLONEL Not a bit! more silvery!

BOTH (*pantomiming*) 'Lock, ho!'

SYLVESTER Who's Margery?

COLONEL Oh, my dear fellow, just your sort—*my* sort—well, hang it,   230
every man's sort! Margery is—oh, how can I explain? If I'd seen a
Margery thirty years ago; well, I should never have been a bachelor!°
Margery is—come, Gerald, what *is* Margery? Margery is a woman,
who—Well, Margery's a woman! That's all Margery is!

GERALD Old Armstrong's daughter. We grew up together. When I was   235
very young, I was considered delicate, and I was sent to the farmhouse at Mapledurham. When I went to Eton, Lady Wargrave took
Margery into her service. There she has remained—

COLONEL And she is coming with your aunt today.

> *Knock at door in flat. Re-enter Wells, followed by Mrs Sylvester,*
> *with a small portfolio*

WELLS Mrs Sylvester! (*Exit, door in flat*)   240

MRS SYLVESTER (*stops short on seeing Sylvester*) Jack!

SYLVESTER This is an unexpected pleasure. (*A cold matrimonial kiss*)
Colonel Cazenove—my old Colonel. Mr Cazenove I think you know.

MRS SYLVESTER Well, of course, Jack! How ridiculous you are! Should
I be here if I didn't know Mr Cazenove?   245

SYLVESTER I haven't the least notion. I only know you wouldn't be at
home.

MRS SYLVESTER I was in all the morning.

SYLVESTER I had business at the Horse Guards.° I shall be home to
dinner, though.   250

MRS SYLVESTER Oh dear, I wish I had known that. There's only
mutton.

SYLVESTER The same mutton?°

MRS SYLVESTER What do you mean by same?

SYLVESTER I mean the mutton I had yesterday.   255

MRS SYLVESTER Did you have mutton yesterday?

SYLVESTER No matter; I'll dine at the club.°

MRS SYLVESTER Thank you, dear.

SYLVESTER Good-bye. (*Kiss*) Good-bye, Mr Cazenove.

COLONEL I will come with you. (*To Gerald*) I am due at your aunt's.   260

GERALD But I shall see you again presently?

COLONEL If I am visible behind Caroline. Madam, your servant. (*Aside
to Sylvester*) Cheer up, Sylvester! I'll join you at the club, and we will
wind the night up at the Empire.°

> *Exit after Sylvester, R of flat*

MRS SYLVESTER That is so like a man! Doesn't say he's coming home,   265
   and then expects six courses and a savoury!

GERALD There is a difference between cold mutton and six courses, to
   say nothing of the savoury.

MRS SYLVESTER It is a fine distinction, and in no way affects the valid-
   ity of my argument.   270

GERALD (*smiling*) You mean, of your statement.

MRS SYLVESTER Husbands are all alike. The ancient regarded his wife
   as a slave, the modern regards her as a cook.

GERALD Then they are *not* alike.

MRS SYLVESTER (*emphatically*) A man thinks of nothing but his   275
   stomach.

GERALD That is another proposition.

MRS SYLVESTER You're very argumentative today. I haven't seen you
   for six weeks, and you've come home in a nasty, horrid temper!

GERALD I have been working so hard.   280

MRS SYLVESTER Why is your face so brown?

GERALD Well, of course, I went out.

MRS SYLVESTER (*takes his hand*) And why are your hands blistered?

GERALD I had a few pulls on the river; and being out of training—

MRS SYLVESTER (*innocently*) Were you stroke? (*Holding his hands*)   285

GERALD Not always. (*Bites his lip*)

MRS SYLVESTER Oh,° then you weren't alone?

GERALD I met an old friend up the river.

MRS SYLVESTER Now I understand why you didn't write to me. (*Drops
   his hand and turns away pettishly*)

GERALD About the book? (*She gives him a quick glance*) Oh, I had noth-   290
   ing to say, except that I was getting on all right. I've written the first
   chapter. (*Produces manuscript*)

MRS SYLVESTER And I've written the last. (*Opening portfolio*) Connot-
   ing the results of our arguments.

GERALD But where are the arguments?   295

MRS SYLVESTER We'll put those in afterwards. (*Gerald looks at her*)
   That's how Victoria always writes her novels. She begins at the
   end.

GERALD But this is a work of philosophy.

MRS SYLVESTER (*pouting*) Oh, you *are* disagreeable!   300

GERALD (*putting manuscript aside*) Don't let us talk philosophy today.
   I want to talk to you about something else.

MRS SYLVESTER (*cheerfully*) Yes!

GERALD I have something to tell you.

MRS SYLVESTER Interesting? (*Smiling*)

GERALD I'm in love.

MRS SYLVESTER Oh! (*From this point her manner changes*)

GERALD Yes, in love, Mrs Sylvester—in real love.

MRS SYLVESTER What do you call real love?

GERALD Something quite different from what we had supposed. We've   310
been on the wrong tack altogether. We have imagined something we
have labelled love; we have put it into a crucible, and reduced it to its
elements.

MRS SYLVESTER And we have found those elements to be, community
of interest and sympathy of soul.   315

GERALD But unfortunately for our theory, the thing we put into the
crucible wasn't love at all.

MRS SYLVESTER How do you know?

GERALD I didn't, till last week.

MRS SYLVESTER It was at Mapledurham you made this discovery?   320

GERALD At Mapledurham.

MRS SYLVESTER And your friend?

GERALD She was the revelation.

MRS SYLVESTER I thought it was a woman.

GERALD That word just describes her. She is a woman—nothing more   325
or less. Away went all my theories into air. My precious wisdom was
stripped bare before me, and in its nakedness I saw my folly. Not with
laborious thought; but in one vivid flash I learned more than I ever
learned at Oxford.

MRS SYLVESTER Really?   330

GERALD A woman! that is what one wants—that's all. Birth, brains,
accomplishments—pshaw! vanities! community of interest—
sympathy of soul? mere dialectics! That's not love.

MRS SYLVESTER What *is*, then?

GERALD It defies analysis. You can't put love into a crucible. You   335
only know that there is something empty in you; and you don't
know what fills it; but that's love. There's no mistake about the real
thing.

MRS SYLVESTER Is she good-looking?

GERALD In *my* eyes.   340

MRS SYLVESTER A lady?

GERALD In social station, beneath me. But what's social station?

MRS SYLVESTER This is infatuation. Some riverside coquette—

GERALD Simplicity itself.

MRS SYLVESTER Of course you think so; but you don't know women.   345

The simple woman hasn't yet been born. This isn't love, Mr Cazenove. This is the temporary victory of the baser side of your nature.
The true alliance is the union of souls.°

GERALD Of man and woman.

MRS SYLVESTER But of soul and soul; not a mere sensual temptation.   350

GERALD Nor is this. A week ago I thought so. I know better now.

MRS SYLVESTER Happily the weeks are not all over yet. In a few more
you will have forgotten her as completely as she will have forgotten
you.

GERALD In a few more, I hope that she will be my wife.   355

MRS SYLVESTER You contemplate a *mésalliance?*°

GERALD There is no *mésalliance* where there's love.

MRS SYLVESTER You, of whom everyone expects so much, to throw
away your opportunities, and to begin your life hindered and ham-
pered by a foolish marriage.   360

GERALD If she will only marry me.

MRS SYLVESTER (*looks at him, pained*) I may still be your friend? (*Offers
him her hands, which he takes a little reluctantly. Re-enter Wells*)

WELLS Lady Wargrave. (*Exit*)
        *Enter Lady Wargrave leaning on the Colonel's arm. She walks
        with a crutch-stick, and is followed by Margery, who carries a
        cushion. Mrs Sylvester retires up,° so that she is not immediately
        seen by Lady Wargrave*

GERALD (*a little tentatively*) My dear aunt!
        They shake hands

LADY WARGRAVE You may kiss me.   365
        *He kisses her, then casts a glance of gratitude at Margery. Mean-
        while Margery has prepared a chair for her, into which she is
        placed by Gerald and the Colonel, who is now subdued and defer-
        ential, in marked contrast to his last scene. Margery takes up her
        position in the background*

COLONEL I was so fortunate as to meet the carriage.

LADY WARGRAVE Theodore was late as usual.

COLONEL Only ten minutes, Caroline; but, as you know, time, tide,
and your aunt wait for no man.

LADY WARGRAVE Now, Gerald, let me look at you. Your face to the   370
light, please. (*Gerald stands for inspection. She takes a long look through
her eye-glass*) I don't like that necktie.

GERALD (*smiling and bowing*) It shall be changed tomorrow, aunt.

LADY WARGRAVE Today. (*Gerald bows. She takes another look*) That
will do, Gerald. (*Gerald salutes. She drops her glasses*)   375

COLONEL Stand at ease! Dismiss!°

LADY WARGRAVE Theodore, this is not a barracks!

COLONEL True. (*Bows*) Peccavi!°

LADY WARGRAVE (*addressing Gerald*) I need hardly say with what pleasure I have followed your career at Oxford. It is worthy of a Cazenove.   380

COLONEL Brilliant—magnificent!

LADY WARGRAVE It is worthy of a Cazenove; that is all.

> *Colonel subsides, bowing*

GERALD Yes, aunt, I flatter myself—

LADY WARGRAVE Don't do that. You did your duty. Nothing more.   385

GERALD By the way, did you receive my poem?

LADY WARGRAVE Poem?

GERALD That won the Newdigate.° I sent you a copy—to Rome.

LADY WARGRAVE Ah, I remember; I received the document. Tell me, were there many competitors?   390

GERALD A dozen or so.

LADY WARGRAVE Is it possible that Oxford can produce eleven worse poems than yours?

GERALD My dear aunt!

> *Colonel turns aside, chuckling, and finds himself face to face with*
> *Margery, laughing; both become suddenly serious*

MRS SYLVESTER (*advancing*) It is a work of genius—none but a true poet—   395

LADY WARGRAVE (*half rising. Margery steps forward to help her*) I ask your pardon. Gerald, you haven't introduced me!

GERALD Forgive me, Mrs Sylvester—forgive me, aunt, but in the excitement of seeing you—   400

LADY WARGRAVE Sylvester!

COLONEL Wife of my old lieutenant. Captain now.

LADY WARGRAVE Wife of Jack Sylvester! I am pleased to meet you. I have known your husband almost from a boy. But I don't see him. (*Looking round*)

GERALD (*confused*) He has just gone. (*Lady Wargrave looks from one to another. Slight pause*)   405

MRS SYLVESTER Mr Cazenove and I are collaborating.

LADY WARGRAVE Oh! Captain Sylvester's wife is collaborating with *you*?

GERALD On the ethics of marriage.

MRS SYLVESTER Viewed from the standpoint of the higher morality.   410

LADY WARGRAVE Ah! (*Drops back into her seat, helped by Margery*)

That will be a very interesting work. (*Margery retires up*) Did you do very much down at Mapledurham?

GERALD Not *very* much, I'm afraid.

MRS SYLVESTER Mr Cazenove met a friend up the river.   415

LADY WARGRAVE A friend? Margery, you didn't tell me that.

MARGERY (*advancing, and with a slight curtsey*) I didn't know, my lady.

MRS SYLVESTER An old friend.

COLONEL Perhaps the old friend was Margery herself?

MRS SYLVESTER (*perplexed and curious*) Your maid was at Maple-   420
durham?

LADY WARGRAVE Her father lives there. Theodore, don't you think
Margery looks all the better for her holiday?

COLONEL (*with enthusiasm*) If it is possible—

LADY WARGRAVE (*aside to him, stopping his mouth with her fan*)   425
Theodore!

COLONEL (*subsides. Sotto voce*°) Peccavi!

LADY WARGRAVE Doesn't she look brown?

GERALD Well, up the river everybody does. It was hot weather, too.

LADY WARGRAVE It must have been. You should have seen her hands.   430
They were all over blisters.

COLONEL Ah, that was the rowing! (*Pantomime as before*)

LADY WARGRAVE Margery! (*Margery casts down her eyes*) You were
rowing?

MARGERY Sometimes, my lady.   435

MRS SYLVESTER Stroke.° (*Looking at Gerald*)
        Lady Wargrave, watching Mrs Sylvester, motions to Margery,
        who retires up

COLONEL (*aside to Lady Wargrave*) Caroline, you took the water very
neatly.

LADY WARGRAVE (*aside to Colonel*) The higher morality has caught a
crab.°   440

MRS SYLVESTER (*gathers up manuscript into her portfolio*) I will not tres-
pass any longer, Mr Cazenove. No doubt, your aunt has much to say
to you.

GERALD But won't you stay to tea?

MRS SYLVESTER Thanks. Captain Sylvester dines early.   445

COLONEL (*aside*) At the club!

MRS SYLVESTER Good day to you, Lady Wargrave. (*Lady Wargrave is
about to rise*) Pray don't rise. (*Bows to the Colonel and goes to door in
flat where Gerald is waiting for her*) Don't trouble; I know my way.
(*Exit*)

LADY WARGRAVE Poor Sylvester! He was such a nice boy! (*Gerald*   450
   comes down) Gerald, can Margery wait in the next room?
     Gerald opens door R. Exit Margery R
GERALD (*returning*) And how have you been, aunt? You never mentioned your health in your letters. Are you better?
LADY WARGRAVE I mustn't complain; but Providence is really most
   unjust. Here am I, who have lived a life of temperance, in my old   455
   age—
COLONEL Middle age, Caroline! (*Bowing*)
LADY WARGRAVE (*smiling*) A chronic invalid; while this old transgres-
   sor who has denied himself nothing (*Colonel grins*), and committed
   every sin in the Decalogue° (*Colonel chuckles*), is as hale and as hearty   460
   as I am infirm.
COLONEL Never felt better, never!
LADY WARGRAVE But how have *you* been, Gerald? *We* belong to the
   past—
COLONEL Caroline!   465
LADY WARGRAVE *You* belong to the future, and the future belongs to
   you.
GERALD Oh, I've been all right! (*A little recklessly*)
LADY WARGRAVE Quite sure you suffer from nothing?
GERALD What do you mean?   470
LADY WARGRAVE Your letters have told me a great deal—more than
   perhaps you know; but I have read them very carefully; and when you
   asked me to come home—
GERALD I didn't, aunt.
LADY WARGRAVE Between the lines.   475
GERALD (*laughing*) What did I say to you between the lines? (*Kneeling
   by her*)
LADY WARGRAVE You told me that you had learned everything Oxford
   has to teach worth learning, and that you were in danger of becom-
   ing—well (*laying her hand on his head*)—shall we say, *tête montée?*°
COLONEL Yes, Caroline! I should certainly say, *tête montée.*   480
LADY WARGRAVE Cure yourself, Gerald. Knowledge is not wisdom.
   (*Stroking his head*) Forgive me, dear; but I have known so many men
   who have never survived the distinctions of their youth, who are
   always at Oxford, and even in their manhood play with rattles. Now,
   forget Oxford—go into the world—lay books aside, and study men.   485
COLONEL *And* women.
LADY WARGRAVE Yes—and *women.* (*Knock without*°)
GERALD (*rising*) Just what I'm doing!

Female voices in altercation. Re-enter Wells, door in flat

WELLS Miss Bethune, Miss Vivash.

Enter Enid and Victoria, in hot argument. They take opposite sides of the stage and continue the discussion without taking the slightest notice of anybody.° Lady Wargrave looks from the one to the other in amazement. Exit Wells, door in flat

ENID I can't agree with you! Say what you will, I can't agree with you!   490

VICTORIA That doesn't alter the fact. A woman has just as much right to a latchkey as a man.

ENID But a man has no right to a latchkey.

VICTORIA That's ridiculous!

ENID Rudeness is not argument!   495

VICTORIA Why make distinctions?

ENID I make no distinctions. I admit that a woman has just as much right to come home with the milk° as a man: but I say, a man has no right to come home with the milk; and I say more—no woman who respects herself has any *desire* to come home with the milk!   500

VICTORIA Bother the milk! It isn't a question of milk. It's a question of making artificial distinctions between the sexes.

ENID I say that there ought to be *no* distinction! Why should a man be allowed to commit sins—

VICTORIA And woman not be given an opportunity?   505

ENID Then do you *want* to commit sins?

VICTORIA I want to be allowed to do as *men* do.

ENID Then you ought to be ashamed of yourself; there!

VICTORIA I only say, I ought to be allowed.

ENID And *I* say that a man, reeking with infamy, ought not to be   510
allowed to marry a pure girl—

VICTORIA Certainly not! *She* ought to reek with infamy as well.

ENID Victoria! (*Knock without*)

VICTORIA What is the difference between man and woman?

ENID There is *no* difference.   515

Re-enter Wells, door in flat

WELLS Dr Mary Bevan.° (*Exit Wells. Enter Dr Mary Bevan*)

VICTORIA Why should a woman have children and a man have none?

ENID But a man *has* children!

DOCTOR Only vicariously.   520

VICTORIA Here's Dr Mary! (*Rushing up to Doctor. Enid has rushed up to the other side of her*)

DOCTOR (*pragmatically*) But I am not without hope that, when the

attention of science is directed to the unequal incidence of the burden
of maternity, some method of re-adjustment may be devised.

LADY WARGRAVE (*who has risen*) Pardon me, ladies; but if you are   525
about to consult your physician, you would no doubt prefer to be
alone.°

> *They turn and see her for the first time*

VICTORIA Pray, don't move.

GERALD My aunt, Lady Wargrave. Colonel Cazenove.

DOCTOR These matters are best discussed openly. A morbid modesty   530
has too long closed our eyes. But the day of awakening has come.
Sylvester, in her *Aspirations after a Higher Morality*, Bethune, in her
Man, the Betrayer, Vivash, in her *Foolish Virgins*, have postulated the
sexual problem from every conceivable point of view; and I have
myself contributed to the discussion a modest little treatise—   535

ENID No, no, not modest!

VICTORIA Profound!

DOCTOR *Naked and Unashamed!*

ENID Man has done all the talking up to now—

VICTORIA He has had things all his own way—   540

DOCTOR And a nice mess he's made of them!

ENID Now it is our turn.

VICTORIA We mean to put things right!

DOCTOR Man has departed. Woman has arrived.

LADY WARGRAVE Excuse my ignorance, but I have been away from Eng-   545
land for so many years. Can this be the New Woman I have read about?

COLONEL Everything's New nowadays!° We have a New Art—

ENID A New Journalism—

VICTORIA A New Political Economy—

DOCTOR A New Morality—   550

COLONEL A New Sex!

LADY WARGRAVE (*smiling*) Ah!

DOCTOR Do you object to modernity?

LADY WARGRAVE I've only one objection to new things; they are so old.

VICTORIA Not the New Woman!   555

LADY WARGRAVE No; *she* is generally middle-aged.

> *Colonel turns to Gerald, to hide his chuckles*

ENID Then, do you take Man's part in the discussion?

LADY WARGRAVE I take no part in it.

DOCTOR Do you deny that Woman has arrived, Man has departed?

LADY WARGRAVE I don't wonder at it. But Man has an awkward habit   560
of coming back again.

TRIO Never!

LADY WARGRAVE Then Woman will go after him.

> *Colonel roars out aloud—the Women survey him with disgust.*
> *Re-enter Wells, L, and whispers to Gerald*

GERALD Tea is quite ready, ladies!

ENID Ah! A cup of tea! (*Exit L, followed by Victoria, Doctor Mary, and* 565
Wells)

LADY WARGRAVE Theodore, your arm. These ladies interest me.
Besides, they sadly want a chaperone.

COLONEL They want a husband°—that's what *they* want, badly!

LADY WARGRAVE Gerald, call Margery. (*Gerald goes to door R*) Well,
they are looking for one. (*Glancing after Gerald*)   570

COLONEL And they've found *you*, Caroline.

> *Exeunt both, laughing, L. Each time the door, L, is opened, a*
> *babel° of female voices is heard from within, and such phrases as*
> *'Peter Robinson's', 'Swan and Edgar's', 'Stagg and Mantle's',°*
> *are distinctly audible above the clink of teacups, etc. Re-enter*
> *Margery, R, she goes straight to Lady Wargrave's chair, and is*
> *about to carry the cushion into the room, L, when Gerald, who has*
> *stood back, watching her, advances*

GERALD Margery! (*Margery drops the cushion and turns*) Thank you!
God bless you!

MARGERY For what, sir?

GERALD You have not told my aunt.   575

MARGERY Of course I haven't told her! (*Slight pause*) May I go?

GERALD Not yet. Margery, can you ever forgive me?

MARGERY For being a man? Oh yes!

GERALD Can you ever respect me again?

MARGERY I do respect you, sir.   580

GERALD Not as I do you, Margery. You don't know what you did for me
that day. If you had rounded on me, I should not have cared—but to
be silent—to do nothing—to forgive me!

MARGERY I had a reason for forgiving you.

GERALD What?   585

MARGERY That's my business.

GERALD But, Margery, you do forgive me?

MARGERY Don't let's talk about it.

GERALD *Really* forgive me?

MARGERY Really!   590

GERALD Prove it to me.

MARGERY How can I?

GERALD (*still° holding her*) Be my wife!

MARGERY (*recoiling*) Mr Cazenove!

GERALD My name is Gerald.   595

MARGERY Mr Gerald!°

GERALD Gerald! Call me so, Margery.

MARGERY I couldn't, sir. Don't ask me!

GERALD Then you refuse me? (*Margery is silent—he turns away*) Well,
I don't deserve you.   600

MARGERY (*approaching him*) Oh, don't think I mean that! Do you suppose you are the only man that's ever made love to me?° It's a man's
business to make love; and it's a woman's business to stop him—
when he makes love too hard. But if we can't be lovers, Mr Gerald, we
can be friends.   605

GERALD It's got past friendship with me, Margery. Since I came back to
town, everything's changed. My pursuits all feel so empty and so
meaningless; every woman I meet seems different from what she was:
and oh, how different from *you*!

MARGERY Gentry *are* different. We're different breeds. That's why we   610
can't be lovers.

GERALD We can be man and wife!

MARGERY Isn't that being lovers?

GERALD In my case, it would be!

MARGERY Hush! Mr Gerald, that's impossible. My lady will be asking   615
for me. Let me go!

GERALD Not till I've told you how I love you, Margery. Seeing you
again is breathing the pure air. It seems a younger and a sweeter
world, now you have come again. Nothing else matters. All my life
beside appears a folly and a waste of time. My real life was lived with   620
you down yonder, out in the fields, and rambling through the woods
and listening to the music of the weir. The life that we began together
so pleasantly, cannot we live together to the end? I was quite honest
when I said I loved you. And couldn't you love *me*,—just a little bit?

MARGERY You oughtn't to ask that!   625

GERALD I mean to have an answer.

MARGERY Please, Mr Gerald, don't! It makes it very hard for me—

GERALD Answer me! Could you love me, Margery?

MARGERY Oh, what's the use of asking? You only want to make me tell
a lie.   630

GERALD Answer me!

MARGERY I *have* answered you!

GERALD Margery, then you do!

MARGERY That is what made it easy to forgive you. Now let me go.

GERALD Not till you've said that you will be my wife.   635

MARGERY Oh, Mr Gerald.

GERALD Gerald! say Gerald!

MARGERY It's no use. I can't!

GERALD Say you will marry me!

MARGERY If you will let me call you 'Mr Gerald'. (*Embrace*)   640

COLONEL (*off, opens door L*) Margery! where are you?
   Re-enter L, just as Margery is withdrawing from Gerald's arms,
   stands thunderstruck. Exit Margery, L

GERALD It's all right, uncle.

COLONEL All right, you call it? Look here, you young cub! None of
your higher morality with Margery!

GERALD I tell you, it's all right. Margery's going to be your niece—my   645
wife.

COLONEL Margery, your wife! (*Slight pause*) You're a damned lucky
dog!

GERALD That I am, uncle!

COLONEL 'Gad, sir, you're a man; and I thought you were a monkey.   650
I congratulate you!

GERALD (*shaking hands*) *You* don't object then?

COLONEL I thought a Cazenove would come right side up.

GERALD But what will aunt say?

COLONEL (*suddenly collapses*) I was forgetting Caroline!   655

GERALD She must be told.

COLONEL But cautiously. Courage! I'll back you up!

GERALD I'll tell her now!

COLONEL Stay! Don't do anything rash! I wouldn't risk a private interview. Safety in numbers.   660

GERALD I will tell them all!

COLONEL Sht! what a bomb-shell! Courage!

GERALD Courage, yourself! You're shaking all over.

COLONEL No matter. I'll stand by you!

LADY WARGRAVE (*opening door, L*) Gerald!   665

COLONEL Form square!° Prepare to receive cavalry! (*Retires up*)
   Re-enter Lady Wargrave, L

LADY WARGRAVE Where are you? Why have you deserted me? To
leave me at the mercy of that crew! My poor, dear, Gerald! however
did you get into this set?

GERALD It was my poem did it.   670

LADY WARGRAVE I thought, that crime would bring its punishment.

20

Now, they're upon the marriage service! As though *that* concerned
them! Gerald, if you marry any of that tribe, you'll really break my
heart!

>   *Colonel comes down R of Gerald*

GERALD I hope I shall never do that!   675

LADY WARGRAVE Marry a *woman*, whatever else she is.

COLONEL (*aside to Gerald*) Courage!

GERALD Or isn't, aunt! (*Effusively*)

COLONEL (*aside to Gerald*) Caution! (*Retires up*)

LADY WARGRAVE Or isn't!   680

>   *The door L is thrown open, and re-enter Dr Mary, Enid, and*
>   *Victoria, all talking, followed by Margery, who takes up her*
>   *original position at the back*

DOCTOR 'Obey,' forsooth!°

VICTORIA To promise to love is ridiculous, for how can one control the
mysterious expansions of the heart?

DOCTOR It is the brain that loves. A still more complicated mechanism.

ENID It is impossible to honour a man who has invariably lived a revolt-   685
ing, ante-nuptial life—

VICTORIA But to 'obey!'

>   *Colonel works down stage,° interested*

DOCTOR Lady Wargrave, even *you* surely wouldn't promise to 'obey' a
man?

LADY WARGRAVE Not till he asked me, certainly.   690

COLONEL Ha! ha!

>   *The trio turn on him; he retires up*

LADY WARGRAVE Gerald, I must be going.

DOCTOR So must I.

ENID And I.

DOCTOR I have a clinical lecture—   695

VICTORIA I have an engagement.

GERALD One moment, ladies! Stay one moment, aunt! Before you go
I want to tell you all of *my* engagement.

LADY WARGRAVE Your engagement, Gerald?

GERALD Yes, I am going to be married. (*Pause*)   700

ENID (*with jealousy*) To Agnes Syl—? Oh, I forgot; she's married.

LADY WARGRAVE To whom? (*All stand expectantly*)

GERALD To Margery.

>   *All stand transfixed. Exit Colonel, door in flat*

DOCTOR Mr Cazenove, I offer you my congratulations. Having a clinical lecture to deliver, you will excuse me if I say good afternoon.   705

ENID Wait for me, Doctor. (*Exit Dr Mary, door in flat*) You have my best wishes. (*Exit, door in flat*)

VICTORIA And thank you for the plot of my next novel. (*Exit, door in flat*)

LADY WARGRAVE Gerald, is this a trick?

GERALD No, aunt; it is the truth.   710

LADY WARGRAVE And you, a Cazenove! It is out of the question! I won't permit it! I forbid it, Gerald!

GERALD But, my dear aunt, you said only just now—

LADY WARGRAVE No matter!

GERALD Marry a woman—   715

LADY WARGRAVE Don't repeat my words! A Cazenove marry Margery! Ridiculous!

GERALD But, aunt—

LADY WARGRAVE Silence! You said just now, you hoped that you would never break my heart. Well, Gerald, you have broken it. A   720
Cazenove! (*Exit, door in flat*)

     Margery takes up the cushion, and is about to follow

GERALD Put that thing down. (*She puts it down*) You are mine now; not hers.

MARGERY Yes, Mr Gerald.

GERALD (*sits, drawing her to him*) For better, for worse, Margery.   725

MARGERY For better, for worse.

GERALD You are not frightened?

MARGERY Not now, Mr Gerald.

GERALD Then call me, Gerald.

MARGERY Gerald! (*Dropping on her knee by his side*)   730

GERALD *You're* not afraid to make those promises!

MARGERY No, Gerald!

GERALD To love—to honour.

MARGERY And obey! (*Looking up at him*)

CURTAIN

2

Twelve months have elapsed.

SCENE *Study at Gerald's, opening upon a little boudoir, through curtains which are drawn across part of the stage at back. Doors, R, and LUE. Mantelpiece, between doors, R*

Gerald discovered, seated at a writing table, with his back to the curtains, writing busily. Margery's head appears through the curtains, which she holds closely round it, so that only her face is visible. She watches Gerald for a few moments, with a broad smile on her face

MARGERY Bo! (*Withdraws her head*)

GERALD (*starts and looks round*) Margery, of course!
    Resumes his writing. A peal of laughter behind the curtains, and Margery's head reappears, laughing. Gerald throws down his pen

MARGERY (*running in*) Did I startle you?

GERALD Not much; I'm getting used to it.

MARGERY Well, don't be cross!   5

GERALD I'm not cross, dear; but these repeated interludes make composition rather difficult.

MARGERY Oh, bother! you've been all the morning at that stupid book, and I'm so happy, I can't help it. Kiss me, and say that you forgive me!

GERALD Of course I forgive you!   10

MARGERY Kiss me, then!

GERALD My dear—

MARGERY Gerald! will you kiss me?

GERALD (*kisses her*) How many times does that make?

MARGERY Only three this morning. You used to like kissing me.   15

GERALD Yes, dear, but—

MARGERY What?

GERALD This isn't writing my book.

MARGERY No, but it's being happy, and that's worth all the books that ever were written.   20

GERALD Yes—being happy—that's the great thing. (*Sighs*)

MARGERY Why do you sigh?

GERALD Did I sigh? (*Smiling*)

MARGERY Yes.

GERALD I didn't know I sighed. Writing's hard work.   25

MARGERY   Then put the book away! (*Thrusts the manuscript aside*) I've such news for you!

GERALD   News?

MARGERY   Such good news. Guess what it is. I'll give you three tries.

GERALD (*deprecatingly*)   Margery!

MARGERY   You'll never guess!

GERALD   Then what's the use of trying?

MARGERY   Because I want you to guess wrong.

GERALD   I shan't do that!

MARGERY   You will! I'm sure you will!

GERALD   I'm sure I shan't, because I am not going to guess at all.

MARGERY (*grimaces*)   Cross again! You'd better not be, or you know the penalty!

GERALD   Come! what is the good news?

MARGERY   That's the good news. (*Gives him a card*)

GERALD (*with real pleasure*)   Margery!

MARGERY (*pouting*)   You might have guessed!

GERALD   A card from Lady Wargrave! And addressed to you!

MARGERY   Asking us to a party at her house.

GERALD   Don't say a party, Margery!

MARGERY   Well, isn't it a party?

GERALD   Call it an At Home.

MARGERY   Oh, that's another lesson! Never call things by their right names, it's vulgar!°

GERALD   This is an olive-branch,° and no mistake! So aunt is thawing at last.

MARGERY   Stop a bit, Gerald!

GERALD   Wait a moment, Margery!

MARGERY   Is that another lesson? Never use one syllable when two will do? Very well, Gerald, I'll remember that. But what do you mean by olive-branch?

GERALD (*looks at her, and sighs again*)   Oh, never mind!

MARGERY   Yes, tell me. I want to make sure as I go along.

GERALD   An overture—a sign of reconciliation—like holding out your hand.

MARGERY   Ah, now I understand! But what a funny thing to call it— olive-branch! (*Bursts into a peal of laughter*)

GERALD (*shivers slightly and goes over to the mantelpiece. Aside°*)   It didn't sound like that in Mapledurham! (*Conquering himself, returns to her*) I'm so glad aunt's come round. You don't know how it's worried me—her estrangement.

MARGERY They've all come round now. They've all recognized me. Oh, I'm so happy, Gerald! It isn't half as hard to be a lady as I thought!

GERALD (*thoughtfully*) Of course you'll have to answer this!   70

MARGERY Of course!

GERALD Show me the answer when you've written it!

MARGERY Oh, I shan't spell it wrong!°

GERALD No, dear, but—

MARGERY I know what you mean. I might use all short words instead of   75
long ones. (*Gerald laughs*) Don't be afraid: I'll pick the longest in the dictionary. (*Kisses him*) Ah, Gerald, dear! short words were good enough for you once! (*Archly*)

GERALD I dare say.

MARGERY Yes; when you said, 'I love you, Margery!' Say it again!   80

GERALD Margery, what nonsense!

MARGERY That's what I like—nonsense. Say it again!

GERALD (*with effort*) I love you, Margery. (*Sits, and resumes his pen*) Now, let me get on with my work!

MARGERY (*goes L. Aside*) Somehow it didn't sound like that in Maple-   85
durham.° (*Brightly*) Well, I suppose his head's full of his book. I wish mine was of mine. Oh, those French verbs! and what's the use of them? Why isn't English good enough for England?
        Enter Wells, L

WELLS Captain Sylvester.
        Gerald flings down his pen in despair. Exit Wells, L. Enter Sylvester

MARGERY Ah, I'm so glad you've come! (*Crosses to him*) I wanted some-   90
body to talk to. Gerald's so busy!
        Takes Sylvester's hat and stick

SYLVESTER Busy? then I'm afraid I intrude.

GERALD (*resignedly*) Oh, not at all! (*Sees Margery at back, who has put Sylvester's hat on, very much askew, and is marching up and down with the stick under her arm*) Good gracious, Margery!
        Margery laughs. Sylvester laughs. Gerald goes up, snatches the hat and stick, and turns to put them down

MARGERY Cross again! (*As Gerald turns again, he finds himself face to   95
face with her, holding her mouth out*) Penalty!

GERALD It is for Captain Sylvester to forgive you.

SYLVESTER Anything. Mrs Cazenove can do no wrong. (*Bows. Margery curtseys*) But where's Agnes? Happening to pass this way, I thought I might perhaps give her a lift home.   100

MARGERY   Oh! Gerald expects Mrs Sylvester—

GERALD   Later on, later on!

SYLVESTER   Then may I wait for her?

GERALD   Oh, certainly! (*Taking up manuscripts*) If you'll excuse me going
on with my work. I've been a good deal interrupted. (*Goes to door, R*)   105

SYLVESTER   By all means, if I may talk to Mrs Cazenove!
*Gerald bows stiffly and exit, R, watched by Margery, who makes
a grimace to audience*

MARGERY   I believe Gerald's jealous!

SYLVESTER (*laughing*) Of *me*?

MARGERY (*laughs*) Just fancy anyone being jealous of *you!* (*Laughs
loudly, then stops suddenly*) Hush! I forgot! We mustn't make so much   110
noise. Clever people don't like noise.

SYLVESTER   Music is noise to some people. I like it!

MARGERY   Ah, but then you're not clever!

SYLVESTER (*laughing*) I'm afraid not!

MARGERY   There's a pair of us!   115

SYLVESTER   And what a pleasure it is to meet somebody who's not
clever. Mrs Cazenove, I think cleverness is the most boring thing in
the world. This planet would be quite a pleasant place but for the
clever people.

MARGERY   Do you mean my husband?   120

SYLVESTER   I was thinking of my wife; she's one of them. I'm not. I'm
only Mrs Sylvester's husband.

MARGERY   Are you sure you're that?

SYLVESTER   I have always been under that impression.

MARGERY   A husband who isn't master of his wife isn't half a husband.   125

SYLVESTER   I am content to be a fraction!

MARGERY   But you're a cipher.

SYLVESTER   You're frank, Mrs Cazenove.

MARGERY   I only say to your face what everybody says behind your
back.   130

SYLVESTER   What do they say?

MARGERY   That Mrs Sylvester's too much alone.

SYLVESTER   Never. She's always with your husband!

MARGERY   Well?

SYLVESTER   As long as *you* don't object—   135

MARGERY   Object? Not I! But that's a very different thing!

SYLVESTER   How so?

MARGERY   I am my husband's wife, and I am not afraid of any woman in
the world.

SYLVESTER You have no need to be. (*With admiration*) And in your pre-   140
eminence resides my safety, Margery.

MARGERY I'm not Margery now!

SYLVESTER (*seriously*) I ask Mrs Cazenove's pardon. (*In a casual tone*)
You don't object to the collaboration, then?

MARGERY I think it's fun! They are so serious over it. As if the world   145
depended on a book! As if there were no Providence or anything, and
they two had to keep creation going by scratching upon little bits of
paper! I love to watch them, biting at their pens, and staring at that
little crack up there. (*Looking at the ceiling. Sylvester looks also*) I often
think to myself, you may well look—there's something there that'll   150
keep the world going round, just as it is, long after your precious book
is dust and ashes.

SYLVESTER Then you do watch them, Margery—Mrs Cazenove?

MARGERY Oh, often, from my room. (*Indicates curtains*) But I can
scarcely keep from laughing all the time. Some day I mean to   155
have such fun with them! I mean to steal in here (*business*°), and put
my head out, so—and just when they are putting the world right, say
Bo!

> *Runs back, and bursts into a peal of laughter. Sylvester laughs*
> *also. Re-enter Wells, L*

WELLS Miss Vivash!

> *Exit Wells, L. Enter Victoria*

VICTORIA Good morning, dear. (*Kisses Margery*) What! Captain   160
Sylvester! you here, and Agnes not?

MARGERY Mrs Sylvester is coming!

VICTORIA No need to apologise! A wife is just as much entitled to entertain another woman's husband as a husband to entertain another
man's wife. You're getting on, dear. That's philosophy!   165

MARGERY Gerald is in the next room!

VICTORIA Then it's not philosophy!

MARGERY I'll go and wake him up. (*Exit, R*)

VICTORIA Humph! (*Sits*) Well, how long do you give it?

SYLVESTER Do you mean philosophy?   170

VICTORIA The Cazenove *ménage*. Another six months? These love-
matches are honeymoon affairs. When once that's over, there's an
end of everything.

SYLVESTER But is it over?

VICTORIA Everybody's talking. Cazenove is bored to death.   175

SYLVESTER I don't think his wife is.

VICTORIA Ah, that will come in time; and when it does, I mean to take

27

Margery in hand. She is neglected shamefully. *She* hasn't discovered
it yet, but all her friends have.

SYLVESTER They're generally first in the field.   180

VICTORIA If a husband ignores his wife, the wife is entitled to ignore
her husband. What would a man do under the same circumstances?

SYLVESTER Is not the question rather, what a man *ought* to do?

VICTORIA That is Utopian. We must take the world as we find it.

SYLVESTER I'm afraid Mrs Cazenove won't be an apt pupil.   185

VICTORIA No spirit—no proper pride. But things can't go on as they're
going along. Margery is on the edge of a volcano. I give it six months.

SYLVESTER Is it as bad as that?

VICTORIA Never at home—and when he is—'in the next room'. Never
takes her anywhere, and I don't wonder at it. Margery is too *gauche*   190
for anything. But what could be expected, when a man throws himself away in that manner? Bless me, there were other women in the
world!

SYLVESTER Oh, plenty, plenty.

VICTORIA Unluckily, he's found that out. (*Aside*) That's one for *him!*   195

SYLVESTER Indeed!

VICTORIA (*gives him a glance of contempt, and produces a cigarette case*)
Do you mind tobacco?°

SYLVESTER Not at all. I like it. (*Re-enter Margery, R*) If Mrs Cazenove—

MARGERY Gerald's so busy, will you please excuse him?

VICTORIA Certainly. Will you join me? (*Offers case*)   200

MARGERY Thank you, I can't smoke.

VICTORIA Then you should learn at once. (*Puts a cigarette in her mouth*)
Could you oblige me with a light? (*Sylvester strikes a match*) Thanks.
(*Lights up at the wrong end of a gold-tipped cigarette°. Margery stands,
arms akimbo, surveying her*)

MARGERY Do you like smoking?

VICTORIA No, but I smoke on principle!   205

SYLVESTER On the wrong principle!

VICTORIA I beg your pardon. Men smoke cigarettes.

SYLVESTER Yes, but they light them at the other end.
> *Victoria takes the cigarette out of her mouth and looks at it.*
> *Margery and Sylvester burst out laughing. She throws it away*
> *viciously. Re-enter Wells, L*

WELLS Miss Bethune.
> *Exit Wells, L. Enter Enid*

ENID How are you dear? (*Kisses Margery*) Victoria! (*Goes to Victoria,*   210
who presents her cheek)

28

SYLVESTER (*to Margery*) Now you have company, I'll say good-day. I've waited for my wife quite long enough!

MARGERY (*with outstretched hand*) But you will come and see me again soon?

Enid and Victoria exchange glances

SYLVESTER (*holding her hand, and in a lower voice*) Shall you be in   215
tomorrow?

MARGERY (*frankly*) Yes. (*Sylvester smiles and presses her hand; she sees her mistake*) If Gerald is.

Enid and Victoria are exchanging whispers

SYLVESTER (*drops her hand; aside*) Women are like Bradshaw°—a guide and a puzzle! (*Exit, L*)   220

ENID Does Captain Sylvester often call, my dear?

MARGERY He has done lately.

ENID Quite a change for him! He must occasionally meet his wife!

VICTORIA (*who has gone to the mantelpiece for a match*) Now that that man has gone—(*Lights another cigarette*)   225

ENID Victoria!

VICTORIA (*offering case to Margery*) Can't I prevail on you?

MARGERY (*takes one*) Well, I don't mind trying.

Lights hers from Victoria's, Victoria putting the case on the table

ENID How *can* you, Margery? I call it shocking! To take a nasty, evil-smelling thing like this (*taking a cigarette out of Victoria's case*)—and   230
put it to your lips—brrh! (*Shudders, but puts it in her mouth. Margery presses her burning cigarette against it till it is alight*) Don't, Margery, don't! I call it horrid—most unladylike!

MARGERY Now puff!

All three sit and puff vigorously. Margery perched on table

VICTORIA Well, dear, and how are you getting on?   235

MARGERY Oh, famously!

ENID I hope you've taken my advice to heart!

VICTORIA And mine! Have you a latchkey yet?

MARGERY Oh, yes!

ENID Margery, you shock me!   240

MARGERY Well, you're easily shocked!

VICTORIA You have a latchkey? (*Triumphantly*)

MARGERY (*simply*) Yes, we have a latchkey!

BOTH (*in different tones*) *We?*

MARGERY What would Gerald do without one?   245

VICTORIA (*with contempt*) Gerald!

MARGERY When he comes home late.

ENID *Does* he come home late?

VICTORIA All men do!

ENID *Before* marriage. Would that were *all* they did. (*Mysteriously*) Has   250
he told you everything?°

MARGERY He's told me everything I've asked him.

VICTORIA (*with curiosity, putting down cigarette*) What have you asked
him?

MARGERY Nothing!   255

ENID Margery! (*Rises*) It's such women as you on whom men prey!
(*Turns off*)

VICTORIA (*rises*) And it's such men as him that women marry! (*Turns
off*)°

MARGERY When they get the chance! (*Grimace at audience*)
        Re-enter Wells, L

WELLS Colonel Cazenove.
        *Enid hides her cigarette behind her back; Margery flings hers
        away, jumps down and runs to meet him. Exit Wells, L. Enter
        Colonel*

MARGERY Uncle!   260
        *Flings her arms round his neck, and gives him three smacking
        kisses. Colonel smiles all over his face. Enid and Victoria
        exchange shrugs*

COLONEL Bless me! what a smell of tobacco! (*Looks about, sniffing, sees
Victoria*) Ah, the foolish—beg pardon!—Miss Vivash! (*Bow*) Dear
me, something burning! (*Sniffs. Victoria sits again*)

ENID (*confused*) Yes, Mr Cazenove—the next room—

COLONEL (*seeing her*) Man the Be—Miss Bethune, I think? (*Holds out*   265
*his hand. Enid has to change the cigarette into her left hand behind her
back; shakes hands, then turns to wipe the nicotine from her lips, unconsciously presenting the burning cigarette to Colonel's eyeglass. Margery
laughs. Colonel grins at audience*)

COLONEL I thought something was burning. (*Enid throws cigarette into
the grate, and covers her face. Colonel lifts his finger*) And you said
Mr Cazenove!

ENID Well, it wasn't a story. He *is* in the next room.

COLONEL So man has not a monopoly of the vices!   270

ENID We're none of us perfect!

COLONEL No, (*rubbing his hands*) thank Heaven! It's the spice of the old
Adam that makes life endurable!

MARGERY (*again embracing him*) Oh, I'm so happy, uncle!

ENID (*aside*) Wish she wouldn't do that!   275

MARGERY Oh, so happy!

COLONEL So am I, Margery. What did I always say? Caroline's a heart of gold. I knew she would come round. I always said I'd stand by you and Gerald.

MARGERY Uncle!

COLONEL I always said so!

MARGERY You ran away!

COLONEL Yes, but I said so. Then you have got her card?

MARGERY (*nodding her head*) Yes! (*Jumps up and gives him another kiss*)

ENID (*aside, jealously*) I do wish she wouldn't!°

COLONEL My doing, Margery—my doing!

ENID I have a card as well!

COLONEL My doing, Miss Bethune!

ENID I've just been ordering my gown!°

COLONEL (*gallantly*) I trust it will be worthy of the wearer. (*Bows. Enid smiles*)

MARGERY Have *you* a card, Miss Vivash?

VICTORIA (*who has sat very quietly, now rises*) If you'll excuse me, dear, I'll say good-morning!

MARGERY (*shakes hands*) Must you go?
　　　　　Exit Victoria, L

MARGERY Excuse *me*, uncle. Gerald doesn't know you're here! (*Exit, R*)

COLONEL Miss Vivash—?

ENID Don't trouble, Colonel! She resents an escort. I have no patience with Victoria. Trying to be a man!

COLONEL And making only a *succès d'estime!* °

ENID I like a woman to be womanly!

COLONEL (*aside*) The best of 'em.

ENID I don't mean weak—like Agnes. She goes to the other extreme. Do you know, I'm getting very anxious about Agnes!

COLONEL Mrs Sylvester?

ENID Haven't you noticed anything? Of course not! You men never do!

COLONEL I am afraid I must plead guilty!

ENID Haven't you observed how much she and your nephew are together?

COLONEL But they're collaborating.

ENID Ah, Colonel, when a man collaborates with a woman, a third person ought always to be present.

COLONEL To protect the man?

ENID (*tapping him, playfully*) You are incorrigible!

31

COLONEL (*cheerfully*) I always was, and at my age reformation is out of
   the question!   315
ENID Oh, you are not so old as all that!
COLONEL Guess.
ENID Fifty!
COLONEL (*pleased*) Add six to it!
ENID Six!   320
COLONEL (*aside*) She might add eight.
ENID I don't believe it, Colonel.
COLONEL (*aside*) *Quite* the best of 'em! (*Sits*) So you have appointed
   yourself the third person?
ENID It's time someone did.   325
COLONEL A sort of Vigilance Committee,° eh?
ENID I simply take the interest of a friend in Agnes.
COLONEL And what is the result of your observations?
ENID I have come to a terrible conclusion.
COLONEL You alarm me!   330
ENID That she is a poor, tempted creature.
COLONEL Bless me! I never regarded her in that light before. I thought
   the boot was on the other leg. (*Corrects himself hurriedly*) Foot!—foot!
   (*Indicating Enid's, which she is carefully showing; aside*) Very neat foot
   she has!   335
ENID Men always stand by one another, so should women. Agnes must
   be protected against herself!
COLONEL Then it's herself, after all? I thought you meant my nephew.
ENID So I do. She is the moth—he is the candle.
COLONEL Really!—   340
ENID Oh, you men, you men! You're all alike—at least, I won't say all!
COLONEL Say all, say all! It really doesn't matter!
ENID No, no, I won't say all!
COLONEL You say so in your book!
ENID (*pleased*) You've read my book?   345
COLONEL (*evading the question*) *Man, the Betrayer?*
ENID Well, you know, Colonel, one has to paint with a broad brush.
   (*Pantomime*)
COLONEL Yes, when one paints with tar! (*Aside*) Very nice arm, too!
   (*Aloud*) Look at your title!
ENID *Man, the Betrayer!*   350
COLONEL (*aside*) Don't know any more!
ENID A mere figure of speech!
COLONEL (*admiring her*) Figure?

32

ENID Mere figure!

COLONEL (*to himself, but aloud*) Damned fine figure, too!   355

ENID Colonel!

COLONEL Ten thousand pardons! I was thinking of something else.
Pray forgive my bad language!

ENID Oh, I'm used to it! Victoria's is much worse!

COLONEL Miss Vivash!   360

ENID Vulgar-minded thing! Learned French on purpose to read Zola's
novels.° I don't suppose that even *you* have read them.

COLONEL Oh, haven't I? Every one!

ENID I don't believe it, Colonel!

COLONEL I'm a shocking old sinner! I never professed to be anything   365
else!

ENID I simply don't believe it! You men exaggerate so! You make yourselves out to be so much worse than you are. Whereas we women pretend to be so much better. That's the worst of us! We are such
hypocrites! Oh, if you knew as much about women as *I* do—   370

COLONEL (*aside, much interested*) Now I'm going to hear something.
(*Meanwhile Margery has crept in, R, behind them. She flings her handkerchief over the Colonel's eyes, and ties it in a knot behind his head, then
skips away from him. Rising*) You rascal! It's that Margery! I know it is!
Where are you? (*Groping about, Margery evading him, and in shrieks of
laughter*) Margery, if I catch you!

MARGERY But you can't!   375

> Enid has risen to evade the Colonel, who is groping all over the
> room—a sort of blind-man's buff—all laughing

COLONEL (*seizing Enid*) I've got you!

> Kisses her. Enid shrieks. Margery roars. Colonel tears off the
> handkerchief and stands aghast. Re-enter Wells, L

WELLS Lady Wargrave.

> Sudden silence. Exit Colonel, R. Enid runs out, C, in confusion.
> Enter Lady Wargrave, L, and comes down. Exit Wells, L. Enid
> re-appears C, and runs across stage behind Lady Wargrave, and
> off, L. Margery stands confused, not knowing how to greet Lady
> Wargrave

LADY WARGRAVE (*putting out both hands*) Margery! (*Holding both
Margery's hands*)

MARGERY Oh, Lady Wargrave!

LADY WARGRAVE Aunt. I've called to make amends to you.   380

MARGERY Amends?

LADY WARGRAVE For my neglect. (*Kisses her*) Forgive me, Margery, but your marriage was a shock to me. However, I've got over it. Perhaps, after all, Gerald has chosen wisely!

MARGERY Thank you for your kind words. I knew you had got over it.   385

LADY WARGRAVE Of course! you had my card.

MARGERY I knew from uncle, too. How good of him to bring it all about!

LADY WARGRAVE Theodore!

MARGERY I mean, to reconcile you!   390

LADY WARGRAVE My dear Margery, your uncle has never presumed to mention the subject?

MARGERY Oh, what a story he has told us! he said it was *his* doing.

LADY WARGRAVE No doubt. When you know Theodore as well as I do, you will have learnt what value to attach to his observations!   395

MARGERY Won't I pay him out? (*Shaking her fist*)

LADY WARGRAVE Never mind your uncle. Tell me about yourself— and about Gerald. I hope your marriage has turned out a happy one.

MARGERY Yes—we're as happy as the day is long.

LADY WARGRAVE That is good news. Then you haven't found your   400
new position difficult?

MARGERY Oh, I'm quite used to it! I'm not a bit shy now. Of course I put my foot in it—I make mistakes sometimes; but even born ladies sometimes make mistakes.

LADY WARGRAVE Yes, Margery. (*Bending her head slightly*) And Ger-   405
ald?

MARGERY Is the best husband in the world to me. Of course, he's very busy—

LADY WARGRAVE Busy?

MARGERY With his book; and sometimes I can't help annoying him.   410
That's nothing. We haven't had a real cross word yet.

LADY WARGRAVE Does he write very much?

MARGERY Oh, morning, noon, and night. He's always got a pen in his hand. I often say I wonder he doesn't wear the ceiling out with looking at it. (*Laughs*)   415

LADY WARGRAVE That isn't writing, Margery.

MARGERY No, but it's thinking—and he's always thinking. (*Falls into a reverie*)

LADY WARGRAVE Do you go out much?

MARGERY We went out a good deal at first, but we got tired of it. I like home best; at any rate, Gerald does. I rather liked going out. Oh, I'm   420
quite a success in society.

LADY WARGRAVE Indeed?

34

MARGERY Of course, aunt, I'm not clever; but I suppose I'm witty
without knowing it!

LADY WARGRAVE Witty?   425

MARGERY At any rate, I make the people laugh. Isn't that being witty?
Then *I* laugh as well, although I don't know what I'm laughing at,
I'm sure! (*Laughs*) Oh, everybody laughs at me—but Gerald. And
he's thinking of his book!

LADY WARGRAVE Do you have many visitors?   430

MARGERY Oh, yes! Miss Vivash—Miss Bethune—Dr Mary—Mrs
Sylvester—and uncle. They're often coming. As for Mrs Sylvester,
she almost lives here!—oh, and Captain Sylvester, he's taken to
calling lately!

LADY WARGRAVE In future, dear, you'll have another visitor. I see 435
I have neglected you too long.° And you must come and see me. We'll
go out together.

MARGERY Oh, that *will* be nice! Then you have *quite* forgiven me?

LADY WARGRAVE But not myself!

MARGERY (*embracing her*) Oh, why is everyone so good to me?   440
      Re-enter Gerald, R, followed by Colonel

GERALD Aunt, this is kind of you! but you were always kind.

LADY WARGRAVE Not always. I ought to have paid this visit earlier.
I made a mistake, Gerald, and I have come to acknowledge it.

COLONEL (*laying his hand on Lady Wargrave's shoulder in an access of
enthusiasm*) Caroline, you're a trump!

LADY WARGRAVE Theodore!   445

COLONEL No other word for it! I always said you'd come round!

LADY WARGRAVE Never!

COLONEL Always!

LADY WARGRAVE Theodore, you *never* said so!

COLONEL To myself. (*Turns off*)   450

GERALD Better late than never, aunt. And thank you for the card for
your At Home. (*Talks to Lady Wargrave*)

MARGERY Oh, uncle, you're a shocking old story,° aren't you?

COLONEL What have I been saying now?

MARGERY You said it was *your* doing!   455

COLONEL So it was!

MARGERY Aunt vows you'd nothing to do with it at all!

COLONEL (*taking Margery aside*) Caroline's a heart of gold; but your
aunt must be managing! So I let her manage, and I manage *her*.

MARGERY You? (*Smiling*)   460

COLONEL But I do it quietly. I influence her, without her knowing it.

Sheer force of character. Chut! not a word! (*Backing away from her, signalling silence; backs into Lady Wargrave*) Ten thousand pardons! (*Bows profusely*)

LADY WARGRAVE Really, Theodore!
   Margery goes up, stifling her laughter; he shakes his handkerchief at her. Re-enter Wells, L

WELLS Mrs Sylvester!   465
   Enter Mrs Sylvester, she hesitates, on seeing Lady Wargrave. Exit Wells, L

GERALD Pray come in, Mrs Sylvester. You know my aunt.

MRS SYLVESTER I think we've met before.

LADY WARGRAVE Yes, at my nephew's chambers. I remember perfectly. You were engaged upon some work or other.

GERALD It's not finished yet. I am so interrupted! (*Glancing at Margery* 470 *who has crept down behind Colonel*)

MARGERY (*whispering in Colonel's ear*) Who kissed Miss Bethune?
   Colonel starts guiltily; Margery roars

GERALD (*angrily*) Margery! (*Margery runs out, L*)

LADY WARGRAVE Not finished yet!

MRS SYLVESTER But we have made great progress.

LADY WARGRAVE And are you satisfied with what you have done? 475

GERALD It is certainly interesting.

LADY WARGRAVE It is not enough for me that a work of my nephew's should be interesting! Tell me, as far as you have gone, do you think it is worthy of a Cazenove?

GERALD It is the work of my life.   480

MRS SYLVESTER And of mine!

LADY WARGRAVE As far as you have gone.° But what is to be the end of it?

GERALD Ah, we've not got there yet.

LADY WARGRAVE Would you admit a third collaborateur?°   485

MRS SYLVESTER (*alarmed*) Who?

LADY WARGRAVE An *old* woman.

GERALD Lady Wargrave's joking!

LADY WARGRAVE Oh, I could put an end to it, I think!

MRS SYLVESTER We don't know what the end will be ourselves. 490

LADY WARGRAVE There I have the advantage. If I can help in any way, my experience is always at your service. Meanwhile, I fear I am another interruption. Theodore, your arm!

GERALD (*follows them to door, L*) Thank you so much for coming. (*Holding his hand out*)

LADY WARGRAVE (*taking it*) And for going? (*Exit with Colonel, L*) 495

MRS SYLVESTER What does she mean?

GERALD Thank her for going?

MRS SYLVESTER And the end of it?

GERALD Aunt always talks in riddles!

MRS SYLVESTER Is it a riddle? 500

GERALD (*avoids her eyes*)° Come, let us get to work. I've done hardly anything today. It's first one interruption, then another. (*Sits*)

MRS SYLVESTER We should be quieter at our house.

GERALD There's your husband!

MRS SYLVESTER Always a husband! 505

GERALD Or a wife. Ah, me! (*Sits with his head between his hands, staring at vacancy; Mrs Sylvester watching him sympathetically*)

MRS SYLVESTER (*comes and kneels by him*) Gerald! (*He starts slightly*) You are not happy. You have realized the truth.

GERALD What truth?

MRS SYLVESTER Your marriage was a mistake from the beginning. 510

GERALD Not from the beginning. It started right enough, but somehow it has taken the wrong turn.

MRS SYLVESTER It was wrong from the first. Mine was the true ideal. The thing that you thought love was a mere passion—an intoxication. Now you have come back to your better self you feel the need of 515 sympathy.

GERALD No, no; my love was real enough, and I love Margery still; but love doesn't seem to bear the wear and tear of marriage—the hourly friction—the continual jar.

MRS SYLVESTER There is no friction in true marriage, Gerald. You say 520 you love your wife, and it is good and loyal of you to deceive yourself, but you can't deceive me. Haven't I made the same mistake myself? I was a thoughtless, inexperienced girl, Jack was a handsome, easygoing man. We married, and for a year or two we jogged along. But I grew up—the girl became a woman. I read, I thought, I felt; my life 525 enlarged. Jack never reads, never thinks—he is just the same. (*Rising*) I am not unhappy, but my soul is starved—(*goes to mantelpiece and stands looking at him*)—as yours is!

> Pause. Margery's face appears between the curtains at the back, wearing a broad smile. She grimaces at them, unobserved, and remains there; then looks at Gerald with a long face of mock sympathy

GERALD Well, we must make the best of it!

MRS SYLVESTER Yes, but what *is* the best? (*Margery grimaces at her*) Is 530

our mistake so hopeless, irremediable? After all, is not true loyalty
loyalty to oneself?

GERALD (*looks at her*) You think so?

MRS SYLVESTER Or what becomes of our philosophy?

GERALD Yes, what becomes of it?   535
> *Another pause. Margery laughs almost audibly. During the next
> passage the laugh subsides into an expression of perplexity*

MRS SYLVESTER What is a promise when the heart's gone out of it?

GERALD Surely it is a promise.

MRS SYLVESTER To an empty phrase must one sacrifice one's life?
Must one stake everything on the judgment of one's youth? By the
decision of a moment must one be bound for ever? Must one go   540
through the world 'with quiet eyes unfaithful to the truth'? Does one
not owe a duty to oneself? There can be but one answer!

GERALD (*absently*) Margery! (*Margery winces as if struck—quite serious
now. Then with energy*) But, Agnes, Margery is impossible! She's no
companion to me! I am all alone! Her very laughter grates upon me!   545
There's no meaning in it! It is the laughter of a tomboy, of a clown!
And she will never learn! She's hopeless, Agnes, hopeless! (*Margery
drops back horror-struck, but her face disappears only by degrees. Mrs Sylvester lays her hand on him. Another pause. The curtains close*) What is
one to do? (*Rising*)

MRS SYLVESTER We are face to face with the problem! Let us confront   550
it boldly. Gerald, do you love me?
> *A thud behind the curtains. Gerald starts guiltily. Pause. They
> stand looking at one another*

GERALD (*in a whisper*) What was that? (*Goes up cautiously and draws curtains back, discovering Margery stretched senseless on the floor*) Margery!

CURTAIN

3

A fortnight later

SCENE *Drawing-room at Lady Wargrave's. Main entrance C,
Conservatory R. Entrance, L, to an inner room. Fireplace, R, up
stage, near which is Lady Wargrave's chair, with the cushion of
Act I.*

*The stage is discovered half-filled with Guests, who stand and sit
in groups, including Colonel, Captain and Mrs Sylvester, and
Gerald. Lady Wargrave is receiving her guests. A buzz of general
conversation; and a band is heard° playing in the inner room,
loudly at first, but softly after the picture is discovered°*

SERVANT (*at entrance C*) Miss Vivash° and Mr Pettigrew!
  *Enter Victoria, followed leisurely by Percy, a very young man
  who is always smiling to himself, unconsciously*

VICTORIA (*going straight to Lady Wargrave and grasping her hand*) Good
  evening, Lady Wargrave, I have taken the liberty of bringing a friend
  whose name is no doubt known to you—Mr Percy Pettigrew. (*Percy
  bows distantly, smiling*)

LADY WARGRAVE Pettigrew, did you say?

PERCY Percy *Bysshe* Pettigrew. (*Smiling*)   5

LADY WARGRAVE Of course! *two* of your names are *quite* well known to
  me; it is only the surname that is unfamiliar.°

PERCY (*smiling*) Pettigrew! (*Turns off*)

GERALD One of my Oxford friends.   10

LADY WARGRAVE (*aside to him*) One of those who are always at Oxford?

VICTORIA His 'Supercilia' are quoted everywhere.

LADY WARGRAVE His——?

GERALD A column Percy does for *The Corset.*°

VICTORIA A newspaper devoted to our cause.   15

GERALD *The Corset* is Percy's organ.

LADY WARGRAVE Ah, his rattle!°

SERVANT Dr Bevan. [*Enter Dr Bevan*]°

DR BEVAN (*shakes hands with Lady Wargrave*) I hope I am not late; but
  I was detained at the hospital. Most interesting case, unhappily unfit   20
  for publication.

SERVANT Miss Bethune. (*Exit Servant*)
  Enter Enid

39

COLONEL (*to Sylvester*) The best of 'em!°
    Enid shakes hands with Lady Wargrave

COLONEL Ah, what a pity, what a pity, Sylvester!

SYLVESTER What is a pity, Colonel?   25

COLONEL That such a figure should be wasted!

SYLVESTER (*in a matter of course voice*) I prefer Mrs Cazenove's. (*Turns off. Colonel eyes him curiously. The other Guests should be so arranged that each man is surrounded by a little group of women.*)

PERCY (*the centre of one group, lolling lazily, always smiling with self-complacency, suddenly sits up and shivers*) No, no! don't mention it. It bores me so. (*Shivers*)

CHORUS And me! (*All shiver*)°   30

VICTORIA The stage has ever been Woman's greatest foe.

GUEST For centuries it has shirked the sexual problem.

SYLVESTER (*who has strolled up*) But doesn't it show signs of repentance?°

PERCY The theatre is dying.   35

SYLVESTER Death–bed repentance, then. That's the one problem it discusses.

GUEST It is the one problem in life.

PERCY The theatre is dying! Dixi!° (*Leans back again*)

DOCTOR The novel will sweep everything before it.   40

SYLVESTER You mean, the female novel?

DOCTOR Nothing can stop it.

SYLVESTER No, it stops at nothing.

DOCTOR Nor will it, till the problem is solved. That solution, I venture to predict, will be on the lines of pure mathematics.   45

SYLVESTER Really? (*Smothering a yawn*)

DOCTOR I put the proposition in this way. The sexes are parallel lines.

SYLVESTER Which are bound to meet.

DOCTOR I must not be taken to admit, that there is any physiological necessity.   50

VOICES Certainly not.

DOCTOR (*to Lady Wargrave, who is passing*) I am sure, Lady Wargrave must agree with us.

LADY WARGRAVE What is that, Doctor?

DOCTOR That there is no physiological necessity—   55

LADY WARGRAVE To discuss physiology? I am quite of your opinion. (*Passes on*)

ENID (*who is in a group surrounding Colonel*) That's where we differ. What is *your* view, Colonel?

COLONEL My dear Miss Bethune, there is no occasion for Man to
express *any* view, when Woman expresses them all. First, you must   60
reconcile your internal differences.

VOICE But we can't.

COLONEL To begin with, you must make up your minds whether you
wish to regenerate us or to degrade yourselves.

ENID Regenerate you, of course.   65

COLONEL Miss Vivash prefers the alternative.

ENID That is Victoria's foible.

COLONEL (*gallantly*) I can admit no foible in a lady.

ENID At any rate, we are agreed on the main point—the equality of the
sexes.   70

COLONEL That, alas, is impossible.

VOICE Impossible?

COLONEL Whilst Woman persists in remaining perfect.

VICTORIA Cannot Man emulate her?

COLONEL I am afraid his strength is only equal to the confession of his   75
unworthiness.

ENID You would confess that? Then you agree with me, that a woman
is entitled to know the whole of a man's past?°

LADY WARGRAVE (*who has joined them*) Would it not be more useful if
she knew something of his future?   80

ENID Women have futures; men have only pasts.

DOCTOR (*still in Sylvester's group*) It stands to reason—pure reason—
there ought not to be one law for women and another for men.

SYLVESTER You mean, that they ought both to be for women?

DOCTOR I mean, that the institution of marriage is in urgent need of   85
reconsideration.

SYLVESTER The sooner, the better.

DOCTOR I am glad you think so.

SYLVESTER When the institution of marriage is reconsidered, man will
have another chance. (*Exit R*)   90

LADY WARGRAVE (*who has joined Percy's group*) What do I think of the
New Woman? There is no New Woman; she is as old as Molière.°
(*Stands listening, amused*)

CHORUS Molière!

VICTORIA A pagan!

PERCY A frank pagan. For pure art we must go to Athens.   95

CHORUS Athens!

PERCY Or the Music Halls. Have you seen Trixy Blinko?°

CHORUS Trixy—oh, charming—sweet!

PERCY   In her alone I find the true Greek spirit. What were the prevailing characteristics of Hellenic culture? (*A sudden silence*) Breadth and   100
centrality, blitheness and repose. All these I find in Trixy.
CHORUS   Little dear!
LADY WARGRAVE   Somewhat *risquée*, isn't she?
PERCY   To the suburban mind.
    Lady Wargrave bows and turns off. Servant enters, L
SERVANT   Signor Labinski has arrived, your ladyship. (*Exit, L*)   105
    Lady Wargrave speaks to one or two of the Guests, and the company disperse, most of them going off, L, but a few, C, and others into the conservatory. During this general movement, the music off, is heard louder. Colonel is left with Dr Mary
COLONEL   Nonsense, my dear Doctor—The fact's just this. The modern woman is prostrated by the discovery of her own superiority; and she is now engaged in one of those hopeless enterprises which *we* have regretfully abandoned. She is endeavouring to understand *herself*. I offer her my respectful sympathy. (*Bows and sits, C*)   110
DOCTOR   (*sits by him*) The truth amounts to this: the one mitigating circumstance about the existence of Man is, that he occasionally co-operates in the creation of a Woman.
COLONEL   His proudest privilege! The mystery to me is, that you ladies haven't found it out before.   115
    Re-enter Enid, C
DOCTOR   Yes, but you shirk the question!
    Colonel is fanning himself, helplessly
ENID   (*aside*) A man in distress! I must help him! (*Advancing sweetly*) What were you saying, Doctor? (*Sits on the other side of Colonel*)
COLONEL   (*aside*) Bethune! the best of 'em!
DOCTOR   You know, from your own experience, that marriage is not a   120
necessity.
COLONEL   No, it's a luxury—an expensive luxury.
ENID   Oh, surely that depends upon the wife.
DOCTOR   It is she who has to associate with him.
ENID   And considering what his past has been—   125.
COLONEL   Suppose it hasn't!
DOCTOR   But it always has!
ENID   I should be sorry to think that.
DOCTOR   Take the Colonel's own case.
COLONEL   (*alarmed*) Doctor!   130
DOCTOR   Do you deny that you have had a past?
COLONEL   Oh, a few trifling peccadilloes!

ENID Then you must never marry.

COLONEL Am I to have no chance of reformation?

ENID It is your own fault.   135

DOCTOR Entirely.

COLONEL One moment, my dear ladies! Excuse me pointing out, that, in the last resort, there must always be a female accomplice!

ENID Poor, tempted creature!

COLONEL *Tempted* by a *man!*   140

DOCTOR We all have our weak moments. (*Sighs*)

ENID All of us! (*Sighs*)

> *As the pair sit with their eyes cast down, silent, Colonel looks from one to the other in dismay, then steals off, R*

COLONEL (*at door*) Getting dangerous! (*Exit R*)

> *When they look up, each with a languorous glance, they find themselves languishing at one another; both rise*

ENID (*putting her arm round Doctor's waist*) My dear, we are missing the music! (*Exeunt L*)   145

> *Re-enter Mrs Sylvester and Gerald, C. Movement of other Guests across stage, during music*

MRS SYLVESTER Where have you been? I have seen nothing of you. What have you been doing?

GERALD Thinking.

MRS SYLVESTER (*jealously*) Of whom?

GERALD Of Margery. (*Movement of Mrs Sylvester*)   150

MRS SYLVESTER Has she said anything?

GERALD No, not a word.

MRS SYLVESTER Of course, she heard?

GERALD What did I say? What did I do? What must she think of me? I can't bear this suspense. For the last fortnight, she's been another 155
woman. So grave—so thoughtful—so unlike herself. There is no laugh to grate upon me now. What would I give to bring it back again?

MRS SYLVESTER Is it she only who has changed?

GERALD Ever since I saw that figure on the ground, I can see nothing else. And it is I who brought it to the dust—I, who had sworn to cher- 160
ish it. Yes, you are right; I too am different; I see things from a differ-ent point of view. And when I think of Margery's young life, so full of hope and joy—Margery, who never asked to be my wife—Margery, whom I compelled to marry me—with all the joy crushed out of her—I feel too much ashamed even to ask forgiveness. And as I watch 165
her move about the house—silent and sorrowful—I ask myself, how much did Margery give up for me? I took her from the station of life

43

in which she was born, and in which she was happy. I set her in another and a strange one. Was mine the only sacrifice? How much of friendship and of old association did she resign for my sake? My life continued as it was before—I had my old friends and my old pursuits. What had she? Nothing—but my love. And I took it away from her. Because she made a few mistakes, and a few people laughed—a few more didn't call—and I mistook a light heart for an empty head. What do all these things matter? what is a man worth who sets such things above a love like hers?°

MRS SYLVESTER   This is pure pity, Gerald.

GERALD   Pity for myself.

MRS SYLVESTER   She was no wife for you. She could be no companion.

GERALD   If she was no companion, did I make her one?

MRS SYLVESTER   Need you tell *me* all this?

GERALD   Yes, Mrs Sylvester, it's best I should. I came to tell it you.

MRS SYLVESTER   Not Agnes now!

GERALD   Forget my folly, and forget your own.

MRS SYLVESTER   Mine was no folly. I, at least, was sincere; the love that isn't based on sympathy is a mere passion.

GERALD   And the love that has no passion in it, isn't worth the name!

MRS SYLVESTER   That's your idea?

GERALD   And what is yours? Let us be frank.

MRS SYLVESTER   Oh, frankness, by all means.

GERALD   Forgive me; but we're face to face with truth. Don't let us flinch from it. We have both made the same mistake—not in our marriages, but in despising them. What we want in a partner is what we lack in ourselves. Not sympathy only, but sex. Strength requires gentleness, sweetness asks for light; and all that is womanly in woman wants all that is manly in man. You think your husband is no mate for you. What I have missed in Margery, have you not missed in him?

MRS SYLVESTER   (*after pause*)   I understand you. It is over.

GERALD   It is for you to say. We have gone too far together for either of us to turn back alone. I have not only made my own hearth desolate, but yours. I owe you all the reparation I can make. I only want you to know the truth. What is left of my life you may command, but my heart is not mine to bestow.°

MRS SYLVESTER   (*turns up, to hide her emotion, and tries to go into the room, L, but half-way she falters and puts out her hand*)   Gerald!

> He goes to her and offers her his arm. Exeunt Gerald and Mrs Sylvester, L. Other Guests cross the stage. Enter Margery, C. Finding herself opposite Lady Wargrave's chair, takes a long look

> *at it, then moves the cushion, and gradually gets into her old posi-*
> *tion behind it. Music heard off, softly, during this passage*

MARGERY Yes, this is how it ought to be. It looks a different world al-   205
together—the real world—the world, when Gerald loved me! (*Comes
down and sits, in a reverie*)
> *Re-enter Sylvester, R*

SYLVESTER Alone, Mrs Cazenove? It isn't often that I find you alone.
I've seen nothing of you lately. You've always been out when I've
called.

MARGERY I was in once.   210

SYLVESTER Only once.

MARGERY It was enough.

SYLVESTER You are cruel.

MARGERY Are you looking for your wife?

SYLVESTER (*laughs*) Agnes and I go very different ways.   215

MARGERY I think you're going the same way, both of you.

SYLVESTER (*still laughing*) But in opposite directions. Mrs Cazenove,
you're quite a philosopher. Why have you grown so serious all at
once?

MARGERY I'm older than I was.   220

SYLVESTER Only a fortnight since you were all vivacity.

MARGERY One can live a long time in a fortnight.

SYLVESTER I hope these ladies haven't converted you.

MARGERY Yes; I am a new woman.

SYLVESTER (*laughs*) Your husband has been reading you his book!   225

MARGERY A good deal of it.

SYLVESTER What is it all about? If I am not too curious.

MARGERY It's about love.

SYLVESTER I thought it was about marriage.

MARGERY Aren't they the same thing? He says they are, and I agree with   230
him. And then he says (*half to herself*) that, when the love is gone, so
is the marriage—and I think he's right! (*Loses herself in thought*)

SYLVESTER (*gazes at her for some moments, then unable to restrain himself*)
Ah, Margery! if Heaven had given me such a wife as you—

MARGERY (*rises*) Heaven didn't, and there's an end of it.

SYLVESTER (*rises*) Forgive me! how can I help admiring you?   235

MARGERY Can't you admire me without telling me? It's well to make
the best of what we have, instead of trying to make the worst of what
we haven't.

SYLVESTER I must be silent!

MARGERY Or not talk in that way. (*Moves away*)   240

45

SYLVESTER (*following, in an outburst*) Gerald doesn't love you (*movement of Margery*)—oh, you said that just now! you mayn't know that you said it, but you did! My wife doesn't love me—I don't love my wife—and yet I must say nothing.

MARGERY What's it to me that you don't love your wife?   245

SYLVESTER I love *you*, Margery.

MARGERY I knew that was coming.

SYLVESTER Honestly love you! I admired you always. It was an empty admiration, perhaps—the admiration a man feels for twenty women—but it grew solid; and the more you repulsed me, the more   250 you attracted me. You mayn't believe me, but at first I *wanted* you to repulse me; then it got past that; and when I saw you sitting there alone—living over in your mind your wasted life—I loved you, and the words sprang to my lips. Nothing could keep them back! I love you, Margery—nobody but you! Why should your life be wasted?   255 Why should mine?

MARGERY Well, have you finished?

SYLVESTER (*seizing her*) No!

MARGERY I can guess the rest. You say Gerald doesn't love me, you don't love your wife, and your wife doesn't love *you*; but you forget   260 one thing—that *I* don't love you either.

SYLVESTER Not now, but by and by. Margery, I would make you love me—I would teach you!

MARGERY So, I'm to *learn* to be unfaithful, is that it? As one learns music? No, Captain Sylvester! Suppose two people are so much in   265 love that they can't help it, Heaven is their judge, not me. But to *begin* to love when they *can* help it—not to resist—to *teach* themselves to love—that's where the wrong is, and there's no gainsaying it.

SYLVESTER Suppose your husband left you?

MARGERY I would have no other!   270

SYLVESTER Why not?
        Re-enter Gerald, L

MARGERY Because I love him, and I don't love you!
        Margery's back is towards Gerald, so that she doesn't see him; but
        Sylvester is facing him and sees him

GERALD (*coming down to Margery*) What has he said?

MARGERY Nothing for your ears!

SYLVESTER Yes, for all the world's! I'll tell you!   275

MARGERY I forbid you! Leave me with my husband.
        Sylvester hesitates a moment, then exit, C

GERALD Margery, speak! I have a right to know.

46

MARGERY You have no right!

GERALD You will not tell me?

MARGERY No!   280

GERALD Then *he shall!* (*Advances on her*)

MARGERY Stand back! You shall not go!

GERALD What, you defend him?

MARGERY Against you, I do! Who are you to question him? Are your own hands clean?   285

GERALD (*drops back as if struck*) Margery!

MARGERY (*holding out her hand*) Good-bye!

GERALD Good-bye?

MARGERY I'm going home.

GERALD To Mapledurham?   290

MARGERY We'll say good-bye now.

GERALD Here—Margery?

MARGERY You needn't be afraid. There'll be no scene; I've done with tears.

GERALD You're (*chokes*) going to leave me?   295

MARGERY Yes.

GERALD For a few days, you mean?

MARGERY I mean, for ever. Gerald, I've had enough of half a home and only half a heart. I'm starving, withering, dying here with you! They love me there! Let me go back to them! Oh, what a world it is! To   300
think that one can get the love of any man except the man one loves!

GERALD You have it, Margery.

MARGERY (*fiercely*) I haven't.

GERALD If you only knew—

MARGERY I know I haven't! what's the use of words? Do you think a   305
woman doesn't know when she's not loved, or is? When you first said you loved me, down in the fields yonder, do you suppose you took me by surprise? You had no need to swear. I knew you loved me, just as certainly as I know now you don't!

GERALD (*much moved*) Oh, what a scoundrel I was, Margery!   310

MARGERY No man's a scoundrel to the woman he loves. Ah, it was easy to forgive your loving me. But I'll do something that is not so easy. I will forgive you for *not* loving me. It's been a struggle. For the last fortnight I haven't said a word, because I wasn't master of myself, and I didn't want to speak till I'd forgiven you. I wasn't listening,   315
Gerald. Heaven knows I would have given all the world not to have heard a word; but when you spoke my name, I couldn't move. The ground seemed slipping underneath my feet, and all the happiness of

all my life went out of it in those three words, 'Margery's hopeless, hopeless!'   320

GERALD Don't! don't! you torture me!

MARGERY Yes, Margery *is* hopeless. Every scrap of hope has gone out of her heart. I heard no more. It was enough. There was the end of all the world for me. (*Gerald groans*) But it was well I heard you. I should have gone blundering along, in my old madcap way, and perhaps not   325 found it out till I had spoilt your life. It's well to know the truth; but, Gerald dear, why didn't you tell it *me* instead of her? Why didn't you tell me I was no companion? I would have gone away. But to pretend you loved me, when you didn't—to let me go on thinking you were happy, when all the time you were regretting your mistake—not to   330 tell *me*, and to tell someone else—oh, it was cruel, when I loved you so!

GERALD How could I tell you, Margery?

MARGERY How could you tell *her!* How could she listen to you? I forgive *you*, Gerald—I didn't at first, but now I understand that there   335 are times when one's heart is so sore, it must cry out to somebody. But *she*—

GERALD It was my fault!

MARGERY You are mistaken there. It was your voice that spoke them, but the words were hers. It's she who's robbed me of your love! It   340 isn't I who've lost it; she has stolen it!

GERALD No, no!

MARGERY Be careful, or she'll steal your honour too. Don't trust to her fine phrases. She deceives herself. She wants your love, that's what that woman wants: not to instruct the world—just to be happy—   345 nothing more or less; but she won't make you happy or herself. If I am no companion, she's a bad one!

GERALD You wrong her, Margery—indeed, you do! *I* was the culprit—

MARGERY Have some pity on me! Don't let the last words I shall hear you say be words defending her! Think what she's done for me!   350 Think how you loved me when you married me—think what our two lives might have been, but for her—think what mine *will* be! for mine won't be like yours. Your love is dead, and you will bury it, but mine's alive—alive! (*Breaks down*)

GERALD And so is mine!   355

MARGERY (*springs up*) Don't soil your lips with lies! I've borne as much as I can bear. I can't bear that!

GERALD If you will only listen—

MARGERY I have heard too much! Don't speak again, or you will make

48

me hate you! My mind's made up. I have no business here! You are   360
above me. I'm no wife for you! I'm dragging you down every day and
hour.

GERALD Margery! you shall not go.

MARGERY (*flinging him off*) Tonight and now! Good-bye! (*Rushes into
conservatory, R*)

GERALD What right have I to stop her? (*Goes up, leans upon chair*)   365
          Re-enter Sylvester, C

SYLVESTER Now, Mr Cazenove, I am at your service.

GERALD You are too late. (*Exit, C*)

SYLVESTER So, he won't speak to me. But I will make him. If he thinks
I am caught, like a rat in a trap, he's made a mistake. There'll be a
scandal—well, so much the better! Better that they should know the   370
truth all round.
          Re-enter Mrs Sylvester, L

MRS SYLVESTER Ah, you are here! I've been looking for you everywhere.

SYLVESTER Looking for *me*?

MRS SYLVESTER I want you to take me home.   375

SYLVESTER I've something to say to you. Sit down.

MRS SYLVESTER Not tonight. I'm tired.

SYLVESTER Yes, tonight. What I'm going to say may be everybody's
property tomorrow. I choose that you should know it now.

MRS SYLVESTER I don't understand you.   380

SYLVESTER But you shall. I've often heard you say that a loveless marriage is no marriage. Well, ours is loveless enough, isn't it?

MRS SYLVESTER It has been.

SYLVESTER It is! I've never understood you; and if there was any good
in me, you've never taken the trouble to find it out.   385

MRS SYLVESTER I can't bear this now.

SYLVESTER You must. Don't think I'm going to reproach you. I take all
the blame on myself. What if I were to tell you that you've made a
convert to your principles where you least expected it?

MRS SYLVESTER What do you mean?   390

SYLVESTER That it's best for us both to put an end to this farce that
we're living. I mean, that I love another woman.

MRS SYLVESTER (*rising*) You!

SYLVESTER Perhaps that seems to you impossible. You thought, perhaps, that I was dull and stupid enough to go on with this empty life   395
of ours to the end. I thought so too, but I was wrong. I love this
woman, and I've told her so—

49

MRS SYLVESTER (*with jealousy*) Who is she?

SYLVESTER And I would tell her husband to his face—

MRS SYLVESTER Then she is married?   400

SYLVESTER As I tell *you*.

MRS SYLVESTER Who is she, I say?

SYLVESTER Margery.

MRS SYLVESTER Margery! Are you all mad, you men? What is it in that
  woman that enslaves you? What is the charm we others don't pos-   405
  sess? Only you men can see it; and you all do! You lose your senses,
  every one of you! What is it in her that bewitches you?

SYLVESTER What you've crushed out of yourself—your womanhood.
  What you're ashamed of is a woman's glory. Philosophy is well
  enough in books; but in a woman a man wants flesh and blood—frank   410
  human nature!

MRS SYLVESTER (*laughing, hysterically*) A mere animal!

SYLVESTER A woman.

MRS SYLVESTER Well, you have found one.

SYLVESTER Yes.°   415

MRS SYLVESTER Take her, then! go your way!

SYLVESTER I will. (*Exit, C*)

MRS SYLVESTER This world was made for such as you and her!

> *Re-enter Margery, R, cloaked*

We have no place in it—we who love with our brains! we have no
  chance of happiness!   420

MARGERY What chance have we? we, who love with our hearts! we,
  who are simply what God made us—women! we, to whom love is not
  a cult—a problem, but just as vital as the air we breathe. Take love
  away from us, and you take life itself. You have your books, your sci-
  ences, your brains! What have we?—nothing but our broken hearts!   425

MRS SYLVESTER Broken hearts heal! The things that *you* call hearts!
  One love is dead, another takes its place; one man is lost, another man
  is found. What is the difference to a love like yours? Oh, there are
  always men for such women as you!

> *By degrees re-enter omnes,° R, L, and C, gradually, except*
> *Gerald*

MARGERY But if the love is not dead? if it's stolen? what is our lot   430
  then—ours, whose love's alive? We, who're not skilled to steal—who
  only want our own—

MRS SYLVESTER Not skilled to steal! have you not stolen mine?

MARGERY I have one husband, and I want no other! (*Murmurs*)

LADY WARGRAVE (*restraining her*) Calm yourself, dear!   435

MARGERY I have been calm too long!°

LADY WARGRAVE Remember, you are my niece.

MARGERY That's what I do remember!° (*Murmurs continue*) I am Gerald's wife! That's what she doesn't forgive me! [Oh, I am not the fool
you think I am. One can't stand for ten years behind a lady's chair   440
without at least learning what a lady is. Oh, I've learnt a lot behind
that chair, better than Greek and Latin and the stuff that you think
knowledge. You I have studied, morning, noon and night. I know
you better than you know yourselves.] (*Addressing Mrs Sylvester*) You
call yourself a New Woman°—you're not New at all. You're just as   445
old as Eve [, and just as hungry for the fruit she plucked]. You only
want one thing—the one thing every woman wants—the one thing
that no woman's life's worth living without! A true man's love! Ah, if
we all had that, there'd be no problem of the sexes then. I had it once.
Heaven help me, I have lost it! I've done my best—it isn't much, but   450
it's the best I can. I give it up! If you° have robbed me of his love, my
own is left to me; and if the future's yours, the past is mine. He loved
me once, and I shall love him always! (*Exit, C*)

CURTAIN

4

A month later

SCENE *An orchard at Mapledurham. Farmhouse at back, C. Paths off, R and L front. A cluster of trees, R, at back. A few stumps of trees to serve as seats.*

Margery discovered, standing on a ladder placed against one of the trees, gathering apples, which she throws into a basket below. She is dressed in peasant costume.

Enter Armstrong, C

ARMSTRONG Margery!

MARGERY Yes, dad!

ARMSTRONG (*comes underneath the tree and roars with laughter*) Here's a slice of luck! That fellow in London wants the grey mare back again! [That screw° he picked up cheap has broken down.]   5

MARGERY (*who has come down*) The grey mare, father?

ARMSTRONG Old Dapple! you remember her?

MARGERY Of course! but what about her?

ARMSTRONG Bless me, haven't I told you? I sold old Dapple to a chap in London.   10

MARGERY (*reproachfully*) You sold old Dapple?

ARMSTRONG She's too good for hereabouts. True, she's a splint° on the off leg, but what's a splint? I sold her without warranty, and buyer took her with all faults, just as she stood.

MARGERY Well, dad?   15

ARMSTRONG Darn me, if the next day he didn't cry off his bargain!

MARGERY (*thoughtfully*) Poor Dapple!

ARMSTRONG Oh, says I, if you're not satisfied with her, I am. So, there's your money; give me back my mare. An Armstrong doesn't stand on warranties.   20

MARGERY No, daddy dear, and you don't mind the splint?

ARMSTRONG But Margery, you should have seen the screw he got in place of her! Ha, ha! she was *all* splints!

MARGERY He's found that out?

ARMSTRONG And wants the old mare back! at my own price!   25

MARGERY This *is* good news! For we were getting hard up, weren't we, father?

ARMSTRONG Ay, farming isn't what it used to be; and now that you
    won't let me take in visitors—

MARGERY I never stopped you.   30

ARMSTRONG How about Captain Sylvester?

MARGERY Oh, him!

ARMSTRONG He's an old customer;° and always seemed a civil-spoken
    gentleman enough.

MARGERY Too civil!   35

ARMSTRONG That's more than you were, Margery. You'd scarce say a
    word.

MARGERY He came for no good.

ARMSTRONG There's no harm in trout fishing—unless it's for the
    trout.   40

MARGERY I was the trout.

ARMSTRONG You? Go on! That's the way with you girls! You think all
    the men are after you. I'm sure he said nothing to hurt you.

MARGERY But he has written since.

ARMSTRONG (scratches his head) I didn't know he'd written.   45

MARGERY Nearly every day.

ARMSTRONG Those letters were from *him?* I thought they were from—
    (*Hesitates*)

MARGERY No! From Captain Sylvester.

ARMSTRONG Of course you haven't answered them?

MARGERY Only the last.   50

ARMSTRONG I shoudn't have done that.

MARGERY Yes, you would, dad!

ARMSTRONG Well, you know best. You always went your own way,
    Margery, and it was always the right road.

MARGERY Where shall I put these apples?   55

ARMSTRONG Nay, I've the broadest shoulders. Give me a hand; I'll
    take 'em.

      Margery helps him to put the basket on his shoulders. Exit, C

MARGERY Dear old dad! We leave our parents, and we return to them;
    they let us go, and they take us back again! How little we think of their
    partings, and how much of our own! (*Sits R*)   60

      Enter Sylvester, L front

SYLVESTER I saw you in the apple-tree, and took a short cut.

MARGERY You got my message then?

SYLVESTER How good of you to send for me! So then my letters have
    had some effect?

MARGERY I sent for you because I want to speak to you.   65

SYLVESTER And I to you. Margery, I've left my wife.

MARGERY Yes, so I heard.

SYLVESTER She was no wife to me. For years our marriage has been a
mockery, and it was best to put an end to it. Now I am free.

MARGERY Because you've left your wife?   70

SYLVESTER It's no use beating about the bush. Things have gone too
far, and I'm too much in earnest. She loves your husband. It is common talk. I've shut my eyes as long as possible, and you've shut yours;
but we both know the truth.

MARGERY That you've deserted her!   75

SYLVESTER What if I have?

MARGERY Go back.

SYLVESTER Back to a wife who is no wife!

MARGERY Back to the woman you promised to protect, and whom you
left when she most needed you.   80

SYLVESTER Because I love you, Margery!

MARGERY That love won't last long. Love can't live on nothing!

SYLVESTER There is no hope for me?

MARGERY No, not a scrap!

SYLVESTER Then what do you propose? To sacrifice your life to an   85
idea—to be true to a phantom? You owe no faith to one who is
unfaithful. Think! You are young—your real life lies before you—
would you end it before it's begun? A widow before you're a wife?

MARGERY I *am* a wife, and I shall not forget it. If I have lost my husband's love, at least I'll save his honour. A public scandal mayn't   90
mean much to *you*, but it means your wife's ruin—it means Gerald's.
Gerald shall not be ruined! You *shall* go back to her!

SYLVESTER Is it a challenge?

MARGERY Challenge or not, you *shall!* It is ignoble to desert her so! You
are a coward to make love to me! If her love was unworthy, what is   95
yours? Is it for you to cast a stone at her?° See! Read your letters!
(*Producing a packet*) Letters to me—love-letters! Letters to a woman
you didn't respect in her grief and persecuted in her loneliness—a
woman who would have none of you—who tells you to your face
you're not a man! Your love's an insult! take the thing away! (*Turns* 100
off. Pause)

SYLVESTER Do you propose to send those to my wife?

MARGERY No! but I want to make you realise you need more mercy
than you show to her. These letters were written for my eye alone; to
open them was to promise secrecy.

SYLVESTER Why have you kept them, then?   105

MARGERY To give them back to you. (*Gives him the packet. Another pause*)

SYLVESTER Margery, everything you say and do makes it more hard to go away from you.

MARGERY You're going, then?

SYLVESTER Your words leave me no choice. 110

MARGERY Where are you going? to her?

SYLVESTER I don't know yet. I don't know if I'm welcome. (*Playing with the packet, mechanically*)

MARGERY That rests with you. You say, she's been no wife to you; but have you been a husband to her?

SYLVESTER Why do you take her part? She's injured you enough. 115

MARGERY Yes; she *has* injured me; but now I know what it is to live without love, and to want it, I can pardon her. Can't you? (*Goes to him and gives him both her hands*) Forgive her, Captain Sylvester—freely as I do you—give her the love that you have offered me—and you will find your wife's a woman just as much as I am. 120

SYLVESTER Margery—I may call you 'Margery'?

MARGERY I'm 'Margery' to everybody now.

SYLVESTER If there were more women like you, there would be fewer men like me. (*Exit, L*)

MARGERY (*looks after him, then goes, R front and looks again*) He'll go 125 back to his wife; and if she isn't happy, it's her fault.° (*Exit, R*)
    Re-enter Armstrong, showing out, C, Lady Wargrave and the Colonel

ARMSTRONG This way, my lady. I'll send Margery to you. (*Exit Armstrong, R*)

COLONEL This must be put right, Caroline.

LADY WARGRAVE I mean to put it right.

COLONEL (*severely*) A Cazenove living apart from his wife! 130

LADY WARGRAVE It is sad—very sad.

COLONEL More than that, Caroline—it's not respectable.

LADY WARGRAVE That doesn't trouble *you*.

COLONEL It shocks me. The institution of marriage is the foundation of society; and whatever tends to cast discredit on that holy 'ordnance'° 135 saps the moral fibre of the community.

LADY WARGRAVE Did you say, 'ordnance'?

COLONEL I did say 'ordnance'. It was a slip of the tongue.

LADY WARGRAVE You are not used to ordinances.°

COLONEL What do you mean, Caroline? Wasn't I baptized—wasn't 140 I confirmed?

LADY WARGRAVE There is another ceremony which, during a somewhat long career, you have systematically avoided.

COLONEL A mere sin of omission, which even now it is not too late to
repair. I am a young man still—   145

LADY WARGRAVE Young man?

COLONEL Comparatively. And everything in the world is comparative.
What cannot be undone in the past can at least be avoided in the
future.

LADY WARGRAVE What is the matter with you, Theodore? You have   150
suddenly become quite a moral martinet, and have developed such a
severity of aspect that I scarcely know my own brother.

COLONEL (*aside*) Shall I tell her? Dare I? Courage!

LADY WARGRAVE I think I liked you better as you were. At any rate,
I was used to you.   155

COLONEL How peaceful it is here, Caroline—how sylvan! ·

LADY WARGRAVE Yes, it's a pretty little place enough.

COLONEL It might have been created expressly for the exchange of
those sacred confidences which are never more becoming than when
shared between a brother and a sister.   160

LADY WARGRAVE Good gracious! you are growing quite sentimental!
I have no confidences to make.

COLONEL But *I* have.

LADY WARGRAVE Theodore! What fresh iniquity—?

COLONEL Caroline, I am going to be married. (*Blows his nose vigorously*) 165

LADY WARGRAVE (*astounded*) Married!

COLONEL Tomorrow.

LADY WARGRAVE To whom, pray?

COLONEL Miss Bethune.

LADY WARGRAVE Give me my smelling salts.   170

COLONEL (*gives her them*) Enid! Pretty name, isn't it? Enid! (*Smiling to
himself*)

LADY WARGRAVE No fool like an old fool!

COLONEL Fifty-six.

LADY WARGRAVE Eight.

COLONEL But don't tell Enid, will you?   175

LADY WARGRAVE There are so many things I mustn't tell Enid!

COLONEL No, Caroline; I've made a clean breast of it.

LADY WARGRAVE *Quite* a clean breast of it?

COLONEL Everything in the world is comparative.

LADY WARGRAVE Then, Miss Bethune has renounced her opinions?   180

COLONEL Oh, no; she's too much of a woman for that.

LADY WARGRAVE How can she reconcile them with your enormities?

COLONEL My peccadilloes? Oh, she doesn't believe them—or she pretends she doesn't—which is the same thing. She says we men exaggerate so; and as for the women, you simply can't believe a word they say! (*Chuckles in his old style*)   185

LADY WARGRAVE At any rate, she means to marry you?

COLONEL Upon the whole, she thinks I have been rather badly used. (*Chuckles again*)

LADY WARGRAVE To marry! after your experience!

COLONEL Way of the world, my dear. My poor old adjutant! went through the Mutiny° unscathed, and killed in Rotten Row!°   190

LADY WARGRAVE Well, it was quite time that you had a nurse! (*Rising and going R front to meet Margery*)

COLONEL Caroline's taken it very well. Nothing like courage in these matters—courage! 'Nurse' was distinctly nasty; but that's Caroline's way.   195

Re-enter Armstrong, R, followed by Margery

ARMSTRONG Found her at last, my lady.

LADY WARGRAVE Leave us together, Armstrong.

Margery drops a curtsey

ARMSTRONG Come with me, Colonel. If you'll step indoors, I'll give you a glass of ale that'll do your heart good.

COLONEL (*putting his arm through Armstrong's*) Caroline takes it very well. (*Quite forgetting himself*)°   200

ARMSTRONG My lady's very welcome.°

COLONEL (*hastily withdrawing his arm*) No, no, no! I was talking to myself. (*Exit Armstrong, C, roaring. Aside, glancing at Lady Wargrave.*) Nurse! (*Exit, C*)   205

LADY WARGRAVE Margery, I've come to scold you.

MARGERY Yes, my lady.

LADY WARGRAVE Aunt. Come and sit down by me. (*Draws her towards seat under the tree, L. Lady Wargrave sits—Margery at her feet*) Yes, Margery, to scold you. Why did you not confide in me? If you had only told me of your troubles, this would never have happened. It was undutiful.   210

MARGERY No, aunt. There are some troubles one can confide to nobody—some griefs which are too sacred to be talked about.

LADY WARGRAVE And is yours one of them? You are young, Margery; and youth exaggerates its sorrows as well as its joys. Nothing has happened that cannot be put right, if you will only trust me and obey me.   215

MARGERY I owe my obedience elsewhere.

LADY WARGRAVE And do you think that you have paid it?

MARGERY Yes.   220

LADY WARGRAVE Gerald *desired* you to leave him?

MARGERY No; but I read his thoughts—just as you used to say I could
read yours—and I obeyed his wishes.

LADY WARGRAVE Then if he wished you to return, you would come
back?   225

MARGERY Not if he'd been talked over; not if he asked me to go back to
him because he thinks it his duty, or I want him. I don't want duty;
I want love.

LADY WARGRAVE You wouldn't see him, if I sent him to you?

MARGERY What is the use of seeing him? You can send Gerald, but not   230
Gerald's heart. I have done all I can—I can't do any more. I've saved
his honour—I've resigned his love. All I ask is, to be left alone with
mine. (*Turning away*)

> Lady Wargrave rises, and as Gerald advances, retires into the
> house, C

GERALD Margery!

MARGERY Gerald!   235

GERALD I am not here to ask you to come back to me. How can I say
what I have come for? I have come—because I cannot keep away from
you. To ask for your forgiveness—

MARGERY You have that.

GERALD And, if it's possible, some place in your esteem. Let me say   240
this, and I will say no more. If, for a little space, my heart strayed from
you, Margery—if, for a moment, words escaped my lips which cannot be recalled, that is my only infidelity. You understand me?

MARGERY Yes.

GERALD That's what I came to say—that's all!   245

MARGERY (*giving him her hand*) Thank you for telling me.

GERALD (*holding her hand*) Not all I want to say, but all I must. I am no
longer a free man. My lips are sealed.

MARGERY What seals them?

GERALD Haven't you heard? Sylvester's left his wife—and it is all my   250
doing.

MARGERY No, it is his.

GERALD His?

MARGERY I may tell you now. He left his wife, not through your fault or
hers, but to make love to me.   255

GERALD He has been here?

MARGERY But he has gone.

GERALD Where?

MARGERY To his wife. I sent him back to her.

GERALD Then, I am free!   260

MARGERY Yes, Gerald.

GERALD Free to say how I love you—how I have always loved you! Yes,
     Margery, I loved you even then—then when I spoke those unjust,
     cruel words; but love's so weird a thing it sometimes turns us against
     those we love. But when I saw you, there upon the ground, my heart   265
     turned back to you—no, it was not my heart, only my lips that were
     unfaithful! My heart was always yours—not half of it, but all—yours
     when I married you, yours when you said good-bye, and never more
     yours, never as much as now, now I have lost you.

MARGERY You have not lost me, if you love me that much! (*Throwing*   270
     her arms round him)

GERALD Margery!

          Lady Wargrave and Colonel re-enter, quietly, C, and stand,
          looking on, at back, amongst the trees

GERALD My wife again!

MARGERY But, Gerald, remember I am nothing more. I don't think
     I shall ever be a lady.°

GERALD Always in my eyes!   275

MARGERY No, not even there. Only a woman.

GERALD I want you to be nothing less or more—only a woman!
          About to kiss her. Lady Wargrave, at back, bows her head, with
          her fan half spread before the Colonel's face.° Gerald kisses
          Margery

          CURTAIN

THE NOTORIOUS
MRS EBBSMITH

A Drama in Four Acts

BY

ARTHUR WING PINERO

THE NOTORIOUS MRS EBBSMITH

The play was first staged at the Garrick Theatre,° London,
on 13 March 1895 with the following cast

Agnes	*Mrs Patrick Campbell°*
Sybil Cleeve	*Miss Eleanor Calhoun*
Gertrude Thorpe	*Miss Ellis Jeffreys*
Nella	*Miss Mary Halsey*
Hephzibah	*Mrs Charles Groves*
Lucas Cleeve	*Mr Johnston Forbes-Robertson°*
Duke of St Olpherts	*Mr John Hare°*
Sir Sandford Cleeve	*Mr Ian Robertson*
Rev. Amos Winterfield	*Mr C. Aubrey Smith°*
Sir George Brodrick	*Mr Joseph Carne*
Dr Kirke	*Mr Fred Thorne*
Fortuné	*Mr Gerald du Maurier°*
Antonio Poppi	*Mr C. F. Caravoglia*

The scenery by Mr W. Harford

*The Scene is laid in Venice—first at the Palazzo Arconati, a
lodging-house on the Grand Canal; afterwards in an apartment
in the Campo S Bartolomeo.*

*It is Easter-tide, a week passes between the events of the First and
Second Acts*

1

*The Scene° is a room in the Palazzo Arconati, on the Grand
Canal, Venice. The room itself is beautiful in its decayed
grandeur, but the furniture and hangings are either tawdry
and meretricious or avowedly modern. The three windows at the
back open on to a narrow covered balcony, or loggia, and through
them can be seen the west side of the canal. Between recessed
double doors on either side of the room is a fireplace out of use and
a marble mantelpiece, but a tiled stove is used for a wood fire.
Breakfast things are laid on a table. The sun streams into the
room.*

*Antonio Poppi and Nella, two Venetian servants, with a touch of
the picturesque in their attire, are engaged in clearing the break-
fast-table*

NELLA (*turning her head*) Ascolta! [Listen!]°

ANTONIO Una gondola allo scalo.° [A gondola at our steps.] (*They open
the centre-window, go out on to the balcony, and look down below*) La
Signora Thorpe. [The Signora Thorpe.]

NELLA Con suo fratello. [With her brother.]   5

ANTONIO (*calling*) Buon di, Signor Winterfield! Iddio la benedica!
[Good day, Signor Winterfield! The blessing of God be upon
you!]

NELLA (*calling*) Buon di, Signora! La Madonna l'assista! [Good day,
Signora! May the Virgin have you in her keeping!]   10

ANTONIO (*returning to the room*) Noi siamo in ritardo di tutto questa
mattina. [We are behindhand with everything this morning.]

NELLA (*following him*) È vero. [That is true.]

ANTONIO (*bustling about*) La stufa! [The stove.]

NELLA (*throwing wood into the stove*) Che tu sia benedetta per rammen-   15
tarmelo! Questi Inglesi non si contentono del sole. [Bless you for
remembering it. These English are not content with the sun.]

*Leaving only a vase of flowers upon the table, they hurry out with
the breakfast things. At the same moment, Fortuné, a man-
servant, enters, showing in Mrs Thorpe and the Rev. Amos Winterfield. Gertrude Thorpe is a pretty, frank-looking young woman
of about seven-and-twenty. She is in mourning, and has sorrowful
eyes and a complexion that is too delicate, but natural cheerfulness
and brightness are seen through all. Amos is about forty—big,*

burly, gruff; he is untidily dressed, and has a pipe in his hand.
Fortuné is carrying a pair of freshly-cleaned tan-coloured boots
upon boot-trees°

GERTRUDE Now, Fortuné, you ought to have told us downstairs that
Dr Kirke is with Mrs Cleeve.

AMOS Come away, Gerty. Mrs Cleeve can't want to be bored with us
just now.   20

FORTUNÉ [(*politely*)] Mrs Cleeve give 'er ordares she is always to be
bored wiz Madame Thorpe and Mr Winterfield.

AMOS Ha, ha!

GERTRUDE (*smiling*) Fortuné!

FORTUNÉ Besides, ze doctares vill go in 'alf a minute, you see.   25

GERTRUDE Doctors!

AMOS What, is there another doctor with Dr Kirke?

FORTUNÉ Ze great physician, Sir Brodrick.

GERTRUDE Sir George Brodrick? Amos!

AMOS Doesn't Mr Cleeve feel so well?   30

FORTUNÉ Oh, yes. But Mrs Cleeve 'appen to read in a newspapare
zat Sir George Brodrick vas in Florence for ze Pâque°—ze Eastare.
Sir Brodrick vas Mr Cleeve's doctare in London, Mrs Cleeve tell me,
so 'e is acquainted wiz Mr Cleeve's inside.

AMOS Ho, ho!   35

GERTRUDE Mr Cleeve's constitution,° Fortuné.

FORTUNÉ Excuse, madame. Zerefore Mrs Cleeve she telegraph for
Sir Brodrick to come to Venise.

AMOS To consult with Dr Kirke, I suppose.

FORTUNÉ (*listening*) 'Ere is ze doctares.   40

Dr Kirke enters, followed by Sir George Brodrick. Kirke is a
shabby, snuff-taking old gentleman—blunt but kind; Sir George,
on the contrary, is scrupulously neat in his dress, and has a suave,
professional manner. Fortuné withdraws

KIRKE Good morning, Mr Winterfield. (*To Gertrude*) How do you do,
my dear? You're getting some colour into your pretty face, I'm glad
to see. (*To Sir George*) Mr Winterfield—Sir George Brodrick. (*Sir*
George and Amos shake hands)

KIRKE (*to Sir George*) Mrs Thorpe. (*Sir George shakes hands with*
Gertrude) Sir George and I started life together in London years ago;   45
now he finds me here in Venice. Well, we can't all win the race°—eh?

SIR GEORGE My dear old friend! (*To Gertrude*) Mr Cleeve has been
telling me, Mrs Thorpe, how exceedingly kind you and your brother
have been to him during his illness.

GERTRUDE Oh, Mr Cleeve exaggerates our little services.   50

AMOS *I've* done nothing.

GERTRUDE Nor I.

KIRKE Now, my dear!

GERTRUDE Dr Kirke, you weren't in Florence with us; you're only a
tale-bearer.   55

KIRKE Well, I've excellent authority for my story of a young woman
who volunteered to share the nursing of an invalid at a time when she
herself stood greatly in need of being nursed.

GERTRUDE Nonsense! (*To Sir George*) You know, Amos—my big
brother over there—Amos and I struck up an acquaintance with   60
Mr and Mrs Cleeve at Florence, at the Hotel d'Italie,° and occasionally one of us would give Mr Cleeve his dose while poor Mrs Cleeve
took a little rest or a drive—but positively that's all.

KIRKE You don't tell us—

GERTRUDE I've nothing more to tell, except that I'm awfully fond of   65
Mrs Cleeve—

AMOS Oh, if you once get my sister on the subject of Mrs Cleeve—
(*Taking up a newspaper*)

GERTRUDE (*to Sir George*) Yes, I always say that if I were a man searching for a wife, I should be inclined to base my ideal on Mrs Cleeve.

SIR GEORGE (*edging away towards Kirke, with a surprised, uncomfortable
smile*) Eh? Really?   70

GERTRUDE [(*following him loftily*)] You conceive a different ideal, Sir
George?

SIR GEORGE Oh—well—

GERTRUDE Well, Sir George?

AMOS Perhaps Sir George has heard that Mrs Cleeve holds regrettable   75
opinions on some points. If so, he may feel surprised that a parson's
sister—

GERTRUDE Oh, I don't share all Mrs Cleeve's views, or sympathise
with them, of course. But they succeed only in making me sad and
sorry. Mrs Cleeve's opinions don't stop me from loving the gentle,   80
sweet woman; admiring her for her patient, absorbing devotion to
her husband; wondering at the beautiful stillness with which she
seems to glide through life—!°

AMOS (*putting down the newspaper, to Sir George and Kirke*) I told you
so! (*To Gertrude*) Gertrude, I'm sure Sir George and Dr Kirke want   85
to be left together for a few minutes.

GERTRUDE (*going up to the window*) I'll sun myself on the balcony.

AMOS And I'll go and buy some tobacco. (*To Gertrude*) Don't be long,

Gerty. (*Nodding to Sir George and Kirke*) Good morning. (*They return his nod; and he goes out*)

GERTRUDE (*on the balcony*) Dr Kirke, I've heard what doctors' con-   90
sultations consist of. After looking at the pictures, you talk about
whist. (*She closes the window and sits outside*)

KIRKE (*producing his snuff-box*) Ha, ha!

SIR GEORGE Why, this lady and her brother evidently haven't the
faintest suspicion of the actual truth, my dear Kirke!

KIRKE (*taking snuff*) Not the slightest.   95

SIR GEORGE The woman made a point of being extremely explicit with
you, you tell me?

KIRKE Yes, she was plain enough with me. At our first meeting she said:
'Doctor, I want you to know so-and-so, and so-and-so, and so-and-
so.'   100

SIR GEORGE Really? Well, it certainly isn't fair of Cleeve and his—his
associate° to trick decent people like Mrs Thorpe and her brother.
Good gracious, the brother is a clergyman too!

KIRKE The rector of some dull hole in the north of England.

SIR GEORGE Really!   105

KIRKE A bachelor; this Mrs Thorpe keeps house for him. She's a widow.

SIR GEORGE Really?

KIRKE Widow of a captain in the army. Poor thing! She's lately lost her
only child and can't get over it.

SIR GEORGE Indeed, really, really? . . . But about Cleeve, now—he had   110
Roman fever° of rather a severe type?

KIRKE In November. And then that fool of a Bickerstaff at Rome
allowed the woman to move him to Florence too soon, and there he
had a relapse. However, when she brought him on here the man was
practically well.   115

SIR GEORGE The difficulty being to convince him of the fact, eh?
A highly-strung, emotional creature?°

KIRKE You've hit him.

SIR GEORGE I've known him from his childhood. Are you still giving
him anything?   120

KIRKE A little quinine°, to humour him.

SIR GEORGE Exactly. (*Looking at his watch*) Where is she? where is she?
I've promised to take my wife shopping in the Merceria° this morning. By-the-by, Kirke—I must talk scandal, I find—*this* is rather an
odd circumstance. Whom do you think I got a bow from as I passed   125
through the hall of the Danieli° last night? (*Kirke grunts and shakes his
head*) The Duke of St Olpherts.°

KIRKE (*taking snuff*) Ah! I suppose you're in with a lot of swells now, Brodrick.

SIR GEORGE No, no; you don't understand me. The Duke is this young fellow's uncle by marriage. His Grace married a sister of Lady Cleeve's—of Cleeve's mother, you know.

KIRKE Oh! This looks as if the family are trying to put a finger in the pie.

SIR GEORGE The Duke may be here by mere chance. Still, as you say, it does look—(*Lowering his voice as Kirke eyes an opening door*) Who's that?

KIRKE [(*in the same tone*)] The woman.°

> *Agnes enters.° She moves firmly but noiselessly—a placid woman, with a sweet, low voice. Her dress is plain to the verge of coarseness; her face, which has little colour, is at the first glance almost wholly unattractive*

AGNES (*looking from one to the other*) I thought you would send for me, perhaps. (*To Sir George*) What do you say about him?

KIRKE One moment. (*Pointing to the balcony*) Mrs Thorpe—

AGNES Excuse me. (*She goes to the window and opens it*)

GERTRUDE Oh, Mrs Cleeve! (*Entering the room*) Am I in the way!

AGNES You are never that, dear. [(*Bringing her down C*)] Run along to my room; I'll call you in a minute or two. (*Gertrude nods, and goes to the door*) Take off your hat and sit with me a little while.

GERTRUDE I'll stay for a bit, but this hat doesn't take off. (*She goes out*)

AGNES (*to Sir George and Kirke*) Yes?

SIR GEORGE We are glad to be able to give a most favourable report. I may say that Mr Cleeve has never appeared to be in better health.

AGNES (*drawing a deep breath*) He will be very much cheered by what you say.

SIR GEORGE (*bowing stiffly*) I'm glad—

AGNES His illness left him with a morbid, irrational impression that he would never be quite his former self again.

SIR GEORGE A nervous man recovering from a scare. I've helped to remove that impression I believe.

AGNES Thank you. We have a troublesome, perhaps a hard time before us; we both need all our health and spirits. (*Turning her head, listening*) Lucas?

> *Lucas enters the room. He is a handsome, intellectual-looking young man of about eight-and-twenty*

LUCAS (*to Agnes, excitedly*) Have you heard what they say of me?

AGNES (*smiling*) Yes.

LUCAS   How good of you, Sir George, to break up your little holiday for the sake of an anxious, fidgety fellow. (*To Agnes*) Isn't it?

AGNES   Sir George has rendered us a great service.

LUCAS (*going to Kirke, brightly*) Yes, and proved how ungrateful I've   165
been to you, doctor.

KIRKE   Don't apologise. People who don't know when they're well are the mainstay of my profession. (*Offering snuff-box*) Here—
>   *Lucas takes a pinch of snuff, laughingly*

AGNES (*in a low voice to Sir George*) He has been terribly hipped° at times. (*Taking up the vase of flowers from the table*) Your visit will have   170
made him another man.
>   *She goes to a table, puts down the vase upon the tray, and commences to cut and arrange the fresh flowers she finds there*

LUCAS (*seeing that Agnes is out of hearing*) Excuse me, Kirke—just for one moment. (*To Sir George*) Sir George—(*Kirke joins Agnes. [Quietly to Sir George]*) You still go frequently to Great Cumberland Place?°

SIR GEORGE [(*assenting*)] Your mother's gout has been rather stubborn   175
lately.

LUCAS   Very likely she and my brother Sandford will get to hear of your visit to me here; in that case you'll be questioned pretty closely, naturally.

SIR GEORGE   My position is certainly a little delicate.   180

LUCAS   Oh, you may be perfectly open with my people as to my present mode of life. Only—(*He motions Sir George to be seated; they sit facing each other*) Only I want you to hear me declare again plainly (*looking towards Agnes*) that but for the care and devotion of that good woman over there, but for the solace of that woman's companionship, I   185
should have been dead months ago—I should have died raving in my awful bedroom on the ground-floor of that foul Roman hotel.° Malarial fever, of course! Doctors don't admit—do they?—that it's possible for strong men to die of miserable marriages. And yet I was dying in Rome, I truly believe, from *my* bitter, crushing disappoint-   190
ment, from the consciousness of my wretched, irretrievable—
>   *Fortuné enters, carrying Lucas's hat, gloves, overcoat, and silk wrap, and, upon a salver, a bottle of medicine and a glass*

LUCAS (*sharply*) Qu'y a-t-il,° Fortuné?

FORTUNÉ   Sir, you 'ave an appointment.

LUCAS (*rising*) At the Danieli at eleven. Is it so late?
>   *Fortuné places the things upon the table. Lucas puts the wrap round his throat; Agnes goes to him and arranges it for him solicitously*

SIR GEORGE (*rising*) I have to meet Lady Brodrick at the Piazzetta. Let   195
me take you in my gondola.

LUCAS Thanks—delighted.

AGNES (*to Sir George*) I would rather Lucas went in the house gondola:
I know its cushions are dry. May he take you to the Piazzetta?

SIR GEORGE (*a little stiffly*) Certainly.   200

AGNES (*to Fortuné*) Mettez les coussins dans la gondole.°

FORTUNÉ Bien, madame.°

> *Fortuné goes out. Agnes begins to measure a dose of medicine*

SIR GEORGE (*to Agnes*) Er—I—ah—

LUCAS (*putting on his gloves*) Agnes, Sir George—

AGNES (*turning to Sir George, the bottle and glass in her hands*) Yes?   205

SIR GEORGE (*constrainedly*) We always make a point of acknowledging
the importance of nursing as an aid to medical treatment. I—I am
sure Mr Cleeve owes you much in that respect.

AGNES Thank you.

SIR GEORGE (*to Lucas*) I have to discharge my gondola; you'll find me   210
at the steps, Cleeve. (*Agnes shifts the medicine bottle from one hand to
the other so that her right hand may be free, but Sir George simply bows°
in a formal way and moves towards the door*) You are coming with us,
Kirke?

KIRKE Yes.

SIR GEORGE Do you mind seeing that I'm not robbed by my gondolier?   215
(*He goes out*)

AGNES (*giving the medicine to Lucas, undisturbed*) Here, dear.

KIRKE (*to Agnes*) May I pop in tonight for my game of chess?

AGNES Do, doctor; I shall be very pleased.

KIRKE (*shaking her hand in a marked way*) Thank you. (*He follows Sir
George*)

AGNES (*looking after him*) Liberal little man.   220

> *She has Lucas's overcoat in her hand: a small pen-and-ink draw-
> ing of a woman's head drops from one of the pockets. They pick it
> up together*

AGNES Isn't that the sketch you made of me in Florence?

LUCAS (*replacing it in the coat-pocket*) Yes.

AGNES You are carrying it about with you?

LUCAS I slipped it into my pocket, thinking it might interest the Duke.

AGNES (*assisting him with his overcoat*) Surely I am too obnoxious in the   225
abstract for your uncle to entertain such a detail as a portrait.

LUCAS It struck me it might serve to correct certain preconceived
notions of my people's.

AGNES Images of a beautiful temptress with peach-blossom cheeks and
stained hair?   230

LUCAS That's what I mean; I assume they suspect a decline of taste on
my part, of that sort. Good-bye, dear.

AGNES Is this mission of the Duke of St Olpherts the final attempt to
part us, I wonder? (*Angrily, her voice hardening*) Why should they
harass and disturb you as they do?   235

LUCAS (*kissing her*) Nothing disturbs me now that I *know* I am strong
and well. Besides, everybody will soon tire of being shocked. Even
conventional morality must grow breathless in the chase.

    He leaves her. She opens the other door and calls

AGNES [(*gentle again*)] Mrs Thorpe! I'm alone now.

    She goes on to the balcony, through the centre window, and looks
    down below. Gertrude enters, and joins her on the balcony

GERTRUDE How well your husband is looking!   240

AGNES Sir George Brodrick pronounces him quite recovered.

GERTRUDE Isn't that splendid! (*Waving her hand and calling*) Buon
giorno, Signor Cleeve! Come molto meglio voi state!° (*Leaving the
balcony, laughing*) Ha, ha, my Italian!

    Agnes waves finally to the gondola below, returns to the room, and
    slips her arm through Gertrude's

AGNES Two whole days since I've seen you.   245

GERTRUDE They've been two of my bad days, dear.

AGNES (*looking into her face*) All right now?

GERTRUDE Oh, 'God's in His heaven'° this morning! When the sun's
out I feel that my little boy's bed in Ketherick Cemetery is warm and
cosy.   250

AGNES (*patting Gertrude's hand*) Ah!—

GERTRUDE [(*walking away and fingering papers on the table*)] The
weather's the same all over Europe, according to the papers. Do you
think it's really going to settle at last? To me these chilly, showery
nights are terrible. You know, I still tuck my child up at night-time;   255
still have my last peep at him before going to my own bed; and it is
awful to listen to these cold rains—drip, drip, drip upon that little
green coverlet of his! (*She goes and stands by the window silently*)

AGNES This isn't strong of you, dear Mrs Thorpe. You mustn't—you
mustn't.   260

    Agnes brings the tray with the cut flowers to the nearer table;
    calmly and methodically she resumes trimming the stalks

GERTRUDE You're quite right. That's over. [(*Brightly*)] Now, then, I'm
going to gabble for five minutes gaily. (*Settling herself comfortably in*

an armchair) What jolly flowers you've got there! What have you been doing with yourself? Amos took me to the Caffè Quadri° yesterday to late breakfast, to cheer me up. Oh, I've something to say to you! At the Caffè, at the next table to ours, there were three English people— two men and a girl—home from India,° I gathered. One of the men was looking out of the window, quizzing° the folks walking in the Piazza, and suddenly he caught sight of your husband. (*Agnes's hands pause in their work*) 'I do believe that's Lucas Cleeve', he said. And then the girl had a peep, and said: 'Certainly it is'. And the man said: 'I must find out where he's stopping; if Minerva is with him, you must call'. 'Who's Minerva?' said the second man. 'Minerva is Mrs Lucas Cleeve', the girl said. 'It's a pet name—he married a chum of mine, a daughter of Sir John Steyning's, a year or so after I went out'.° Excuse me, dear. Do these people really know you and your husband, or were they talking nonsense?

> *Agnes takes the vase of faded flowers, goes on to the balcony, and*
> *empties the contents of the vase into the canal. Then she stands by*
> *the window, her back towards Gertrude*

AGNES No, they evidently know Mr Cleeve.

GERTRUDE Your husband never calls you by that pet-name of yours. Why is it you haven't told me you're a daughter of Admiral Steyning's?

AGNES [(*turning*)] Mrs Thorpe—

GERTRUDE (*warmly*) Oh, I must say what I mean! I have often pulled myself up short in my gossips with you, conscious of a sort of wall between us. (*Agnes comes slowly from the window*) Somehow, I feel now that you haven't in the least made a friend of me. I'm hurt. It's stupid of me; I can't help it.

AGNES (*after a moment's pause*) I am not the lady these people were speaking of yesterday.

GERTRUDE Not—?

AGNES Mr Cleeve is no longer with his wife; he has left her.

GERTRUDE Left—his wife!

AGNES Like yourself, I am a widow. I don't know whether you've ever heard my name—Ebbsmith.° (*Gertrude stares at her blankly*) I beg your pardon sincerely. I never meant to conceal my true position; such a course is opposed to every principle of mine. But I grew so attached to you in Florence and—well, it was contemptibly weak; I'll never do such a thing again. (*She goes back to the table and commences to refill the vase with the fresh flowers*)

GERTRUDE When you say that Mr Cleeve has left his wife, I suppose you mean to tell me you have taken her place?

AGNES Yes, I mean that.   300
      Gertrude rises and walks to the door

GERTRUDE (*at the door*) You knew that I could not speak to you again
    after hearing this?

AGNES I thought it almost certain you would not.°
      After a moment's irresolution, Gertrude returns, and stands by the
      settee

GERTRUDE I can hardly believe you.

AGNES I should like you to hear more than just the bare fact.   305

GERTRUDE (*drumming on the back of the settee*) Why don't you tell me
    more?

AGNES You were going, you know.

GERTRUDE (*sitting*) I won't go quite like that. Please tell me.

AGNES (*calmly*) Well—did you ever read of John Thorold—'Jack   310
    Thorold, the demagogue'? (*Gertrude shakes her head*) I daresay not.
    John Thorold, once a schoolmaster, was my father. In my time he
    used to write for the two or three, so-called, inflammatory journals,
    and hold forth in small lecture-halls, occasionally even from the top
    of a wooden stool in the Park,° upon trade and labour questions, div-   315
    ision of wealth, and the rest of it. He believed in nothing that people
    who go to church are credited with believing in, Mrs Thorpe; his
    scheme for the re-adjustment of things was Force; his pet doctrine,
    the ultimate healthy healing that follows the surgery of Revolution.
    But to me he was the gentlest creature imaginable; and I was very   320
    fond of him, in spite of his—as I then thought—strange ideas.
    Strange ideas! Ha! many of 'em luckily don't sound quite so irrational
    today!°

GERTRUDE (*under her breath*) Oh!

AGNES My home was a wretched one. If dad was violent out of the   325
    house, mother was violent enough in it; with her it was rage, sulk,
    storm, from morning till night; till one day father turned a deaf ear to
    mother and died in his bed. That was my first intimate experience of
    the horrible curse that falls upon so many.

GERTRUDE Curse?   330

AGNES The curse of unhappy marriage. Though really I'd looked on at
    little else all my life. Most of our married friends were cursed in a like
    way;° and I remember taking an oath, when I was a mere child, that
    nothing should ever push me over into the choked-up, seething pit.
    Fool! When I was nineteen I was gazing like a pet sheep into a man's   335
    eyes; and one morning I was married, at St Andrew's Church in
    Holborn,° to Mr Ebbsmith, a barrister.

GERTRUDE In church?

AGNES Yes, in church [(*sitting, facing Gertrude*)]—in church. In spite of
father's unbelief and mother's indifference, at the time I married I   340
was as simple—ay, in my heart as devout—as any girl in a parsonage.° The other thing hadn't soaked into me. Whenever I could
escape from our stifling rooms at home, and slam the front door
behind me, the air blew away uncertainty and scepticism; I seemed
only to have to take a long, deep breath to be full of hope and faith.   345
And it was like this till that man married me.

GERTRUDE Of course, I guess your marriage was an unfortunate one.

AGNES It lasted eight years. For about twelve months he treated me like
a woman in a harem,° for the rest of the time like a beast of burden.
Oh! when I think of it! (*Wiping her brow with her handkerchief*) Phew!   350

GERTRUDE It changed you?

AGNES Oh, yes, it changed me.

GERTRUDE You spoke of yourself just now as a widow. He's dead?

AGNES He died on our wedding day—the eighth anniversary.

GERTRUDE You were free then—free to begin again.   355

AGNES Eh? (*Looking at Gertrude*) Yes; but you don't begin to believe all
over again. (*She gathers up the stalks of the flowers from the tray, and,
kneeling, crams them into the stove*) However, this is an old story. I'm
thirty-three now.

GERTRUDE (*hesitatingly*) You and Mr Cleeve—?   360

AGNES We've known each other since last November—no longer. Six
years of my life unaccounted for, eh? Well, for a couple of years or so
I was lecturing.

GERTRUDE Lecturing?

AGNES Ah, I'd become an out-and-out child of my father by that   365
time—spouting, perhaps you'd call it, standing on the identical little
platforms he used to speak from, lashing abuses with my tongue as he
had done. Oh, and I was fond, too, of warning women.

GERTRUDE Against what?

AGNES Falling into the pit.   370

GERTRUDE Marriage?

AGNES [(*putting logs on the stove*)] The choked-up, seething pit [(*turning to Gertrude*)]—until I found my bones almost through my skin
and my voice too weak to travel across a room.

GERTRUDE From what cause?   375

AGNES Starvation, my dear. [(*Rising*)] So, after lying in a hospital for a
month or two, I took up nursing for a living.° [(*Wiping her hands upon
her handkerchief*)] Last November I was sent for by Dr Bickerstaff to

go through to Rome to look after a young man who'd broken down there, and who declined to send for his friends. My patient was 380 Mr Cleeve—(*taking up the tray*)—and that's where his fortunes—join mine. (*She crosses the room, and puts the tray upon the cabinet*)

GERTRUDE And yet, judging from what that girl said yesterday, Mr Cleeve married quite recently?

AGNES Less than three years ago.° Men don't suffer as patiently as 385 women. In many respects his marriage story is my own, reversed—the man in place of the woman. I endured my hell, though; he broke the gates of his.

GERTRUDE I have often seen Mr Cleeve's name in the papers. His future promised to be brilliant, didn't it? 390

AGNES (*tidying the table, folding the newspapers, &c.*) There's a great career for him still.

GERTRUDE In Parliament—*now*?   .

AGNES No, he abandons that, and devotes himself to writing. We shall write much together, urging our views on this subject of Marriage. 395 We shall have to be poor, I expect, but we shall be content.

GERTRUDE Content!

AGNES Quite content. Don't judge us by my one piece of cowardly folly in keeping the truth from you, Mrs Thorpe. [Our intention is the reverse of deceiving people.] Indeed, it's our great plan to live the life 400 we have mapped out for ourselves, fearlessly, openly; faithful to each other, helpful to each other, for as long as we remain together.

GERTRUDE But tell me—you don't know how I—how I have liked you!—tell me, if Mr Cleeve's wife divorces him he will marry you?

AGNES No 405

GERTRUDE No!

AGNES No. I haven't made you quite understand—Lucas and I don't desire to marry, in your sense.

GERTRUDE But you are devoted to each other!

AGNES Thoroughly. 410

GERTRUDE What, is that the meaning of 'for as long as you are together'? You would go your different ways if ever you found that one of you was making the other unhappy?

AGNES I do mean that. We remain together only to help, to heal, to console. Why should men and women be so eager to grant to each other 415 the power of wasting life? That is what marriage gives—the right to destroy years and years of life. And the right, once given, it *attracts*—*attracts!* We have both suffered from it. So many rich years out of my life have been squandered by it. And out of his life, so much force,

energy—spent in battling with the shrew, the termagant he has now   420
fled from; strength never to be replenished, never to be repaid—all
wasted, wasted!

GERTRUDE Your legal marriage with him might not bring further
miseries.

AGNES Too late! We have done with marriage; we distrust it. We are not   425
now among those who regard marriage as indispensable to union. We
have done with it!

GERTRUDE (*advancing to her*) You know it would be impossible for me,
if I would do so, to deceive my brother as to all this.

AGNES [(*softening*)] Why, of course, dear.   430

GERTRUDE (*looking at her watch*) Amos must be wondering—

AGNES Run away, then.

    Gertrude crosses quickly towards the door

GERTRUDE (*retracing a step or two*) Shall I see you—? Oh!°

AGNES (*shaking her head*) Ah!

GERTRUDE (*going to her, constrainedly*) When Amos and I have talked   435
this over, perhaps—perhaps—

AGNES No, no, I fear not. Come, my dear friend—(*with a smile*)—give
me a shake of the hand.

GERTRUDE (*taking her hand*) What you've told me is dreadful. (*Looking
into Agnes's face*) And yet you're not a wicked woman! (*Kissing Agnes*)   440
In case we don't meet again.

    *The women separate quickly, looking towards the door, as Lucas
    enters*

LUCAS (*shaking hands with Gertrude*) How do you do, Mrs Thorpe? I've
just had a wave of the hand from your brother.

GERTRUDE Where is he?

LUCAS On his back in a gondola,° a pipe in his mouth as usual, gazing   445
skywards. (*Going on to the balcony*) He's within hail. (*Gertrude goes
quickly to the door, followed by Agnes*) There! by the Palazzo Sforza.°
(*He re-enters the room; Gertrude has disappeared. He is going towards
the door*) Let me get hold of him, Mrs Thorpe.

AGNES (*standing before Lucas, quietly*) She knows, Lucas, dear.

LUCAS Does she?   450

AGNES She overheard some gossip at the Caffè Quadri yesterday, and
began questioning me; so I told her.

LUCAS (*taking off his coat*) Adieu to them, then—eh?

AGNES (*assisting him*) Adieu.

LUCAS I intended to write to the brother directly they had left Venice,   455
to explain.

AGNES Your describing me as 'Mrs Cleeve' at the hotel in Florence
helped to lead us into this; after we move from here I must always be,
frankly, 'Mrs Ebbsmith'.

LUCAS These were decent people. You and she had formed quite an   460
attachment?

AGNES Yes. (*She places his coat, &c., on a chair, then fetches her workbasket from the cabinet*)

LUCAS There's something of the man in your nature, Agnes.

AGNES I've anathematised my womanhood often enough. (*She sits at
the table, taking out her work composedly*)

LUCAS Not that every man possesses the power you have acquired—   465
the power of going through life with compressed lips.

AGNES (*looking up, smiling*) A propos?°

LUCAS These people—this woman you've been so fond of. You see
them shrink away with the utmost composure.

AGNES (*threading a needle*) You forget, dear, that you and I have pre-   470
pared ourselves for a good deal of this sort of thing.

LUCAS Certainly, but at the moment—

AGNES One must take care that the regret lasts no longer than a
moment. Have you seen your uncle?

LUCAS A glimpse. He hadn't long risen.   475

AGNES [(*contemptuously*)] He adds sluggishness to other vices, then?

LUCAS (*lighting a cigarette*) He greeted me through six inches of open
door. His toilet has its mysteries.

AGNES A stormy interview?

LUCAS The reverse. He grasped my hand warmly, declared I looked the   480
picture of health, and said it was evident I had been most admirably
nursed.

AGNES (*frowning*) That's a strange utterance. But he's an eccentric,
isn't he?

LUCAS No man has ever been quite satisfied as to whether his oddities   485
are ingrained or affected.

AGNES No man. What about women?

LUCAS Ho! they have had opportunities of closer observation.

AGNES Hah! And they report—?

LUCAS Nothing. They become curiously reticent.   490

AGNES (*scornfully, as she is cutting a thread*) These noblemen!

LUCAS (*taking a packet of letters from his pocket*) Finally, he presented
me with these, expressed a hope that he'd see much of me during the
week, and dismissed me with a fervent God bless you!

AGNES (*surprised*) He remains here, then?   495

LUCAS It seems so.

AGNES What are those, dear?

LUCAS The Duke has made himself the bearer of some letters, from friends. I've only glanced at them: reproaches—appeals—

AGNES Yes, I understand   500

  He sits looking through the letters impatiently, then tearing them up and throwing the pieces upon the table

LUCAS Lord Warminster—my godfather: 'My dear boy, for God's sake—!' (*Tearing up the letter and reading another*) Sir Charles Littlecote: 'Your brilliant future. . . . blasted . . .' (*Another letter*) Lord Froom: 'Promise of a useful political career unfulfilled. . . . cannot an old friend. . . .?' (*Another letter*) Edith Heytesbury. I didn't notice a   505 woman had honoured me. (*In an undertone*) Edie—! (*Slipping the letter into his pocket and opening another*)° Jack Brophy: 'Your great career—' Major Leete: 'Your career—' (*Destroying the rest of the letters without reading them*) My career! my career! That's the chorus, evidently. Well, there goes my career! (*She lays her work aside and goes*   510 *to him*)

AGNES Your career? (*Pointing to the destroyed letters*) True, that one is over. But there's the other, you know—*ours*.

LUCAS (*touching her hand*) Yes, yes. Still, it's just a little saddening, the saying good-bye—(*disturbing the scraps of paper*)—to all this.

AGNES Saddening, dear? Why, this political career of yours—think   515 what it would have been at best? Accident of birth sent you to the wrong side of the House;° influence of family would always have kept you there.

LUCAS (*partly to himself*) But I made my mark. I did make my mark.

AGNES Supporting the Party° that retards; the Party that preserves for   520 the rich, palters with the poor. (*Pointing to the letters again*) Oh, there's not much to mourn for there!

LUCAS Still, it was—success.

AGNES Success!

LUCAS I was talked about, written about, as a Coming Man—*the* Com-   525 ing Man!

AGNES How many 'coming men' has one known. Where on earth do they all go to?

LUCAS Ah, yes, but I allowed for the failures, and carefully set myself to discover the causes of them. And, as I put my finger upon the causes   530 and examined them, I congratulated myself and said, 'Well, I haven't *that* weak point in my armour, or *that*'; and, Agnes, at last I was fool enough to imagine I had no weak point, none whatever.

AGNES It was weak enough to believe that.

LUCAS I couldn't foresee that I was doomed to pay the price all nervous   535
men pay for success; that the greater my success became, the more
cancer-like grew the fear of never being able to continue it, to excel it;
that the triumph of today was always to be the torture of tomorrow!
Oh, Agnes, the agony of success to a nervous, sensitive man; the dismal apprehension that fills his life and gives each victory a voice to cry   540
out 'Hear, hear! Bravo, bravo, bravo! But this is to be your last—
you'll never overtop it!' Ha, yes! I soon found out the weak spot in my
armour—the need of constant encouragement, constant reminder of
my powers; (*taking her hand*) the need of that subtle sympathy which
a sacrificing, unselfish woman alone possesses the secret of. (*Rising*)   545
Well, my very weakness might have been a source of greatness if,
three years ago, it had been to such a woman that I had bound
myself—a woman of your disposition; instead of to—! Ah!°
        She lays her hand upon his arm soothingly

LUCAS Yes, yes. (*Taking her in his arms*) I know I have such a companion now.   550

AGNES Yes—now—

LUCAS You must be everything to me, Agnes—a double faculty, as it
were. When my confidence in myself is shaken, you must try to keep
the consciousness of my poor powers alive in me.

AGNES I shall not fail you in that, Lucas.   555

LUCAS And yet, whenever disturbing recollections come uppermost;
when I catch myself mourning for those lost opportunities of mine; it
is your love that must grant me oblivion—(*kissing her upon the lips*)—
your love!
        She makes no response, and after a pause gently releases herself
        and retreats a step or two

LUCAS (*his eyes following her*) Agnes, you seem to be changing towards   560
me, growing colder to me. At times you seem positively to shrink
from me. I don't understand it. Yesterday I thought I saw you look at
me as if I—frightened you!

AGNES Lucas—Lucas dear, for some weeks, now, I've wanted to say
this to you.   565

LUCAS What?

AGNES Don't you think that such a union as ours would be much
braver, much more truly courageous, if it could but be—be—

LUCAS If it could but be—what?

AGNES (*averting her eyes*) Devoid of passion, if passion had no share in   570
it.°

78

LUCAS Surely this comes a little late, Agnes, between you and me.

AGNES (*leaning upon the back of a chair, staring before her and speaking in a low, steady voice*) What has been was inevitable, I suppose. Still, we have hardly yet set foot upon the path we've agreed to follow. It is not 575 too late for us, in our own lives, to put the highest interpretation upon that word—Love. Think of the inner sustaining power it would give us! (*More forcibly*) We agree to go through the world together, preaching the lessons taught us by our experiences. [You will show yourself fearlessly to the world as one who refuses to endure a misery 580 you have not earned, one who makes a right to end a wretched marriage from which there is no law on your side to release you. And I take my place openly by you—a woman ready to give you, for as long as you ask it, that food of sympathy your talents hunger for to save them from starvation.] We cry out to all people, 'Look at us! Man and 585 woman who are in the bondage of neither law nor ritual! Linked simply by mutual trust! Man and wife, but something better than man and wife! Friends, but even something better than friends!' I say there is that which is noble, finely defiant, in the future we have mapped out for ourselves, if only—if only— 590

LUCAS Yes?

AGNES (*turning from him*) If only it could be free from passion!

LUCAS (*in a low voice*) Yes, but—is that possible?

AGNES (*in the same tone, watching him askance, a frightened look in her eyes*) Why not?

LUCAS Young man and woman . . . youth and love . . .? Scarcely upon 595 this earth, my dear Agnes, such a life as you have pictured.

AGNES I say it can be, it can be—!

> *Fortuné enters, carrying a letter upon a salver, and a beautiful*
> *bouquet of white flowers. He hands the note to Lucas*

LUCAS (*taking the note, glancing at Agnes*) Eh! (*To Fortuné, pointing to the bouquet*) Qu'avez-vous là?°

FORTUNÉ Ah, excuse. (*Presenting the bouquet to Agnes*) Wiz compli- 600 ment. (*Agnes takes the bouquet wonderingly*) Tell Madame ze Duke of St Olphert bring it in person, 'e says.

LUCAS (*opening the note*) Est-il parti?°

FORTUNÉ 'E did not get out of 'is gondola.

LUCAS Bien. (*Fortuné withdraws. Reading the note aloud*) 'While brush- 605 ing my hair, my dear boy, I became possessed of a strong desire to meet the lady with whom you are now improving the shining hour.° Why the devil shouldn't I, if I want to? Without prejudice, as my lawyer says, let me turn up this afternoon and chat pleasantly to her

of Shakespeare, also the musical glasses.° Pray hand her this flag of   610
truce—I mean my poor bunch of flowers—and believe me yours,
with a touch of gout, St Olpherts.' (*Indignantly crushing the note.*) Ah!

AGNES (*frowning at the flowers*) A taste of the oddities, I suppose!

LUCAS He is simply making sport of us. (*Going on to the balcony and
looking out*) There he is. Damn that smile of his!   615

AGNES Where? (*She joins him*)

LUCAS With the two gondoliers.

AGNES Why—that's a beautiful face! How strange!

LUCAS (*drawing her back into the room*) Come away. He is looking up at
us.   620

AGNES Are you sure he sees us?

LUCAS He did.

AGNES He will want an answer—(*She deliberately flings the bouquet°
over the balcony into the canal, then returns to the table and picks up her
work*)

LUCAS (*looking out again cautiously*) He throws his head back and laughs
heartily. (*Re-entering the room*) Oh, of course, his policy is to attempt   625
to laugh me out of my resolves. They send him here merely to laugh
at me, Agnes, to laugh at me—(*coming to Agnes angrily*) laugh at me!°

AGNES He must be a man of small resources. (*Threading her needle*) It is
so easy to mock.

END OF THE FIRST ACT

2

The Scene is the same as that of the previous Act. Through the windows some mastheads and flapping sails are seen in the distance.° [*Within the room, the settee is now RC, set obliquely by the stove.*] *The light is that of late afternoon.*

Agnes, very plainly dressed, is sitting at the table, industriously copying from a manuscript. After a moment or two, Antonio and Nella enter the room, carrying a dressmaker's box, which is corded and labelled

NELLA È permesso, Signora. [Permit us, Signora.]

ANTONIO Uno scatolone per la Signora. [An enormous box for the Signora.]

AGNES (*turning her head*) Eh?

NELLA È venuto colla ferrovia—[It has come by the railway—] 5

ANTONIO (*consulting the label*) Da' Firenze. [From Florence.]

AGNES By railway, from Florence?

NELLA (*reading from the label*) 'Emilia Bardini, Via Rondinelli.'°

AGNES Bardini? That's the dressmaker. There must be some mistake. Non è per me, Nella. [It isn't for me.] 10

    Antonio and Nella carry the box to her animatedly

NELLA Ma guardi, Signora! [But look, Signora!]

ANTONIO Alla Signora Cleeve!

NELLA E poi abbiamo pagato il porto della ferrovia. [Besides, we have paid the railway dues upon it.]

AGNES (*collecting her sheets of paper*) Hush! hush! don't trouble me just 15
now. Mettez-la n'importe où.°

    They place the box on another table

NELLA La corda intaccherebbe la forbice della Signora. Vuole che Antonio la tagli? [The cord would blunt the Signora's scissors. Shall Antonio cut the cord?]

AGNES (*pinning her sheets of paper together*) I'll see about it by and by. 20
Laissez-moi!°

NELLA (*softly to Antonio*) Taglia, taglia! [Cut, cut!]

    Antonio cuts the cord, whereupon Nella utters a little scream

AGNES (*turning, startled*) What is it!

NELLA (*pushing Antonio away*) Questo stupido non ha capito la Signora
e ha tagliata la corda. [The stupid fellow misunderstood the Signora, 25
and has severed the cord.]

AGNES (*rising*) It doesn't matter. Be quiet!

NELLA (*removing the lid from the box angrily*) Ed ecco la scatola aperta contro voglia della Signora! [And now here is the box open against the Signora's wish!] (*Inquisitively pushing aside the paper which covers the contents of the box*) O Dio! Si vede tutto quel che vi é! [O God! and all the contents exposed!] 30

> *When the paper is removed, some beautiful material trimmed with lace, etc., is seen*

NELLA Guardi, guardi, Signora! [Signora, look, look!] (*Agnes examines the contents of the box with a puzzled air*) Oh, che bellezza! [How beautiful!] 35

> *Lucas enters*

ANTONIO (*to Nella*) Il padrone. [The master.]

> *Nella curtsies to Lucas, then withdraws with Antonio*

AGNES Lucas, the dressmaker in the Via Rondinelli at Florence—the woman who ran up the little gown I have on now—

LUCAS (*with a smile*) What of her?

AGNES This has just come from her. Phuh! What does she mean by sending the showy thing to me? 40

LUCAS It is my gift to you.

AGNES (*producing enough of the contents of the box to reveal a very hand-some dress*) This!

LUCAS I knew Bardini had your measurements; I wrote to her, instructing her to make that. I remember Lady Heytesbury in something similar last season. 45

AGNES (*examining the dress*) A mere strap for the sleeve, and sufficiently décolletée,° I should imagine.

LUCAS My dear Agnes, I can't understand your reason for trying to make yourself a plain-looking woman when nature intended you for a pretty one. 50

AGNES Pretty!

LUCAS (*looking hard at her*) You *are* pretty.

AGNES Oh, as a girl I may have been—(*disdainfully*)—pretty. What good did it do anybody? (*Fingering the dress with aversion*) And when would you have me hang this on my bones?° 55

LUCAS Oh, when we are dining, or—

AGNES Dining in a public place?

LUCAS Why not look your best in a public place?

AGNES [(*slowly*)] Look my best! You know, I don't think of this sort of garment in connection with our companionship, Lucas. 60

LUCAS It is not an extraordinary garment for a lady.

AGNES Rustle of silk, glare of arms and throat—they belong, in my mind, to such a very different order of things from that we have set up.   65

LUCAS Shall I appear before you in ill-made clothes, clumsy boots—

AGNES Why? We are just as we always have been, since we've been together. I don't tell you that your appearance is beginning to offend.

LUCAS Offend! Agnes, you—you pain me. I simply fail to understand why you should allow our mode of life to condemn you to perpetual   70 slovenliness.°

AGNES Slovenliness!

LUCAS No, no, shabbiness.

AGNES (*looking down upon the dress she is wearing*) Shabbiness!

LUCAS (*with a laugh*) Forgive me, dear; I'm forgetting you are wearing   75 a comparatively new afternoon-gown.

AGNES At any rate, I'll make this brighter tomorrow with some trim-mings, willingly. (*Pointing to the dressmaker's box*) Then you won't insist on my decking myself out in rags of that kind—eh! There's something in the idea—I needn't explain.   80

LUCAS (*fretfully*) Insist! I'll not urge you again. (*Pointing to the box*) Get rid of it somehow. Are you copying that manuscript of mine?

AGNES I had just finished it.

LUCAS Already! (*Taking up her copy*) How beautifully you write! (*Going to her eagerly*) What do you think of my Essay?   85

AGNES It bristles with truth; it is vital.

LUCAS My method of treating it?

AGNES Hardly a word out of place.

LUCAS (*chilled*) *Hardly* a word?

AGNES Not a word, in fact.   90

LUCAS No, dear, I daresay your 'hardly' is nearer the mark.

AGNES I assure you it is brilliant, Lucas.

LUCAS What a wretch I am ever to find the smallest fault in you! Shall we dine out to night?

AGNES As you wish, dear.   95

LUCAS At the Grünwald?° (*He goes to the table to pick up his manuscript; when his back is turned she looks at her watch quickly*) We'll solemnly toast this, shall we, in Montefiascone?°

AGNES (*eyeing him askance*) You are going out for your chocolate° this afternoon as usual, I suppose?   100

LUCAS Yes, but I'll look through your copy first, so that I can slip it into the post at once. You are not coming out?

AGNES Not till dinner-time.

LUCAS (*kissing her on the forehead*) I talked over the points of this—
(*tapping the manuscript*)—with a man this morning; he praised some   105
of the phrases warmly.

AGNES A man? (*In an altered tone*) The Duke?

LUCAS Er—yes.

AGNES (*with assumed indifference, replacing the lid on the dressmaker's box*)
You have seen him again today, then?

LUCAS We strolled about together for half an hour on the Piazza.°   110

AGNES (*replacing the cord around the box*) You—you don't dislike him as
much as you did?

LUCAS [(*moving away*)] He's somebody to chat to. [(*Going up R*)] I suppose one gets accustomed even to a man one dislikes.

AGNES (*almost inaudibly*) I suppose so.   115

LUCAS As a matter of fact, he has the reputation of being rather a pleasant companion; though I—I confess—I—I `don't find him very
entertaining.

> *He goes out. She stands staring at the door through which he has*
> *disappeared. There is a knock at the opposite door*

AGNES (*rousing herself*) Fortuné! (*Raising her voice*) Fortuné!

> *The door opens, and Gertrude enters hurriedly*

GERTRUDE Fortuné is complacently smoking a cigarette in the   120
Campo.°

AGNES Mrs Thorpe!

GERTRUDE (*breathlessly*, [*sitting*]) Mr Cleeve is out, I conclude?

AGNES No. [*Gertrude rises quickly*]° He is later than usual in going out
this afternoon.   125

GERTRUDE (*irresolutely*) I don't think I'll wait, then.

AGNES But do tell me: you have been crossing the streets to avoid me
during the past week; what has made you come to see me now?

GERTRUDE I *would* come. I've given poor Amos the slip; he believes I'm
buying beads for the Ketherick school-children.   130

AGNES (*shaking her head*) Ah, Mrs Thorpe—!

GERTRUDE Of course, it's perfectly brutal to be underhanded. But
we're leaving for home tomorrow; I couldn't resist it.

AGNES (*coldly*) Perhaps I'm very ungracious—

GERTRUDE (*taking Agnes's hand*) The fact is, Mrs Cleeve—oh, what do   135
you wish me to call you?

AGNES (*withdrawing her hand*) Well—you're off tomorrow. Agnes will
do.

GERTRUDE Thank you. The fact is, it's been a bad week with me—rest-
less, fanciful. And I haven't been able to get you out of my head.   140

AGNES I'm sorry.

GERTRUDE Your story, your present life; you, yourself—such a contradiction to what you profess! Well, it all has a sort of fascination for
me.

AGNES My dear, you're simply not sleeping again. (*Turning away*)   145
You'd better go back to the ammonia° Kirke prescribed for you.

GERTRUDE (*taking a card from her purse, with a little, light laugh*) You
want to physic me, do you, after worrying my poor brain as you've
done? (*Going to her*) 'The Rectory, Daleham, Ketherick Moor.'
Yorkshire, you know. There can be no great harm in your writing to   150
me sometimes.

AGNES (*refusing the card*) No; under the circumstances I can't promise
that.

GERTRUDE (*wistfully*) Very well.

AGNES (*facing her*) Oh, can't you understand that it can only be—dis-   155
turbing to both of us for an impulsive, emotional creature like yourself to keep up acquaintanceship with a woman who takes life as I do?
We'll drop each other, leave each other alone. (*She walks away, and
stands leaning upon the stove, her back towards Gertrude*)

GERTRUDE (*replacing the card in her purse*) As you please. Picture me,
sometimes, in that big, hollow shell of a rectory at Ketherick,   160
strolling about my poor dead little chap's empty room.

AGNES (*under her breath*) Oh!

GERTRUDE (*turning to go*) God bless you.

AGNES Gertrude! (*With altered manner*) You—you have the trick of
making me lonely also. (*Going to Gertrude, taking her hands and*   165
fondling them) I'm tired of talking to the walls! And your blood is
warm to me! [(*Leaving Gertrude and pacing the room*)] Shall I tell you,
or not—or not?

GERTRUDE [(*watching her*)] Do tell me.

AGNES [(*returning to Gertrude, swiftly*)] There is a man here, in Venice,   170
who is torturing me—flaying me alive.

GERTRUDE Torturing you?

AGNES He came here about a week ago; he is trying to separate us.

GERTRUDE You and Mr Cleeve?

AGNES Yes.   175

GERTRUDE You are afraid he will succeed?

AGNES Succeed! What nonsense you talk!

GERTRUDE What upsets you, then?

AGNES After all, it's difficult to explain—the feeling is so indefinite. It's
like—something in the air. This man is influencing us both oddly.   180

Lucas is as near illness again as possible; I can *hear* his nerves vibrating. And I—you know what a fish-like thing I am as a rule—just look at me now, as I'm speaking to you.

GERTRUDE [(*sitting*)] But don't you and Mr Cleeve—talk to each other?

AGNES As children do when the lights are put out—of everything but   185
what's uppermost in their minds.

GERTRUDE You have met the man?

AGNES I intend to meet him.

GERTRUDE Who is he?

AGNES A relation of Lucas's—the Duke of St Olpherts.   190

GERTRUDE He has right on his side, then?

AGNES If you choose to think so.

GERTRUDE ([*rising, approaching Agnes, leaning over the back of the sofa,*]
deliberately) Supposing he *does* succeed in taking Mr Cleeve away
from you?

AGNES (*staring at Gertrude*) What, *now*, do you mean?   195

GERTRUDE Yes. (*There is a brief pause; then Agnes walks across the room,
wiping her brow with her handkerchief*)

AGNES I tell you, that idea's—preposterous.

GERTRUDE Oh, I can't understand you.

AGNES [(*facing her*)] You'll respect my confidence?

GERTRUDE Agnes!   200

AGNES (*sitting [LC; slowly, as if collecting her thoughts]*) Well, I fancy
this man's presence here has simply started me thinking of a time—
oh, it may never come!—a time when I may cease to be—necessary to
Mr Cleeve.° Do you understand?

GERTRUDE I remember what you told me of your being prepared to   205
grant each other freedom if—

AGNES Yes, yes; and for the past few days this idea has filled me with a
fear of the most humiliating kind.

GERTRUDE What fear?

AGNES The fear lest, after all my beliefs and protestations, I should   210
eventually find myself loving Lucas in the helpless, common way of
women—

GERTRUDE (*under her breath*) I see.

AGNES The dread that the moment may arrive some day when, should
it be required of me, *I shan't feel myself able to give him up easily.* (*Her*   215
head drooping, uttering a low moan) Oh—!

> *Lucas, dressed for going out, enters, carrying Agnes's copy of his*
> *manuscript, rolled and addressed for the post. Agnes rises.*
> [*Gertrude walks away to RC*]

86

AGNES (*to Lucas*) Mrs Thorpe starts for home tomorrow; she has called
to say good-bye.

LUCAS (*to Gertrude*) It is very kind. Is your brother quite well?

GERTRUDE (*embarrassed*) Thanks: quite.   220

LUCAS (*smiling*) I believe I have added to his experience of the obscure
corners of Venice during the past week.

GERTRUDE I—I don't—Why?

LUCAS By so frequently putting him to the inconvenience of avoiding
me.   225

GERTRUDE Oh, Mr Cleeve, we—I—I—

LUCAS Please tell your brother I asked after him.

GERTRUDE I—I can't; he—doesn't know I've—I've—

LUCAS [(*dryly*)] Ah! really? (*With a bow*) Good-bye.
        He goes out, Agnes accompanying him to the door

GERTRUDE (*to herself*) Brute! (*To Agnes*) Oh, I suppose Mr Cleeve has   230
made me look precisely as I feel.

AGNES How?

GERTRUDE Like people deserve to feel who do godly, mean things.
        Fortuné appears

FORTUNÉ (*to Agnes, significantly*) Me Cleeve 'as jus' gone out.

AGNES Vous savez, n'est-ce pas?°   235

FORTUNÉ (*glancing at Gertrude*) But Madame is now engagé.

GERTRUDE (*to Agnes*) Oh, I am going.

AGNES (*to Gertrude*) Wait. (*Softly to her*) I want you to hear this little
comedy. Fortuné shall repeat my instructions. (*To Fortuné*) Les
ordres que je vous ai donnés, répétez-les.°   240

FORTUNÉ (*speaking in an undertone*) On ze left 'and side of ze Campo—

AGNES Non, non—tout haut.°

FORTUNÉ (*aloud, with a slight shrug of the shoulders*) On ze left 'and side
of ze Campo—

AGNES Yes.   245

FORTUNÉ In one of ze doorways between Fiorentini's and ze leetle
lamp-shop—ze—ze—h'm—ze person.

AGNES Precisely. Dépêchez-vous.° (*Fortuné bows and retires*) Fortuné
flatters himself he is engaged in some horrid intrigue. You guess
whom I am expecting?   250

GERTRUDE The Duke?

AGNES (*ringing a bell*) I've written to him asking him to call upon me
this afternoon while Lucas is at Florian's°. (*Referring to her watch*) He
is to kick his heels about the Campo till I let him know I am alone.

GERTRUDE Will he obey you?   255

87

AGNES A week ago he was curious to see the sort of animal I am. If he holds off now, I'll hit upon some other plan. I will come to close quarters with him, if only for five minutes.

GERTRUDE Good-bye. (*They embrace, then walk together to the door*) You still refuse my address? 260

AGNES You bat! Didn't you see me make a note of it?

GERTRUDE You!

AGNES (*her hand on her heart*) Here.

GERTRUDE (*gratefully*) Ah! (*She goes out*)

AGNES (*at the open door*) Gertrude! 265

GERTRUDE (*outside*) Yes?

AGNES (*in a low voice*) Remember, in my thoughts I pace that lonely little room of yours with you. (*As if to stop Gertrude from re-entering*) Hush! No, no. (*She closes the door sharply. Nella appears*)

AGNES (*pointing to the box on the table*) Portez ce carton dans ma 270 chambre.°

NELLA (*trying to peep into the box as she carries it*) Signora, se Ella si mettesse questo magnifico abito! Oh! quanto sarebbe più bella! (*Signora, if you were to wear this magnificent dress, oh how much more beautiful you would be!*) 275

AGNES (*listening*) Sssh! Sssh! (*Nella goes out. Fortuné enters*) Eh, bien?
       Fortuné glances over his shoulder. The Duke of St Olpherts
       enters; the wreck of a very handsome man, with delicate features,
       a transparent complexion, a polished manner, and a smooth,
       weary voice. He limps, walking with the aid of a cane. Fortuné
       retires

AGNES Duke of St Olpherts?°

ST OLPHERTS (*bowing*) Mrs Ebbsmith?

AGNES Mr Cleeve would have opposed this rather out-of-the-way proceeding of mine. He doesn't know I have asked you to call on me 280 today.

ST OLPHERTS So I conclude. It gives our meeting a pleasant air of adventure.

AGNES I shall tell him directly he returns.°

ST OLPHERTS (*gallantly*) And destroy a cherished secret. 285

AGNES You are an invalid. (*Motioning him to be seated*) Pray don't stand. (*Sitting*) Your Grace is a man who takes life lightly. It will relieve you to hear that I wish to keep sentiment out of any business we have together.

ST OLPHERTS I believe I haven't the reputation of being a sentimental 290 man. (*Seating himself*) You send for me, Mrs Ebbsmith—

AGNES To tell you I have come to regard the suggestion you were good
enough to make a week ago—

ST OLPHERTS Suggestion?

AGNES Shakespeare, the musical glasses, you know—   295

ST OLPHERTS Oh, yes. Ha! ha!

AGNES I've come to think it a reasonable one. At the moment I considered it a gross impertinence.

ST OLPHERTS Written requests are so dependent on a sympathetic
reader.   300

AGNES That meeting might have saved you time and trouble.

ST OLPHERTS I grudge neither.

AGNES It might perhaps have shown your Grace that your view of life is
too narrow; that your method of dealing with its problems wants
variety; that, in point of fact, your employment upon your present   305
mission is distinctly inappropriate. Our meeting today may serve the
same purpose.

ST OLPHERTS My view of life?

AGNES That all men and women may safely be judged by the standards
of the casino and the dancing-garden.   310

ST OLPHERTS I have found those standards not altogether untrust-
worthy. My method—?

AGNES To scoff, to sneer, to ridicule.

ST OLPHERTS Ah! And how much is there, my dear Mrs Ebbsmith,
belonging to humanity that survives being laughed at?   315

AGNES More than you credit, Duke. For example, I—I think it possible
you may not succeed in grinning away the compact between
Mr Cleeve and myself.

ST OLPHERTS Compact?

AGNES Between serious man and woman.   320

ST OLPHERTS [(*acquiescing politely*)] Serious *woman*.

AGNES Ah! at least you must see that—serious woman. (*Rising, facing
him*) You can't fail to realise, even from this slight personal knowledge of me, that you are not dealing just now with some poor, feeble
ballet-girl.°   325

ST OLPHERTS But how well you put it! (*Rising*) And how frank of you
to furnish, as it were, a plan of the fortifications to the—the—

AGNES Why do you stick at 'enemy'?

ST OLPHERTS It's not the word. Opponent! For the moment, perhaps,
opponent. I am never an enemy, I hope, where your sex is concerned.   330

AGNES No, I am aware that you are not over-nice in the bestowal of your
patronage—where my sex is concerned.

ST OLPHERTS You regard my appearance in an affair of morals as a quaint one?

AGNES Your Grace is beginning to know me.   335

ST OLPHERTS Dear lady, you take pride, I hear, in belonging to—The People. You would delight me amazingly by giving me an inkling of the popular notion of my career.

AGNES (*walking away*) Excuse me.

ST OLPHERTS (*following her*) Please! It would be instructive, perhaps   340
chastening. I entreat.

AGNES No.

ST OLPHERTS You are letting sentiment intrude itself. (*Sitting, in pain*)
I challenge you.°

AGNES At Eton you were curiously precocious. The head-master,   345
referring to your aptitude with books, prophesied a brilliant future
for you; your tutor, alarmed by your attachment to a certain cottage
at Ascot which was minus a host,° thanked his stars to be rid of you.
At Oxford you closed all books, except, of course, betting-books.

ST OLPHERTS I detected the tendency of the age—scholarship for the   350
masses. I considered it my turn to be merely intuitively intelligent.

AGNES You left Oxford a gambler and spendthrift. A year or two in
town established you as an amiable, undisguised debauchee. The rest
is modern history.

ST OLPHERTS Complete your sketch. Don't stop at the—rude outline.   355

AGNES Your affairs falling into disorder, you promptly married a
wealthy woman—the poor, rich lady who has for some years honoured you by being your duchess at a distance. This burlesque of
marriage helped to reassure your friends, and actually obtained for
you an ornamental appointment for which an over-taxed nation pro- 360
vides a handsome stipend. But, to sum up, you must always remain
an irritating source of uneasiness to your own order, as, luckily, you
will always be a sharp-edged weapon in the hands of mine.

ST OLPHERTS (*with a polite smile*) Yours! Ah, to that small, unruly section to which I understand you particularly attach yourself. To the—   365

AGNES (*with changed manner, flashing eyes, harsh voice, and violent
gestures*) The sufferers, the toilers; that great crowd of old and
young—old and young stamped by excessive labour and privation all
of one pattern—whose backs bend under burdens, whose bones ache
and grow awry, whose skins, in youth and in age, are wrinkled and
yellow; those from whom a fair share of the earth's space and of the   370
light of day is withheld. (*Looking down upon him fiercely*) The half-
starved who are bidden to stand with their feet in the kennel° to

watch gay processions in which you and your kind are borne high.
Those who would strip the robes from a dummy aristocracy and cast
the broken dolls into the limbo of a nation's discarded toys. Those   375
who—mark me!—are already upon the highway, marching, marching; whose time is coming as surely as yours is going!°

ST OLPHERTS (*clapping his hands gently*) Bravo! bravo! Really a flash of
the old fire. Admirable! (*She walks away to the window with an impatient exclamation*) Your present *affaire du coeur* does not wholly   380
absorb you, then, Mrs Ebbsmith. Even now the murmurings of love
have not entirely superseded the thunderous denunciations of—
h'm—You once bore a nickname, my dear.

AGNES (*turning sharply*) Ho! so you've heard *that*, have you?

ST OLPHERTS Oh, yes.   385

AGNES Mad—Agnes? (*He bows deprecatingly*) We appear to have studied each other's history pretty closely.

ST OLPHERTS Dear lady, this is not the first time the same roof has
covered us.

AGNES No?   390

ST OLPHERTS Five years ago, on a broiling night in July, I joined a
party of men who made an excursion from a club-house in St James's
Street to the unsavoury district of St Luke's.

AGNES Oh, yes.

ST OLPHERTS A depressin' building; the Iron Hall, Barker Street—   395
no—Carter Street.°

AGNES Precisely.

ST OLPHERTS We took our places amongst a handful of frowsy folks
who cracked nuts and blasphemed. On the platform stood a gaunt,
white-faced young lady resolutely engaged in making up by extrava-   400
gance of gesture for the deficiencies of an exhausted voice. 'There',
said one of my companions, 'that is the notorious Mrs Ebbsmith'.
Upon which a person near us, whom I judged from his air of leaden
laziness to be a British working man, blurted out, 'Notorious
Mrs Ebbsmith! Mad Agnes! That's the name her sanguinary° friends   405
give her—Mad Agnes!' At that moment the eye of the panting
oratress caught mine for an instant, and [(*bowing*)] you and I first met.

AGNES (*passing her hand across her brow, thoughtfully*) Mad—Agnes. . . .
(*To him, with a grim smile*) We have both been criticised, in our time,
pretty sharply, eh, Duke?   410

ST OLPHERTS [(*with humility*)] Yes. Let that reflection make you more
charitable to a poor peer.

    A knock at the door

AGNES Entrez!

> *Fortuné and Antonio enter, Antonio carrying tea, etc., upon a*
> *tray*

AGNES (*to St Olpherts*) You drink tea—fellow-sufferer?

> *He signifies assent. Fortuné places the tray on the table, then*
> *withdraws with Antonio. Agnes pours out tea*

ST OLPHERTS (*producing a little box from his waistcoat pocket*) No milk,   415
dear lady. And may I be allowed—saccharine?°

> *She hands him his cup of tea; their eyes meet*

AGNES (*scornfully*) Tell me now—really—why do the Cleeves send a
rip° like you to do their serious work?

ST OLPHERTS (*laughing heartily*) Ha, ha, ha! Rip! ha, ha! [(*Limping over*
to RC cup in hand and taking up position by stove)] Poor solemn family!   420
Oh, set a thief to catch a thief, you know. That, I presume, is their
motive.   .

AGNES (*pausing in the act of pouring out tea, and staring at him*) What do
you mean?

ST OLPHERTS (*sipping his tea*) Set a thief to catch a thief. And by deduc-   425
tion, set one sensualist—who, after all, doesn't take the trouble to
deceive himself—to rescue another who does.

AGNES If I understand you, that is an insinuation against Mr Cleeve.

ST OLPHERTS Insinuation!—

AGNES (*looking at him fixedly*) Make yourself clearer.   430

ST OLPHERTS You have accused me, Mrs Ebbsmith, of narrowness of
outlook. In the present instance, dear lady, it is *your* judgement
which is at fault.

AGNES Mine?

ST OLPHERTS It is not I who fall into the error of confounding you with   435
the designing *danseuse* of commerce;° it is, strangely enough, you
who have failed in your estimate of Mr Lucas Cleeve.

AGNES What is my estimate?

ST OLPHERTS I pay you the compliment of believing that you have
looked upon my nephew as a talented young gentleman whose future   440
was seriously threatened by domestic disorder; a young man of a certain courage and independence, with a share of the brain and spirit of
those terrible human pests called reformers; the one young gentleman, in fact, most likely to aid you in advancing your vivacious social
and political tenets. You have had such thoughts in your mind?   445

AGNES I don't deny it.

ST OLPHERTS Ah! But what is the real, the actual Lucas Cleeve?

AGNES Well—what is the real Lucas Cleeve?

ST OLPHERTS Poor dear fellow! I'll tell you. (*Going to the table to deposit his cup there; [his back is towards her] while she watches him, her hands tightly clasped, a frightened look in her eyes. [Softly]*) The real Lucas 450
Cleeve. (*Coming back to her*) An egoist. An egoist.

AGNES An egoist. Yes.

ST OLPHERTS Possessing ambition without patience, self-esteem without self-confidence.

AGNES Well? 455

ST OLPHERTS Afflicted with a desperate craving for the opium-like drug, adulation; persistently seeking the society of those whose white, pink-tipped fingers fill the pernicious pipe° most deftly and delicately. Eh?

AGNES I didn't—Pray, go on. 460

ST OLPHERTS Ha! I remember they looked to his marriage to check his dangerous fancy for the flutter of lace, the purr of pretty women. And now, here he is—loose again.

AGNES (*suffering*) Oh!—

ST OLPHERTS In short, in intellect still nothing but a callow boy; in 465
body, nervous, bloodless, hysterical; in morals—an epicure.°

AGNES Have done! Have done!

ST OLPHERTS 'Epicure' offends you. A vain woman would find consolation in the word.

AGNES Enough of it! Enough! Enough! 470

> *She turns away, beating her hands together. The light in the room° has gradually become subdued; the warm tinge of sunset now colours the scene outside the windows*

ST OLPHERTS (*with a shrug of his shoulders*) The real Lucas Cleeve.

AGNES No, no! Untrue, untrue! (*Lucas enters. The three remain silent for a moment*) The Duke of St Olpherts calls in answer to a letter I wrote to him yesterday. I wanted to make his acquaintance. (*She goes out*)

LUCAS (*after a brief pause*) By a lucky accident the tables were crowded 475
at Florian's; I might have missed the chance of welcoming you. In God's name, Duke, why must you come here?

ST OLPHERTS (*fumbling in his pockets for a note*) In God's name? You bring the orthodoxy into this queer firm, then, Lucas? (*Handing the note to Lucas*) A peremptory summons. 480

LUCAS You need not have obeyed it. (*St Olpherts takes a cigarette from his case and limps away*) I looked about for you just now. I wanted to see you.

ST OLPHERTS (*lighting his cigarette*) How fortunate—!

LUCAS To tell you that this persecution must come to an end. It has   485
made me desperately wretched for a whole week.

ST OLPHERTS Persecution?

LUCAS Temptation.

ST OLPHERTS Dear Lucas, the process of inducing a man to return to
his wife isn't generally described as temptation.   490

LUCAS Ah, I won't hear another word of that proposal. (*St Olpherts
shrugs his shoulders*) I say my people are offering me, through you, a
deliberate temptation to be a traitor. To which of these two women—
my wife or— (*pointing to the door*)—to her—am I really bound now?
It may be regrettable, scandalous, but the common rules of right and   495
wrong have ceased to apply here. Finally, Duke—and this is my message—I intend to keep faith with the woman who sat by my bedside
in Rome, the woman to whom I shouted my miserable story in my
delirium, the woman whose calm, resolute voice healed me, hardened me, renewed in me the desire to live.   500

ST OLPHERTS Ah, Oh, these modern nurses, in their greys, or browns,
and snowy bibs! They have much to answer for, dear Lucas.

LUCAS No, no! Why will you persist, all of you, in regarding this as a
mere morbid infatuation, bred in the fumes of pastilles? It isn't so!
Laugh, if you care to; but this is a meeting of affinities, of the solitary   505
man and the truly sympathetic woman.

ST OLPHERTS And oh—oh these sympathetic women!

LUCAS No! Oh, the unsympathetic women! There you have the cause
of half the world's misery. The unsympathetic women—you should
have loved one of them.   510

ST OLPHERTS I dare say I've done that in my time.

LUCAS Love one of these women—*I* know!—worship her, yield yourself to the intoxicating day-dreams that make the grimy world
sweeter than any heaven ever imagined. How your heart leaps with
gratitude for your good fortune! how compassionately you regard   515
your unblest fellow-men! What may you not accomplish with such a
mate beside you; how high will be your aims, how paltry every obstacle that bars your way to them; how sweet is to be the labour, how
divine the rest! Then—you marry her. Marry her, and in six months,
if you've pluck enough to do it, lag behind your shooting-party and   520
blow your brains out, by accident, at the edge of a turnip-field. You
have found out by that time all that there is to look for—the daily
diminishing interest in your doings, the poorly-assumed attention as
you attempt to talk over some plan for the future; then the yawn, and,
by degrees, the covert sneer, the little sarcasm, and finally, the frank,   525

open stare of boredom. Ah, Duke, when you all carry out your repressive legislation against women of evil lives, don't fail to include in your schedule the Unsympathetic Wives. They are the women whose victims show the sorriest scars; they are the really 'bad women' of the world: all the others are snow-white in comparison!   530

ST OLPHERTS Yes, you've got a great deal of this in that capital Essay you quoted from this morning. Dear fellow, I admit your home discomforts; but to jump out of that frying-pan into this confounded—what does she call it?—compact!

LUCAS Compact?   535

ST OLPHERTS A vague reference, as I understand, to your joint crusade against the blessed institution of Marriage.

LUCAS (*an alteration in his manner*) Oh—ho, that idea! What—what has she been saying to you?

ST OLPHERTS Incidentally she pitched into me, dear Lucas; she   540
attacked my moral character. You must have been telling tales.

LUCAS Oh, I—I hope not. Of course, we—

ST OLPHERTS Yes, yes—a little family gossip, to pass the time while she has been dressing her hair, or—By-the-by, she doesn't appear to spend much time in dressing her hair.°   545

LUCAS (*biting his lip*) Really?

ST OLPHERTS Then she denounced the gilded aristocracy generally. Our day is over; we're broken wooden dolls, and are going to be chucked. The old tune; but I enjoyed the novelty of being so near the instrument. I assure you, dear fellow, I was within three feet of her   550
when she deliberately Trafalgar Squared me.°

LUCAS (*with an uneasy laugh*) You're the red rag,° Duke. This spirit of revolt in her—it's ludicrously extravagant; but it will die out in time, when she has become used to being happy and cared for—(*partly to himself, with clenched hands*)—yes, cared for.°   555

ST OLPHERTS Die out? Bred in the bone, dear Lucas.

LUCAS On some topics she's a mere echo of her father—if you mean that?

ST OLPHERTS The father—[a threadbare, unclean socialistic ranter;] one of these public-park vermin, eh?   560

LUCAS [(*impatiently*)] Dead years ago.

ST OLPHERTS [And she took over the business as a going concern.] I once heard her bellowing in a dirty little shed in St Luke's. I told you?

LUCAS Yes, you've told me.

ST OLPHERTS I sat there again, it seemed, this afternoon. The orator   565
not quite so lean perhaps—a little less witch-like; but—

LUCAS She was actually in want of food in those days! Poor girl! (*Partly to himself*) I mean to remind myself of that constantly. Poor girl!

ST OLPHERTS *Girl!* Let me see—you're considerably her junior?°

LUCAS No, no; a few months perhaps.   570

ST OLPHERTS Oh, come!

LUCAS Well, years—two or three.

ST OLPHERTS [That's it; if women are to get stout, they begin to show it at her time of life.]° The voice remains rather raucous.

LUCAS [(*bringing his hand down heavily on the table*)] By God, the voice   575
is sweet!

ST OLPHERTS Well—considering the wear and tear. Really, my dear fellow, I do believe this—I do believe that if you gowned her respectably—

LUCAS (*impulsively*) Yes, yes, I say so. I tell her that.   580

ST OLPHERTS (*with a smile*) Do you? That's odd, now. [(*Walking away to RC*) At present, I suspect, her toilette is closely influenced by the estimable Dr Jaeger.°]

LUCAS What a topic. Poor Agnes's dress!

ST OLPHERTS Your taste used to be rather aesthetic. Even your own   585
wife is one of the smartest women in London.

LUCAS Ha, well, I must contrive to smother these aesthetic tastes of mine.

ST OLPHERTS It's a pity that other people will retain their sense of the incongruous.   590

LUCAS (*snapping his fingers*) Other people—!

ST OLPHERTS The public.

LUCAS The public?

[ST OLPHERTS You don't flatter yourself that Mrs Ebbsmith's ebul-
lient disposition will allow her to remain in this—h'm—honorable   595
retirement for any length of time?

LUCAS You mean—?]

ST OLPHERTS Come, you know well enough that unostentatious immodesty is no part of your partner's programme. Of course, you will find yourself by and by in a sort of perpetual public parade with   600
your crack-brained visionary—

LUCAS You shall not speak of her so! You shall not.

ST OLPHERTS (*unconcernedly*) Each of you bearing a pole of the soiled banner of Free Union.° [Isn't that what this fanaticism is called?

LUCAS Whatever term describes it, I ask you to go, to leave me to it.]   605

ST OLPHERTS Free Union for the People! Ho, my dear Lucas!

LUCAS Good heavens, Duke, do you imagine, now that I am in sound health and mind again, that I don't see the hideous absurdity of these views of hers?

ST OLPHERTS Then why the deuce don't you listen a little more patiently to *my* views?   610

LUCAS No, no. I tell you I intend to keep faith with her, as far as I am able. She's so earnest, so pitiably earnest. If I broke faith with her entirely, it would be too damnably cowardly.

ST OLPHERTS Cowardly! [Why is it that courage, like charity, so seldom begins at home?]   615

LUCAS (*pacing the room agitatedly*) Besides, we shall do well together, after all, I believe—she and I. In the end we shall make concessions to each other and settle down, somewhere abroad, peacefully.

ST OLPHERTS Hah! And they called you a Coming Man at one time, didn't they?   620

LUCAS Oh, I—I shall make as fine a career with my pen as that other career would have been. At any rate, I ask you to leave me to it all—to leave me!

    Fortuné enters. The shades of evening have now deepened; the
    glow of sunset comes into the room

FORTUNÉ I beg your pardon, sir.

LUCAS Well?   625

FORTUNÉ It is pas' ze time for you to dress for dinner.

LUCAS I'll come.

    Fortuné goes out

ST OLPHERTS When do we next meet, dear fellow?

LUCAS No, no—please not again.

    Nella enters, excitedly

NELLA (*speaking over her shoulder*) Si, Signora; ecco il Signore. [Yes, Signora; here is the Signor.] (*To Cleeve*) Scusi, Signore. Quando la vedrá come é cara—! [Pardon, Signor. When you see her you'll see how sweet she looks—!]   630

    Agnes's voice is heard

AGNES (*outside*) Am I keeping you waiting, Lucas?

    She enters, handsomely gowned, her throat and arms bare, the
    fashion of her hair roughly altered. She stops abruptly upon seeing
    St Olpherts; a strange light comes into her eyes; her voice,
    manner, bearing, all express triumph. The two men stare at her
    blankly. She appears to be a beautiful woman°

AGNES (*to Nella*) Un petit châle noir tricoté—cherchez-le.° (*Nella withdraws*) Ah, you are not dressed, Lucas dear.   635

LUCAS What—what time is it? (*He goes towards the door, still staring at Agnes*)

ST OLPHERTS (*looking at her, and speaking in an altered tone*) I fear my gossiping has delayed him. You—you dine out?

AGNES At the Grünwald. Why don't you join us? (*Turning to Lucas, lightly*) Persuade him, Lucas.

      Lucas pauses at the door

ST OLPHERTS Er—impossible. Some—friends of mine may arrive to-night. (*Lucas goes out*) I am more than sorry.

AGNES (*mockingly*) Really? You are sure you are not shy of being seen with a notorious woman?

ST OLPHERTS My dear Mrs Ebbsmith—!

AGNES No, I forget—that would be unlike you. *Mad* people scare you, perhaps?

ST OLPHERTS [(*softly*)] Ha, ha! Don't be too rough.

AGNES [(*between her teeth*)] Come, Duke, confess—isn't there more sanity in me than you suspected?

ST OLPHERTS (*in a low voice, eyeing her*) Much more. I think you are very clever.

      Lucas quietly re-enters the room; he halts upon seeing that St
      Olpherts still lingers

ST OLPHERTS (*with a wave of the hand to Lucas*) Just off, dear fellow. (*He offers his hand to Agnes; she quickly places hers behind her back*) You—you are charming. (*He walks to the door, then looks round at the pair*) Au'voir! (*St Olpherts goes out*)

AGNES Au'voir! (*Her head drooping suddenly, her voice hard and dull*) You had better take me to Fulici's before we dine, and buy me some gloves.

LUCAS (*coming to her, and seizing her hand*) Agnes dear!

AGNES (*releasing herself and sitting with a heavy, almost sullen, look upon her face*) Are you satisfied?

LUCAS (*by her side*) You have delighted me! How sweet you look!°

AGNES Ah!

LUCAS You shall have twenty new gowns now; you shall see the women envying you, the men envying me. Ah, ha! fifty new gowns!° You will wear them?

AGNES Yes.

LUCAS Why, what has brought about this change in you?

AGNES What!

LUCAS What?

AGNES I know.

LUCAS You know?

AGNES Exactly how you regard me.

LUCAS I don't understand you—   675

AGNES Listen. Long ago, in Florence, I began to suspect that we had
made a mistake, Lucas. Even there I began to suspect that your
nature was not one to allow you to go through life sternly, severely,
looking upon me more and more each day as a fellow-worker, and less
and less as—a woman. I suspected this—oh, proved it!—but still   680
made myself believe that this companionship of ours would gradually become, in a sense, colder—more temperate, more impassive.
(*Beating her brow*) Never! never! Oh, a few minutes ago this man, who
means to part us if he can, drew your character, disposition, in a
dozen words.   685

LUCAS You believe *him*! You credit what *he* says of me!

AGNES I declared it to be untrue. Oh, but—

LUCAS But—but—!

AGNES (*rising, seizing his arm*) The picture he paints of you is not wholly
a false one. Sssh! Lucas. Hark! attend to me! I resign myself to it all!   690
Dear, I must resign myself to it!

LUCAS Resign yourself? Has life with me become so distasteful?

AGNES Has it? Think! Why, when I realised the actual conditions of our
companionship—why didn't I go on my own way stoically? Why
don't I go at this moment?   695

LUCAS You really *love* me, do you mean—as simple, tender women are
content to love?° (*She looks at him, nods slowly, then turns away and
droops over the table. He raises her, and takes her in his arms*) My dear
girl! My dear, cold, warm-hearted girl! Ha! You couldn't bear to see
me packed up in one of the Duke's travelling boxes and borne back to   700
London—eh? (*She shakes her head; her lips form the word 'No'*) No
fear of that, my—my sweetheart!

AGNES (*gently pushing him from her*) Quick—dress—take me out.

LUCAS You are shivering; go and get your thickest wrap.

AGNES That heavy brown cloak of mine?   705

LUCAS Yes.

AGNES It's an old friend, but—dreadfully *shabby*. You will be ashamed
of me again.

LUCAS Ashamed!—

AGNES I'll write to Bardini about a new one tomorrow. I won't oppose   710
you—I won't repel you any more.

LUCAS Repel me! I only urged you to reveal yourself as what you are—
a beautiful woman.

AGNES Ah! Am I—that?

LUCAS (*kissing her*) Beautiful—beautiful!   715

AGNES (*with a gesture of abandonment*) I—I'm glad.
>   *She leaves him and goes out. He looks after her for a moment*
>   *thoughtfully, then suddenly passes his hands across his brow and*
>   *opens his arms widely as if casting a burden from him*

LUCAS Oh!—oh! (*Turning away alertly*) Fortuné—

END OF THE SECOND ACT

3

The Scene is the same as before, but it is evening, and the lamps are lighted within the room, while outside is bright moonlight.

Agnes, dressed as at the end of the preceding Act, is lying upon the settee propped up by pillows. A pretty silk shawl, with which she plays restlessly, is over her shoulders. Her face is pale, but her eyes glitter, and her voice has a bright ring in it. Kirke is seated at a table writing. Gertrude, without hat or mantle, is standing behind the settee, looking down smilingly upon Agnes

KIRKE (*writing*) H'm—(*To Agnes*) Are you often guilty of this sort of thing?

AGNES (*laughing*) I've never fainted before in my life; I don't mean to do so again.

KIRKE (*writing*) Should you alter your mind about that, do select a suitable spot on the next occasion. What was it your head came against? 5

GERTRUDE A wooden chest, Mr Cleeve thinks.

AGNES With beautiful, rusty, iron clamps. (*Putting her hand to her head, and addressing Gertrude*) The price of vanity.

KIRKE Vanity? 10

AGNES Lucas was to take me out to dinner. While I was waiting for him to dress I must needs stand and survey my full length in a mirror.

KIRKE (*glancing at her*) A very excusable proceeding.

AGNES Suddenly the room sank and left me—so the feeling was—in air.

KIRKE Well, most women can manage to look into their pier-glasses° 15 without swooning—eh, Mrs Thorpe?

GERTRUDE (*smiling*) How should I know, doctor?

KIRKE (*blotting his writing*) There. How goes the time?

GERTRUDE Half past eight.

KIRKE I'll leave this prescription at Mantovani's myself. I can get it 20 made up tonight.

AGNES (*taking the prescription out of his hand playfully*) Let me look.

KIRKE (*protesting*) Now, now!

AGNES (*reading the prescription*) Ha, ha! After all, what humbugs doctors are! 25

KIRKE You've never heard me deny it.

AGNES (*returning the prescription to him*) But I'll swallow it—for the dignity of my old profession. (*She reaches out her hand to take a cigarette*)

KIRKE Don't smoke too many of those things.°

AGNES They never harm me. It's a survival of the time in my life when   30
the cupboard was always empty. (*Striking a match*) Only it had to be
stronger tobacco in those days, I can tell you.

> *She lights her cigarette. Gertrude is assisting Kirke with his over-*
> *coat. Lucas enters, in evening dress, looking younger, almost boyish*

LUCAS (*brightly*) Well?

KIRKE She's to have a cup of good *bouillon*°—Mrs Thorpe is going
to look after that—and anything else she fancies. She's all right.   35
(*Shaking hands with Agnes*) The excitement of putting on that pretty
frock—(*Agnes gives a hard little laugh. Shaking hands with Lucas*) I'll
look in tomorrow. (*Turning to Gertrude*) Oh, just a word with you,
nurse.

> *Lucas has been bending over Agnes affectionately; he now sits by*
> *her, and they talk in undertones; he lights a cigarette from hers*

KIRKE (*to Gertrude*) There's many a true word, *et cetera*.   40

GERTRUDE Excitement?

KIRKE Yes, and that smart gown's connected with it too.

GERTRUDE It is extraordinary to see her like this.

KIRKE Not the same woman.

GERTRUDE No, nor is he quite the same man.   45

KIRKE How long can you remain with her?

GERTRUDE Till eleven—if you will let my brother know where I am.

KIRKE What, doesn't he know?

GERTRUDE I simply sent word, about an hour ago, that I shouldn't be
back to dinner.   50

KIRKE Very well.

GERTRUDE Look here! I'll get you to tell him the truth.

KIRKE The truth—oh?

GERTRUDE I called here this afternoon, unknown to Amos, to bid her
good-bye. Then I pottered about, rather miserably, spending money.   55
Coming out of Naya's, the photographer's,° I tumbled over Mr
Cleeve, who had been looking for you, and he begged me to come
round here again after I had done my shopping.

KIRKE I understand.

GERTRUDE Doctor, have you ever seen Amos look dreadfully stern and   60
knit about the brows—like a bishop who is put out?

KIRKE No.

GERTRUDE Then you will.

KIRKE Well, this is a pretty task—! (*He goes out. Gertrude comes to Agnes.*
Lucas rises)

GERTRUDE I am going down into the kitchen to see what these people   65
can do in the way of strong soup.

LUCAS You are exceedingly good to us, Mrs Thorpe. I can't tell you
how ashamed I am of my bearishness this afternoon.

GERTRUDE (*arranging the shawl about Agnes's shoulders*) Hush, please!

AGNES Are you looking at my shawl? Lucas brought it in with him, as a   70
reward for my coming out of that stupid faint. I—I have always
refused to be—spoilt in this way, but now—now—

LUCAS (*breaking in deliberately*) Pretty work upon it, is there not,
Mrs Thorpe?

GERTRUDE Charming. (*Going to the door, which Lucas opens for her*)   75
Thank you. (*She passes out. Agnes rises*)

LUCAS Oh, my dear girl!—

AGNES (*throwing her cigarette under the stove*) I'm quite myself again,
Lucas dear. Watch me—look! (*Walking firmly*)

LUCAS No trembling?   80

AGNES Not a flutter. (*Watching her open hand*) My hand is absolutely
steady. (*He takes her hand and kisses it upon the palm*) Ah!—

LUCAS (*looking at her hand*) No, it is shaking.

AGNES Yes, when you—when you—oh, Lucas!—(*She sinks into a
chair, turning her back upon him, and covering her face with her hands;
her shoulders heaving*)

LUCAS (*going to her*) Agnes dear!   85

AGNES (*taking out her handkerchief*) Let me—let me—

LUCAS (*bending over her*) I've never seen you—

AGNES No, I've never been a crying woman. But some great change has
befallen me, I believe. What is it? That swoon—it wasn't mere faint-
ness, giddiness; it was this change coming over me!°   90

LUCAS You are not unhappy?

AGNES (*wiping her eyes*) No, I—I don't think I am. Isn't that strange?

LUCAS My dearest, I'm glad to hear you say that, for you've made me
very happy.

AGNES Because I—?   95

LUCAS Because you love me—naturally, that's one great reason.

AGNES [(*steadily*)] I have always loved you.

LUCAS But never so utterly, so absorbingly, as you confess you do now.
Do you fully realise what your confession does? It strikes off the
shackles from me, from us—sets us free. (*With a gesture of freedom*)   100
Oh, my dear Agnes, free!

AGNES (*staring at him*) Free?

LUCAS Free from the burden of that crazy plan of ours of trumpeting our relations to the world. Forgive me—crazy is the only word for it. Thank heaven, we've at last admitted to each other that we're ordin- 105 ary man and woman! Of course, I was ill—off my head. I didn't know what I was entering upon. And you, dear—living a pleasureless life, letting your thoughts dwell constantly on old troubles; that is how cranks are made. Now that I'm strong again, body and mind, I can protect you, keep you right. Ha, ha! What were we to pose as? 110 Examples of independence of thought and action! (*Laughing*) Oh, my darling, we'll be independent in thought and action still; but we won't make examples of ourselves—eh?

AGNES (*who has been watching him with wide-open eyes*) Do you mean that all idea of our writing together, working together, defending our 115 position, and the positions of such as ourselves, before the world, is to be abandoned?

LUCAS Why, of course.

AGNES *I—I* didn't quite mean that.

LUCAS Oh, come, come! We'll furl what my uncle calls the banner of 120 Free Union finally. (*Going to her and kissing her hair lightly*) For the future, mere man and woman. (*Pacing the room excitedly*) The future! I've settled everything already. The work shall fall wholly on *my* shoulders. My poor girl, you shall enjoy a little rest and pleasure.

AGNES (*in a low voice*) Rest and pleasure— 125

LUCAS We'll remain abroad. One can live unobserved abroad, without actually hiding. (*She rises slowly*) We'll find an ideal retreat. No more English tourists prying round us! And there, in some beautiful spot, alone except for your company, I'll work! (*As he paces the room, she walks slowly to and fro,° listening, staring before her*) I'll work. My new 130 career!° I'll write under a *nom de plume*. My books, Agnes, shall never ride to popularity on the back of a scandal. Our life! The mornings I must spend by myself, of course, shut up in my room. In the after-noon we will walk together. After dinner you shall hear what I've written in the morning; and then a few turns round our pretty gar- 135 den, a glance at the stars with my arms round your waist—(*she stops abruptly, a look of horror on her face*)—while you whisper to me words of tenderness, words of—(*There is the distant sound of music from man-dolin and guitar*) Ah! (*To Agnes*) Keep your shawl over your shoul-ders. (*Opening the window, and stepping out; the music becoming louder*) 140 Some mandolinisti in a gondola. (*Listening at the window, his head turned from her*) How pretty, Agnes! Now, don't those mere sounds, in such surroundings, give you a sensation of hatred for revolt and turmoil! Don't they conjure up alluringly pictures of peace and

pleasure, of golden days and star-lit nights—pictures of beauty and 145
of love?

AGNES (*sitting on the settee, staring before her, speaking to herself*) My
marriage—the early days of my marriage—all over again!°

LUCAS (*turning to her*) Eh? (*Closing the window and coming to her, as the
music dies away*) Tell me that those sounds thrill you. 150

AGNES Lucas—

LUCAS (*sitting beside her*) Yes?

AGNES For the first few months of my marriage—(*Breaking off abruptly
and looking into his face wonderingly*) Why, how young you seem to
have become; you look quite boyish! 155

LUCAS (*laughing*) I believe that this return of our senses will make us
both young again.

AGNES Both? (*With a little shudder*) You know, I'm older than you.

LUCAS Tsch!

AGNES (*passing her hand through his hair*) Yes, I shall feel that *now*. 160
(*Stroking his brow tenderly*) Well—so it has come to this.

LUCAS I declare you have colour in your cheeks already.

AGNES The return of my senses?

LUCAS My dear Agnes, we've both been to the verge of madness, you
and I—driven there by our troubles. (*Taking her hand*) Let us agree, 165
in so many words, that we have completely recovered. Shall we?

AGNES Perhaps mine is a more obstinate case. My enemies called me
mad years ago.

LUCAS (*with a wave of the hand*) Ah, but the future, the future. No more
thoughts of reforming unequal laws from public platforms, no more 170
shrieking in obscure magazines. No more beating of bare knuckles
against stone walls. Come, say it!

AGNES (*with an effort*) Go on.

LUCAS (*looking before him—partly to himself, his voice hardening*) I'll
never be mad again—never. (*Throwing his head back*) By heavens! (*To* 175
her, in an altered tone) You don't say it.

AGNES (*after a pause*) I—I will never be mad again.

LUCAS (*triumphantly*) Hah! ha, ha! (*She deliberately removes the shawl
from her shoulders, and, putting her arms round his neck, draws him to
her*) Ah, my dear girl!

AGNES (*in a whisper, with her head on his breast*) Lucas. 180

LUCAS Yes?

AGNES Isn't *this* madness?

LUCAS I don't think so.

AGNES Oh! oh! oh! I believe, to be a woman is to be mad.

LUCAS   No, to be a woman trying not to be a woman—*that* is to be mad.   185
        She draws a long, deep breath, then, sitting away from him,
        resumes her shawl mechanically

AGNES   Now, you promised me to run out to the Capello Nero° to get a
        little food.

LUCAS   Oh, I'd rather—

AGNES   (*rising*) Dearest, you need it.

LUCAS   (*rising*) Well—Fortuné shall fetch my hat and coat.   190

AGNES   Fortuné! Are you going to take *all* my work from me? (*She is
        walking towards the door; the sound of his voice stops her*)

LUCAS   Agnes! (*She returns*) A thousand thoughts have rushed through
        my brain this last hour or two. I've been thinking—my wife—

AGNES   Yes?

LUCAS   My wife—she will soon get tired of her present position. If, by   195
        and by, there should be a divorce, there would be nothing to prevent
        our marrying.

AGNES   Our—marrying!

LUCAS   (*sitting, not looking at her, as if discussing the matter with himself*) It
        might be to my advantage to settle again in London some day. After   200
        all, scandals quickly lose their keen edge. What would you say?

AGNES   Marriage—

LUCAS   Ah, remember, we're rational beings for the future. However,
        we needn't talk about it now.

AGNES   No.   205

LUCAS   Still, I assume you wouldn't oppose it. You would marry me if
        I wished it?

AGNES   (*in a low voice*) Yes.

LUCAS   That's a sensible girl! By Jove, I *am* hungry! (*He lights a cigarette
        as she walks slowly to the door, then throws himself idly back on the settee*)

AGNES   (*to herself, in a whisper*) My old life—my old life coming all over   210
        again! (*She goes out.*)
        He lies watching the wreaths of tobacco smoke. After a moment or
        two Fortuné enters, closing the door behind him carefully

LUCAS   Eh?

FORTUNÉ   (*after a glance round, dropping his voice*) Ze Duke of St
        Olphert 'e say 'e vould like to speak a meenit alone.
        Lucas rises, with a muttered exclamation of annoyance

LUCAS   Priez Monsieur le Duc d'entrer.°   215
        Fortuné goes to the door and opens it. The Duke of St Olpherts
        enters; he is in evening dress. Fortuné retires

ST OLPHERTS   Quite alone?

LUCAS For the moment

ST OLPHERTS My excuse to Mrs Ebbsmith for not dining at the Grünwald—it was a perfectly legitimate one, dear Lucas. I was really
expecting visitors.   220

LUCAS (*wonderingly*) Yes?

ST OLPHERTS (*with a little cough and a drawn face*) Oh, I am not so well
tonight. Damn these people for troubling me! Damn 'em for keeping
me hopping about! Damn 'em for every shoot I feel in my leg. Visitors from England—they've arrived.   225

LUCAS But what—?

ST OLPHERTS I shall die of gout some day, Lucas. Er—your wife is
here.

LUCAS Sybil!

ST OLPHERTS She's come through with your brother. Sandford's a   230
worse prig than ever—and I'm in shockin' pain.

LUCAS This—this is your doing!

ST OLPHERTS Yes. Damn you, don't keep me standing!

> *Agnes enters with Lucas's hat and coat. She stops abruptly on
> seeing St Olpherts*

ST OLPHERTS (*by the settee—playfully, through his pain*) Ah, my dear
Mrs Ebbsmith, how can you have the heart to deceive an invalid, a   235
poor wretch who begs you—(*sitting on the settee*)—to allow him to sit
down for a moment?

> *Agnes deposits the hat and coat*

AGNES Deceive—?

ST OLPHERTS My friends arrive, I dine scrappily with them, and hurry
to the Grünwald thinking to catch you over your Zabajone.° Dear   240
lady, you haven't been *near* the Grünwald.

AGNES Your women faint sometimes, don't they?

ST OLPHERTS My—? (*In pain*) Oh, what *do* you mean?

AGNES The women in your class of life?

ST OLPHERTS Faint? Oh yes, when there's occasion for it.   245

AGNES I'm hopelessly low-born; I fainted involuntarily.

ST OLPHERTS (*moving nearer to her*) Oh, my dear, pray forgive me.
You've recovered? (*She nods*) Indisposition agrees with you, evidently. Your colouring tonight is charming. (*Coughing*) You are—
delightful—to—look at.   250

> *Gertrude enters, carrying a tray on which are a bowl of soup, a
> small decanter of wine, and accessories. She looks at St Olpherts
> unconcernedly, then turns away and places the tray on a table*

ST OLPHERTS (*quietly to Agnes*) Not a servant?

AGNES Oh, no.

ST OLPHERTS (*rising promptly*) Good God! I beg your pardon. A
friend?

AGNES Yes.   255

ST OLPHERTS (*looking at Gertrude, critically*) Very nice.° (*Still looking
at Gertrude, but speaking to Agnes in undertones*) Married or—? (*Turning to Agnes*) Married or—? (*Agnes has walked away*)

GERTRUDE (*to Lucas, looking around*) It is draughty at this table.

LUCAS (*going to the table near the settee, and collecting the writing materials*) Here—   260
        Agnes joins Gertrude

ST OLPHERTS (*quietly to Lucas*) Lucas—(*Lucas goes to him*) Who's that
gal?

LUCAS (*to St Olpherts*) An hotel acquaintance we made in Florence—
Mrs Thorpe.

ST OLPHERTS Where's the husband?   265

LUCAS A widow.

ST OLPHERTS You might—
        Gertrude advances with the tray

LUCAS Mrs Thorpe, the Duke of St Olpherts wishes to be introduced
to you.
        *Gertrude inclines her head to the Duke. Lucas places the writing
        materials on another table*

ST OLPHERTS (*limping up to Gertrude and handling the tray*) I beg to be   270
allowed to help you. (*At the table*) The tray here?

GERTRUDE Thank you.

ST OLPHERTS [Shall we lay this little white cloth, you and I?]° Ha, how
clumsy I am! [The cruet there—] We think it so gracious of you to
look after our poor friend here who is not quite herself today. (*To   275
Agnes*) Come along, dear lady—everything is prepared for you. (*To
Gertrude*) You are here with—with your mother, I understand.

GERTRUDE My brother.

ST OLPHERTS Brother. Now do tell me whether you find your—your
little hotel comfortable.   280

GERTRUDE (*looking at him steadily*) We don't stay at one.

ST OLPHERTS Apartments?

GERTRUDE Yes.

ST OLPHERTS Do you know, dear Mrs Thorpe, I have always had the
very strongest desire to live in lodgings in Venice?   285

GERTRUDE You should gratify it. Our quarters are rather humble; we
are in the Campo San Bartolomeo.°

ST OLPHERTS But how delightful!

GERTRUDE [(*with deliberation*)] Why not come and see our rooms?

ST OLPHERTS (*bowing*) My dear young lady! (*Producing a pencil and*   290
writing upon his shirt-cuff °) Campo San Bartolomeo—

GERTRUDE Five—four—nought—two.

ST OLPHERTS (*writing*) Five—four—nought—two. Tomorrow afternoon? (*She inclines her head*) Four o'clock?

GERTRUDE Yes; that would give the people ample time to tidy and clear   295
up after us.

ST OLPHERTS After you—?

GERTRUDE After our departure. My brother and I leave early tomorrow morning.°

ST OLPHERTS (*after a brief pause, imperturbably*) A thousand thanks.   300
May I impose myself so far upon you as to ask you to tell your landlord to expect me? (*Taking up his hat and stick*) We are allowing this
soup to get cold. (*Joining Lucas*) Dear Lucas, you have something to
say to me—?

LUCAS (*opening the door*) Come into my room. (*They go out. The two*   305
women look at each other significantly)

AGNES You're a splendid woman.

GERTRUDE That's rather a bad man, I think. Now, dear—(*She places*
Agnes on the settee, and sets the soup, etc., before her. Agnes eats)

GERTRUDE (*watching her closely*) So you have succeeded in coming to
close quarters, as you expressed it, with him.

AGNES (*taciturnly*) Yes.   310

GERTRUDE His second visit here today, I gather.

AGNES [(*breaking bread*)] Yes.

GERTRUDE His attitude towards you—his presence here under any
circumstances—it's all rather queer.

AGNES His code of behaviour is peculiarly his own.   315

GERTRUDE However, are you easier in your mind?

AGNES (*quietly, but with intensity*) I shall defeat him. I shall defeat him.

GERTRUDE Defeat him? You will succeed in holding Mr Cleeve, you
mean?

AGNES [(*uneasily*)] Oh, if you put it in that way—   320

GERTRUDE [(*sitting RC, still watching Agnes*)] Oh, come, I remember all
you told me this afternoon. (*With disdain*) So it has already arrived,
then, at a simple struggle to hold Mr Cleeve?

> There is a pause. Agnes, without answering, stretches out her hand
> to the wine. Her hand shakes—she withdraws it helplessly

GERTRUDE What do you want—wine?

> *Agnes nods. Gertrude pours out wine and gives her the glass.*
> *Agnes drains it eagerly and replaces it*

GERTRUDE Agnes—   325

AGNES Yes?

GERTRUDE You are dressed very beautifully.

AGNES Do you think so?

GERTRUDE Don't you know it? Who made you that gown?

AGNES Bardini.   330

GERTRUDE I shouldn't have credited the little woman with such excellent ideas.

AGNES Oh, Lucas gave her the idea when he—when he—

GERTRUDE When he ordered it?

AGNES Yes.   335

[GERTRUDE The bodice is faulty; it wrinkles very much there.

AGNES I—I haven't been fitted for it.]   •

GERTRUDE Oh, the whole thing came as a surprise to you?

AGNES Er—quite.

GERTRUDE I noticed the box this afternoon, when I called.   340

AGNES Mr Cleeve wishes me to appear more like—more like—

GERTRUDE An ordinary smart woman. (*Contemptuously*) Well, you
ought to find no difficulty in managing that. You can make yourself
very charming, it appears.

> *Agnes again reaches out a hand towards the wine. Gertrude pours*
> *a very little wine into the wine-glass and takes up the glass; Agnes*
> *holds out her hand to receive it*

GERTRUDE Do you mind my drinking from your glass?   345

AGNES (*staring at her*) No. (*Gertrude empties the glass and then places it, in*
a marked way, on the side of the table farthest from Agnes)

GERTRUDE (*with a little shudder*) Ugh! Ugh! (*Agnes moves away*
from Gertrude, to the end of the settee, her head bowed, her hands
clenched) I have something to propose. Come home with me
tomorrow.

AGNES (*after a pause, raising her head*) Home—?   350

GERTRUDE Ketherick. The very spot for a woman who wants to shut
out things. Miles and miles of wild moorland! For company, purple
heath and moss-covered granite, in summer; in winter, the moor-
fowl and the snow glistening on top of the crags. Oh, and for open-air
music, our little church owns the sweetest little peal of old bells—!   355
(*Agnes rises, disturbed*) Ah, I can't promise you *their* silence! Indeed,
I'm very much afraid that on a still Sunday you can even hear the
sound of the organ quite a long distance off. I am the organist when

I'm at home. That's Ketherick. Will you come? (*The distant tinkling of mandolin and guitar is again heard*)

AGNES Listen to that. The mandolinisti! You talk of the sound of your   360
church organ, and I hear *his* music.

GERTRUDE His music?

AGNES The music he is fond of; the music that gives him the thoughts
that please him, soothe him.

GERTRUDE (*listening—humming the words of the air, contemptuously*)

> 'Bell' amore deh! porgi l'orecchio,   365
> Ad un canto che parte dal cuore—'°

Love-music!

AGNES (*in a low voice, staring upon the ground*) Yes, love-music.
> *The door leading from Lucas's room opens, and St Olpherts and*
> *Lucas are heard talking. Gertrude hastily goes out. Lucas enters;*
> *the boyishness of manner has left him—he is pale and excited*

AGNES (*apprehensively*) What is the matter?

LUCAS My wife is revealing quite a novel phase of character.   370

AGNES Your wife—?

LUCAS The submissive mood. It's right that you should be told, Agnes.
She is here, at the Danieli, with my brother Sandford. (*St Olpherts
enters slowly*) Yes, positively! It appears that she has lent herself to a
scheme of Sandford's—(*glancing at St Olpherts*)—and of—and of—   375

ST OLPHERTS Of Sandford's

LUCAS (*to Agnes*) A plan of reconciliation. (*To St Olpherts*) Tell Sybil
that the submissive mood comes too late, by a year or so! (*He paces to
and fro. Agnes sits, with an expressionless face*)

AGNES (*quietly to St Olpherts*) The 'friends' you were expecting, Duke?

ST OLPHERTS (*meekly*) Yes. (*She smiles at him scornfully*)   380

LUCAS Agnes dear, you and I leave here early tomorrow.

AGNES Very well, Lucas.

LUCAS (*to St Olpherts*) Duke, will you be the bearer of a note from me to
Sandford?

ST OLPHERTS Certainly.   385

LUCAS (*going to the door of his room*) I'll write it at once.

ST OLPHERTS (*raising his voice*) You won't see Sandford, then, dear
Lucas, for a moment or two?

LUCAS No, no; pray excuse me. (*He goes out*)
> *St Olpherts advances to Agnes. The sound of the music dies away*

ST OLPHERTS (*slipping his cloak off° and throwing it upon the head of the
settee*) Upon my soul, I think you've routed us!   390

AGNES Yes.

ST OLPHERTS (*sitting, breaking into a laugh*) Ha, ha! he, he, he! Sir
Sandford and Mrs Cleeve will be so angry. Such a devil of a journey
for nothing! Ho! (*Coughing*) Ho, ho, ho!

AGNES This was to be your *grand coup*.   395

ST OLPHERTS I admit it—I *have* been keeping this in reserve.

AGNES I see. A further term of cat-and-dog life for Lucas and this
lady—but it would have served to dispose of *me*, you fondly imagined. I see.

ST OLPHERTS I knew your hold on him was weakening. (*She looks at*   400
him) *You* knew it too. (*She looks away*) He was beginning to find out
that a dowdy demagogue is not the cheeriest person to live with. I
repeat, you're a dooced° clever woman, my dear. (*She rises, with an*
impatient shake of her body, and walks past him, he following her with his
eyes) And a handsome one, into the bargain.

AGNES Tsch!   405

ST OLPHERTS Tell me, when did you make up your mind to transform
yourself?

AGNES Suddenly, after our interview this afternoon; after what you
said—

ST OLPHERTS Oh—!   410

AGNES (*with a little shiver*) An impulse.

ST OLPHERTS Impulse doesn't account for the possession of those
gorgeous trappings.

AGNES These rags? A surprise gift from Lucas, today.

ST OLPHERTS Really, my dear, I believe I've helped to bring about my   415
own defeat. (*Laughing softly*) Ho, ho, ho! How disgusted the Cleeve
family will be! Ha, ha! (*Testily*) Come, why don't you smile—laugh?
You can afford to do so! Show your pretty white teeth! Laugh!

AGNES (*hysterically*) Ha, ha, ha! Ha!

ST OLPHERTS (*grinning*) That's better!   420

> Pushing the cigarette-box towards him, she takes a cigarette and
> places it between her lips. He also takes a cigarette gaily. They
> smoke—she standing, with an elbow resting upon the top of the
> stove, looking down upon him.

ST OLPHERTS (*as he lights his cigarette*) This isn't explosive, I hope? No
nitric and sulphuric acid, with glycerine°—eh? (*Eyeing her wonder-*
ingly and admiringly) By Jove! Which is *you*—the shabby, shapeless
rebel who entertained me this afternoon or—(*kissing the tips of his*
fingers to her)—or *that*?   425

AGNES [(*after a little pause*)] This—this. (*Seating herself, slowly and*

thoughtfully, facing the stove, her back turned to him. [*In a low voice*])
My sex has found me out.

ST OLPHERTS [(*still gazing at her*)] Ha! tsch! (*Between his teeth*) Damn
it, for your sake I almost wish Lucas was a different sort of feller!

AGNES (*partly to herself, with intensity*) Nothing matters now—not even 430
that. He's mine. He would have died but for me. I gave him life. He is
my child, my husband, my lover, my bread, my daylight—all—
everything. Mine! Mine!

ST OLPHERTS (*rising and limping over to her.* [*RC behind her chair*])
Good luck, my girl!

AGNES Thanks! 435

ST OLPHERTS I'm rather sorry for you. This sort of triumph is short-
lived, you know.

AGNES (*turning to him.* [*Quietly*]) I know. But I shall fight for every
moment that prolongs it. This is my hour.°

ST OLPHERTS Your hour—? 440

AGNES There's only one hour in a woman's life.

ST OLPHERTS [(*humouring her*)] One—?

AGNES One supreme hour. Her poor life is like the arch of a crescent; so
many years lead up to that hour, so many weary years decline from it.
No matter what she may strive for, there is a moment when Circum- 445
stance taps her upon the shoulder and says, 'Woman, this hour is the
best that Earth has to spare you'. It may come to her in calm or in tem-
pest, lighted by a steady radiance or by the glitter of evil stars; but
however it comes, be it good or evil, *it is her hour*—let her dwell upon
every second of it! 450

ST OLPHERTS And this little victory of yours—the possession of this
man; you think this is the best that Earth can spare you? (*She nods
slowly and deliberately, with fixed eyes*) Dear me, how amusin' you
women are! And in your dowdy days you had ambitions? (*She looks at
him suddenly*) They were of a queer, gun-powder-and-faggot sort— 455
but they were ambitions.

AGNES (*starting up*) Oh—! (*Putting her hands to her brows*) Oh—!
(*Facing him*) Ambitions! Yes, yes! You're right! Once, long ago,
I hoped that my hour would be very different from this. Ambitions!
I have seen myself, standing, humbly-clad, looking down upon a 460
dense, swaying crowd—a scarlet flag for my background. I have seen
the responsive look upon thousands of white, eager, hungry faces,
[responsive to a single voice that has struck out through the air,
straight and swift, like the flight of a myriad of birds from one small
nest,] and I've heard the great hoarse shout of welcome as I have 465

seized my flag and hurried down amongst the people—to be given a place with their leaders! I! With the leaders, the leaders! Yes, that is what I once hoped would be my hour! (*Her voice sinking*) But this *is* my hour.

ST OLPHERTS Well, my dear, when it's over, you'll have the satisfac-   470
tion of counting the departing footsteps of a ruined man.

AGNES Ruined—!

ST OLPHERTS Yes, there's great compensation in that—for women. [There are two or three living who would each give a limb to see this gouty one of mine shrivel up.]   475

AGNES (*sitting*) Why do you suggest he'll be ruined through me? (*Uneasily*) At any rate, he'd ended his old career before we met.

ST OLPHERTS Pardon me; it's not too late now for him to resume that career. The threads are not quite broken yet.

AGNES Oh, the scandal in London—   480

ST OLPHERTS Would be dispelled by this sham reconciliation with his wife.

AGNES (*looking at him*) Sham—?

ST OLPHERTS Why, of course. All we desired to arrange was that for the future their household should be conducted strictly *à la mode*.°   485

AGNES *À la mode*?

ST OLPHERTS (*behind the settee, looking down upon her*) Mr Cleeve in one quarter of the house, Mrs Cleeve in another.

AGNES [(*quietly*)] Oh, yes.

ST OLPHERTS A proper aspect to the world, combined with freedom on   490
both sides. It's a more decorous system than the aggressive Free Union you once advocated; and it's much in vogue at my end of the town.°

AGNES Your plan was a little more subtle than I gave you credit for. This was to be your method of getting rid of me!   495

ST OLPHERTS No, no. Don't you understand? With regard to yourself, we could have arrived at a compromise.

AGNES [(*calmly*)] A compromise?

ST OLPHERTS It would have made us quite happy to see you placed upon a—upon a somewhat different footing.   500

AGNES What kind of—footing?

ST OLPHERTS The suburban villa, the little garden, a couple of discreet servants—everything *à la mode*.

> *There is a brief pause. Then she rises and walks across the room, outwardly calm but twisting her hands*

AGNES Well, you've had Mr Cleeve's answer to *that*.

ST OLPHERTS Yes.

AGNES [(*her back to him, passing her hand over her brow*)] Which finally disposes of the whole matter—disposes of it—

ST OLPHERTS Completely. (*Struck by an idea*) Unless *you*—

AGNES (*turning to him*) Unless *I*—

ST OLPHERTS Unless you—

AGNES (*after a moment's pause*) What did Lucas say to you when you—?

ST OLPHERTS He said he knew you'd never make that sacrifice for him. (*She pulls herself up rigidly*) So he declined to pain you by asking you to do it.

AGNES (*crossing swiftly to the settee, and speaking straight into his face*) That's a lie!

ST OLPHERTS Keep your temper, my dear.

AGNES (*passionately*) His love may not last—it won't!—but at this moment he loves me better than that! He wouldn't make a mere light thing of me!

ST OLPHERTS Wouldn't he? You try him!

AGNES What!

ST OLPHERTS You put him to the test!

AGNES (*with her hands to her brows*) Oh—!

ST OLPHERTS [(*quickly hobbling after her*)] No, no—don't!

AGNES ([*facing him,*] *faintly*) Why?

ST OLPHERTS I like you. Damn *him*—you deserve to live your hour!
        Lucas enters with a letter in his hand. Agnes sits

LUCAS (*giving St Olpherts the letter*) Thanks.
        *St Olpherts pockets the letter and picks up his cloak, Lucas assist-
        ing him*

AGNES (*outwardly calm*) Oh—Lucas—

LUCAS Yes?

AGNES The Duke has been—has been—telling me—

LUCAS What, dear?

AGNES The sort of arrangement proposed for your going back to London.

LUCAS Oh, my brother's brilliant idea!

AGNES Acquiesced in by your wife.
        St Olpherts strolls away from them

LUCAS Certainly; as I anticipated, she has become intensely dissatisfied with her position.

AGNES And it would be quite possible, it seems, for you to resume your old career?

LUCAS   Just barely possible—well, for the moment, quite possible.

AGNES   Quite possible.

LUCAS   I haven't, formally, made a sign to my political friends yet. It's a task one leaves to the last. I shall do so now—at once. My people have been busying themselves, it appears, in reporting that I shall return   545
to London directly my health is fully re-established.

AGNES   In the hope—? Oh, yes.

LUCAS   Hoping they'd be able to separate us before it was too—too late.

AGNES   Which hope they've now relinquished?

LUCAS   Apparently.   550

AGNES   They're prepared to accept a—a compromise, I hear?

LUCAS   Ha!—yes.

AGNES   A compromise in my favour?

LUCAS   (*hesitatingly*) They suggest—

AGNES   Yes, yes, I know. (*Looking at him searchingly*) After all, your old   555
career was—a success. You made your mark, as you were saying the other day. You did make your mark. (*He walks up and down restlessly, abstractedly, her eyes following him*) You were generally spoken of, accepted, as a Coming Man. *The* Coming Man, often, wasn't it?

LUCAS   (*with an impatient wave of the hand*) That doesn't matter!   560

AGNES   And now you are giving it up—giving it all up.

> *He sits on the settee, resting his elbow on his knee, pushing his hand through his hair*

LUCAS   But—but you believe I shall succeed equally well in this new career of mine?

AGNES   (*stonily*) There's the risk, you must remember.

LUCAS   [(*anxiously*)] Obviously, there's the risk. [(*Raises his head*)] Why   565
do you say all this to me now?

AGNES   Because *now* is the opportunity to—to go back.

LUCAS   (*scornfully*) Opportunity—?

AGNES   An excellent one. You're so strong and well now.

LUCAS   Thanks to you.   570

AGNES   (*staring before her*) Well—I did nurse you carefully, didn't I?

LUCAS   But I don't understand you. You are surely not proposing to—to—break with me?

AGNES   No—I—I—I was only thinking that you—you might see something in this suggestion of a compromise.   575

> [*There is a pause.*] Lucas glances at St Olpherts, whose back is turned to them. St Olpherts instinctively looks round, then goes and sits by the window

LUCAS   (*looking at her searchingly*) Well, but—*you*—?

AGNES (*with assumed indifference*) Oh, I—

LUCAS *You?*

AGNES Lucas, don't—don't make *me* paramount.

> [*There is another brief pause, then*] *he moves to the end of the settee, showing by a look that he desires her to sit by him. After a moment's hesitation she takes her place beside him*

LUCAS (*in an undertone*) I do make you paramount. I do. [(*A pause*)] My dear girl, under any circumstances you would still be everything to me—always. (*She nods with a vacant look*) There would have to be this pretence of an establishment of mine—that would have to be faced; the whited sepulchre,° the mockery of dinners and receptions and so on. But it would be to you I should fly for sympathy, encouragement, rest.   580   585

AGNES [(*in an expressionless tone*)] Even if you were ill again—

LUCAS [(*awkwardly*)] Even then, if it were practicable—if it could be— if it—[(*A pause*)]

AGNES (*looking him in the face*) Well—?   590

LUCAS (*avoiding her gaze*) Yes, dear?

AGNES What do you say, then, to asking the Duke to give you back that letter to your brother?

LUCAS [(*pushing his hands through his hair again*)] It wouldn't settle matters, simply destroying that letter. Sandford begs me to go round to the Danieli tonight, to—to—   595

AGNES To see him? (*Lucas nods*) And her? (*He shrugs his shoulders*) At what time? Was any time specified?

LUCAS Half-past nine.

AGNES I—I haven't my watch on.   600

LUCAS (*referring to his watch*) Nine twenty-five.

AGNES You can almost manage it—if you'd like to go.

LUCAS Oh, let them wait a few minutes for me; that won't hurt them.

AGNES (*dazed*) Let me see—I did fetch your hat and coat—(*She rises and walks mechanically, stumbling against a chair. Lucas looks up, alarmed; St Olpherts rises*)

AGNES (*replacing the chair*) It's all right; I didn't notice this. (*Bringing Lucas's hat and coat, and assisting him with the latter*) How long will you be?   605

LUCAS Not more than half an hour. An hour at the outside.

AGNES (*arranging his neckhandkerchief*) Keep this so.

LUCAS Er—if—if I—if we—   610

AGNES The Duke is waiting.

> *Lucas turns away, and joins St Olpherts*

LUCAS (*to him, in a low voice*) I am going back to the hotel with you.

ST OLPHERTS Oh, are you?

> *The door opens and Fortuné enters, followed by Amos Winter-*
> *field. Fortuné retires*

AMOS (*to Lucas, sternly*) Is my sister still here, may I ask?

> *Lucas looks to Agnes interrogatively. She inclines her head*

AMOS I should like her to know that I am waiting for her.   615

> *Agnes goes out*

LUCAS (*to Amos*) Pray excuse me.

> *Amos draws back. St Olpherts passes out. At the door, Lucas*
> *pauses, and bows slightly to Amos, who returns his bow in the same*
> *fashion; then Lucas follows St Olpherts. Gertrude enters, wearing*
> *her hat and mantle. Agnes follows; her movements are unsteady,*
> *and there is a wild look in her eyes*

GERTRUDE You've come to fetch me, Amos?

> *He assents by a nod*

AMOS (*to Agnes*) I'm sorry to learn from Dr Kirke that you've been ill.
I hope you're better.

AGNES (*turning away, Gertrude watching her*) Thank you, I am quite   620
well.

AMOS (*gruffly*) Are you ready, Gertrude?

GERTRUDE No, dear, not yet. I want you to help me.

AMOS In what way?

GERTRUDE I want you to join me in persuading Mrs Ebbsmith—*my*   625
friend, Mrs Ebbsmith—to come to Ketherick with me.

AMOS My dear sister—!

GERTRUDE (*firmly*) Please, Amos!

AGNES Stop a moment! Mr Winterfield, your sister doesn't in the least
understand how matters are with me. I am returning to England, but   630
with Mr Cleeve. (*Recklessly*) Oh, you'd hear of it eventually! He is
reconciled to his wife.

GERTRUDE Oh—! Then, surely, you—!

AGNES No. The reconciliation goes no further than mere outward
appearances. He relies upon me as much as ever. (*Beating her hands*   635
together passionately) He can't spare me—can't spare me!

> [(*There is a moment's silence*)]

AMOS (*in a low voice to Gertrude*) Are you satisfied?

GERTRUDE I suspected something of the kind. (*Going to Agnes, gripping*
her wrist tightly) Pull yourself out of the mud! Get up out of the mud!

AGNES I have no will to—no desire to!   640

GERTRUDE You mad thing!

AGNES (*releasing herself, facing Gertrude and Amos*) You are only breaking in upon my hour.

GERTRUDE Your hour—?

AGNES (*waving them away*) I ask you to go—to go!   645
    Gertrude returns to Amos

AMOS My dear Gertrude, you see what our position is here. If Mrs Ebbsmith asks for our help it is our duty to give it.

GERTRUDE It is especially *my* duty, Amos.

AMOS And I should have thought it especially mine. However, Mrs Ebbsmith appears to firmly decline our help. And at this point, I confess,   650
I would rather you left it—*you*, at least.

GERTRUDE You would rather *I* left it—I, the virtuous, unsoiled
woman! Yes, I am a virtuous woman, Amos; and it strikes you as odd,
I suppose, my insisting upon friendship with her. But look here, both
of you. I'll tell you a secret. You never knew it, Amos, my dear. I   655
never allowed anybody to suspect it—

AMOS Never knew what?

GERTRUDE The sort of married life *mine* was. It didn't last long, but it
was dreadful, almost intolerable.

AMOS Gertrude!   660

GERTRUDE After the first few weeks—weeks, not months!—after the
first few weeks of it, my husband treated me as cruelly—(*turning to
Agnes*)—just as cruelly, I do believe, as your husband treated *you*.
(*Amos makes a movement, showing astonishment*) Wait! Now, then!
There was another man—one I loved—one I couldn't help loving! I   665
could have found release with him, perhaps happiness of a kind. I
resisted, came through it. They're dead—the two are dead! And here
I am, a virtuous, reputable woman; saved by the blessed mercy of
Heaven!° There, you are not surprised any longer, Amos! (*Pointing to
Agnes*) 'My friend, Mrs Ebbsmith!' (*Bursting into tears*) Oh! Oh, if my   670
little boy had been spared to me, he should have grown up tender to
women—tender to women! he should, he should—! (*She sits upon the
settee, weeping. There is a short silence*)

AMOS Mrs Ebbsmith, when I came here tonight I was angry with
Gertrude—not altogether, I hope, for being in your company. But I
was certainly angry with her for visiting you without my knowledge.   675
I think I sometimes forget that she is eight-and-twenty, not eighteen.
Well, now I offer to delay our journey home for a few days, if you hold
out the faintest hope that her companionship is likely to aid you in
any way.

    Agnes, standing motionless, makes no response. Amos crosses to

> *her, and as he passes Gertrude, he lets his hand drop over her*
> *shoulder; she clasps it, then rises and moves to a chair, where she*
> *sits, crying silently*

AMOS (*by Agnes's side—in a low voice*) You heard what she said. Saved   680
by the mercy of Heaven.

AGNES Yes, but she can feel that.

AMOS You felt so once.

AGNES Once—!°

AMOS You have, in years gone by, asked for help upon your knees.   685

AGNES It never came.

AMOS Repeat your cry!

AGNES There would be no answer.

AMOS Repeat it!

AGNES (*turning upon him*) If miracles *could* happen! If 'help', as you term   690
it, *did* come! Do you know what 'help' would mean to *me*?

AMOS What—?

AGNES It would take the last crumb from me!

AMOS This man's—protection?

AGNES (*defiantly*) Yes!   695

AMOS Oh, Mrs Ebbsmith—!

AGNES ([*coming swiftly to C below settee,*] *pointing to the door*) Well, I've
asked you both to leave me, haven't I! (*Pointing at Gertrude, who
has risen*) The man *she* loves is dead and gone! She can moralise—!
(*Sitting, beating upon the settee with her hands*) Leave me!   700
> *Amos joins Gertrude*

GERTRUDE [(*quietly*)] We'll go, Amos.
> *He takes from his pocket a small leather-bound book;° the cover is*
> *well-worn and shabby*

AMOS (*writing upon the fly-leaf of the book with a pencil*) I am writing our
address here, Mrs Ebbsmith.

AGNES (*in a hard voice*) I already have it.
> *Gertrude glances at the book over Amos's shoulder, and looks at*
> *him wonderingly*

AMOS (*laying the book on the settee by Agnes's side*) You might forget it.   705
> *She stares at the book, with knitted brows, for a moment, then*
> *stretches out her hand and opens it*

AGNES (*withdrawing her hand sharply*) No—I don't accept your gift.

AMOS The address of two friends is upon the fly-leaf.

AGNES I thank both of you; but you shall never be troubled again by me.
(*Rising, pointing to the book*) Take that away! (*Sitting facing the*
stove, the door of which she opens, replenishing the fire—excitedly)

Mr Cleeve may be back soon; it would be disagreeable to you all to   710
meet again.

>   *Gertrude gently pushes Amos aside, and picking up the book from*
>   *the settee, places it upon the table*

GERTRUDE (*to Agnes, pointing to the book*) This frightens you. Simple
print and paper, so you pretend to regard it; but *it frightens you.* (*With
a quick movement, Agnes twists her chair round and faces Gertrude
fiercely*) I called you a mad thing just now. A week ago I did think you
half-mad—a poor, ill-used creature, a visionary, a moral woman   715
living immorally; yet, in spite of all, a woman to be loved and pitied.
But now I'm beginning to think that you're only frail—wanton. Oh,
you're not so mad as not to know you're wicked! (*Tapping the book
forcibly*) And so this frightens you.

AGNES You're right! Wanton! That's what I've become! And I'm in my   720
right senses, as you say. I suppose I *was* mad once for a little time,
years ago. And do you know what drove me so? (*Striking the book with
her fist*) It was *that—that!*

GERTRUDE That!

AGNES I'd trusted in it, clung to it, and it failed me. Never once did it   725
stop my ears to the sounds of a curse; when I was beaten it didn't
make the blows a whit the lighter; it never healed my bruised flesh,
my bruised spirit! Yes, that drove me distracted for a while; but I'm
sane now—*now* it is *you* that are mad, mad to believe! You foolish
people, not to know—(*beating her breast and forehead*)—that Hell or   730
Heaven is here and here! (*Pointing to the book*) Take it!

>   *Gertrude turns away and joins Amos, and they walk quickly to*
>   *the door*

AGNES (*frantically*) I'll not endure the sight of it—!

>   *As they reach the door, Gertrude looks back and sees Agnes hurl*
>   *the book into the fire.° They go out. Agnes starts to her feet and*
>   *stands motionless for a moment, her head bent, her fingers twisted*
>   *in her hair. Then she raises her head; the expression of her face has*
>   *changed to a look of fright and horror. Uttering a loud cry, she*
>   *hastens to the stove, and, thrusting her arm into the fire, drags out*
>   *the book. Gertrude and Amos re-enter quickly in alarm*

GERTRUDE Agnes—!

>   *They stand looking at Agnes, who is kneeling upon the ground,*
>   *clutching the charred book*

END OF THE THIRD ACT

4

*The Scene is an apartment in the Campo San Bartolomeo. The
walls are of plaster; the ceiling is frescoed in cheap modern Italian
fashion. At the end of the room is a door leading to Agnes's bedroom; to the left is an exit on to a landing, while a nearer door, on
the same side, opens into another room. The furniture and the few
objects attached to the walls are characteristic of a moderate-
priced Venetian lodging. Placed about the room, however, are
photographs in frames and pretty knick-knacks personal to
Gertrude, and a travelling-trunk and bag are also to be seen. The
shutters of the two nearer windows are closed; a broad stream of
moonlight,° coming through the further window, floods the upper
part of the room, [suggesting the shutter is open.]*

*Hephzibah, a grey-haired north-country woman dressed as a
lady's maid [in black alpaca, white apron etc.,] is collecting the
knick-knacks and placing them in the travelling-bag. After a
moment or two, Gertrude enters by the further door*

GERTRUDE (*at the partly-closed door, speaking into the further room*) I'll
come back to you in a little while, Agnes. (*Closing the door, and
addressing Hephzibah*) How are you getting on, Heppy?

HEPHZIBAH A'reet,° Miss Gerty. I'm puttin' together a' the sma'
knick-knacks, to lay them wi' the claes i' th' trunks.   5

GERTRUDE (*taking some photographs from the table and bringing them to
Hephzibah*) We leave here at a quarter to eight in the morning; not a
minute later.

HEPHZIBAH Aye. Will there be much to pack for Mistress Cleeve?

GERTRUDE Nothing at all. Besides her handbag, she has only the one
box.   10

HEPHZIBAH (*pointing to the trunk*) Nay, nobbut° that thing!

GERTRUDE Yes, nobbut that. [(*Bringing other articles to Hephzibah*)]
I packed that for her at the Palazzo.

HEPHZIBAH Eh, it won't gi' us ower much trouble to maid Mistress
Cleeve when we get her hame.   15

GERTRUDE Heppy, we are not going to call—my friend—'Mrs Cleeve'.

HEPHZIBAH Nay! what will thee call her?

GERTRUDE I'll tell you—by and by. Remember, she must never, never
be reminded of the name.

122

HEPHZIBAH Aye, I'll be maist carefu'. Poor leddy! After the way she   20
tended that husband o' hers in Florence neet and day, neet and day!

GERTRUDE The world's full of unhappiness, Heppy.

HEPHZIBAH The world's full o' husbands. I canna' bide 'em. They're
true eneugh when they're ailin'—but a lass can't keep her Jo° always
sick. Hey, Miss Gerty! Do forgi'e your auld Heppy!   25

GERTRUDE For what?

HEPHZIBAH Why, your own man, so I've heered, ne'er had as much as
a bit headache till he caught his fever and died o't.

GERTRUDE No, I never knew Captain Thorpe to complain of an ache or
a pain.   30

HEPHZIBAH And *he* was a rare, bonny husband to thee, if a' tales be
true.

GERTRUDE Yes, Heppy. (*Listening, startled*) Who's this?

HEPHZIBAH (*going and looking*) Maister Amos.
          Amos enters briskly

AMOS (*to Gertrude*) How is she?   35

GERTRUDE (*assisting him to remove his overcoat*) More as she used to
be—so still, so gentle. She's reading.

AMOS (*looking at her significantly*) Reading?°

GERTRUDE [(*responding to his look*)] Reading.
          *He sits, humming a tune, while Heppy takes off his shoes and gives
          him his slippers*

HEPHZIBAH Eh, Maister Amos, it's good to see thee sae gladsome.   40

AMOS Home, Heppy, home!

HEPHZIBAH Aye, hame!

AMOS With our savings!

HEPHZIBAH Thy savings—!

AMOS Tsch! get on with your packing.   45
          *Hephzibah goes out, carrying the travelling-bag and Amos's
          shoes. He exchanges the coat he is wearing for a shabby little black
          jacket which Gertrude brings him*

GERTRUDE (*filling Amos's pipe*) Well, dear! Go on!

AMOS Well, I've seen them.

GERTRUDE Them—

AMOS The Duke and Sir Sandford Cleeve.

GERTRUDE At the hotel.   50

AMOS I found them sitting together in the hall, smoking, listening to
some music.

GERTRUDE Quite contented with the arrangement they believed they
had brought about.

AMOS Apparently so. Especially the Baronet—a poor, cadaverous   55
creature.

GERTRUDE Where was Mr Cleeve?

AMOS He had been there, had an interview with his wife, and departed.

GERTRUDE Then by this time he has discovered that Mrs Ebbsmith has
left him?   60

AMOS I suppose so.

GERTRUDE Well, well! the Duke and the cadaverous Baronet?

AMOS Oh, I told them I considered it my duty to let them know that the
position of affairs had suddenly become altered—(*she puts his pipe in
his mouth, and strikes a match*)—that, in point of fact, Mrs Ebbsmith   65
had ceased to be an element in their scheme for re-establishing
Mr Cleeve's household.

GERTRUDE (*holding a light to his pipe*) Did they inquire as to her move-
ments?

AMOS The Duke did—guessed we had taken her.   70

GERTRUDE What did they say to that?

AMOS The Baronet asked whether I was the chaplain of a Home for—°
(*angrily*)—ah!

GERTRUDE Brute! [(*Walking about*)] And then?

AMOS Then they suggested that I ought hardly to leave *them* to make   75
the necessary explanation to their relative, Mr Lucas Cleeve.

GERTRUDE Yes—well?

AMOS I replied that I fervently hoped I should never set eyes on their
relative again.

GERTRUDE (*gleefully*) Ha!   80

AMOS But that Mrs Ebbsmith had left a letter behind her at the Palazzo
Arconati, addressed to that gentleman, which I presumed contained
as full an explanation as he could desire.

GERTRUDE Oh, Amos—!

AMOS Eh?   85

GERTRUDE You're mistaken there, dear; it was no letter.

AMOS No letter—?

GERTRUDE Simply four shakily-written words.

AMOS Only four words!

GERTRUDE 'My—hour—is—over.'   90

　　　Hephzibah enters with a card on a little tray. Gertrude reads the
　　　card and utters an exclamation

GERTRUDE (*taking the card and speaking under her breath*) Amos!
　　　He goes to her; they stare at the card together

AMOS (*to Hephzibah*) Certainly!

*Hephzibah goes out, then returns with the Duke of St Olpherts,
and retires. St Olpherts bows graciously to Gertrude and more
formally to Amos*

AMOS Pray, sit down.

St Olpherts seats himself on the settee. [*Gertrude retires up LC by
the stove*]

ST OLPHERTS Oh, my dear sir!—if I may use such an expression in
your presence—here is the devil to pay!   95

AMOS (*to St Olpherts*) You don't mind my pipe. (*St Olpherts waves a
hand pleasantly*) And I don't mind your expression—(*sitting by the
table*)—the devil to pay?

ST OLPHERTS This, I daresay well-intentioned, interference of yours
has brought about some very unpleasant results. Mr Cleeve   100
returns to the Palazzo Arconati and finds that Mrs Ebbsmith has
flown.

AMOS That result, at least, was inevitable.

ST OLPHERTS Whereupon he hurries back to the Danieli and de-
nounces us all for a set of conspirators.   105

AMOS Your Grace doesn't complain of the injustice of that charge?

ST OLPHERTS (*smilingly*) No, no, *I* don't complain. But the brother—
the wife! Just when they imagined they had bagged the truant—
there's the sting!

GERTRUDE Oh, then Mr Cleeve now refuses to carry out his part of the   110
shameful arrangement?

ST OLPHERTS Absolutely. (*Rising, taking a chair, and placing it by the
settee*) Come into this, dear Mrs Thorn—!

AMOS Thorpe.

ST OLPHERTS Come into this! ([*Gertrude hesitatingly comes down C*].   115
Sitting again) *You* understand the sort of man we have to deal with in
Mr Cleeve.

GERTRUDE (*sitting*) A man who prizes a woman when he has lost her.

ST OLPHERTS Precisely.

GERTRUDE Men don't relish, I suppose, being cast off by women.   120

ST OLPHERTS It's an inversion of the picturesque; the male abandoned
is not a pathetic figure.° At any rate, our poor Lucas is now raving
fidelity to Mrs Ebbsmith.

GERTRUDE (*indignantly*) Ah—!

ST OLPHERTS If you please, he cannot, will not, exist without her.   125
Reputation, fame, fortune are nothing when weighed against—
Mrs Ebbsmith. And we may go to perdition, so that he recovers—
Mrs Ebbsmith.

AMOS Well—to be plain—you're not asking us to sympathise with   130
Mrs Cleeve and her brother-in-law over their defeat?

ST OLPHERTS Certainly not. All I ask, Mr Winterfield, is that you will
raise no obstacle to a meeting between Mrs Cleeve and—and—

GERTRUDE No!

    St Olpherts signifies assent; Gertrude makes a movement

ST OLPHERTS (*to her*) Don't go.

AMOS The object of such a meeting?   135

ST OLPHERTS Mrs Cleeve desires to make a direct, personal appeal to
Mrs Ebbsmith.

GERTRUDE [(*remaining*)] Oh, what kind of woman can this Mrs Cleeve be!

ST OLPHERTS A woman of character, who sets herself to accomplish a
certain task—   140

GERTRUDE Character!

AMOS Hush, Gerty!

ST OLPHERTS And who gathers her skirts tightly round her and gently
tiptoes into the mire.

AMOS To put it clearly: in order to get her unfaithful husband back to   145
London, Mrs Cleeve would deliberately employ this weak, unhappy
woman as a lure.

ST OLPHERTS Perhaps Mrs Cleeve is an unhappy woman.

GERTRUDE What work for a wife!

ST OLPHERTS Wife—nonsense! She is only married to Cleeve.   150

AMOS ([*rising and*] *walking up and down*) It is proposed that this meeting should take place—when?

ST OLPHERTS I have brought Sir Sandford and Mrs Cleeve with me.
([*Gertrude rises; Amos pauses in his walk*.] *Pointing towards the outer
door*) They are—

AMOS If I decline?   155

ST OLPHERTS It's known you leave for Milan at a quarter to nine in the
morning; there might be some sort of foolish, inconvenient scene at
the station.

AMOS Surely your Grace—?

ST OLPHERTS Oh, no, *I* shall be in bed at that hour. I mean, between   160
the women, perhaps—and Mr Cleeve. Come, come, sir, you can't
abduct Mrs Ebbsmith—nor can we. Nor must you gag her. (*Amos
appears angry and perplexed*) Pray be reasonable. Let her speak out for
herself—here, finally—and settle the business. Come, sir, come!

AMOS (*going to Gertrude and speaking in a low voice*) Ask her. (*Gertrude*   165
goes out) Cleeve! Where is he while this poor creature's body and soul
are being played for? You have told him that she is with us?

ST OLPHERTS No, *I* haven't.

AMOS He must suspect it.

ST OLPHERTS Well, candidly, Mr Winterfield, Mr Cleeve is just now   170
employed in looking for Mrs Ebbsmith elsewhere.

AMOS Elsewhere?

ST OLPHERTS Sir Sandford recognised that, in his brother's present
mood, the young man's presence might be prejudicial to the success
of these delicate negotiations.   175

AMOS So some lie has been told him, to keep him out of the way?

ST OLPHERTS Now, Mr Winterfield—!

AMOS Good heavens! Duke—forgive me for my roughness—you
appear to be fouling your hands, all of you, with some relish!

ST OLPHERTS [(*coming down*)] I must trouble you to address remarks of   180
that nature to Sir Sandford Cleeve. [(*Testily*)] I am no longer a prime
mover in the affair. I am simply standing by.

AMOS But how can you 'stand by'?

ST OLPHERTS Confound it, sir, if you will trouble yourself to rescue
people, there is a man to be rescued here as well as a woman; a man,   185
by the way, who is a—a sort of relative of mine.

AMOS The woman first!

ST OLPHERTS Not always. You can rescue this woman in a few weeks'
time; it can make no difference.

AMOS (*indignantly*) Ah—!   190

ST OLPHERTS Oh, you are angry!

AMOS I beg your pardon. One word. I assure your Grace that I truly
believe this wretched woman is at a fatal crisis in her life. I believe that
if I lose her now there is every chance of her slipping back into a misery and despair out of which it will be impossible to drag her. Oh, I'll   195
be perfectly open with you. At this moment we—my sister and I—
are not sure of her. Her affection for this man may still induce her to
sacrifice herself utterly for him; she is still in danger of falling to the
lowest depth a woman can attain. Come, Duke, don't help these
people. And don't 'stand by'! Help me and my sister. For God's sake!°   200

ST OLPHERTS My good Mr Winterfield, believe me or not, I—I
positively like this woman.

AMOS (*gladly*) Ah!

ST OLPHERTS She attracts me curiously. And if she wanted assistance—   205

AMOS Doesn't she?

ST OLPHERTS Money—

AMOS No, no.

ST OLPHERTS She should have it. But as for the rest—well—

AMOS Well?   210

ST OLPHERTS [(*with a strange dignity*)] Well, sir, you must understand
me. It is a failing of mine; I can't approach women—I never could—
in the missionary spirit.

> *Gertrude re-enters; the men turn to face her*

AMOS (*to Gertrude*) Will she—?

GERTRUDE Yes. (*St Olpherts limps out of the room, bowing to Gertrude as*   215
he passes) Oh, Amos!

AMOS Are we to lose the poor soul after all, Gerty?

GERTRUDE I—I can't think so. Oh! but I'm afraid.

> *St Olpherts returns, and Sir Sandford Cleeve enters with Sybil*
> *Cleeve. Sandford is a long, lean, old-young man with a pinched*
> *face. Sybil is a stately, handsome young woman, beautifully*
> *gowned and thickly veiled*   •

ST OLPHERTS Mrs Thorpe—Mr Winterfield.

> *Sandford and Sybil bow distantly to Gertrude and Amos*

AMOS (*to Sandford and Sybil, indicating the settee*) Will you—? (*Sybil sits*   220
on settee; Sandford takes the chair beside her) Gertrude—(*Gertrude goes*
out)

SIR SANDFORD (*pompously*) Mr Winterfield, I find myself engaged
upon a peculiarly distasteful task.

AMOS I have no hope, Sir Sandford, that you will not have strength to
discharge it.   225

SIR SANDFORD We shall object to loftiness of attitude on your part, sir.
You would do well to reflect that we are seeking to restore a young
man to a useful and honourable career.

AMOS You are using very honourable means, Sir Sandford.

SIR SANDFORD I shall protest against any perversion of words, Mr   230
Winterfield—

> *The door of the further room opens, and Gertrude comes in, then*
> *Agnes. The latter is in a rusty, ill-fitting, black, stuff dress°; her*
> *hair is tightly drawn from her brows; her face is haggard, her eyes*
> *are red and sunken. A strip of linen binds her right hand*

ST OLPHERTS (*speaking into Sybil's ear*) The lean witch again! The
witch of the Iron Hall at St Luke's.

SYBIL (*in a whisper*) Is *that* the woman?

ST OLPHERTS You see only one of 'em—there are *two* there.   235

> *Sandford rises as Agnes comes slowly forward accompanied by*
> *Gertrude. Amos joins Gertrude; and they go together into the*
> *adjoining room, Gertrude giving Agnes an appealing look*

SIR SANDFORD ([*after a pause*] *to Agnes*) I—I am Mr Lucas Cleeve's brother—(*with a motion of the hand towards Sybil*)—this is—this is— (*He swallows the rest of the announcement and retires to the back of the room, where he stands before the stove. St Olpherts strolls away and disappears*)

SYBIL (*to Agnes, in a hard, dry, disdainful voice*) I beg that you will sit down. (*Agnes sits mechanically, with an expressionless face*) I—I don't need to be told that this is a very—a very unwomanly proceeding on 240 my part.

SIR SANDFORD I can't regard it in that light, under the peculiar circumstances.

SYBIL I'd rather you wouldn't interrupt me, Sandford. (*To Agnes*) But the peculiar circumstances, to borrow my brother-in-law's phrase, 245 are not such as develop sweetness and modesty, I suppose.

SIR SANDFORD Again I say you wrong yourself there, Sybil—

SYBIL (*impatiently*) Oh, please let me wrong myself, for a change. (*To Agnes*) When my husband left me, and I heard of his association with you, I felt sure that his vanity would soon make an openly irregular 250 life intolerable to him. Vanity is the cause of a great deal of virtue in men; the vainest are those who like to be thought respectable.

SIR SANDFORD Really, I must protest—

SYBIL But Lady Cleeve—the mother—and the rest of the family have not had the patience to wait for the fulfilment of my prophecy. And 255 so I have been forced to undertake this journey.

SIR SANDFORD I demur to the expression 'forced', Sybil—

SYBIL Cannot we be left alone?° Surely—! (*Sandford bows stiffly and moves away, following St Olpherts*) However—there's this to be said for them, poor people—whatever is done to save my husband's 260 prospects in life must be done *now*. It is no longer possible to play fast and loose with friends and supporters—to say nothing of enemies. His future now rests upon a matter of days—hours almost. (*Rising and walking about agitatedly*. [*Stopping at certain points to address Agnes*]) That is why I am sent here—well, why I *am* here.

AGNES (*in a low quavering voice*) What is it you are all asking me to do now? 265

SYBIL We are asking you to continue to—to exert your influence over him for a little while longer.

AGNES (*rising unsteadily*) Ah—! (*She makes a movement to go, falters, and irresolutely sits again*) My influence—mine!

SYBIL (*with a stamp of the foot*) You wouldn't underrate your power if 270 you had seen him, heard him, about an hour ago—(*mockingly*) after he had discovered his bereavement.

AGNES   He will soon forget *me*.

SYBIL   Yes—if you don't forsake him.

AGNES   I am going to England, into Yorkshire; according to your show-   275
ing, that should draw him back.

SYBIL   Oh, I've no doubt we shall hear of him—in Yorkshire! You'll
find him dangling about your skirts in Yorkshire!

AGNES   [(*clenching her hands*)]   And *he* will find that I am determined—
strong.   280

SYBIL   Ultimately he will tire, of course. But when? And what assurance
have we that he returns to us when he has wearied of pursuing you?
Besides, don't I tell you that we must make sure of him *now*? It's of no
use his begging us, in a month's time, to patch up home and reputation. It must be *now*—and *you* can end our suspense. Come, hideous   285
as it sounds, this is not much to ask.

AGNES   (*shrinking from her*)   Oh—!

SYBIL   Oh, don't regard me as the wife! That's an unnecessary sentiment, I pledge you my word. It's a little late in the day, too, for such
considerations. So, come, help us!   290

AGNES   I will not.

SYBIL   He has an old mother—

AGNES   Poor woman!

SYBIL   And remember, *you* took him away—!

AGNES   I!   295

SYBIL   Practically you did—with your tender nursing and sweet com-
passion. Isn't it straining a point—to shirk bringing him back?

AGNES   (*rising* [*and going to C*])   I did not take him from you. You—you
sent him to me.

SYBIL   [(*rising*)]   Ho, yes! that tale has been dinned into your ears often   300
enough, I can quite believe. *I* sent him to you—my coldness, heart-
lessness, selfishness sent him to you. The unsympathetic wife—eh?
[(*Approaching her*)]   Yes, but you didn't put yourself to the trouble of
asking for *my* version of the story before you mingled your woes with
his. (*Agnes faces her suddenly*)   You know him now. Have I been al-   305
together to blame, do you still think? Unsympathetic! Because I've so
often had to tighten my lips, and stare blankly over his shoulder, to
stop myself from crying out in weariness of his vanity and pettiness?
Cruel! Because, occasionally, patience became exhausted at the mere
contemplation of a man so thoroughly, greedily self-absorbed? Why,   310
you married miserably, the Duke of St Olpherts tells us! Before you
made yourself my husband's champion and protector, why didn't
you let your experience speak a word for *me*? (*Agnes quickly turns*

away and sits upon the settee, her hands to her brow) However, I didn't
come here to revile you. ([*Following her and*] *standing by her*) They   315
say that you're a strange woman—not the sort of woman one generally
finds doing such things as you have done; a woman with odd ideas.
I hear—oh, I'm willing to believe it!—that there's good in you.

    Agnes breaks into a low peal of hysterical laughter

AGNES Who tells you—that?

SYBIL The Duke.   320

AGNES Ha, ha, ha! A character°—from him! ha, ha, ha!

SYBIL (*her voice and manner softening*) Well, if there *is* pity in you,
help us to get my husband back to London, to his friends, to his old
ambitions.

AGNES Ha, ha, ha, ha! your husband!   325

SYBIL The word slips out. I swear to you that he and I can never be
more to each other than companion figures in a masquerade. The
same roof may cover us; but between two wings of a house, as you
may know, there often stretches a wide desert. I despise him; he hates
me. (*Walking away, her voice breaking*) Only—I did love him once. . . .   330
I don't want to see him utterly thrown away—wasted. . . . I don't
quite want to see that. . . .

    [*There is a pause, then*] *Agnes rises and approaches Sybil, fear-*
    fully

AGNES (*in a whisper*) Lift your veil for a moment. (*Sybil raises her veil*)
Tears—tears—° (*With a deep groan*)—Oh—! (*Sybil turns away*) I—
I'll do it. . . . I'll go back to the Palazzo. . . . at once . . . . (*Sybil draws* 335
herself up suddenly) I've wronged you! wronged you! O God! O God!
(*She totters away and goes into her bedroom. For a moment or two Sybil*
stands still, a look of horror and repulsion upon her face. Then she turns
and goes towards the outer door [*quickly*])

SYBIL (*calling*) Sandford! Sandford! [(*She comes down C in agitation*)]
    Sir Sandford Cleeve and the Duke of St Olpherts enter

SIR SANDFORD (*to Sybil*) Well—?

SYBIL She is going back to the Palazzo.

SIR SANDFORD You mean that she consents to—?   340

SYBIL (*stamping her foot*) I mean that she will go back to the Palazzo.
(*Sitting and leaning her head upon her hands*) Oh! oh!

SIR SANDFORD Need we wait longer, then?

SYBIL These people—these people who are befriending her! Tell
them.   345

SIR SANDFORD Really, it can hardly be necessary to consult—

SYBIL ([*looking up,*] *fiercely*) I will have them told! I will have them told!

*Sandford goes to the door of the adjoining room and knocks,
returning to Sybil as Gertrude and Amos enter. Sybil draws down
her veil*

GERTRUDE (*looking round*) Mrs Ebbsmith—? [(*Crossing quickly to RC*)]
Mrs Ebbsmith—!

SIR SANDFORD Er—many matters have been discussed with Mrs Ebb-   350
smith. Undoubtedly she has, for the moment, considerable influence
over my brother. She has consented to exert it, to induce him to
return at once to London.

AMOS I think I understand you!

Agnes appears at the door of her room dressed in bonnet and cloak

GERTRUDE Agnes—!   355

*Agnes comes forward, stretches out her hand to Gertrude, and
throws herself upon the settee*

SYBIL (*to Sandford, clutching his arm*) Take me away.

They turn to go

GERTRUDE (*to Sybil*) Mrs Cleeve—! (*Looking down upon Agnes*) Mrs
Cleeve, we—my brother and I—hoped to save this woman. She was
worth saving. You have utterly destroyed her.°

*Sybil makes no answer, but walks slowly away with Sandford,
then stops and turns abruptly*

SYBIL (*with a gasp*) Oh—! [(*Firmly*)] No—I will not accept the service of   360
this wretched woman. I loathe myself for doing what I have done.
(*Coming to Agnes*) Look up! Look at me! [*Agnes raises her head.*]
Proudly—lifting her veil) I decline your help—I decline it. (*To Gertrude
and Amos*) You hear me—you—and you? I unsay all that I've said to
her. It's too degrading. I will not have such an act upon my conscience.   365
(*To Agnes*) Understand me! If you rejoin this man I shall consider it a
fresh outrage upon me. I hope you will keep with your friends.

Gertrude holds out her hand to Sybil; Sybil touches it distantly

AGNES (*clutching at Sybil's skirts*) Forgive me! forgive—!

SYBIL (*retreating*) Ah, please—! (*Turning and confronting Sandford*)
Tell your mother I have failed. I am not going back to England.   370

*Lucas enters quickly; he and Sybil come face to face. They stand
looking at each other for a moment, then she sweeps past him and
goes out. Sandford follows her*

LUCAS (*coming to Agnes*) Agnes—(*To Agnes, in rapid, earnest undertones*)
They sent me to the railway station; my brother told me you were
likely to leave for Milan tonight. I ought to have guessed sooner that
you were in the hands of this meddling parson and his sister. Why has
my wife been here—?   375

AGNES (*in a low voice, rocking herself gently to and fro*) Your wife—your wife—!

LUCAS And the others? What scheme is afoot now? Why have you left me? Why didn't you tell me outright that I was putting you to too severe a test? You tempted me, you led me on, to propose that I should patch up my life in that way. (*She rises, with an expressionless face*) But it has had one good result. I know now how much I depend upon you. Oh, I have had it all out with myself, pacing up and down that cursed railway station. (*Laying his hand upon her arm and speaking into her ear*) I don't deceive myself any longer. Agnes, *this* is the great cause of the unhappiness I've experienced of late years—I'm not fit for the fight and press of life. I wear no armour; I am too horribly sensitive. My skin bleeds at a touch; even flattery wounds me. Oh, the wretchedness of it! But *you* can be strong—at your weakest, there is a certain strength in you. With you, in time, I feel *I* shall grow stronger. Only I must withdraw from the struggle for a while; you must take me out of it and let me rest—recover breath, as it were. Come! Forgive me for having treated you ungratefully, almost treacherously. Tomorrow we will begin our search for our new home. Agnes!

AGNES [(*steadily*)] I have already found a home.

LUCAS Apart from me, you mean?

AGNES Apart from you.

LUCAS No, no. You'll not do that!

AGNES Lucas, this evening, two or three hours ago, you planned out the life we were to lead in the future. We had done with 'madness', if you remember; henceforth we were to be 'mere man and woman'.

LUCAS You agreed—

AGNES Then. But we hadn't looked at each other clearly then, as mere man and woman. You, the man—what are you? You've confessed—

LUCAS I lack strength; I shall gain it.

AGNES Never from me—never from me. For what am I? Untrue to myself, as you are untrue to yourself; false to others, as you are false to others; passionate, unstable, like yourself; like yourself, a coward. A coward. I—I was to lead women! *I* was to show them, in your company, how laws—laws made and laws that are natural°—may be set aside or slighted; how men and women may live independent and noble lives without rule, or guidance, or sacrament. *I* was to be the example—the figure set up for others to observe and imitate. But the figure was made of wax—it fell awry at the first hot breath that touched it! You and I! What a partnership it has been! How base, and gross, and wicked, almost from the very beginning! We know each other now thoroughly—how base and wicked it would remain! No, go your way, Lucas, and let me go mine.

LUCAS Where—where are you going? 420

AGNES To Ketherick—to think. (*Wringing her hands*) Ah! I have to think too, now, of the woman I have wronged.

LUCAS Wronged?

AGNES Your wife; the woman I have wronged, who came here tonight, and—spared me. Oh, go! 425

LUCAS Not like this, Agnes! not like this!

AGNES (*appealingly*) Gertrude! ([*Gertrude comes down C and stands behind chair.*] *Lucas looks round—first at Gertrude then at Amos—and, with a hard smile upon his face, turns to go. Suddenly Agnes touches his sleeve.* [*To him in a low voice*]) Lucas, when I have learnt to pray again, I will remember you, every day of my life.

LUCAS (*staring at her*) Pray! . . . you! . . .° 430
          She inclines her head twice, slowly; without another word he walks away and goes out. Agnes sinks upon the settee; Amos and Gertrude remain, stiffly and silently, in the attitude of people who are waiting for the departure of a disagreeable person

ST OLPHERTS (*after watching Lucas's departure,* [*coming down*]) Now I wonder whether, if he hurried to his wife at this moment, repentant, and begged her to relent—I wonder whether—whether she would—whether—(*looking at Amos and Gertrude, a little disconcerted*)—I beg your pardon—you're not interested? 435

AMOS Frankly, we are not.

ST OLPHERTS No; other people's affairs *are* tedious. (*Producing his gloves*) Well! A week in Venice—and the weather has been delightful. (*Shaking hands with Gertrude, whose expression remains unchanged*) A pleasant journey! (*Going to Agnes, offering his hand*) Mrs Ebb-smith—? (*She lifts her maimed hand*) Ah! An accident? (*She nods 440 wearily*) I'm sorry . . . I . . . (*He turns away and goes out, bowing to Amos as he passes*)

THE END

VOTES FOR WOMEN!
A Dramatic Tract
in Three Acts

BY

ELIZABETH ROBINS

VOTES FOR WOMEN!

*The play was first produced at the Royal Court Theatre°
on 9 April 1907, with the following cast*

Lord John Wynnstay	*Mr Athol Forde°*
The Hon. Geoffrey Stonor	*Mr Aubrey Smith°*
Mr St John Greatorex	*Mr E. Holman Clark*
Mr Richard Farnborough	*Mr P. Clayton Greene*
Mr Freddy Tunbridge	*Mr Percy Marmont*
Mr Allen Trent	*Mr Lewis Casson°*
* Mr Walker°	*Mr Edmund Gwenn*
Lady John Wynnstay°	*Miss Maud Milton*
Mrs Heriot	*Miss Frances Ivor°*
Miss Vida Levering°	*Miss Wynne-Matthison*
* Miss Beatrice Dunbarton°	*Miss Jean MacKinlay*
Mrs Freddy Tunbridge	*Miss Gertrude Burnett*
Miss Ernestine Blunt°	*Miss Dorothy Minto*
A Working Woman°	*Miss Agnes Thomas*

*Act 1   Wynnstay House in Hertfordshire
Act 2   Trafalgar Square, London
Act 3   Eaton Square, London*

*The Entire Action of the Play takes place between Sunday noon
and six o'clock in the evening of the same day.*

* In the text these characters have been altered to Mr Pilcher and Miss Jean
Dunbarton.

1

SCENE° *Hall of Wynnstay House. Twelve o'clock, Sunday morning, end of June.*

With the rising of the Curtain, enter the Butler. As he is going, with majestic port, to answer the door L, enter briskly from the garden, by lower French window, Lady John Wynnstay, flushed, and flapping a garden hat to fan herself. She is a pink-cheeked woman of fifty-four, who has plainly been a beauty, keeps her complexion, but is 'gone to fat'

LADY JOHN Has Miss Levering come down yet?

BUTLER (*pausing C*) I haven't seen her, m'lady.

LADY JOHN (*almost sharply as Butler turns L*) I won't have her disturbed if she's resting. (*To herself as she goes to writing-table*) She certainly needs it.   5

BUTLER Yes, m'lady.

LADY JOHN (*sitting at writing-table, her back to front door*) But I want her to know the moment she comes down that the new plans arrived by the morning post.

BUTLER (*pausing nearly at the door*) Plans, m'la—   10

LADY JOHN She'll understand. There they are. (*Glancing at the clock*) It's very important she should have them in time to look over before she goes—(*Butler opens the door L. Over her shoulder*) Is that Miss Levering?

BUTLER No, m'lady. Mr Farnborough. (*Exit Butler*)   15
        Enter the Hon R. Farnborough. He is twenty-six; reddish hair, high-coloured, sanguine, self-important

FARNBOROUGH I'm afraid I'm scandalously early. It didn't take me nearly as long to motor over as Lord John said.

LADY JOHN (*shaking hands*) I'm afraid my husband is no authority on motoring—°and he's not home yet from church.

FARNBOROUGH It's the greatest luck finding *you*. I thought Miss Levering was the only person under this roof who was ever allowed to observe Sunday as a real Day of Rest.   20

LADY JOHN If you've come to see Miss Levering—

FARNBOROUGH Is she here? I give you my word I didn't know it.

LADY JOHN (*unconvinced*) Oh?   25

FARNBOROUGH Does she come every week-end?

137

LADY JOHN   Whenever we can get her to. But we've only known her a couple of months.

FARNBOROUGH   And I have only known her three weeks! Lady John, I've come to ask you to help me.°   30

LADY JOHN (*quickly*)   With Miss Levering? I can't do it!

FARNBOROUGH   No, no—all that's no good. She only laughs.

LADY JOHN (*relieved*)   Ah!—she looks upon you as a boy.

FARNBOROUGH (*firing up*)   Such rot!° What do you think she said to me in London the other day?   35

LADY JOHN   That she was four years older than you?

FARNBOROUGH   Oh, I knew that. No. She said she knew she was all the charming things I'd been saying, but there was only one way to prove it—and that was to marry some one young enough to be her son. She'd noticed that was what the *most* attractive women did—and she   40 named names.

LADY JOHN (*laughing*)   *You* were too old!

FARNBOROUGH (*nods*)   Her future husband, she said, was probably just entering Eton.

LADY JOHN   Just like her!   45

FARNBOROUGH (*waving the subject away*)   No. I wanted to see you about the Secretaryship.°

LADY JOHN   You didn't get it, then?

FARNBOROUGH   No. It's the grief of my life.

LADY JOHN   Oh, if you don't get one you'll get another.   50

FARNBOROUGH   But there *is* only one.

LADY JOHN   Only one vacancy?

FARNBOROUGH   Only one man I'd give my ears to work for.

LADY JOHN (*smiling*)   I remember.

FARNBOROUGH (*quickly*)   Do I always talk about Stonor? Well, it's a   55 habit people have got into.

LADY JOHN   I forget, do you know Mr Stonor personally, or (*smiling*) are you just dazzled from afar?

FARNBOROUGH   Oh, I know him. The trouble is he doesn't know me. If he did he'd realise he can't be sure of winning his election without my   60 valuable services.

LADY JOHN   Geoffrey Stonor's re-election° is always a foregone con-clusion.

FARNBOROUGH   That the great man shares that opinion is precisely his weak point. (*Smiling*) His only one.   65

LADY JOHN   You think because the Liberals swept the country the last time—°

FARNBOROUGH How can we be sure any Conservative seat is safe
after—(*As Lady John smiles and turns to her papers*) Forgive me, I
know you're not interested in politics *qua* politics. But this concerns   70
Geoffrey Stonor.

LADY JOHN And you count on my being interested in him like all the
rest of my sex.

FARNBOROUGH (*leans forward*) Lady John, I've heard the news.

LADY JOHN What news?   75

FARNBOROUGH That your little niece—the Scotch heiress—is going
to become Mrs Geoffrey Stonor.

LADY JOHN Who told you that?

FARNBOROUGH Please don't mind my knowing.

LADY JOHN (*visibly perturbed*) She had set her heart upon having a few   80
days with just her family in the secret, before the flood of congratulations breaks loose.

FARNBOROUGH Oh, that's all right. I always hear things before other
people.

LADY JOHN Well, I must ask you to be good enough to be very circum-   85
spect. I wouldn't have my niece think that I—

FARNBOROUGH Oh, of course not.

LADY JOHN She will be here in an hour.

FARNBOROUGH (*jumping up delighted*) What? Today? The future Mrs
Stonor!   90

LADY JOHN (*harassed*) Yes. Unfortunately we had one or two people
already asked for the week-end—°

FARNBOROUGH And I go and invite myself to luncheon! Lady John,
you can buy me off. I'll promise to remove myself in five minutes if
you'll—   95

LADY JOHN No, the penalty is you shall stay and keep the others
amused between church and luncheon, and so leave me free. (*Takes
up the plan*) Only *remember*—

FARNBOROUGH Wild horses won't get a hint out of me! I only mentioned it to you because—since we've come back to live in this part of   100
the world you've been so awfully kind—I thought, I hoped maybe
you—you'd put in a word for me.

LADY JOHN With—[my niece]?°

FARNBOROUGH With your nephew that is to be. Though I'm *not* the
slavish satellite people make out, you can't doubt—   105

LADY JOHN Oh, I don't doubt. But you know Mr Stonor inspires a
similar enthusiasm in a good many young—

FARNBOROUGH They haven't studied the situation as I have. They

don't know what's at stake. They don't go to that hole Dutfield as I
did just to hear his Friday speech.   110

LADY JOHN Ah! But you were rewarded. Jean°—my niece—wrote me
it was 'glorious'.

FARNBOROUGH (*judicially*) Well, you know, *I* was disappointed. He's
too content just to criticise, just to make his delicate pungent fun of
the men who are grappling—very inadequately, of course—still   115
grappling with the big questions. There's a carrying power (*gets up
and faces an imaginary audience*)—some of Stonor's friends ought to
point it out—there's a driving power in the poorest constructive
policy that makes the most brilliant criticism look barren.

LADY JOHN (*with good-humoured malice*) Who told you that?   120

FARNBOROUGH You think there's nothing in it because *I* say it. But now
that he's coming into the family, Lord John or somebody really ought
to point out—Stonor's overdoing his *rôle* of magnificent security.

LADY JOHN I don't see even Lord John offering to instruct Mr Stonor.

FARNBOROUGH Believe me, that's just Stonor's danger! Nobody say-   125
ing a word, everybody hoping he's on the point of adopting some def-
inite line, something strong and original that's going to fire the public
imagination and bring the Tories back into power.

LADY JOHN So he will.

FARNBOROUGH (*hotly*) Not if he disappoints meetings—goes calmly   130
up to town—and leaves the field to the Liberals.

LADY JOHN When did he do anything like that?

FARNBOROUGH Yesterday! (*With a harassed air*) And now that he's got
this other preoccupation—

LADY JOHN You mean—   135

FARNBOROUGH Yes, your niece—that spoilt child of Fortune. Of
course! (*Stopping suddenly*) She kept him from the meeting last night.
Well! (*sits down*) if that's the effect she's going to have it's pretty
serious!

LADY JOHN (*smiling*) *You* are!   140

FARNBOROUGH I can assure you the election agent's more so. He's
simply tearing his hair.

LADY JOHN (*more gravely and coming nearer*) How do you know?

FARNBOROUGH He told me so himself—yesterday. I scraped acquaintance with the agent just to see if—if—   145

LADY JOHN It's not only here that you manoeuvre for that Secretaryship!

FARNBOROUGH (*confidentially*) You can never tell when your chance
might come! That election chap's promised to keep me posted.°

The door flies open and Jean Dunbarton rushes in

JEAN Aunt Ellen—here I—   150

LADY JOHN (*astonished*) My dear child!

> *They embrace. Enter Lord John from the garden—a benevolent,*
> *silver-haired despot of sixty-two*

LORD JOHN I thought that was you running up the avenue.

> *Jean greets her uncle warmly, but all the time she and her aunt*
> *talk together. 'How did you get here so early?' 'I knew you'd be*
> *surprised—wasn't it clever of me to manage it? I don't deserve all*
> *the credit.' 'But there isn't any train between—' 'Yes, wait till I*
> *tell you.' 'You walked in the broiling sun—' 'No, no.' 'You must*
> *be dead. Why didn't you telegraph? I ordered the carriage to meet*
> *the 1.10. Didn't you say the 1.10? Yes, I'm sure you did—here's*
> *your letter.'*

LORD JOHN (*has shaken hands with Farnborough and speaks through the*
torrent) Now they'll tell each other for ten minutes that she's an hour
earlier than we expected. (*Lord John leads Farnborough towards the*
garden*)

FARNBOROUGH The Freddy Tunbridges said *they* were coming to you   155
this week.

LORD JOHN Yes, they're dawdling through the park with the Church
Brigade.°

FARNBOROUGH Oh! (*With a glance back at Jean*) I'll go and meet them.
(*Exit Farnborough*)

LORD JOHN (*as he turns back.*) That discreet young man will get on.   160

LADY JOHN (*to Jean*) But *how* did you get here?

JEAN (*breathless*) 'He' motored me down.

LADY JOHN Geoffrey Stonor? (*Jean nods*) Why, where is he, then?

JEAN He dropped me at the end of the avenue and went on to see a
supporter about something.   165

LORD JOHN You let him go off like that without—

LADY JOHN (*taking Jean's two hands*) Just tell me, my child, is it all
right?

JEAN My engagement? (*Radiantly*) Yes, absolutely.

LADY JOHN Geoffrey Stonor isn't going to be—a little too old for you?   170

JEAN (*laughing*) Bless me, am I such a chicken?

LADY JOHN Twenty-four used not to be so young—but it's become so.

JEAN Yes, we don't grow up so quick. (*Gaily*) But on the other hand we
stay up longer.

LORD JOHN You've got what's vulgarly called 'looks', my dear, and   175
that will help to *keep* you up!

JEAN (*smiling*) I know what Uncle John's thinking. But I'm not the only girl who's been left 'what's vulgarly called' money.

LORD JOHN You're the only one of our immediate circle who's been left so beautifully much.°   180

JEAN Ah, but remember Geoffrey could—everybody *knows* he could have married any one in England.

LADY JOHN (*faintly ironic*) I'm afraid everybody does know it—not excepting Mr Stonor.

LORD JOHN Well, how spoilt is the great man?   185

JEAN Not the least little bit in the world. You'll see! He so wants to know my best-beloved relations better. (*Another embrace*) An orphan has so few belongings, she has to make the most of them.

LORD JOHN (*smiling*) Let us hope he'll approve of us on more intimate acquaintance.°   190

JEAN (*firmly*) He will. He's an angel. Why, he gets on with my grandfather!

LADY JOHN *Does* he? (*Teasing*) You mean to say Mr Geoffrey Stonor isn't just a tiny bit—'superior' about Dissenters.°

JEAN (*stoutly*) Not half as much as Uncle John and all the rest of you!   195 My grandfather's been ill again, you know, and rather difficult— bless him! (*Radiantly*) But Geoffrey—(*Clasps her hands*)

LADY JOHN He must have powers of persuasion!—to get that old Covenanter to let you come in an abhorred motor-car°—on Sunday, too!   200

JEAN (*half whispering*) Grandfather didn't know!

LADY JOHN Didn't know?

JEAN I honestly meant to come by train. Geoffrey met me on my way to the station. We had the most glorious run. Oh, Aunt Ellen, we're so happy! (*Embracing her*. [*Pressing her cheek against Lady John's shoul-   205 der*]°) I've so looked forward to having you to myself the whole day just to talk to you about—

LORD JOHN (*turning away with affected displeasure*) Oh, very well—

JEAN (*catches him affectionately by the arm*) *You'd* find it dreffly° dull to hear me talk about Geoffrey the whole blessed day!   210

LADY JOHN Well, till luncheon, my dear, [(*a glance at the clock*)] you mustn't mind if I—(*To Lord John, as she goes to writing-table*) Miss Levering wasn't only tired last night, she was ill.

LORD JOHN I thought she looked very white.

JEAN Who is Miss—You don't mean to say there are other people?   215

LADY JOHN One or two. Your uncle's responsible for asking that old cynic, St John Greatorex, and I—

JEAN (*gravely*) Mr Greatorex—he's a Radical, isn't he?

LORD JOHN (*laughing*) *Jean!* Beginning to 'think in parties'!°

LADY JOHN It's very natural now that she should—   220

JEAN I only meant it was odd he should be here. Naturally at my grand-father's—

LORD JOHN It's all right, my child. Of course we expect now that you'll begin to think like Geoffrey Stonor, and to feel like Geoffrey Stonor, and to talk like Geoffrey Stonor. And quite proper too.   225

JEAN (*smiling*) Well, if I do think with my husband and feel with him—as, of course, I shall°—it will surprise me if I ever find myself talking a tenth as well—(*Following her uncle to the French window*) You should have heard him at Dutfield°—(*Stopping short, delighted*) Oh! The Freddy Tunbridges. What? Not Aunt Lydia! Oh-h! (*Looking back*   230
reproachfully at Lady John, who makes a discreet motion 'I couldn't help it')
> *Enter the Tunbridges. Mr Freddy, of no profession and of*
> *independent means. Well-groomed, pleasant-looking; of few*
> *words. A 'nice man' who likes 'nice women', and has married one*
> *of them. Mrs Freddy is thirty. An attractive figure, delicate face,*
> *intelligent grey eyes, over-sensitive mouth, and naturally curling*
> *dust-coloured hair*

MRS FREDDY What a delightful surprise!

JEAN (*shaking hands warmly*) I'm so glad. How d'ye do, Mr Freddy?
> *Enter Lady John's sister, Mrs Heriot—smart, pompous, fifty—*
> *followed by Farnborough*

MRS HERIOT My dear Jean! My darling child!

JEAN How do you do, aunt?

MRS HERIOT (*sotto voce*) *I* wasn't surprised. I always prophesied—   235

JEAN Sh! *Please!*

FARNBOROUGH We haven't met since you were in short skirts. I'm Dick Farnborough.

JEAN Oh, I remember. (*They shake hands*)

MRS FREDDY (*looking round*) Not down yet—the Elusive One?   240

JEAN Who is the Elusive One?

MRS FREDDY Lady John's new friend.

LORD JOHN (*to Jean*) Oh, I forgot you hadn't seen Miss Levering; such a nice creature! (*to Mrs Freddy*)—don't you think?

MRS FREDDY Of course I do. You're lucky to get her to come so often.   245
She won't go to other people.

LADY JOHN She knows she can rest here.

FREDDY (*who has joined Lady John near the writing-table*) What does she do to tire her?

LADY JOHN She's been helping my sister and me with a scheme of ours.   250
MRS HERIOT She certainly knows how to inveigle money out of the men.
LADY JOHN It would sound less equivocal, Lydia, if you added that the money is to build baths in our Shelter for Homeless Women.
MRS FREDDY Homeless women?   255
LADY JOHN Yes, in the most insanitary part of Soho.
FREDDY Oh—a—really.
FARNBOROUGH It doesn't sound quite in Miss Levering's line!
LADY JOHN My dear boy, you know as little about what's in a woman's line as most men.   260
FREDDY (*laughing*) Oh, I say!
LORD JOHN (*indulgently to Mr Freddy and Farnborough*) Philanthropy in a woman like Miss Levering is a form of restlessness. But she's a *nice* creature; all she needs is to get some 'nice' fella to marry her.
MRS FREDDY (*laughing as she hangs on her husband's arm*) Yes, a woman   265
needs a balance wheel°—if only to keep her from flying back to town on a hot day like this.
LORD JOHN Who's proposing anything so—
MRS FREDDY The Elusive One.
LORD JOHN Not Miss—   270
MRS FREDDY Yes, before luncheon!
       Exit Farnborough to garden
LADY JOHN She must be in London by this afternoon, she says.
LORD JOHN What for in the name of—
LADY JOHN Well, *that* I didn't ask her. But (*consults watch*) I think I'll just go up and see if she's changed her plans. (*Exit Lady John*)   275
LORD JOHN Oh, she must be *made* to. Such a nice creature! All she needs—
       Voices outside. Enter fussily, talking and gesticulating, St John Greatorex, followed by Miss Levering and Farnborough. Greatorex is sixty, wealthy, a county magnate, and Liberal M.P. He is square, thick-set, square-bearded. His shining bald pate has two strands of coal-black hair trained across his crown from left ear to right and securely pasted there. He has small, twinkling eyes and a reputation for telling good stories after dinner when ladies have left the room. He is carrying a little book for Miss Levering. She (parasol over shoulder), an attractive, essentially feminine, and rather 'smart' woman of thirty-two, with a somewhat foreign grace; the kind of whom men and women alike say, 'What's her story? Why doesn't she marry?'°

GREATOREX I protest! Good Lord! what are the women of this country coming to? I *protest* against Miss Levering being carried off to discuss anything so revolting. Bless my soul! what can a woman like you *know* 280 about it?

MISS LEVERING (*smiling*) Little enough. Good morning.

GREATOREX (*relieved*) I should think so indeed!

LORD JOHN (*aside*) You aren't serious about going—

GREATOREX (*waggishly breaking in*) We were so happy out there in the 285 summer-house, weren't we?

MISS LEVERING Ideally.

GREATOREX And to be haled out to talk about Public *Sanitation* forsooth! (*Hurries after Miss Levering as she advances to speak to the Freddys, etc.*) Why, God bless my soul, do you realise that's *drains?* 290

MISS LEVERING I'm dreadfully afraid it is! (*Holds out her hand for the small book Greatorex is carrying*)

> Greatorex returns Miss Levering's book open; he has been keeping
> the place with his finger. She opens it and shuts her handkerchief in

GREATOREX And we in the act of discussing Italian literature! Perhaps you'll tell me that isn't a more savoury topic for a lady.

MISS LEVERING But for the tramp population less conducive to savouriness, don't you think, than—baths? 295

GREATOREX No, I can't understand this morbid interest in vagrants. *You're* much too—leave it to the others.

JEAN What others?

GREATOREX (*with smiling impertinence*) Oh, the sort of woman who smells of indiarubber.° The typical English spinster. (*To Miss Lever-* 300 *ing*) *You* know—Italy's full of her. She never goes anywhere without a mackintosh and a collapsible bath—rubber. When you look at her, it's borne in upon you that she doesn't only smell of rubber. *She's* rubber too.

LORD JOHN (*laughing*) This is my niece, Miss Jean Dunbarton, Miss 305 Levering.

JEAN How do you do? (*They shake hands*)

GREATOREX (*to Jean*) I'm sure *you* agree with me.

JEAN About Miss Levering being too—

GREATOREX For that sort of thing—*much* too— 310

MISS LEVERING What a pity you've exhausted the more eloquent adjectives.

GREATOREX But I haven't!

MISS LEVERING Well, you can't say to me as you did to Mrs Freddy: 'You're too young and too happily married—and too—(*Glances* 315

round smiling at Mrs Freddy, who, oblivious, is laughing and talking to
her husband and Mrs Heriot)

JEAN   For what was Mrs Freddy too happily married and all the rest?

MISS LEVERING (*lightly*) Mr Greatorex was repudiating the horrid
rumour that Mrs Freddy had been speaking in public; about
Women's Trade Unions°—wasn't that what you said, Mrs Heriot?

LORD JOHN (*chuckling*) Yes, it isn't made up as carefully as your aunt's   320
parties usually are. Here we've got Greatorex (*takes his arm*) who
hates political women, and we've got in that mild and inoffensive-
looking little lady—(*Motion over his shoulder towards Mrs Freddy*)

GREATOREX (*shrinking down stage in comic terror*) You don't mean she's
really—   325

JEAN (*simultaneously and gaily rising*) Oh, and you've got me!

LORD JOHN (*with genial affection*) My dear child, he doesn't hate the
charming wives and sweethearts who help to win seats.   ·

Jean makes her uncle a discreet little signal of warning

MISS LEVERING Mr Greatorex objects only to the unsexed creatures
who—a—   330

LORD JOHN (*hastily to cover up his slip*) Yes, yes, who want to act inde-
pendently of men.

MISS LEVERING Vote, and do silly things of that sort.

LORD JOHN (*with enthusiasm*) Exactly.

MRS HERIOT It will be a long time before we hear any more of *that* non-   335
sense.

JEAN You mean that rowdy scene in the House of Commons?°

MRS HERIOT Yes. No decent woman will be able to say 'Suffrage' without blushing for another generation, thank Heaven!

MISS LEVERING (*smiling*) Oh? I understood that so little I almost   340
imagined people were more stirred up about it than they'd ever been
before.

GREATOREX (*with a quizzical affectation of gallantry*) Not people like you.

MISS LEVERING (*teasingly*) How do you know?

GREATOREX (*with a start*) God bless my soul!   345

LORD JOHN She's saying that only to get a rise out of you.

GREATOREX Ah, yes, your frocks aren't serious enough.

MISS LEVERING I'm told it's an exploded notion that the Suffrage
women are all dowdy and dull.

GREATOREX Don't you believe it!   350

MISS LEVERING Well, of course we know you've been an authority on
the subject for—let's see, how many years is it you've kept the House
in roars whenever Woman's Rights are mentioned?

GREATOREX (*flattered but not entirely comfortable*) Oh, as long as I've
known anything about politics there have been a few discontented   355
old maids and hungry widows—

MISS LEVERING 'A few'! That's really rather forbearing of you, Mr
Greatorex. I'm afraid the number of the discontented and the hungry
was 96,000—among the mill operatives alone. (*Hastily*) At least the
papers said so, didn't they?°   360

GREATOREX Oh, don't ask me; that kind of woman doesn't interest me,
I'm afraid. Only I am able to point out to the people who lose their
heads and seem inclined to treat the phenomenon seriously that
there's absolutely nothing new in it. There have been women for the
last forty years who haven't had anything more pressing to do than   365
petition Parliament.

MISS LEVERING (*reflectively*) And that's as far as they've got.

LORD JOHN (*turning on his heel*) It's as far as they'll ever get. (*Meets the
group up R coming down*)

MISS LEVERING (*chaffing Greatorex*) Let me see, wasn't a deputation
sent to you not long ago? (*Sits C*)   370

GREATOREX H'm! (*Irritably*) Yes, yes.

MISS LEVERING (*as though she has just recalled the circumstances*) Oh, yes,
I remember. I thought at the time, in my modest way, it was nothing
short of heroic of them to go asking audience of their arch opponent.

GREATOREX (*stoutly*) It didn't come off.   375

MISS LEVERING (*innocently*) Oh! I thought they insisted on bearding
the lion in his den.

GREATOREX Of course I wasn't going to be bothered with a lot of—

MISS LEVERING You don't mean you refused to go out and face them!

GREATOREX (*with a comic look of terror*) I wouldn't have done it for   380
worlds. But a friend of mine went and had a look at 'em.

MISS LEVERING (*smiling*) Well, did he get back alive?

GREATOREX Yes, but he advised me not to go. 'You're quite right', he
said. 'Don't you think of bothering', he said. 'I've looked over the
lot', he said, 'and there isn't a week-ender° among 'em'.   385

JEAN (*gaily precipitates herself into the conversation*) You remember Mrs
Freddy's friend who came to tea here in the winter? (*To Greatorex*)
He was a member of Parliament too—quite a little young one—he
said women would never be respected till they had the vote!

> Greatorex snorts, the other men smile and all the women except
> Mrs Heriot

MRS HERIOT (*sniffing*) I remember telling him that he was too young to   390
know what he was talking about.

147

LORD JOHN Yes, I'm afraid you all sat on the poor gentleman.

LADY JOHN (*entering*) Oh, *there* you are! [I hope you slept.] (*Greets Miss Levering*)

JEAN It was such fun. He was flat as a pancake when we'd done with him. Aunt Ellen told him with her most distinguished air she didn't want to be 'respected'.   395

MRS FREDDY (*with a little laugh of remonstrance*) My *dear* Lady John!

FARNBOROUGH Quite right! Awful idea to think you're *respected!*

MISS LEVERING (*smiling*) Simply revolting.

[LORD JOHN (*contentedly*) I'm afraid the new-fangled seed fell on   400
barren ground in my old-fashioned garden (*with a bow*) pace° Mrs Freddy.

JEAN° (*gaily to Miss Levering*) Poor little man. And he thought he was being so agreeable.

MISS LEVERING Instead of which it was you.   405

JEAN Me?

MISS LEVERING (*caustic but smiling*) You had the satisfaction of knowing you'd made yourself popular with all the other men.

JEAN I hope you don't think I did it for that reason.]

LADY JOHN (*at writing-table*) Now, you frivolous people, go away.   410
We've only got a few minutes to talk over the terms of the late Mr Soper's° munificence before the carriage comes for Miss Levering—

MRS FREDDY (*to Farnborough*) Did you know she'd got that old horror to give Lady John £8,000 for her charity before he died?

FREDDY° Who got him to?   415

LADY JOHN Miss Levering. He wouldn't do it for me, but she brought him round.

FREDDY Yes. Bah-ee Jove!° I expect so.

MRS FREDDY (*turning enthusiastically to her husband*) Isn't she wonderful?   420

LORD JOHN (*aside*) Nice creature. All she needs is—°
> *Mr and Mrs Freddy and Farnborough stroll off to the garden.*
> *Lady John on far side of the writing-table. Mrs Heriot at the top.*
> *Jean and Lord John, L*

GREATOREX (*on divan C, aside to Miss Levering*) Too 'wonderful' to waste your time on the wrong people.

MISS LEVERING I shall waste less of my time after this.

GREATOREX I'm relieved to hear it. I can't see you wheedling money for   425
shelters and rot of that sort out of retired grocers.

MISS LEVERING You see, you call it rot. We couldn't have got £8,000 out of *you.*

GREATOREX (*very low*) I'm not sure.
        Miss Levering looks at him
GREATOREX If I gave you that much—for your little projects—what   430
        would you give me?
MISS LEVERING (*speaking quietly*) Soper didn't ask that.°
GREATOREX (*horrified*) Soper! I should think not!
LORD JOHN (*turning to Miss Levering*) Soper? You two still talking
        Soper? How flattered the old beggar'd be! (*Lower*) Did you hear what   435
        Mrs Heriot said about him? 'So kind; so munificent—so *vulgar*, poor
        soul, we couldn't know him in London—*but we shall meet him in
        heaven.*'
        Greatorex and Lord John go off laughing
LADY JOHN (*to Miss Levering*) Sit over there, my dear. (*Indicating chair
        in front of writing-table*) You needn't stay, Jean. This won't interest   440
        you.
MISS LEVERING (*in the tone of one agreeing*) It's only an effort to meet
        the greatest evil in the world?
JEAN (*pausing as she's following the others*) What do you call the greatest
        evil in the world?   445
        Looks pass between Mrs Heriot and Lady John
MISS LEVERING (*without emphasis*) The helplessness of women.
        Jean stands still
LADY JOHN (*rising and putting her arm about the girl's shoulder*) Jean, dar-
        ling, I know you can think of nothing but (*aside*) him—so just go and—
JEAN (*brightly*) Indeed, indeed, I can think of everything better than I
        ever did before. He has lit up everything for me—made everything   450
        vivider, more—more significant.
MISS LEVERING (*turning round*) Who has?
JEAN Oh, yes, I don't care about other things less but a thousand times
        more.
LADY JOHN You *are* in love.   455
MISS LEVERING Oh, that's it! (*Smiling at Jean*) I congratulate you.
LADY JOHN (*returning to the outspread plan*) Well—*this*, you see, obvi-
        ates the difficulty you raised.
MISS LEVERING Yes, quite.
MRS HERIOT But it's going to cost a great deal more.   460
MISS LEVERING It's worth it.
MRS HERIOT We'll have nothing left for the organ at St Pilgrim's.
LADY JOHN My dear Lydia, we're putting the organ aside.
MRS HERIOT (*with asperity*) We can't afford to 'put aside' the elevating
        effect of music.   465

LADY JOHN What we must make for, first, is the cheap and humanely conducted lodging-house.

MRS HERIOT There are several of those already, but poor St Pilgrim's—

MISS LEVERING There are none for the poorest women. 470

LADY JOHN No, even the excellent Soper was for multiplying Rowton Houses.° You can never get men to realise—you can't always get women—

MISS LEVERING It's the work least able to wait.

MRS HERIOT I don't agree with you, and I happen to have spent a great 475
deal of my life in works of charity.

MISS LEVERING Ah, then you'll be interested in the girl I saw dying in a Tramp Ward° a little while ago. *Glad* her cough was worse—only she mustn't die before her father. Two reasons. Nobody but her to keep the old man out of the workhouse—and 'father is so proud'. If 480
she died first, he would starve; worst of all he might hear what had happened up in London to his girl.

MISS HERIOT She didn't say, I suppose, how she happened to fall so low.

MISS LEVERING Yes, she had been in service. She lost the train back one Sunday night and was too terrified of her employer to dare ring 485
him up after hours. The wrong person found her crying on the platform.°

MRS HERIOT She should have gone to one of the Friendly Societies.°

MISS LEVERING At eleven at night?

MRS HERIOT And there are the Rescue Leagues.° I myself have been 490
connected with one for twenty years—

MISS LEVERING (*reflectively*) 'Twenty years'! Always arriving 'after the train's gone'—after the girl and the Wrong Person have got to the journey's end.

Mrs Heriot's eyes flash

JEAN Where is she now? 495

LADY JOHN Never mind.

MISS LEVERING Two nights ago she was waiting at a street corner in the rain.

MRS HERIOT Near a public-house, I suppose.

MISS LEVERING Yes, a sort of 'public-house'. She was plainly dying— 500
she was told she shouldn't be out in the rain. 'I mustn't go in yet', she said. '*This* is what he gave me', and she began to cry. In her hand were two pennies silvered over to look like half-crowns.

MRS HERIOT I don't believe that story. It's just the sort of thing some sensation-monger trumps up—now, who tells you such— 505

MISS LEVERING Several credible people. I didn't believe them till—

JEAN Till—?

MISS LEVERING Till last week I saw for myself.

LADY JOHN *Saw?* Where?

MISS LEVERING In a low lodging-house not a hundred yards from the   510
church you want a new organ for.

MRS HERIOT How did *you* happen to be there?

MISS LEVERING I was on a pilgrimage.

JEAN A pilgrimage?

MISS LEVERING Into the Underworld.°   515

LADY JOHN *You* went?

JEAN How *could* you?

MISS LEVERING I put on an old gown and a tawdry hat—(*Turns to Lady
John*) You'll never know how many things are hidden from a woman
in good clothes. The bold, free look of a man at a woman he believes   520
to be destitute—you must *feel* that look on you before you can understand—a good half of history.

MRS HERIOT (*rises*) Jean!—°

JEAN But where did you go—dressed like that?

MISS LEVERING Down among the homeless women—on a wet night   525
looking for shelter.

LADY JOHN (*hastily*) No wonder you've been ill.

JEAN (*under breath*) And it's like that?

MISS LEVERING No.

JEAN No?   530

MISS LEVERING It's so much worse I dare not tell about it—even if you
weren't here I couldn't.

MRS HERIOT (*to Jean*) You needn't suppose, darling, that those
wretched creatures feel it as we would.

MISS LEVERING The girls who need shelter and work aren't all serving-   535
maids.

MRS HERIOT (*with an involuntary flash*) We know that all the women
who—*make mistakes* aren't.

MISS LEVERING (*steadily*) That is why *every* woman ought to take an
interest in this—every girl too.   540

JEAN
LADY JOHN } (*simultaneously*) { Yes—oh, yes!
No. This is a matter for us older—

MRS HERIOT (*with an air of sly challenge*) Or for a person who has some
special knowledge. (*Significantly*) *We* can't pretend to have access to
such sources of information as Miss Levering.   545

MISS LEVERING (*meeting Mrs Heriot's eye steadily*) Yes, for I can give you access. As you seem to think, I have some first-hand knowledge about homeless girls.

LADY JOHN (*cheerfully turning it aside*) Well, my dear, it will all come in convenient. (*Tapping the plan*) 550

MISS LEVERING It once happened to me to take offence at an ugly thing that was going on under my father's roof. Oh, *years* ago! I was an impulsive girl. I turned my back on my father's house—°

LADY JOHN (*for Jean's benefit*) That was ill-advised.

MRS HERIOT Of course, if a girl does *that*— 555

MISS LEVERING That was what all my relations said (*with a glance at Jean*), and I couldn't explain.

JEAN Not to your mother?

MISS LEVERING She was dead. I went to London to a small hotel and tried to find employment. I wandered about all day and every day 560 from agency to agency. I was supposed to be educated. I'd been brought up partly in Paris; I could play several instruments, and sing little songs in four different tongues. (*Slight pause*)

JEAN Did nobody want you to teach French or sing the little songs?

MISS LEVERING The heads of schools thought me too young. There 565 were people ready to listen to my singing, but the terms—they were too hard. Soon my money was gone. I began to pawn my trinkets. *They* went.

JEAN And still no work?

MISS LEVERING No; but by that time I had some real education—an 570 unpaid hotel bill, and not a shilling in the world. (*Slight pause*) Some girls think it hardship to have to earn their living. The horror is not to be allowed to—

JEAN (*bending forward*) What happened?

LADY JOHN (*rises*) My dear (*to Miss Levering*), have your things been 575 sent down? Are you quite ready?

MISS LEVERING Yes, all but my hat.

JEAN Well?

MISS LEVERING Well, by chance I met a friend of my family.

JEAN That was lucky. 580

MISS LEVERING I thought so. He was nearly ten years older than I. He said he wanted to help me. (*Pause*)

JEAN And didn't he?

Lady John lays her hand on Miss Levering's shoulder

MISS LEVERING Perhaps after all he did. (*With sudden change of tone*) Why do I waste time over myself? I belonged to the little class of 585 armed women. My body wasn't born weak, and my spirit wasn't broken by the *habit* of slavery. But, as Mrs Heriot was kind enough to hint, I do know something about the possible fate of homeless girls. I found there were pleasant parks, museums, free libraries in our great rich London—and not one single place where destitute women can be sure of work that isn't killing or food that isn't worse than prison fare. That's why women ought not to sleep o' nights till this Shelter stands spreading out wide arms.

JEAN No, no—

MRS HERIOT (*gathering up her gloves, fan, prayerbook, &c.*) Even when it's built—you'll see! Many of those creatures will prefer the life they lead. They *like* it.

MISS LEVERING A woman told me—one of the sort that knows—told me many of them 'like it' so much that they are indifferent to the risk of being sent to prison. '*It gives them a rest*', she said.

LADY JOHN A rest!

> *Miss Levering glances at the clock as she rises to go upstairs. Lady John and Mrs Heriot bend their heads over the plan, covertly talking*

JEAN (*intercepting Miss Levering*) I want to begin to understand something of—I'm horribly ignorant.

MISS LEVERING (*looks at her searchingly*) I'm a rather busy person—

JEAN (*interrupting*) I have a quite special reason for wanting *not* to be ignorant. (*Impulsively*) I'll go to town tomorrow, if you'll come and lunch with me.

MISS LEVERING Thank you—I (*catches Mrs Heriot's eye*)—I must go and put my hat on. (*Exit upstairs*)

MRS HERIOT (*aside*) How little she minds [talking about] all these horrors!

LADY JOHN They turn me cold. Ugh! (*Rising, harassed*) I wonder if she's signed the visitors' book!

MRS HERIOT For all her Shelter schemes, she's a hard woman.

JEAN Miss Levering is?

MRS HERIOT Oh, of course *you* won't think so. She has angled very adroitly for your sympathy.

JEAN She doesn't look hard.

LADY JOHN (*glancing at Jean and taking alarm*) I'm not sure but what she does. Her mouth—always like this . . . as if she were holding back something by main force!

MRS HERIOT (*half under her breath*) Well, so she is.°

> *Exit Lady John into the lobby to look at the visitors' book*

JEAN Why haven't I seen her before?

153

MRS HERIOT Oh, she's lived abroad. (*Debating with herself*) You don't
    know about her, I suppose?   625

JEAN I don't know how Aunt Ellen came to know her.

MRS HERIOT That was my doing. But I didn't bargain for her being
    introduced to you.

JEAN She seems to go everywhere. And why shouldn't she?

MRS HERIOT (*quickly*) You mustn't ask her to Eaton Square.°   630

JEAN I have.

MRS HERIOT Then you'll have to get out of it.

JEAN (*with a stubborn look*) I must have a reason. And a very good
    reason.

MRS HERIOT Well, it's not a thing I should have preferred to tell you,   635
    but I know how difficult you are to guide . . . so I suppose you'll have
    to know. (*Lowering her voice*) It was ten or twelve years ago. I found
    her horribly ill in a lonely Welsh farmhouse. We had taken the Manor
    for that August. The farmer's wife was frightened, and begged me to
    go and see what I thought. I soon saw how it was—I thought she was   640
    dying.

JEAN *Dying!* What was the—

MRS HERIOT I got no more out of her than the farmer's wife did. She
    had had no letters. There had been no one to see her except a man
    down from London, a shady-looking doctor—nameless, of course.   645
    And then this result. The farmer and his wife, highly respectable
    people, were incensed. They were for turning the girl out.°

JEAN *Oh!* but—

MRS HERIOT Yes. Pitiless some of these people are! I insisted they
    should treat the girl humanely, and we became friends . . . that is,   650
    'sort of'. In spite of all I did for her—

JEAN What did you do?

MRS HERIOT I—I've told you, and I lent her money. No small sum
    either.

JEAN Has she never paid it back?   655

MRS HERIOT Oh, yes, after a time. But I *always* kept her secret—as
    much as I knew of it.

JEAN But you've been telling me!

MRS HERIOT That was my duty—and I *never* had her full confidence.

JEAN Wasn't it natural she—   660

MRS HERIOT Well, all things considered, she might have wanted to tell
    me who was responsible.

JEAN Oh! Aunt Lydia!

MRS HERIOT All she ever said was that she was ashamed—(*losing her*

temper and her fine feeling for the innocence of her auditor)—ashamed 665
that she 'hadn't had the courage to resist'—not the original temptation but the pressure brought to bear on her 'not to go through with
it', as she said.

JEAN (*wrinkling her brows*) You are being so delicate—I'm not sure I
understand.° 670

MRS HERIOT (*irritably*) The only thing you need understand is that
she's not a desirable companion for a young girl.

 Pause

JEAN When did you see her after—after—

MRS HERIOT (*with a slight grimace*) I met her last winter at the Bishop's.
(*Hurriedly*) She's a connection of his wife's. They'd got her to help 675
with some of their work. Then she took hold of ours. Your aunt and
uncle are quite foolish about her, and I'm debarred from taking any
steps, at least till the Shelter is out of hand.

JEAN I do rather wonder she can bring herself to talk about—the unfortunate women of the world. 680

MRS HERIOT The effrontery of it!

JEAN Or . . . the courage! (*Puts her hand up to her throat as if the sentence
had caught there*)

MRS HERIOT Even presumes to set *me* right! Of course I don't *mind* in
the least, poor soul . . . but I feel I owe it to your dead mother to tell
you about her, especially as you're old enough now to know some- 685
thing about life—

JEAN (*slowly*)—and since a girl needn't be very old to suffer for her
ignorance. (*Moves a little away*) I *felt* she was rather wonderful.

MRS HERIOT *Wonderful!*

JEAN (*pausing*) . . . To have lived through *that* when she was . . . how 690
old?

MRS HERIOT (*rising*) Oh, nineteen or thereabouts.

JEAN Five years younger than I. To be abandoned and to come out of it
like this!

MRS HERIOT (*laying her hand on the girl's shoulder*) It was too bad to have 695
to tell you such a sordid story today of all days.

JEAN It is a very terrible story, but this wasn't a bad time. I feel very
sorry today for women who aren't happy. (*Motor horn heard faintly.
Jumping up*) That's Geoffrey!

MRS HERIOT Mr Stonor! What makes you think . . .? 700

JEAN Yes, yes. I'm sure, I'm sure—(*Checks herself as she is flying off.
Turns and sees Lord John entering from the garden. Motor horn louder°*)

LORD JOHN Who do you think is motoring up the drive?

JEAN (*catching hold of him*) Oh, dear! how am I ever going to be able to
behave like a girl who isn't engaged to the only man in the world
worth marrying? 705

MRS HERIOT You were expecting Mr Stonor all the time!

JEAN He promised he'd come to luncheon if it was humanly possible;
but I was afraid to tell you for fear he'd be prevented.

LORD JOHN (*laughing as he crosses to the lobby*) You felt we couldn't have
borne the disappointment. 710

JEAN I felt I couldn't.

> *The lobby door opens. Lady John appears radiant, followed by a
> tall figure in a dustcoat,° &c., no goggles. He has straight, firm
> features, a little blunt; fair skin, high-coloured; fine, straight
> hair, very fair; grey eyes, set somewhat prominently and heavy
> when not interested; lips full, but firmly moulded. Geoffrey
> Stonor is heavier than a man of forty should be, but otherwise in
> the pink of physical condition. The Footman stands waiting to
> help him off with his motor coat*

LADY JOHN Here's an agreeable surprise!

> *Jean has gone forward only a step, and stands smiling at the
> approaching figure*

LORD JOHN How do you do? (*As he comes between them and briskly
shakes hands with Stonor*)

> *Farnborough appears at the French window*

FARNBOROUGH Yes, by Jove! (*Turning to the others clustered round the
window*) What gigantic luck! 715

> *Those outside crane and glance, and then elaborately turn their
> backs and pretend to be talking among themselves, but betray as far
> as manners permit the enormous sensation the arrival has created*

STONOR How do you do?

> *Shakes hands with Mrs Heriot, who has rushed up to him with
> both hers outstretched. He crosses to Jean, who meets him half
> way; they shake hands, smiling into each other's eyes*

JEAN Such a long time since we met!

LORD JOHN (*to Stonor, [observing the group half in half out of the French
window]*) You're growing very enterprising. I could hardly believe
my ears when I heard you'd motored all the way from town to see a
supporter on Sunday. 720

STONOR I don't know how we covered the ground in the old days. (*To
Lady John*) It's no use to stand for your borough any more. The
American, you know, he 'runs' for Congress. By and by we shall all be
flying after the thing we want. (*Smiles at Jean*)

JEAN Sh! (*Smiles and then glances over her shoulder and speaks low*) All   725
sorts of irrelevant people here.

FARNBOROUGH (*unable to resist the temptation, comes forward*) How do
you do, Mr Stonor?

STONOR Oh—how d'you do.

FARNBOROUGH Some of them were arguing in the smoking-room   730
last night whether it didn't hurt a man's chances going about in a
motor.

LORD JOHN Yes, we've been hearing a lot of stories about the unpopu-
larity of motor-cars—among the class that hasn't got 'em, of course.
What do you say?   735

LADY JOHN I'm sure you gain more votes by being able to reach so
many more of your constituency than we used—

STONOR Well, I don't know—I've sometimes wondered whether the
charm of our presence wasn't counterbalanced by the way we tear
about smothering our fellow-beings in dust and running down their   740
pigs and chickens, not to speak of their children.

LORD JOHN (*anxiously*) What on the whole are the prospects?
        Farnborough cranes forward

STONOR (*gravely*) We shall have to work harder than we realised.

FARNBOROUGH Ah! (*Retires towards group*)

JEAN (*in a half-aside as she slips her arm in her uncle's and smiles at Geoffrey*) He says he believes I'll be able to make a real difference to his   745
chances. Isn't it angelic of him?

STONOR (*in a jocular tone*) Angelic? Machiavellian. I pin all my hopes
on your being able to counteract the pernicious influence of my
opponent's glib wife.

JEAN You want me to have a *real* share in it all, don't you, Geoffrey?   750

STONOR (*smiling into her eyes*) Of course I do.
        *Farnborough drops down again on pretence of talking to Mrs
        Heriot*

[LADY JOHN (*to Stonor*) As to the seat, you and I must have a good talk
after luncheon.°]

LORD JOHN I don't gather you're altogether sanguine. Any complica-
tion?   755
        *Jean and Lady John stand close together C, the girl radiant,
        following Stonor with her eyes and whispering to the sympathetic
        elder woman*

STONOR Well (*taking Sunday paper out of pocket*), there's this agitation
about the Woman Question. Oddly enough, it seems likely to affect
the issue.

LORD JOHN Why should it? Can't you do what the other four hundred have done?   760

STONOR (*laughs*) Easily. But, you see, the mere fact that four hundred and twenty members have been worried into promising support— and then once in the House have let the matter severely alone—

LORD JOHN (*to Stonor*) Let it alone! Bless my soul, I should think so indeed.   765

STONOR Of course. Only it's a device that's somewhat worn.

> *Enter Miss Levering, with hat on; gloves and veil in her hand*

LORD JOHN Still if they think they're getting a future Cabinet Minister on their side—

STONOR . . . it will be sufficiently embarrassing for the Cabinet Minister.   770

> *Stonor turns to speak to Jean. Stops dead seeing Miss Levering*

JEAN (*smiling*) You know one another?°

MISS LEVERING (*looking at Stonor with intentness but quite calmly*) Everybody in this part of the world knows Mr Stonor, but he doesn't know me.

LORD JOHN Miss Levering.

> *They bow. Enter Greatorex, sidling in with an air of giving Mrs Freddy a wide berth*

JEAN (*to Miss Levering with artless enthusiasm*) Oh, have you been hear-   775
ing him speak?

MISS LEVERING Yes, I was visiting some relations near Dutfield. They took me to hear you.

STONOR Oh—the night the Suffragettes made their customary row.

MISS LEVERING The night they asked you—   780

STONOR (*flying at the first chance of distraction, shakes hands with Mrs Freddy*) Well, Mrs Freddy, what do you think of your friends now?

MRS FREDDY My friends?

STONOR (*offering her the Sunday paper*) Yes, the disorderly women.

MRS FREDDY (*with dignity*) They are not my friends, but I don't think you must call them—   785

STONOR Why not? (*Laughs*) I can forgive them for worrying the late Government. But they *are* disorderly.

MISS LEVERING (*quietly*) Isn't the phrase consecrated to a different class?

GREATOREX (*who has got hold of the Sunday paper*) He's perfectly right.   790
How do you do? Disorderly women! That's what they are!

FARNBOROUGH (*reading over his shoulder*) Ought to be locked up! every one of 'em.

GREATOREX (*assenting angrily*) Public nuisances! Going about with dog
whips and spitting in policemen's faces.°   795

MRS FREDDY (*with a harassed air*) I wonder if they did spit?

GREATOREX (*exulting*) Of *course* they did.

MRS FREDDY (*turns on him*) You're no authority on what they do. *You*
run away.

GREATOREX (*trying to turn the laugh*) Run away? Yes. (*Backing a few*   800
paces) And if ever I muster up courage to come back, it will be to vote
for better manners in public life, not worse than we have already.

MRS FREDDY (*meekly*) So should I. Don't think that *I* defend the Suffragette methods.

JEAN (*with cheerful curiosity*) Still you *are* an advocate of the Suffrage, 805
aren't you?

MRS FREDDY Here? (*Shrugs*) I don't beat the air.

GREATOREX (*mocking*) Only policemen.

MRS FREDDY (*plaintively*) If you cared to know the attitude of the real
workers in the reform, you might have noticed in any paper last week   810
we lost no time in dissociating ourselves from the little group of° hysterical—(*Catches her husband's eye, and instantly checks her flow of words*)

MRS HERIOT They have lowered the whole sex in the eyes of the entire
world.

JEAN (*joining Geoffrey Stonor*) I can't quite see what they want—those   815
Suffragettes.

GREATOREX Notoriety.

FARNBOROUGH What they want? A good thrashin'—that's what I'd
give 'em.

MISS LEVERING (*murmurs*) Spirited fellow!   820

LORD JOHN Well, there's one sure thing—they've dished their goose.
(*Greatorex chuckles, still reading the account*) I believe these silly
scenes are a pure joy to you.

GREATOREX Final death-blow to the whole silly business!

JEAN (*mystified, looking from one to the other*) The Suffragettes don't   825
seem to *know* they're dead.

GREATOREX They still keep up a sort of death-rattle. But they've done
for themselves.

JEAN (*clasping her hands with fervour*) Oh, I hope they'll last till the
election's over.   830

FARNBOROUGH (*stares*) Why?

JEAN Oh, we want them to get the working man to—(*stumbling and a*
little confused)—to vote for . . . the Conservative candidate. Isn't that
so? (*Looking round for help. General laughter*)

LORD JOHN Fancy, Jean—!   835

GREATOREX The working man's a good deal of an ass, but even he
    won't listen to—

JEAN (*again appealing to the silent Stonor*) But he *does* listen like any-
    thing! I asked why there were so few at the Long Mitcham meeting,
    and I was told, 'Oh, they've all gone to hear Miss—'   840

STONOR Just for a lark, that was.

LORD JOHN It has no real effect on the vote.

GREATOREX Not the smallest.

JEAN (*wide-eyed, to Stonor*) Why, I thought you said—

STONOR (*hastily, rubbing his hand over the lower part of his face and speak-
    ing quickly*) I've a notion a little soap and water wouldn't do me any 845
    harm.

LORD JOHN I'll take you up. You know Freddy Tunbridge.
        Stonor pauses to shake hands. Exeunt all three

JEAN (*perplexed, as Stonor turns away, says to Greatorex*) Well, if women
    are of no importance in politics, it isn't for the reason you gave. There
    is now and then a week-ender among them.   850

GREATOREX (*shuffles about uneasily*) Hm—Hm. (*Finds himself near Mrs
    Freddy*) Lord! The perils that beset the feet of man! (*With an air of
    comic caution, moves away, L*)

JEAN (*to Farnborough, aside, laughing*) Why does he behave like that?

FARNBOROUGH His moral sense is shocked.

JEAN Why, I saw him and Mrs Freddy together at the French Play the   855
    other night—as thick as thieves.

MISS LEVERING Ah, that was before he knew her revolting views.

JEAN What revolting views?

GREATOREX Sh! Sunday.° (*As Greatorex sidles cautiously further away*)

JEAN (*laughing in spite of herself*) I can't believe women are so helpless 860
    when I see men so afraid of them.

GREATOREX The great mistake was in teaching them to read and write.

JEAN (*over Miss Levering's shoulder, whispers*) *Say* something.

MISS LEVERING (*to Greatorex, smiling*) Oh no, that wasn't the worst
    mistake.   865

GREATOREX Yes, it was.

MISS LEVERING No. Believe me. The mistake was in letting women
    learn to talk.

GREATOREX *Ah!* (*Wheels about with sudden rapture*) I see now what's to
    be the next great reform.   870

MISS LEVERING (*holding up the little volume*) When women are all
    dumb, no more discussions of the 'Paradiso'.°

GREATOREX (*with a gesture of mock rapture*) The thing itself!° (*Aside*)
That's a great deal better than talking about it, as I'm sure *you* know.

MISS LEVERING Why do you think I know?   875

GREATOREX Only the plain women are in any doubt.

> *Jean joins Miss Levering*

GREATOREX Wait for me, Farnborough. I cannot go about unpro-
tected.

> *Exeunt Farnborough and Greatorex*

MRS FREDDY It's true what that old cynic says. The scene in the House
has put back the reform a generation.   880

JEAN [It must have been awfully exciting.] I wish I'd been there.

MRS FREDDY I *was*.

JEAN Oh, was it like the papers said?

MRS FREDDY Worse. I've never been so moved in public. No tragedy,
no great opera ever gripped an audience as the situation in the House   885
did that night. There we all sat breathless—with everything more
favourable to us than it had been within the memory of women.
Another five minutes and the Resolution would have passed. Then
. . . all in a moment—

LADY JOHN (*to Mrs Heriot*) Listen—they're talking about the female   890
hooligans.

MRS HERIOT No, thank you! (*Sits apart with the 'Church Times'°*)

MRS FREDDY (*excitedly*) All in a moment a horrible dingy little flag was
poked through the grille of the Woman's Gallery—cries—insults—
scuffling—the police—the ignominious turning out of the women—   895
us as well as the—Oh, I can't *think* of it without—(*Jumps up and
walks to and fro. Pauses*) Then the next morning! The people gloating.
Our friends antagonised—people who were wavering—nearly won
over—all thrown back—heart-breaking! Even my husband!
Freddy's been an angel about letting me take my share when I felt I   900
must—but of course I've always known he doesn't really like it. It
makes him shy. I'm sure it gives him a horrid twist inside when he
sees my name among the speakers on the placards.° But he's always
been an angel about it before this. After the disgraceful scene he said,
'It just shows how unfit women are for any sort of coherent thinking   905
or concerted action'.

JEAN To think that it should be women who've given the Cause the
worst blow it ever had!

MRS FREDDY The work of forty years destroyed in five minutes!

JEAN They must have felt pretty sick when they woke up the next   910
morning—the Suffragettes.

MRS FREDDY I don't waste any sympathy on *them*. I'm thinking of the
penalty *all* women have to pay because a handful of° hysterical—

JEAN Still I think I'm sorry for them. It must be dreadful to find you've
done such a lot of harm to the thing you care most about in the world.   915

MISS LEVERING Do you picture the Suffragettes sitting in sackcloth?°

MRS FREDDY Well, they can't help realising *now* what they've done.

MISS LEVERING (*quietly*) Isn't it just possible they realise they've
woken up interest in the Woman Question so that it's advertised in
every paper and discussed in every house from Land's End to John   920
o'Groats?° Don't you think *they* know there's been more said and
written about it in these ten days since the scene, than in the ten years
before it?

MRS FREDDY You aren't saying you think it was a good way to get what
they wanted?   925

MISS LEVERING (*shrugs*) I'm only pointing out that it seems not such a
bad way to get it known they *do* want something—and (*smiling*) 'want
it bad'.

JEAN (*getting up*) Didn't Mr Greatorex say women had been politely
petitioning Parliament for forty years?   930

MISS LEVERING And men have only laughed.

JEAN But they'd come round. (*She looks from one to the other*) Mrs Tunbridge says, before that horrid scene, everything was favourable at
last.

MISS LEVERING At last? Hadn't it been just as 'favourable' before?   935

MRS FREDDY No. We'd never had so many members pledged to our
side.

MISS LEVERING I thought I'd heard somebody say the Bill had got as
far as that, time and time again.

JEAN Oh no. Surely not—   940

MRS FREDDY (*reluctantly*) Y-yes. This [last thing] was only a Resolution. The Bill° passed a second reading thirty-seven years ago.

JEAN (*with wide eyes*) And what difference did it make?

MISS LEVERING The men laughed rather louder.

MRS FREDDY Oh, it's got as far as a second reading several times—but   945
we never had so many friends in the House before—

MISS LEVERING (*with a faint smile*) 'Friends'!

JEAN Why do you say it like that?

MISS LEVERING Perhaps because I was thinking of a funny story—he
said it was funny—a Liberal Whip told me the other day. A Radical   950
Member went out of the House after his speech in favour of the
Woman's Bill, and as he came back half an hour later, he heard some

Members talking in the Lobby about the astonishing number who were going to vote for the measure. And the Friend of Woman dropped his jaw and clutched the man next him: 'My God!' he said, 955 'you don't mean to say they're going to give it to them!'

JEAN Oh!

MRS FREDDY You don't think all men in Parliament are like that!

MISS LEVERING I don't think all men are burglars, but I lock my doors.

JEAN (*below her breath*) You think that night of the scene—you think 960 the men didn't *mean* to play fair?

MISS LEVERING (*her coolness in contrast to the excitement of the others*) Didn't the women sit quiet till ten minutes to closing time?

JEAN Ten minutes to settle a question like that!

MISS LEVERING (*quietly to Mrs Freddy*) Couldn't you see the men were at their old game? 965

LADY JOHN (*coming forward*) You think they were just putting off the issue till it was too late?

MISS LEVERING (*in a detached tone*) *I* wasn't there, but I haven't heard anybody deny that the women waited till ten minutes to eleven. Then they discovered the policeman who'd been sent up at the psycho- 970 logical moment to the back of the gallery. Then, I'm told, when the women saw they were betrayed once more, they utilised the few minutes left, to impress on the country at large the fact of their demands—did it in the only way left them. (*Sits leaning forward reflectively smiling, chin in hand*) It does rather look to the outsider as 975 if the well-behaved women had worked for forty years and made less impression on the world than those fiery young women made in five minutes.

MRS FREDDY Oh, come, be fair!

MISS LEVERING Well, you must admit that, next day, every newspaper 980 reader in Europe and America knew there were women in England in such dead earnest about the Suffrage that the men had stopped laughing at last, and turned them out of the House. Men even adver- tised how little they appreciated the fun by sending the women to gaol in pretty sober earnest. And all the world was talking about it. 985

Mrs Heriot lays down the 'Church Times' and joins the others

LADY JOHN I have noticed, whenever the men aren't there, the women sit and discuss that scene.

JEAN (*cheerfully*) *I* shan't have to wait till the men are gone. (*Leans over Lady John's shoulder and says half aside*) He's in sympathy.

LADY JOHN How do you know? 990

JEAN He told the interrupting women so.

163

Mrs Freddy looks mystified. The others smile

LADY JOHN Oh!

*Mr Freddy and Lord John appear by the door they went out of.
They stop to talk*

MRS FREDDY Here's Freddy! (*Lower, hastily to Miss Levering*) You're
judging from the outside. Those of us who have been working for
years . . . we all realise it was a perfectly lunatic proceeding. Why,   995
think! The only chance of our getting what we want is by *winning over*
the men. (*Her watchful eye, leaving her husband for a moment, catches
Miss Levering's little involuntary gesture*) What's the matter?

MISS LEVERING 'Winning over the men' has been the woman's way for
centuries.° Do you think the result should make us proud of our   1000
policy? Yes? Then go and walk in Piccadilly at midnight.° (*The older
women glance at Jean*) No, I forgot—

MRS HERIOT (*with majesty*) Yes, it's not the first time you've forgotten.

MISS LEVERING I forgot the magistrate's ruling. He said no decent
woman had any business to be in London's main thoroughfare at   1005
night unless she has *a man with her*. I heard that in Nine Elms,° too.
'You're obliged to take up with a chap!' was what the woman said.

MRS HERIOT (*rising*) JEAN! Come!

*She takes Jean by her arm and draws her to the window, where
she signals Greatorex and Farnborough. Mrs Freddy joins her
husband and Lord John*

LADY JOHN (*kindly, aside to Miss Levering*) My dear, I think Lydia
Heriot's right. We oughtn't to do anything or *say* anything to encour-   1010
age this ferment of feminism, and I'll tell you why: it's likely to bring
a very terrible thing in its train.

MISS LEVERING What terrible thing?

LADY JOHN Sex antagonism.

MISS LEVERING (*rising*) It's here.   1015

LADY JOHN (*very gravely*) Don't say that.

*Jean has quietly disengaged herself from Mrs Heriot, and the
group at the window returns and stands behind Lady John, looking up into Miss Levering's face*

MISS LEVERING (*to Lady John*) You're so conscious it's here, you're
afraid to have it mentioned.

LADY JOHN (*turning and seeing Jean. Rising hastily*) If it's here, it is the
fault of those women agitators.   1020

MISS LEVERING (*gently*) No woman *begins* that way. (*Leans forward
with clasped hands looking into vacancy*) Every woman's in a state of
natural subjection (*smiles at Jean*)—no, I'd rather say allegiance to

her idea of romance and her hope of motherhood. They're embodied
for her in man. They're the strongest things in life—till man kills
them. (*Rousing herself and looking into Lady John's face*) Let's be fair.
Each woman knows why that allegiance died.

> *Lady John turns hastily, sees Lord John coming down with Mr*
> *Freddy and meets them at the foot of the stairs. Miss Levering has*
> *turned to the table looking for her gloves, &c., among the papers;*
> *unconsciously drops the handkerchief she had in her little book*

JEAN (*in a low voice to Miss Levering*) All this talk against the wicked
Suffragettes—it makes me want to go and hear what they've got to
say for themselves.

MISS LEVERING (*smiling with a non-committal air as she finds the veil she's
been searching for*) Well, they're holding a meeting in Trafalgar
Square at three o'clock.

JEAN This afternoon? But that's no use to people out of town—Unless
I could invent some excuse . . .

LORD JOHN (*benevolently*) Still talking over the Shelter plans?

MISS LEVERING No. We left the Shelter some time ago.

LORD JOHN (*to Jean*) Then what's all the chatterment about?

> *Jean, a little confused, looks at Miss Levering*

MISS LEVERING The latest thing in veils. (*Ties hers round her hat*)

GREATOREX The invincible frivolity of woman!

LORD JOHN (*genially*) Don't scold them. It's a very proper topic.

MISS LEVERING (*whimsically*) Oh, I was afraid you'd despise us for it.

BOTH MEN (*with condescension*) Not at all—not at all.

JEAN (*to Miss Levering as Footman appears*) Oh, they're coming for you.
Don't forget your book. (*Footman holds out a salver with a telegram on
it for Jean*) Why, it's for me!

MISS LEVERING But it's time I was—(*Crosses to table*)

JEAN (*opening the telegram*) May I? (*Reads, and glances over the paper at
Miss Levering*) I've got your book. (*Crosses to Miss Levering, and, looking at the back of the volume*) Dante! Whereabouts are you? (*Opening
at the marker*) Oh, the 'Inferno'.

MISS LEVERING No; I'm in a worse place.

JEAN I didn't know there was a worse.

MISS LEVERING Yes; it's worse with the Vigliacchi.

JEAN I forget. Were they Guelf or Ghibelline?°

MISS LEVERING (*smiling*) They weren't either, and that was why Dante
couldn't stand them. (*More gravely*) He said there was no place in
Heaven nor in Purgatory—not even a corner in Hell—for the souls
who had stood aloof from strife. (*Looking steadily into the girl's eyes*)

He called them 'wretches who never lived', Dante did, because they'd never felt the pangs of partisanship.° And so they wander homeless on the skirts of limbo among the abortions° and off-scourings of Creation. 1060

JEAN (*a long breath after a long look. When Miss Levering has turned away to make her leisurely adieux Jean's eyes fall on the open telegram*) Aunt Ellen, I've got to go to London.

>   *Stonor, re-entering, hears this, but pretends to talk to Mr Freddy,*
>   *&c*

LADY JOHN My dear child! 1065

MRS HERIOT Nonsense! Is your grandfather worse?

JEAN (*folding the telegram*) No-o. I don't think so. But it's necessary I should go, all the same.

MRS HERIOT Go away when Mr Stonor—

JEAN He said he'd have to leave directly after luncheon. 1070

LADY JOHN I'll just see Miss Levering off, and then I'll come back and talk about it.

LORD JOHN (*to Miss Levering*) Why are you saying goodbye as if you were never coming back?

MISS LEVERING (*smiling*) One never knows. Maybe I shan't come back. 1075
(*To Stonor*) Goodbye.

>   *Stonor bows ceremoniously. The others go up laughing. Stonor*
>   *comes down*

JEAN (*impulsively*) There mayn't be another train! Miss Levering—

STONOR (*standing in front of her*) What if there isn't? I'll take you back in the motor.

JEAN (*rapturously*) Will you? (*Inadvertently drops the telegram*) I must be 1080
there by three!

STONOR (*picks up the telegram and a handkerchief lying near, glances at the message*) Why, it's only an invitation to dine—Wednesday!

JEAN Sh! (*Takes the telegram and puts it in her pocket*)

STONOR Oh, I see! (*Lower, smiling*) It's rather dear of you to arrange our going off like that. You *are* a clever little girl! 1085

JEAN It's not that I was arranging. I want to hear those women in Trafalgar Square—the Suffragettes.

STONOR (*incredulous, but smiling*) How perfectly absurd! (*Looking after Lady John*) Besides, I expect she wouldn't like my carrying you off like that. 1090

JEAN Then she'll have to make an excuse and come too.

STONOR Ah, it wouldn't be quite the same—

JEAN (*rapidly thinking it out*) We could get back here in time for dinner.

Geoffrey Stonor glances down at the handkerchief still in his
hand, and turns it half mechanically from corner to corner

JEAN (*absent-mindedly*) Mine?

STONOR (*hastily, without reflection*) No. (*Hands it to Miss Levering as she*   1095
passes) Yours.

Miss Levering, on her way to the lobby with Lord John seems not
to notice

JEAN (*takes the handkerchief to give to her, glancing down at the embroi-*
dered corner; stops) But that's not an L! It's Vi—!

Geoffrey Stonor suddenly turns his back and takes up the news-
paper

LADY JOHN (*from the lobby*) Come, Vida, since you will go.

MISS LEVERING Yes; I'm coming. (*Exit Miss Levering*)

JEAN *I* didn't know her name was Vida; how did you?°   1100

Stonor stares silently over the top of his paper

CURTAIN

2

SCENE° *The north side of the Nelson Column in Trafalgar Square. The Curtain rises on an uproar. The crowd, which momentarily° increases, is composed chiefly of weedy youths and wastrel old men. There are a few decent artisans; three or four 'beery' out-o'-works; three or four young women of the domestic servant or Strand restaurant cashier class; one aged woman in rusty black peering with faded, wondering eyes, consulting the faces of the men and laughing nervously and apologetically from time to time; one or two quiet-looking, business-like women, thirty to forty; two middle-class men, who stare and whisper and smile. A quiet old man with a lot of unsold Sunday papers under one arm stands in an attitude of rapt attention, with the free hand round his deaf ear. A brisk-looking woman of forty-five or so, wearing pince-nez, goes round with a pile of propagandist literature on her arm. Many of the men smoking cigarettes—the old ones pipes. On the outskirts of this crowd, of several hundred, a couple of smart men in tall shining hats hover a few moments, single eyeglass up, and then saunter off. Against the middle of the Column, where it rises above the stone platform, is a great red banner, one support-ing pole upheld by a grimy sandwichman, the other by a small, dirty boy of eight. If practicable only the lower portion of the ban-ner need be seen, bearing the final words of the legend—*

'VOTES FOR WOMEN!'

in immense white letters. It will be well to get, to the full, the effect of the height above the crowd of the straggling group of speakers on the pedestal platform. These are, as the Curtain rises, a working-class woman who is waving her arms and talking very earnestly, her voice for the moment blurred in the uproar. She is dressed in brown serge and looks pinched and sallow. At her side is the Chairman urging that she be given a fair hearing. Allen Trent is a tall, slim, brown-haired man of twenty-eight, with a slight stoop, an agreeable aspect, well-bred voice, and the gleaming brown eye of the visionary. Behind these two, looking on or talk-ing among themselves, are several other carelessly dressed women; one, better turned out than the rest, is quite young, very slight and

*gracefully built, with round, very pink cheeks, full, scarlet lips,
naturally waving brown hair, and an air of childish gravity. She
looks at the unruly mob with imperturbable calm. The Chairman's voice is drowned*

WORKING WOMAN (*with lean, brown finger out and voice raised shriller
now above the tumult*) I've got boys o' me own and we laugh at all sorts
o' things, but I should be ashymed and so would they if ever they was
to be'yve as you're doin' tod'y.° (*In laughter the noise dies*) People 'ave
been sayin' this is a middle-class woman's movement. It's a libel. I'm
a workin' woman myself, the wife of a working man. (*Voice: 'Pore   5
devil!'*) I'm a Poor Law Guardian° and a—

NOISY YOUNG MAN Think of that, now—gracious me!° (*Laughter and
interruption*)

OLD NEWSVENDOR (*to the noisy young man near him*) Oh, shut up,
cawn't yer?

NOISY YOUNG MAN Not fur *you!*   10

VOICE Go 'ome and darn yer old man's stockens!

VOICE Just clean yer *own* doorstep!°

WORKING WOMAN It's a pore sort of 'ousekeeper that leaves 'er
doorstep till Sunday afternoon. Maybe that's when you would do
your doorstep. I do mine in the mornin' before you men are awake.   15

OLD NEWSVENDOR It's true, wot she says!—every word.

WORKING WOMAN You say we women 'ave got no business servin' on
boards and thinkin' about politics. Wot's *politics?* (*A derisive roar*)
It's just 'ousekeepin' on a big scyle. 'Oo among you workin' men 'as
the most comfortable 'omes? Those of you that gives yer wives yer   20
wyges. (*Loud laughter and jeers*)

VOICES That's it! Wantin' our money. Lord 'Igh 'Ousekeeper of England.

WORKING WOMAN If it wus only to use fur *our* comfort, d'ye think
many o' you workin' men would be found turnin' over their wyges to   25
their wives? No! Wot's the reason thousands do—and the best and
the soberest? Because the workin' man knows that wot's a pound to
'im is twenty shillin's to 'is wife. And she'll myke every penny in
every one o' them shillin's *tell*. She gets more fur 'im out of 'is wyges
than wot 'e can! Some o' you know wot the 'omes is like w'ere the men   30
don't let the women manage. Well, the Poor Laws and the 'ole Government is just in the syme muddle because the men 'ave tried to do
the national 'ousekeepin' without the women. (*Roars*) But, like I told
you before, it's a libel to say it's only the well-off women wot's wantin' the vote. Wot about the 96,000 textile workers? Wot about the   35

Yorkshire tailoresses? I can tell you wot plenty o' the poor women think about it. I'm one of them, and I can tell you we see there's reforms needed. *We ought to 'ave the vote* (*jeers*), and we know 'ow to appreciate the other women 'oo go to prison° fur tryin' to get it fur us!

> *With a little final bob of emphasis and a glance over shoulder at the old woman and the young one behind her, she seems about to retire, but pauses as the murmur in the crowd grows into distinct phrases.° 'They get their 'air cut free',° 'Naow they don't, that's only us!', 'Silly Suffragettes!', 'Stop at 'ome!', ''Inderin' police-men—mykin' rows in the streets!'*

VOICE (*louder than the others*) They sees yer ain't fit t'ave—   40

OTHER VOICES 'Ha, ha!' 'Shut up!' 'Keep quiet, cawn't yer?' (*General uproar*)

CHAIRMAN You evidently don't know what had to be done by *men* before the extension of the Suffrage in '67. If it hadn't been for demonstrations of violence—(*His voice is drowned*)

WORKING WOMAN (*coming forward again, her shrill note rising clear*)   45
You s'y woman's plyce is 'ome! Don't you know there's a third of the women o' this country can't afford the luxury of stayin' in their 'omes? They *got* to go out and 'elp make money to p'y the rent and keep the 'ome from bein' sold up. Then there's all the women that 'aven't got even miseerable 'omes. They 'aven't got any 'omes *at all*.   50

NOISY YOUNG MAN You said *you* got one. W'y don't you stop in it?

WORKING WOMAN Yes, that's like a man. If one o' you is all right, he thinks the rest don't matter. We women—

NOISY YOUNG MAN The lydies! God bless 'em! (*Voices drown her and the Chairman*)

OLD NEWSVENDOR (*to Noisy Young Man*) Oh, take that extra 'alf pint   55
'ome and *sleep it off!*

WORKING WOMAN P'r'aps *your* 'omes are all right. P'r'aps you aren't livin', old and young, married and single, in one room. I come from a plyce where many fam'lies 'ave to live like that if they're to go on livin' *at all*. If you don't believe me, come and let me show you! (*She   60
spreads out her lean arms*) Come with me to Canning Town!—come with me to Bromley—come to Poplar and to Bow!° No. You won't even *think* about the overworked women and the underfed children and the 'ovels they live in. And you want that we shouldn't think neither—   65

A VAGRANT We'll do the thinkin'. You go 'ome and nuss the byby.

WORKING WOMAN I do nurse my byby! I've nursed seven. What 'ave you done for yours? P'r'aps your children never goes 'ungry, and

maybe you're satisfied—though I must say I wouldn't a' thought it
from the *look* o' you.   70

VOICE Oh, I s'y!

WORKING WOMAN But we women are not satisfied. We don't only
want better things for our own children. We want better things for
all. *Every* child is our child. We know in our 'earts we oughtn't to rest
till we've mothered 'em every one.   75

VOICE 'Women'—'children'—wot about the *men*? Are *they* all 'appy?
(*Derisive laughter and 'No! no!', 'Not precisely', "Appy? Lord!"*)

WORKING WOMAN No, there's lots o' you men I'm sorry for (*Shrill
Voice: 'Thanks awfully!'*), an' we'll 'elp you if you let us.

VOICE 'Elp us? You tyke the bread out of our mouths. You women are
black-leggin' the men!°   80

WORKING WOMAN *W'y* does any woman tyke less wyges than a man
for the same work? Only because we can't get anything better. That's
part the reason w'y we're yere tod'y. Do you reely think we tyke them
there low wyges because we got a *lykin'* for low wyges? No. We're just
like you. We want as much as ever we can get. (*"Ear! 'Ear!" and   85
laughter*) We got a gryte deal to do with our wyges, we women has.
We got the children to think about. And w'en we get our rights, a
woman's flesh and blood won't be so much cheaper than a man's that
employers can get rich on keepin' you out o' work, and sweatin' us. If
you men only could see it, we got the *syme* cause, and if you 'elped us   90
you'd be 'elpin yerselves.

VOICES 'Rot!', 'Drivel!'

OLD NEWSVENDOR True as gospel!

> *She retires against the banner with the others. There is some
> applause*

A MAN (*patronisingly*) Well, now, that wusn't so bad—fur a woman.

ANOTHER N-naw. *Not fur a woman.*   95

CHAIRMAN (*speaking through this last*) Miss Ernestine Blunt will now
address you.

> *Applause, chiefly ironic, laughter, a general moving closer and
> knitting up of attention. Ernestine Blunt is about twenty-four, but
> looks younger. She is very downright, not to say pugnacious—the
> something amusing and attractive about her is there, as it were,
> against her will, and the more fetching for that. She has no con-
> ventional gestures, and none of any sort at first. As she warms to
> her work she uses her slim hands to enforce her emphasis, but as
> though unconsciously. Her manner of speech is less monotonous
> than that of the average woman-speaker, but she, too, has a*

> *fashion of leaning all her weight on the end of the sentence. She*
> *brings out the final word or two with an effort of underscoring, and*
> *makes a forward motion of the slim body as if the better to drive*
> *the last nail in. She evidently means to be immensely practical—*
> *the kind who is pleased to think she hasn't a grain of sentimental-*
> *ity in her composition, and whose feeling, when it does all but*
> *master her, communicates itself magnetically to others*

MISS ERNESTINE BLUNT Perhaps I'd better begin by explaining a little
about our 'tactics'. (*Cries of 'Tactics! We know!', 'Mykin' trouble!',*
'Public scandal!') To make you understand what we've done, I must   100
remind you of what others have done. Perhaps you don't know that
women first petitioned Parliament for the Franchise as long ago as
1866.

VOICE How do *you* know?

> *She pauses a moment, taken off her guard by the suddenness of the*
> *attack*

VOICE You wasn't there!   105

VOICE That was the trouble. Haw! haw!

MISS ERNESTINE BLUNT And the petition was presented—

VOICE Give 'er a 'earin' now she 'as got out of 'er crydle.

MISS ERNESTINE BLUNT —presented to the House of Commons by
that great Liberal, John Stuart Mill.° (*Voice: 'Mill? Who is he when*   110
he's at home?°) Bills or Resolutions have been before the House on
and off for the last thirty-six years. That, roughly, is our history. We
found ourselves, towards the close of the year 1905,° with no assurance that if we went on in the same way any girl born into the world
in this generation° would live to exercise the rights of citizenship,   115
though she lived to be a hundred. So we said all this has been in vain.
We must try some other way. How did the working man get the Suffrage, we asked ourselves? Well, we turned up the records, and we
saw—

VOICES 'Not by scratching people's faces!', 'Disraeli give it 'em!',   120
'Dizzy? Get out!', 'Cahnty Cahncil scholarships!', 'Oh, Lord, this
education!', 'Chartist riots, she's thinkin' of!'° (*Noise in the*
crowd)

MISS ERNESTINE BLUNT But we don't *want* to follow such a violent
example. We would much rather *not*—but if that's the only way we
can make the country see we're in earnest, we are prepared to show   125
them.

VOICE An' they'll show you!—Give you another month 'ard.°

MISS ERNESTINE BLUNT Don't think that going to prison has any fears

for us. We'd go *for life* if by doing that we could get freedom for the
rest of the women.   130

VOICES 'Hear, hear!', 'Rot!', 'W'y don't the men 'elp ye to get your
rights?'

MISS ERNESTINE BLUNT Here's some one asking why the men don't
help. It's partly they don't understand yet—they *will* before
we've done! (*Laughter*) Partly they don't understand yet what's at   135
stake—

RESPECTABLE OLD MAN (*chuckling*) Lord, they're a 'educatin' of us!

VOICE Wot next?

MISS ERNESTINE BLUNT —and partly that the bravest man is afraid of
ridicule. Oh, yes; we've heard a great deal all our lives about the   140
timidity and the sensitiveness of women. And it's true. We *are* sensitive. But I tell you, ridicule crumples a man up. It steels a woman.
[(*A motor horn is heard*)] We've come to know the value of ridicule.
We've educated ourselves so that we welcome ridicule. We owe our
sincerest thanks to the comic writers. The cartoonist is our uncon-   145
scious friend. Who cartoons people who are of no importance? What
advertisement is so sure of being remembered?

POETIC YOUNG MAN I admit that.°

MISS ERNESTINE BLUNT If we didn't know it by any other sign, the
comic papers would tell us *we've arrived!* But our greatest debt of   150
gratitude we owe, to the man who called us female hooligans. (*The
crowd bursts into laughter*) We aren't hooligans, but we hope the fact
will be overlooked. If everybody said we were nice, well-behaved
women, who'd come to hear us? *Not the men.* (*Roars*) Men tell us it
isn't womanly for us to care about politics. How do they know what's   155
womanly? It's for women to decide that. Let the men attend to being
manly. It will take them all their time.

VOICE Are we down-'earted? Oh no!

MISS ERNESTINE BLUNT And they say it would be dreadful if we got
the vote, because then we'd be pitted against men in the economic   160
struggle. But that's come about already. Do you know that out of
every hundred women in this country eighty-two are wage-earning
women? It used to be thought unfeminine for women to be students
and to aspire to the arts—that bring fame and fortune. But nobody
has ever said it was unfeminine for women to do the heavy drudgery   165
that's badly paid. That kind of work had to be done by *some*body—
and the men didn't hanker after it. Oh, no. (*Laughter and interruption*)

A MAN ON THE OUTER FRINGE She can *talk*—the little one can.

ANOTHER Oh, they can all 'talk'.

A BEERY, DIRTY FELLOW OF FIFTY I wouldn't like to be 'er 'usban'.   170
   Think o' comin' 'ome to *that!*

HIS PAL I'd soon learn 'er!

MISS ERNESTINE BLUNT (*speaking through the noise*) Oh, no! *Let* the
   women scrub and cook and wash. That's all right! But if they want to
   try their hand at the better paid work of the liberal professions—oh,   175
   very unfeminine indeed! Then there's another thing. Now I want
   you to listen to this, because it's *very* important. Men say if we persist
   in competing with them for the bigger prizes, they're dreadfully
   afraid we'd lose the beautiful protecting chivalry that—Yes, I don't
   wonder you laugh. *We* laugh. (*Bending forward with lit eyes*) But the   180
   women I found at the Ferry Tin Works working for five shillings a
   week—I didn't see them laughing. The beautiful chivalry of the
   employers of women doesn't prevent them from paying women ten-
   pence a day for sorting coal and loading and unloading carts—
   doesn't prevent them from forcing women to earn bread in ways   185
   worse still. So we won't talk about chivalry. It's being over-sarcastic.
   We'll just let this poor ghost of chivalry go—in exchange for a little
   plain justice.

VOICE If the House of Commons won't give you justice, why don't you
   go to the House of Lords?   190

MISS ERNESTINE BLUNT What?

VOICE Better 'urry up. Case of early closin'.° (*Laughter. A man at the
   back asks the speaker something*)

MISS ERNESTINE BLUNT (*unable to hear*) You'll be allowed to ask any
   question you like at the end of the meeting.

NEWCOMER (*boy of eighteen*) Oh, is it question time? I s'y, Miss, 'oo   195
   killed cock robin?°
            She is about to resume, but above the general noise the voice of a
            man at the back reaches her indistinct but insistent. She leans for-
            ward trying to catch what he says. While the indistinguishable
            murmur has been going on Geoffrey Stonor has appeared on the
            edge of the crowd, followed by Jean and Lady John in motor
            veils

JEAN (*pressing forward eagerly and raising her veil*) Is she one of them?
   That little thing!

STONOR (*doubtfully*) I—I suppose so.

JEAN Oh, ask some one, Geoffrey. I'm so disappointed. I did so hope   200
   we'd hear one of the—the worst.

MISS ERNESTINE BLUNT (*to the interrupter—on the other side*) What?
   What do you say? (*She screws up her eyes with the effort to hear, and puts*

a hand up to her ear. A few indistinguishable words between her and the man)

LADY JOHN (*who has been studying the figures on the platform through her lorgnon,° turns to a working man beside her*) Can you tell me, my man, which are the ones that—a—that make the disturbances?   205

WORKING MAN The one that's doing the talking—she's the disturbingest o' the lot.

JEAN (*craning to listen*) Not that nice little—

WORKING MAN Don't you be took in, Miss.

MISS ERNESTINE BLUNT Oh, yes—I see. There's a man over here   210
asking—

A YOUNG MAN *I've* got a question, too. Are—you—married?

ANOTHER (*sniggering*) Quick! There's yer chawnce. 'E's a bachelor.
(*Laughter*)

MISS ERNESTINE BLUNT (*goes straight on as if she had not heard*)—man
asking: if the women get full citizenship, and a war is declared, will   215
the women fight?

POETIC YOUNG MAN No, really—no, really, now! (*The Crowd: 'Haw!
Haw!', 'Yes!', 'Yes, how about that?'*)

MISS ERNESTINE BLUNT (*smiling*) Well, you know, some people say
the whole trouble about us is that we *do* fight. But it is only hard
necessity makes us do that. We don't *want* to fight—as men seem   220
to—just for fighting's sake. Women are for peace.

VOICE Hear, hear.

MISS ERNESTINE BLUNT And when we have a share in public affairs
there'll be less likelihood of war. But that's not to say women can't
fight. The Boer women did.° The Russian women face conflicts   225
worse than any battlefield can show.° (*Her voice shakes a little, and the
eyes fill, but she controls her emotion gallantly, and dashes on*) But we
women know all that is evil, and we're for peace. Our part—we're
proud to remember it—our part has been to go about after you men
in war-time, and—*pick up the pieces!* (*A great shout*) Yes—seems   230
funny, doesn't it? You men blow them to bits, and then we come
along and put them together again. If you know anything about military
nursing, you know a good deal of our work has been done in the
face of danger—*but it's always been done.*

OLD NEWSVENDOR That's so. That's so.   235

MISS ERNESTINE BLUNT You complain that more and more we're taking
away from you men the work that's always been yours. You can't
any longer keep women out of the industries. The only question is
upon what terms shall she continue to be in? As long as she's in on bad

terms, she's not only hurting herself—she's hurting you. But if   240
you're feeling discouraged about our competing with you, we're willing to leave you your trade in war. *Let* the men take life! We *give* life!
(*Her voice is once more moved and proud*) No one will pretend ours
isn't one of the dangerous trades either. I won't say any more to you
now, because we've got others to speak to you, and a new woman-   245
helper that I want you to hear. (*She retires to the sound of clapping.
There's a hurried consultation between her and the Chairman. Voices in
the Crowd: 'The little 'un's all right', 'Ernestine's a corker', etc.*)

JEAN (*looking at Stonor to see how he's taken it*) Well?

STONOR (*smiling down at her*) Well—

JEAN Nothing reprehensible in what *she* said, was there?

STONOR (*shrugs*) Oh, reprehensible!   250

JEAN It makes me rather miserable all the same.

STONOR (*draws her hand protectingly through his arm*) You mustn't take
it as much to heart as all that.

JEAN I can't help it—I can't indeed, Geoffrey. I shall *never* be able to
make a speech like that!   255

STONOR (*taken aback*) I hope not, indeed.

JEAN Why, I thought you said you wanted me—?

STONOR (*smiling*) To make nice little speeches with composure—so I
did!—So I—(*Seems to lose his thread as he looks at her*)

JEAN (*with a little frown*) You *said*—   260

STONOR That you have very pink cheeks? Well, I stick to that.

JEAN (*smiling*) Sh! Don't tell everybody.

STONOR And you're the only female creature I ever saw who didn't
look a fright in motor things.

JEAN (*melted and smiling*) I'm glad you don't think me a fright.   265

CHAIRMAN I will now ask (*name indistinguishable*) to address the
meeting.

JEAN (*as she sees Lady John moving to one side*) Oh, don't go yet, Aunt
Ellen!

LADY JOHN Go? Certainly not. I want to hear another. (*Craning her*   270
neck) I can't believe, you know, she was really one of the worst.

> *A big, sallow Cockney has come forward. His scanty hair grows in
> wisps on a great bony skull*

VOICE That's Pilcher.°

ANOTHER 'Oo's Pilcher?

ANOTHER If you can't afford a bottle of Tatcho,° w'y don't you get yer
'air cut.   275

MR PILCHER (*not in the least discomposed*) I've been addressin' a big meetin' at 'Ammersmith this morning, and w'en I told 'em I wus comin' 'ere this awfternoon to speak fur the women—well—then the usual thing began! (*An appreciative roar from the crowd*) In these times if you want peace and quiet at a public meetin'—(*The crowd fills in the hiatus with laughter*) There was a man at 'Ammersmith, too, talkin' about women's sphere bein' 'ome. 'Ome do you call it? You've got a kennel w'ere you can munch your tommy.° You've got a corner w'ere you can curl up fur a few hours till you go out to work again. No, my man, there's too many of you ain't able to *give* the women 'omes—fit to live in, too many of you in that fix fur you to go on jawin' at those o' the women 'oo want to myke the 'omes a little decenter.

VOICE If the vote ain't done us any good, 'ow'll it do the women any good?

MR PILCHER Look 'ere! Any men here belongin' to the Labour Party?° (*Shouts and applause*) Well, I don't need to tell these men the vote 'as done us *some* good. They know it. And it'll do us a lot more good w'en you know 'ow to use the power you got in your 'and.

VOICE Power! It's those fellers at the bottom o' the street° that's got the power.

MR PILCHER It's you, and men like you, that gave it to 'em. You carried the Liberals into Parliament Street on your own shoulders.° (*Complacent applause*) You believed all their fine words. You never asked yourselves, '*Wot's a Liberal, anyw'y?*'

A VOICE He's a jolly good fellow. (*Cheers and booing*)

MR PILCHER No, 'e ain't, or if 'e is jolly, it's only because 'e thinks you're such silly codfish you'll go swellin' his majority again. (*Laughter, in which Stonor joins*) It's enough to make any Liberal jolly to see sheep like you lookin' on, proud and 'appy, while you see° Liberal leaders desertin' Liberal principles. (*Voices in agreement and protest*) You show me a Liberal, and I'll show you a Mr Fycing-both-W'ys. Yuss. (*Stonor moves closer with an amused look*) 'E sheds the light of 'is warm and 'andsome smile on the working man, and round on the other side 'e's tippin' a wink to the great land-owners. That's to let 'em know 'e's standin' between them and the Socialists. Huh! Socialists. Yuss, *Socialists! (General laughter, in which Stonor joins)* The Liberal, 'e's the judicial sort o' chap that sits in the middle—

VOICE On the fence!

MR PILCHER Tories on one side—Socialists the other. Well it ain't always so comfortable in the middle. You're like to get squeezed. Now, I s'y to the women, the Conservatives don't promise you much but what they promise they *do!*

177

STONOR (*to Jean*) This fellow isn't half bad.

MR PILCHER The Liberals—they'll promise you the earth, and give
yer . . . the whole o' nothing. (*Roars of approval*)   320

JEAN *Isn't* it fun? Now, aren't you glad I brought you?

STONOR (*laughing*) This chap's rather amusing!

MR PILCHER We men 'ave seen it 'appen over and over. But the women
can tyke a 'int quicker'n what we can. They won't stand the nonsense
men do. Only they 'aven't got a fair chawnce even to agitate fur their   325
rights. As I wus comin' up 'ere I 'eard a man sayin', 'Look at this big
crowd. W'y, we're all *men!* If the women want the vote w'y ain't they
'ere to s'y so?' Well, I'll tell you w'y. It's because they've 'ad to get the
dinner fur you and me, and now they're washin' up the dishes.

A VOICE D'you think *we* ought to st'y 'ome and wash the dishes?   330

MR PILCHER (*laughs good-naturedly*) If they'd leave it to us once or
twice per'aps we'd understand a little more about the Woman Question. I know w'y *my* wife isn't here. It's because she *knows* I ain't
much use round the 'ouse, and she's 'opin' I can talk to some purpose.
Maybe she's mistaken. Any'ow, here I am to vote for her and all the   335
other women. ('*Hear! hear!*', '*Oh-h!*') And to tell you men what
improvements you can expect to see when women 'as the share in
public affairs they *ought* to 'ave!

VOICE What do you know about it? You can't even talk grammar.

MR PILCHER (*is dashed a fraction of a moment, for the first and only time*)
I'm not 'ere to talk grammar but to talk Reform. I ain't defendin' my   340
grammar—but I'll say in pawssing that if my mother 'ad 'ad 'er
rights, maybe my grammar would have been better.°

> *Stonor and Jean exchange smiles. He takes her arm again and*
> *bends his head to whisper something in her ear. She listens with*
> *lowered eyes and happy face. The discreet love-making goes on*
> *during the next few sentences. Interruption. One voice insistent*
> *but not clear. The speaker waits only a second and then resumes.*
> '*Yes, if the women*', *but he cannot instantly make himself heard.*
> *The boyish Chairman looks harassed and anxious. Miss Ernestine*
> *Blunt alert, watchful*

MR PILCHER Wait a bit—'arf a minute, my man!

VOICE 'Oo yer talkin' to? I ain't your man.

MR PILCHER Lucky for me!° There seems to be a *gentleman* 'ere who   345
doesn't think women ought to 'ave the vote.

VOICE *One?* Oh-h! (*Laughter*)

MR PILCHER Per'aps 'e doesn't know much about women? (*Indistinguishable repartee*) Oh, the gentleman says 'e's married. Well, then,

fur the syke of 'is wife we mustn't be too sorry 'e's 'ere. No doubt 350
she's s'ying: ''Eaven by prysed those women are mykin' a
Demonstrytion in Trafalgar Square, and I'll 'ave a little peace and
quiet at 'ome for one Sunday in my life'. (*The crowd laughs and there
are jeers for the interrupter—and at the speaker. Pointing*) Why, *you're*
like the man at 'Ammersmith this morning. 'E was awskin' me: ''Ow 355
would you like men to st'y at 'ome and do the fam'ly washin'?'
(*Laughter*) I told 'im I wouldn't advise it. I 'ave too much respect
fur—me clo'es.

VAGRANT It's their place—the women ought to do the washin'.

MR PILCHER I'm not sure you ain't right. For a good many o' you 360
fellas, from the look o' you—you cawn't even wash yerselves.
(*Laughter*)

VOICE (*threatening*) 'Oo are you talkin' to?

> *Chairman more anxious than before—movement in the crowd*

THREATENING VOICE Which of us d'you mean?

MR PILCHER (*coolly looking down*) Well, it takes about ten of your sort
to myke a man, so you may take it I mean the lot of you. 365

> *Angry indistinguishable retorts and the crowd sways. Miss Ernestine Blunt, who has been watching the fray with serious face, turns suddenly, catching sight of some one just arrived at the end of the platform. Miss Blunt goes R with alacrity, saying audibly to Pilcher as she passes, 'Here she is', and proceeds to offer her hand helping some one to get up the improvised steps. Laughter and interruption in the crowd*

LADY JOHN Now, there's another woman going to speak.

JEAN Oh, is she? Who? Which? I do hope she'll be one of the wild ones.

MR PILCHER (*speaking through this last. Glancing at the new arrival whose hat appears above the platform R*) That's all right, then. (*Turns to the left*) When I've attended to this microbe that's vitiating the air on my right—(*Laughter and interruptions from the crowd*) 370

STONOR (*staring R, one dazed instant, at the face of the new arrival, his own changes. Jean withdraws her arm from his and quite suddenly presses a shade nearer the platform. Stonor moves forward and takes her by the arm*) We're going now.

JEAN Not yet—oh, please not yet. (*Breathless, looking back*) Why I—I do believe—

STONOR (*to Lady John, with decision*) I'm going to take Jean out of this mob. Will you come? 375

LADY JOHN What? Oh yes, if you think—(*Another look through her glasses*) But isn't that—*surely* it's—!!!

> *Vida Levering comes forward R. She wears a long, plain, dark green dust-cloak. Stands talking to Ernestine Blunt and glancing a little apprehensively at the crowd*

JEAN Geoffrey!

STONOR (*trying to draw Jean away*) Lady John's tired—

JEAN But you don't see who it is, Geoffrey—! (*Looks into his face, and is arrested by the look she finds there*)   380

> *Lady John has pushed in front of them amazed, transfixed, with glass up. Geoffrey Stonor restrains a gesture of annoyance, and withdraws behind two big policemen. Jean from time to time turns to look at him with a face of perplexity*

MR PILCHER (*resuming through a fire of indistinct interruption*) I'll come down and attend to that microbe while a lady will say a few words to you (*raises his voice*)—if she can myke 'erself 'eard. (*Pilcher retires in the midst of booing and cheers*)

CHAIRMAN (*harassed and trying to create a diversion*) Some one suggests—and it's such a good idea I'd like you to listen to it—(*noise dies down*) that a clause shall be inserted in the next Suffrage Bill that shall expressly reserve to each Cabinet Minister, and to any respectable man, the power to prevent the Franchise being given to the female members of his family on his public declaration of their lack of sufficient intelligence to entitle them to vote.   385   390

VOICES Oh! oh!

CHAIRMAN Now, I ask you to listen, as quietly as you can, to a lady who is not accustomed to speaking—a—in Trafalgar Square—or a . . . as a matter of fact, at all.

VOICES 'A dumb lady', 'Hooray!', 'Three cheers for the dumb lady!'   395

CHAIRMAN A lady who, as I've said, will tell you, if you'll behave yourselves, her impressions° of the administration of police-court justice in this country.

> *Jean looks wondering at Stonor's sphinx-like face as Vida Levering comes to the edge of the platform*

MISS LEVERING Mr Chairman, men and women—

VOICES (*off*) Speak up.   400

> *She flushes, comes quite to the edge of the platform and raises her voice a little*

MISS LEVERING I just wanted to tell you that I was—I was—present in the police-court when the women were charged for creating a disturbance.

VOICE Y'oughtn't t' get mixed up in wot didn't concern you.

MISS LEVERING I—I—(*Stumbles and stops*)   405

> *Talking and laughing increases. 'Wot's 'er name?', 'Mrs or Miss?', 'Ain't seen this one before.'*

CHAIRMAN (*anxiously*) Now, see here, men; don't interrupt—

A GIRL (*shrilly*) I like this one's 'at. Ye can see she ain't one of 'em.

MISS LEVERING (*trying to recommence*) I—

VOICE They're a disgrace—them women be'ind yer.

A MAN WITH A FATHERLY AIR It's the w'y they goes on as mykes the   410
Government keep ye from gettin' yer rights.

CHAIRMAN (*losing his temper*) It's the way *you* go on that—

> *Noise increases. Chairman drowned, waves his arms and moves his lips. Miss Levering discouraged, turns and looks at Ernestine Blunt and pantomimes 'It's no good. I can't go on.' Ernestine Blunt comes forward, says a word to the Chairman, who ceases gyrating, and nods*

MISS ERNESTINE BLUNT (*facing the crowd*) Look here. If the Government withhold the vote because they don't like the way some of us ask for it—*let them give it to the Quiet Ones*. Does the Government want   415
to punish *all* women because they don't like the manners of a handful? Perhaps that's you men's notion of justice. It isn't women's.

VOICES Haw! haw!

MISS LEVERING Yes. Th-this is the first time I've ever 'gone on', as you call it, but they never gave me a vote.   420

MISS ERNESTINE BLUNT (*with energy*) No! And there are one—two—three—four women on this platform. Now, we all want the vote, as you know. Well, we'd agree to be disfranchised all our lives, if they'd give the vote to all the other women.

VOICE Look here, you made one speech, give the lady a chawnce.   425

MISS ERNESTINE BLUNT (*retires smiling*) That's *just* what I wanted *you* to [say]!°

MISS LEVERING Perhaps you—you don't know—you don't know—

VOICE (*sarcastic*) 'Ow're we goin' to know if you can't tell us?

MISS LEVERING (*flushing and smiling*) Thank you for that. We couldn't   430
have a better motto. How *are* you to know if we can't somehow manage to tell you? (*With a visible effort she goes on*) Well, I certainly didn't know before that the sergeants and policemen are instructed to deceive the people as to the time such cases are heard. You ask, and you're sent to Marlborough Police Court instead of to Marylebone.°   435

VOICE They ought ter sent yer to 'Olloway°—do y' good.

OLD NEWSVENDOR You go on, Miss, don't mind 'im.

VOICE Wot d'you expect from a pig but a grunt?

MISS LEVERING You're told the case will be at two o'clock, and it's

181

really called for eleven. Well, I took a great deal of trouble, and I 440
didn't believe what I was told—(*Warming a little to her task*) Yes,
that's almost the first thing we have to learn—to get over our touching faith that, because a man tells us something, it's true. I got to the
right court, and I was so anxious not to be late, I was too early.
The case before the Women's was just coming on. I heard a noise. At 445
the door I saw the helmets of two policemen, and I said to myself:
'What sort of crime shall I have to sit and hear about? Is this a burglar
coming along between the two big policemen, or will it be a mur-
derer? What sort of felon is to stand in the dock before the women
whose crime is they ask for the vote?' But, try as I would, I couldn't 450
see the prisoner. My heart misgave me. Is it a woman, I wondered?
Then the policemen got nearer, and I saw—(*she waits an instant*)—a
little, thin, half-starved boy. What do you think he was charged with?
Stealing. What had he been stealing—that small criminal? *Milk*. It
seemed to me as I sat there looking on, that the men who had the 455
affairs of the world in their hands from the beginning, and who've
made so poor a business of it—

VOICES Oh! oh! Pore benighted man! Are we down-'earted? *Oh*, no!

MISS LEVERING —so poor a business of it as to have the poor and
the unemployed in the condition they're in today—when your only 460
remedy for a starving child is to hale him off to the police-court—
because he had managed to get a little milk—well, I *did* wonder that
the men refuse to be helped with a problem they've so notoriously
failed at. I began to say to myself: 'Isn't it time the women lent a
hand?' 465

A VOICE Would you have women magistrates?
        She is stumped by the suddenness of the demand

VOICES Haw! Haw! Magistrates!

ANOTHER Women! Let 'em prove first they deserve—

A SHABBY ART STUDENT (*his hair longish, soft hat, and flowing tie*) They
study music by thousands; where's their Beethoven? Where's their 470
Plato? Where's the woman Shakespeare?

ANOTHER Yes—what 'a' they ever *done*?
        *The speaker clenches her hands, and is recovering her presence of
        mind, so that by the time the Chairman can make himself heard
        with, 'Now men, give this lady a fair hearing—don't interrupt'—
        she, with the slightest of gestures, waves him aside with a low 'It's
        all right'.*

MISS LEVERING (*steadying and raising her voice*) These questions are
quite proper! They are often asked elsewhere; and I would like to ask

in return: Since when was human society held to exist for its handful   475
of geniuses? How many Platos are there here in this crowd?

A VOICE (*very loud and shrill*) Divil a wan! (*Laughter*)

MISS LEVERING Not one. Yet that doesn't keep you men off the
register. How many Shakespeares are there in all England today?
Not one. Yet the State doesn't tumble to pieces. Railroads and   480
ships are built—homes are kept going, and babies are born. The
world goes on! (*bending over the crowd*) It goes on *by virtue of its common people*.

VOICES (*subdued*) Hear! hear!

MISS LEVERING I am not concerned that you should think we women
can paint great pictures, or compose immortal music, or write good   485
books. I am content that we should be classed with the common
people—who keep the world going. But (*straightening up and taking a
fresh start*), I'd like the world to go a great deal better. We were talking about justice. I have been inquiring into the kind of lodging the
poorest class of homeless women can get in this town of London. I   490
find that only the men of that class are provided for. Some measure to
establish Rowton Houses for women has been before the London
County Council°. They looked into the question 'very carefully', so
their apologists say. And what did they decide? They decided that
they could do nothing.   495

LADY JOHN (*having forced her way to Stonor's side*) Is that true?

STONOR (*speaking through Miss Levering's next words*) I don't know.

MISS LEVERING Why could that great, all-powerful body do nothing?
Because, if these cheap and decent houses were opened, they said, the
homeless women in the streets would make use of them! You'll think   500
I'm not in earnest. But that was actually the decision and the reason
given for it. Women that the bitter struggle for existence has forced
into a life of horror—

STONOR (*sternly to Lady John*) You think this is the kind of thing—
(*A motion of the head towards Jean*)

MISS LEVERING —the outcast women might take advantage of the   505
shelter these decent, cheap places offered. But the *men*, I said! Are all
who avail themselves of Lord Rowton's hostels, are *they* all angels?
Or does wrong-doing in a man not matter? Yet women are recom-
mended to depend on the chivalry of men.

> The two policemen, who at first had been strolling about, have
> stood during this scene in front of Geoffrey Stonor. They turn now
> and walk away, leaving Stonor exposed. He, embarrassed, moves
> uneasily, and Vida Levering's eye falls upon his big figure. He

still has the collar of his motor coat turned up to his ears. A change
passes over her face, and her nerve fails her an instant

MISS LEVERING Justice and chivalry!! (*she steadies her voice and hurries*   510
on)—they both remind me of what those of you who read the police-
court news—(I have begun only lately to do that)—but you've seen
the accounts of the girl who's been tried in Manchester lately for the
murder of her child. Not pleasant reading. Even if we'd noticed it, we
wouldn't speak of it in my world. A few months ago I should have   515
turned away my eyes and forgotten even the headline as quickly as I
could. But since that morning in the police-court, I read these things.
This, as you'll remember, was about a little working girl—an orphan
of eighteen—who crawled with the dead body of her new-born child
to her master's back-door, and left the baby there. She dragged her-   520
self a little way off and fainted. A few days later she found herself in
court, being tried for the murder of her child. Her master—a married
man—had of course reported the 'find' at his back-door to the police,
and he had been summoned to give evidence. The girl cried out to
him in the open court, 'You are the father!' He couldn't deny it. The   525
Coroner at the jury's request censured the man, and regretted that
the law didn't make him responsible. But he went scot-free. And that
girl is now serving her sentence in Strangeways Gaol.°

Murmuring and scraps of indistinguishable comment in the crowd,
through which only Jean's voice is clear

JEAN (*who has wormed her way to Stonor's side*) Why do you dislike her
so?   530

STONOR I? Why should you think—

JEAN (*with a vaguely frightened air*) I never saw you look as you did—as
you do.

CHAIRMAN Order, please—give the lady a fair—

MISS LEVERING (*signing to him 'It's all right'*) Men make boast that an   535
English citizen is tried by his peers. What woman is tried by hers?
(*A sombre passion strengthens her voice and hurries her on*) A woman is
arrested by a man, brought before a man judge, tried by a jury of men,
condemned by men, taken to prison by a man, and by a man she's
hanged! Where in all this were *her* 'peers'? Why did men so long ago°   540
insist on trial by 'a jury of their peers'? So that justice shouldn't mis-
carry—wasn't it? A man's peers would best understand his circumstances, his temptation, the degree of his guilt. Yet there's no such
unlikeness between different classes of men as exists between man
and woman. What man has the knowledge that makes him a fit judge   545
of woman's deeds at that time of anguish—that hour—(*lowers her*

voice and bends over the crowd)—that hour that some woman struggled through to put each man here into the world. I noticed when a
previous speaker quoted the Labour Party you applauded. Some of
you here—I gather—call yourselves Labour men. Every woman who   550
has borne a child is a Labour woman. No man among you can judge
what she goes through in her hour of darkness—

JEAN (*with frightened eyes on her lover's set, white face, whispers*)
Geoffrey—

MISS LEVERING (*catching her fluttering breath, goes on very low*)—in
that great agony when, even under the best conditions that money   555
and devotion can buy, many a woman falls into temporary mania, and
not a few go down to death. In the case of this poor little abandoned
working girl, what man can be the fit judge of her deeds in that awful
moment of half-crazed temptation? Women know of these things as
those know burning who have walked through fire. (*Stonor makes a*   560
motion towards Jean and she turns away fronting the audience. Her hands
go up to her throat as though she suffered a choking sensation. It is in her
face that she 'knows'. Miss Levering leans over the platform and speaks
with a low and thrilling earnestness) I would say in conclusion to the
women here, it's not enough to be sorry for these our unfortunate sisters. We must get the conditions of life made fairer. We women must
organise. We must learn to work together. We have all (rich and poor,
happy and unhappy) worked so long and so exclusively for *men*, we   565
hardly know how to work for one another. But we must learn. Those
who can, may give money—

VOICES (*grumbling*) Oh, yes—Money! Money!

MISS LEVERING Those who haven't pennies to give—even those
people aren't so poor they can't give some part of their labour—some   570
share of their sympathy and support. (*Turns to hear something the*
Chairman is whispering to her)

JEAN (*low to Lady John*) Oh, I'm glad I've got power!

LADY JOHN (*bewildered*) Power!—*you?*

JEAN Yes, all that money—
              Lady John tries to make her way to Stonor

MISS LEVERING (*suddenly turning from the Chairman to the crowd*) Oh,   575
yes, I hope you'll all join the Union.° Come up after the meeting and
give your names.

LOUD VOICE You won't get many men.

MISS LEVERING (*with fire*) Then it's to the women I appeal! (*She is*
about to retire when, with a sudden gleam in her lit eyes, she turns for the
last time to the crowd, silencing the general murmur and holding the

people by the sudden concentration of passion in her face) I don't mean to   580
say it wouldn't be better if men and women did this work together—
shoulder to shoulder.° But the mass of men won't have it so. I only
hope they'll realise in time the good they've renounced and the spirit
they've aroused. For I know as well as any man could tell me, it would
be a bad day for England if all women felt about all men *as I do*.   585

> *She retires in a tumult. The others on the platform close about her.*
> *The Chairman tries in vain to get a hearing from the excited*
> *crowd. Jean tries to make her way through the knot of people*
> *surging round her*

STONOR (*calls*) Here!—Follow me!

JEAN No—no—I—

STONOR You're going the wrong way.

JEAN *This* is the way I must go.°

STONOR You can get out quicker on this side.   590

JEAN I don't *want* to get out.

STONOR What! Where are you going?

JEAN To ask that woman to let me have the honour of working with her.

  (*She disappears in the crowd*)

CURTAIN

3

SCENE *The drawing-room at old Mr Dunbarton's house in Eaton Square. Six o'clock the same evening.*

As the Curtain rises the door L opens and Jean appears on the threshold. She looks back into her own sitting-room, then crosses the drawing-room, treading softly on the parquet spaces between the rugs. She goes to the window and is in the act of parting the lace curtains when the folding doors C are opened by the Butler

JEAN (*to the Servant*) Sh! (*She goes softly back to the door she has left open and closes it carefully. When she turns, the Butler has stepped aside to admit Geoffrey Stonor, and departed, shutting the folding doors. Stonor comes rapidly forward. Before he gets a word out*) Speak low, please.

STONOR (*angrily*) I waited about a whole hour for you to come back. (*Jean turns away as though vaguely looking for the nearest chair*) If you didn't mind leaving *me* like that, you might have considered Lady John.

JEAN (*pausing*) Is she here with you?

STONOR No. My place was nearer than this, and she was very tired. I left her to get some tea. We couldn't tell whether you'd be here, or *what* had become of you.

JEAN Mr Trent got us a hansom.

STONOR Trent?

JEAN The Chairman of the meeting.

STONOR 'Got us—'?

JEAN Miss Levering and me.

STONOR (*incensed*) Miss L—

BUTLER (*opens the door and announces*) Mr Farnborough.

Enter Mr Richard Farnborough—more flurried than ever

FARNBOROUGH (*seeing Stonor*) At last! You'll forgive this incursion, Miss Dunbarton, when you hear—(*Turns abruptly back to Stonor*) They've been telegraphing you all over London. In despair they set me on your track.

STONOR Who did? What's up?

FARNBOROUGH (*lays down his hat and fumbles agitatedly in his breast-pocket*) There was the devil to pay at Dutfield last night. The Liberal chap tore down from London and took over your meeting!

187

STONOR Oh?—Nothing about it in the Sunday paper *I* saw.

FARNBOROUGH Wait till you see the Press tomorrow morning! There was a great rally and the beggar made a rousing speech.

STONOR What about?

FARNBOROUGH Abolition of the Upper House—°.   30

STONOR They were at that when I was at Eton!

FARNBOROUGH Yes. But this new man has got a way of putting things!—the people went mad. (*Pompously*) The Liberal platform as defined at Dutfield is going to make a big difference.

STONOR (*drily*) You think so.   35

FARNBOROUGH Well, your agent says as much. (*Opens telegram*)

STONOR My—(*Taking telegram*) 'Try find Stonor'—Hm! Hm!

FARNBOROUGH (*pointing*) —'tremendous effect of last night's Liberal manifesto ought to be counteracted in tomorrow's papers.' (*Very earnestly*) You see, Mr Stonor, it's a battle-cry we want.   40

STONOR (*turns on his heel*) Claptrap!

FARNBOROUGH (*a little dashed*) Well, they've been saying we have nothing to offer but personal popularity. No practical reform. No—

STONOR No truckling to the masses, I suppose. (*Walks impatiently away*)

FARNBOROUGH (*snubbed*) Well, in these democratic days—(*Turns to* 45
Jean for countenance) I hope you'll forgive my bursting in like this. (*Struck by her face*) But I can see you realise the gravity—(*Lowering his voice with an air of speaking for her ear alone*) It isn't as if he were going to be a mere private member. Everybody knows he'll be in the Cabinet.   50

STONOR (*drily*) It may be a Liberal Cabinet.

FARNBOROUGH Nobody thought so up to last night. Why, even your brother—but I am afraid I'm seeming officious. (*Takes up his hat*)

STONOR (*coldly*) What about my brother?

FARNBOROUGH I met Lord Windlesham° as I rushed out of the   55
Carlton.°

STONOR Did he say anything?

FARNBOROUGH I told him the Dutfield news.

STONOR (*impatiently*) Well?

FARNBOROUGH He said it only confirmed his fears.   60

STONOR (*half under his breath*) Said that, did he?

FARNBOROUGH Yes. Defeat is inevitable, he thinks, unless—(*Pause. Geoffrey Stonor, who has been pacing the floor, stops but doesn't raise his eyes*)—unless you can 'manufacture some political dynamite within the next few hours'. Those were his words.

STONOR (*resumes his walking to and fro, raises his head and catches sight of Jean's white, drawn face. Stops short*) You are very tired.   65

JEAN No. No.

STONOR (*to Farnborough*) I'm obliged to you for taking so much trouble. (*Shakes hands by way of dismissing Farnborough*) I'll see what can be done.

FARNBOROUGH (*offering the reply-paid form*) If you'd like to wire I'll   70
take it.

STONOR (*faintly amused*) You don't understand, my young friend. Moves of this kind are not rushed at by responsible politicians. I must have time for consideration.

FARNBOROUGH (*disappointed*) Oh, well, I only hope someone else won't   75
jump into the breach before you—(*watch in hand*) I tell you. (*To Jean*) I'll find out what time the newspapers go to press on Sunday. Good-bye. (*To Stonor*) I'll be at the Club just *in case* I can be of any use.

STONOR (*firmly*) No, don't do that. If I should have anything new to
say—   80

FARNBOROUGH (*feverishly*) B-b-but with our party, as your brother said—'heading straight for a vast electoral disaster—'

STONOR If I decide on a counterblast I shall simply telegraph to head-quarters. Goodbye.

FARNBOROUGH Oh—a—g-goodbye. (*A gesture of 'The country's going*   85
to the dogs'. Jean rings the bell. Exit Farnborough)

STONOR (*studying the carpet*) 'Political dynamite', eh? (*Pause*) After all
. . . women are much more conservative than men—aren't they?° (*Jean looks straight in front of her, making no attempt to reply*) Espe-cially the women the property qualification would bring in. (*He glances at Jean as though for the first time conscious of her silence*) You   90
see now (*he throws himself into the chair by the table*) one reason why I've encouraged you to take an interest in public affairs. Because people like us don't go screaming about it, is no sign we don't (some of us) see what's on the way. However little they want to, women of our class will have to come into line. All the best things in the world—   95
everything that civilisation has won will be in danger if—when this change comes—the only women who have practical political training are the women of the lower classes. Women of the lower classes, and (*his brows knit heavily*)—women inoculated by the Socialist virus.

JEAN Geoffrey.   100

STONOR (*draws the telegraph form towards him*) Let us see, how we shall put it—when the time comes—shall we? (*He detaches a pencil from his watch chain and bends over the paper, writing*)

*Jean opens her lips to speak, moves a shade nearer the table and
then falls back upon her silent, half-incredulous misery*

STONOR (*holds the paper off, smiling*) Enough dynamite in that! Rather
too much, isn't there, little girl?°

JEAN Geoffrey, I know her story.   105

STONOR Whose story?

JEAN Miss Levering's.

STONOR *Whose?*

JEAN Vida Levering's. (*Stonor stares speechless. Slight pause. The words
escaping from her in a miserable cry*) Why did you desert her?   110

STONOR (*staggered*) I? *I?*

JEAN Oh, why did you do it?

STONOR (*bewildered*) What in the name of—What has she been saying
to you?

JEAN Some one else told me part. Then the way you looked when you   115
saw her at Aunt Ellen's—Miss Levering's saying you didn't know
her—then your letting out that you knew even the curious name on
the handkerchief—Oh, I pieced it together—

STONOR (*with recovered self-possession*) Your ingenuity is undeni-
able!   120

JEAN —and then, when she said that at the meeting about 'the dark
hour' and I looked at your face—it flashed over me—Oh, *why* did
you desert her?

STONOR I *didn't* desert her!

JEAN Ah-h! (*Puts her hands before her eyes. Stonor makes a passionate* 125
motion towards her, is checked by her muffled voice saying) I'm glad—
I'm glad! (*He stares bewildered. Jean drops her hands in her lap and
steadies her voice*) She went away from you, then?

STONOR You don't expect me to enter into—

JEAN She went away from you?   130

STONOR (*with a look of almost uncontrollable anger*) Yes!

JEAN Was that because you wouldn't marry her?

STONOR I couldn't marry her—and she knew it.

JEAN Did you want to?

STONOR (*an instant's angry scrutiny and then turning away his eyes*) I 135
thought I did—*then*. It's a long time ago.

JEAN And why 'couldn't' you?

STONOR (*a movement of strong irritation cut short*) Why are you catechis-
ing me? It's a matter that concerns another woman.

JEAN If you're saying that it doesn't concern me, you're saying—(*her*   140
lip trembles)—that *you* don't concern me.

STONOR (*commanding his temper with difficulty*) In those days I—I was
absolutely dependent on my father.

JEAN Why, you must have been thirty, Geoffrey.

STONOR (*slight pause*) What? Oh—thereabouts.   145

JEAN And everybody says you're so clever.

STONOR Well, everybody's mistaken.

JEAN (*drawing nearer*) It must have been terribly hard—(*Stonor turns
towards her*) for you both—(*he arrests his movement and stands stonily*)
that a man like you shouldn't have had the freedom that even the   150
lowest seem to have.

STONOR Freedom?

JEAN To marry the woman they choose.

STONOR She didn't break off our relations because I couldn't marry
her.   155

JEAN Why was it, then?

STONOR You're too young to discuss such a story. (*Half turns away*)

JEAN I'm not so young as she was when—

STONOR (*wheeling upon her*) Very well, then, if you will have it! The
truth is, it didn't seem to weigh upon her, as it seems to on you, that I 160
wasn't able to marry her.

JEAN Why are you so sure of that?

STONOR Because she didn't so much as hint such a thing when she
wrote that she meant to break off the—the—

JEAN What made her write like that?   165

STONOR (*with suppressed rage*) Why *will* you go on talking of what's so
long over and ended?

JEAN What reason did she give?

STONOR If your curiosity has so got the upper hand—*ask her.*

JEAN (*her eyes upon him*) You're afraid to tell me.   170

STONOR (*putting pressure on himself to answer quietly*) I still hoped—at
that time—to win my father over. She blamed me because (*goes to
window and looks blindly out and speaks in a low tone*) if the child had
lived it wouldn't have been possible to get my father to—to overlook
it.   175

JEAN (*faintly*) You wanted it *overlooked?* I don't underst—

STONOR (*turning passionately back to her*) Of course you don't. (*He
seizes her hand and tries to draw her to him*) If you did, you wouldn't be
the beautiful, tender, innocent child you are—

JEAN (*has withdrawn her hand and shrunk from him with an impulse—slight
as is its expression—so tragically eloquent, that fear for the first
time catches hold of him*) I am glad you didn't mean to desert her,   180

Geoffrey. It wasn't your fault after all—only some misunderstanding that can be cleared up.

STONOR *Cleared up?*

JEAN Yes. Cleared up.

STONOR (*aghast*) You aren't thinking that this miserable old affair I'd as   185
good as forgotten—

JEAN (*in a horror-struck whisper, with a glance at the door which he doesn't see*) Forgotten!

STONOR No, no. I don't mean exactly forgotten. But you're torturing me so I don't know what I'm saying. (*He goes closer*) You aren't—
Jean! you—you aren't going to let it come between you and me!   190

JEAN (*presses her handkerchief to her lips, and then, taking it away, answers steadily*) I can't make or unmake what's past. But I'm glad, at least, that you didn't *mean* to desert her in her trouble. You'll remind her of that first of all, won't you? (*Moves to the door, L*)

STONOR Where are you going? (*Raising his voice*) Why should I remind anybody of what I want only to forget?   195

JEAN (*finger on lip*) Sh!

STONOR (*with eyes on the door*) You don't mean that *she's*—

JEAN Yes. I left her to get a little rest. (*He recoils in an access of uncontrollable rage. She follows him. Speechless, he goes down R to get his hat*)
Geoffrey, don't go before you hear me. I don't know if what I think matters to you now—but I hope it does. (*With tears*) You can still   200
make me think of you without shrinking—if you will.

STONOR (*fixes her a moment with his eyes. Then sternly*) What is it you are asking of me?

JEAN To make amends, Geoffrey.

STONOR (*with an outburst*) You poor little innocent!   205

JEAN I'm poor enough. But (*locking her hands together*) I'm not so innocent but what I know you must right that old wrong now, if you're ever to right it.

STONOR You aren't insane enough to think I would turn round in these few hours and go back to something that ten years ago was ended for   210
ever! Why, it's stark, staring madness!

JEAN No. (*Catching on his arm*) What you did ten years ago—*that* was mad. This is paying a debt.

STONOR Look here, Jean, you're dreadfully wrought up and excited—tired too—   215

JEAN No, not tired—though I've travelled so far today, [as far as Tarsus is from Damascus and seen a sign in the heavens].° I know you smile at sudden conversions. You think they're hysterical—worse—

vulgar. But people must get their revelation how they can. And, Geoffrey, if I can't make you see this one of mine—I shall know your love could never mean strength to me. Only weakness. And I shall be afraid. So afraid I'll never dare to give you the *chance* of making me loathe myself. I shall never see you again.

STONOR How right *I* was to be afraid of that vein of fanaticism in you. (*Moves towards the door*)

JEAN Certainly you couldn't make a greater mistake than to go away now and think it any good ever to come back. (*He turns*) Even if I came to feel different, I couldn't *do* anything different. I should know all this couldn't be forgotten. I should know that it would poison my life in the end. Yours too.

STONOR (*with suppressed fury*) She has made good use of her time! (*With a sudden thought*) What has changed her? Has *she* been seeing visions too?

JEAN What do you mean?

STONOR Why is she intriguing to get hold of a man that, ten years ago, she flatly refused to see, or hold any communication with?

JEAN 'Intriguing to get hold of'? She hasn't mentioned you!

STONOR *What!* Then how in the name of Heaven do you know—that she wants—what you ask?

JEAN (*firmly*) There can't be any doubt about that.

STONOR (*with immense relief*) You absurd, ridiculous child! Then all this is just your own unaided invention. Well—I could thank God! (*Falls into the nearest chair and passes his handkerchief over his face*)

JEAN (*perplexed, uneasy*) For what are you thanking God?

STONOR (*trying to think out his plan of action*) Suppose—(I'm not going to risk it)—but suppose—(*He looks up and at the sight of Jean's face a new tenderness comes into his own. He rises suddenly*) Whether I deserve to suffer or not—it's quite certain *you* don't. Don't cry, dear one. It never was the real thing. I had to wait till I knew you before I understood.

JEAN (*lifts her eyes brimming*) Oh, is that true? (*Checks her movement towards him*) Loving you has made things clear to me I didn't dream of before. If I could think that because of me you were able to do this—

STONOR (*seizes her by the shoulders and says hoarsely*) Look here! Do you seriously ask me to give up the girl I love—to go and offer to marry a woman that even to think of—

JEAN You cared for her once. You'll care about her again. She is beautiful and brilliant—everything. I've heard she could win any man she set herself to—

STONOR (*pushing Jean from him*) She's bewitched you!

JEAN Geoffrey, Geoffrey, you aren't going away like that. This isn't *the end!* 260

STONOR (*darkly—hesitating*) I suppose even if she refused me, you'd—

JEAN She won't refuse you.

STONOR She did once.

JEAN She didn't refuse to *marry* you—(*Jean is going to the door L*)

STONOR (*catches her by the arm*) Wait!—a—(*Hunting for some means of gaining time*) Lady John is waiting all this while for the car to go back with a message. 265

JEAN *That's* not a matter of life and death—

STONOR All the same—I'll go down and give the order.

JEAN (*stopping quite still on a sudden*) Very well. (*Sits C*) You'll come back if you're the man I pray you are. (*Breaks into a flood of silent tears, her elbows on the table C her face in her hands*) 270

STONOR (*returns, bends over her, about to take her in his arms*) Dearest of all the world—

> Door L opens softly and Vida Levering appears. She is arrested at sight of Stonor, and is in the act of drawing back when, upon the slight noise, Stonor looks round. His face darkens, he stands staring at her and then with a look of speechless anger goes silently out C. Jean, hearing him shut the door, drops her head on the table with a sob. Vida Levering crosses slowly to her and stands a moment silent at the girl's side

MISS LEVERING What is the matter?

JEAN (*lifting her head and drying her eyes*) I—I've been seeing Geoffrey. 275

MISS LEVERING (*with an attempt at lightness*) Is this the effect seeing Geoffrey has?

JEAN You see, I know now (*as Miss Levering looks quite uncomprehending*)—how he (*drops her eyes*)—how he spoiled some one else's life.

MISS LEVERING (*quickly*) Who tells you that? 280

JEAN Several people have told me.

MISS LEVERING Well, you should be very careful how you believe what you hear.

JEAN (*passionately*) You *know* it's true.

MISS LEVERING I know that it's possible to be mistaken. 285

JEAN I see! You're trying to shield him—

MISS LEVERING Why should I—what is it to me?

JEAN (*with tears*) Oh—h, how you must love him!

MISS LEVERING Listen to me—

JEAN (*rising*) What's the use of your going on denying it? (*Miss Levering,* 290 *about to break in, is silenced*) Geoffrey doesn't. (*Jean, struggling to command her feelings, goes to window. Vida Levering relinquishes an impulse to follow, and sits left centre. Jean comes slowly back with her eyes bent on the floor, does not lift them till she is quite near Vida. Then the girl's self-absorbed face changes*) Oh, don't look like that! I shall bring him back to you! (*Drops on her knees beside the other's chair*)

MISS LEVERING You would be impertinent° (*softening*) if you weren't a romantic child. You can't bring him back.

JEAN Yes, he—

MISS LEVERING But there's something you *can* do—

JEAN What?

MISS LEVERING Bring him to the point where he recognises that he's in our debt.

JEAN In *our* debt?

MISS LEVERING In debt to women. He can't repay the one he robbed—

JEAN (*wincing and rising from her knees*) Yes, yes.

MISS LEVERING (*sternly*) No, he can't repay the dead. But there are the living. There are the thousands with hope still in their hearts and youth in their blood. Let him help *them*. Let him be a Friend to Women.

JEAN (*rising on a wave of enthusiasm*) Yes, yes—I understand. That too!
　　　The door opens. As Stonor enters with Lady John, he makes a slight gesture towards the two as much as to say, 'You see'.

JEAN (*catching sight of him*) Thank you!

LADY JOHN (*in a clear, commonplace tone to Jean*) Well, you rather gave us the slip. Vida, I believe Mr Stonor wants to see you for a few minutes (*glances at watch*)—but I'd like a word with you first, as I must get back. (*To Stonor*) Do you think the car—your man said something about re-charging.

STONOR (*hastily*) Oh, did he?—I'll see about it.
　　　As Stonor is going out he encounters the Butler. Exit Stonor

BUTLER Mr Trent has called, Miss, to take Miss Levering to the meeting.

JEAN Bring Mr Trent into my sitting-room. I'll tell him—you can't go tonight.
　　　Exeunt Butler C, Jean L

LADY JOHN (*hurriedly*) I know, my dear, *you're* not aware of what that impulsive girl wants to insist on.

MISS LEVERING Yes, I am aware of it.

LADY JOHN But it isn't with your sanction, surely, that she goes on making this extraordinary demand.

MISS LEVERING (*slowly*) I didn't sanction it at first, but I've been think- 325
ing it over.

LADY JOHN Then all I can say is I am greatly disappointed in you. You
threw this man over years ago for reasons—whatever they were—
that seemed to you good and sufficient. And now you come between
him and a younger woman—just to play Nemesis,° so far as I can 330
make out!

MISS LEVERING Is that what he says?

LADY JOHN He says nothing that isn't fair and considerate.

MISS LEVERING I can see he's changed.

LADY JOHN And you're unchanged—is that it? 335

MISS LEVERING I've changed even more than he.

LADY JOHN But (*pity and annoyance blended in her tone*)—you care
about him still, Vida?

MISS LEVERING No.

LADY JOHN I see. It's just that you wish to marry somebody— 340

MISS LEVERING Oh, Lady John, there are no men listening.

LADY JOHN (*surprised*) No, I didn't suppose there were.

MISS LEVERING Then why keep up that old pretence?

LADY JOHN What pre—

MISS LEVERING That to marry *at all costs* is every woman's dear- 345
est ambition till the grave closes over her. You and I *know* it isn't
true.

LADY JOHN Well, but—Oh! it was just the unexpected sight of him
bringing it back—*That* was what fired you this afternoon! (*With an
honest attempt at sympathetic understanding*) Of course. The memory 350
of a thing like that can never die—can never even be dimmed—*for the
woman*.

MISS LEVERING I mean her to think so.

LADY JOHN (*bewildered*) Jean!
     Miss Levering nods

LADY JOHN And it *isn't* so? 355

MISS LEVERING You don't seriously believe a woman with anything
else to think about, comes to the end of ten years still *absorbed* in a
memory of that sort?

LADY JOHN (*astonished*) You've got over it, then!

MISS LEVERING If the newspapers didn't remind me I shouldn't 360
remember once a twelvemonth that there was ever such a person as
Geoffrey Stonor in the world.

LADY JOHN (*with unconscious rapture*) Oh, I'm *so* glad!

MISS LEVERING (*smiles grimly*) Yes, I'm glad too.

LADY JOHN And if Geoffrey Stonor offered you—what's called 365
   'reparation'—you'd refuse it?

MISS LEVERING (*smiles a little contemptuously*) Geoffrey Stonor! For me
   he's simply one of the far-back links in a chain of evidence. It's certain I think a hundred times of other women's present unhappiness,
   to once that I remember that old unhappiness of mine that's past. I 370
   think of the nail and chain makers of Cradley Heath. The sweated
   girls° of the slums. I think of the army of ill-used women whose very
   existence I mustn't mention—

LADY JOHN (*interrupting hurriedly*) Then why in Heaven's name do
   you let poor Jean imagine— 375

MISS LEVERING (*bending forward*) Look—I'll trust you, Lady John. I
   don't suffer from that old wrong as Jean thinks I do, but I shall coin
   her sympathy into gold for a greater cause than mine.

LADY JOHN I don't understand you.

MISS LEVERING Jean isn't old enough to be able to care as much about 380
   a principle as about a person. But if my half-forgotten pain can turn
   her generosity into the common treasury—

LADY JOHN What do you propose she shall do, poor child?

MISS LEVERING Use her hold over Geoffrey Stonor to make him help
   us! 385

LADY JOHN Help you?

MISS LEVERING The man who served one woman—God knows how
   many more—very ill, shall serve hundreds of thousands well. Geoffrey Stonor shall make it harder for his son, harder still for his grandson, to treat any woman as he treated me. 390

LADY JOHN How will he do that?

MISS LEVERING By putting an end to the helplessness of women.

LADY JOHN (*ironically*) You must think he has a great deal of power—

MISS LEVERING Power? Yes, men have too much over penniless and
   frightened women. 395

LADY JOHN (*impatiently*) What nonsense! You talk as though the
   women hadn't their share of human nature. *We* aren't made of ice any
   more than the men.

MISS LEVERING No, but all the same we have more self-control.

LADY JOHN Than men? 400

MISS LEVERING You know we have.

LADY JOHN (*shrewdly*) I know we mustn't admit it.

MISS LEVERING For fear they'd call us fishes!°

LADY JOHN (*evasively*) They talk of our lack of self-control—but it's
   the last thing they *want* women to have. 405

MISS LEVERING Oh, we know what they want us to have. So we make shift to have it. If we don't, we go without hope—sometimes we go without bread.

LADY JOHN (*shocked*) Vida—do you mean to say that you—

MISS LEVERING I mean to say that men's vanity won't let them see it,   410
but the thing's largely a question of economics.

LADY JOHN (*shocked*) You *never* loved him, then!

MISS LEVERING Oh, yes, I loved him—*once*. It was my helplessness turned the best thing life can bring, into a curse for both of us.

LADY JOHN I don't understand you—   415

MISS LEVERING Oh, being 'understood'!—that's too much to expect. When people come to know I've joined the Union—

LADY JOHN But you won't—

MISS LEVERING —who is there who will resist the temptation to say, 'Poor Vida Levering! What a pity she hasn't got a husband and a baby   420
to keep her quiet'? The few who know about me, they'll be equally sure that it's not the larger view of life I've gained—my own poor little story is responsible for my new departure. (*Leans forward and looks into Lady John's face*) My best friend, she will be surest of all, that it's a private sense of loss, or, lower yet, a grudge—! But I tell you   425
the only difference between me and thousands of women with hus-bands and babies is that I'm free to say what I think. *They aren't*.°

LADY JOHN (*rising and looking at her watch*) I must get back—my poor ill-used guests.

MISS LEVERING (*rising*) I won't ring. I think you'll find Mr Stonor   430
downstairs waiting for you.

LADY JOHN (*embarrassed*) Oh—a—he will have left word about the car in any case.

> *Miss Levering has opened the door C. Allen Trent is in the act of saying goodbye to Jean in the hall*

MISS LEVERING Well, Mr Trent, I didn't expect to see you this evening.   435

TRENT (*comes and stands in the doorway*) Why not? Have I ever failed?

MISS LEVERING Lady John, this is one of our allies. He is good enough to squire me through the rabble from time to time.

LADY JOHN Well, I think it's very handsome of you, after what she said today about men. (*Shakes hands*)   440

TRENT I've no great opinion of most men myself. I might add—or of most women.

LADY JOHN Oh! Well, at any rate I shall go away relieved to think that Miss Levering's plain speaking hasn't alienated *all* masculine regard.

TRENT Why should it? 445

LADY JOHN That's right, Mr Trent! Don't believe all she says in the heat of propaganda.

TRENT I do believe all she says. But I'm not cast down.

LADY JOHN (*smiling*) Not when she says—

TRENT (*interrupting*) Was there never a misogynist of my sex who 450
ended by deciding to make an exception?

LADY JOHN (*smiling significantly*) Oh, if *that's* what you build on!

TRENT Well, why shouldn't a man-hater on your side prove equally open to reason?

MISS LEVERING That part of the question doesn't concern me. I've 455
come to a place where I realise that the first battles of this new campaign must be fought by women alone. The only effective help men could give—amendment of the law—they refuse. The rest is nothing.

LADY JOHN Don't be ungrateful, Vida. Here's Mr Trent ready to face 460
criticism in publicly championing you.

MISS LEVERING It's an illusion that I as an individual need Mr Trent. I am quite safe in the crowd. Please don't wait for me, and don't come for me again.

TRENT (*flushes*) Of course if you'd rather— 465

MISS LEVERING And that reminds me. I was asked to thank you and to tell you, too, that they—the women of the Union—they won't need your chairmanship any more—though that, I beg you to believe, has nothing to do with any feeling of mine.

TRENT (*hurt*) Of course, I know there must be other men ready—better 470
known men—

MISS LEVERING It isn't that. It's simply that they find a man can't keep a rowdy meeting in order as well as a woman.
He stares

LADY JOHN You aren't serious?

MISS LEVERING (*to Trent*) Haven't you noticed that all their worst dis- 475
turbances come when men are in charge?

TRENT Well—a—(*laughs a little ruefully as he moves to the door*) I hadn't connected the two ideas. Goodbye.

MISS LEVERING Good bye.
Jean takes him downstairs, right centre

LADY JOHN (*as Trent disappears*) That nice boy's in love with you. 480
Miss Levering simply looks at her

LADY JOHN Goodbye. (*They shake hands*) I wish you hadn't been so unkind to that nice boy!

MISS LEVERING Do you?

LADY JOHN Yes, for then I would be more certain of your telling Geof-   485
frey Stonor that intelligent women don't nurse their wrongs and lie
in wait to punish them.

MISS LEVERING You are *not* certain?

LADY JOHN (*goes close up to Vida*) Are you?

> *Vida stands with her eyes on the ground, silent, motionless. Lady
> John, with a nervous glance at her watch and a gesture of extreme
> perturbation, goes hurriedly out. Vida shuts the door. She comes
> slowly back, sits down and covers her face with her hands. She
> rises and begins to walk up and down, obviously trying to master
> her agitation. Enter Geoffrey Stonor*

MISS LEVERING Well, have they primed you? Have you got your lesson
(*with a little broken laugh*) by heart at last?   490

STONOR (*looking at her from immeasurable distance*) I am·not sure I
understand you. (*Pause*) However unpropitious your mood may
be—I shall discharge my errand. (*Pause. Her silence irritates him*) I
have promised to offer you what I believe is called 'amends'.°

MISS LEVERING (*quickly*) You've come to realise, then—after all these   495
years—that you owed me something?

STONOR (*on the brink of protest, checks himself*) I am not here to deny it.

MISS LEVERING (*fiercely*) Pay, then—*pay*.

STONOR (*a moment's dread as he looks at her, his lips set. Then stonily*) I
have promised that, if you exact it, I will.   500

MISS LEVERING Ah! If I insist you'll 'make it all good'! (*Quite low*) Then
don't you know you must pay me in kind?

STONOR What do you mean.

MISS LEVERING Give me back what you took from me: my old faith.
Give me that.   505

STONOR Oh, if you mean to make phrases—(*A gesture of scant patience*)

MISS LEVERING (*going closer*) Or give me back mere kindness—or even
tolerance. Oh, I don't mean *your* tolerance! [I mean mine.] Give me
back the power to think fairly of my brothers—not as mockers—
thieves.   510

STONOR I have not mocked you. And I have asked you—

MISS LEVERING Something you knew I should refuse! Or (*her eyes
blaze*) did you dare to be afraid I wouldn't?

STONOR I suppose, if we set our teeth, we could—

MISS LEVERING I couldn't—not even if I set my teeth. And you   515
wouldn't dream of asking me, if you thought there was the smallest
chance.

STONOR I can do no more than make you an offer of such reparation as is in my power. If you don't accept it—(*He turns with an air of 'That's done'*)

MISS LEVERING Accept it? No! . . . Go away and live in debt! Pay and   520
pay and pay—and find yourself still in debt!—for a thing you'll never be able to give me back. (*Lower*) And when you come to die, say to yourself, 'I paid all creditors but one'.

STONOR I'm rather tired, you know, of this talk of debt. If I hear that you persist in it I shall have to—   525

MISS LEVERING What? (*She faces him*)

STONOR No. I'll keep to my resolution. (*Turning to the door*)

MISS LEVERING (*intercepting him*) What resolution?

STONOR I came here, under considerable pressure, to speak of the future—not to re-open the past.   530

MISS LEVERING The Future and the Past are one.

STONOR You talk as if that old madness was mine alone. It is the woman's way.

MISS LEVERING I know. And it's not fair. Men suffer as well as we by the woman's starting wrong. We are taught to think the man a sort of   535
demigod. If he tells her: 'go down into Hell'—down into Hell she goes.

STONOR Make no mistake. Not the woman alone. *They go down together.*

MISS LEVERING Yes, they go down together, but the man comes up alone. As a rule. It is more convenient so—for him. And for the Other   540
Woman.

    The eyes of both go to Jean's door°

STONOR (*angrily*) My conscience is clear. I know—and so do you—that most men in my position wouldn't have troubled themselves. I gave myself endless trouble.

MISS LEVERING (*with wondering eyes*) So you've gone about all these   545
years feeling that you'd discharged every obligation.

STONOR Not only that. I stood by you with a fidelity that was nothing short of Quixotic. If, woman-like, you *must* recall the Past—I insist on your recalling it correctly.

MISS LEVERING (*very low*) You think I don't recall it correctly?   550

STONOR Not when you make—other people believe that I deserted you. (*With gathering wrath*) It's a curious enough charge when you stop to consider—(*Checks himself, and with a gesture of impatience sweeps the whole thing out of his way*)

MISS LEVERING Well, when we *do*—just for five minutes out of ten years—when we do stop to consider—
    555

STONOR We remember it was *you* who did the deserting! Since you had to rake the story up, you might have had the fairness to tell the facts.

MISS LEVERING You think 'the facts' would have excused you! (*She sits*)

STONOR No doubt you've forgotten them, since Lady John tells me you wouldn't remember my existence once a year if the newspapers didn't— 560

MISS LEVERING Ah, you minded that!

STONOR (*with manly spirit*) I minded your giving false impressions. (*She is about speak, he advances on her*) Do you deny that you returned my letters unopened? 565

MISS LEVERING (*quietly*) No.

STONOR Do you deny that you refused to see me—and that, when I persisted, you vanished?

MISS LEVERING I don't deny any of those things.

STONOR Why, I had no trace of you for years! 570

MISS LEVERING I suppose not.

STONOR Very well, then. What *could* I do?

MISS LEVERING Nothing. It was too late to do anything.

STONOR It wasn't too late! You knew—since you 'read the papers'— that my father died that same year. There was no longer any barrier 575 between us.

MISS LEVERING Oh yes, there was a barrier.

STONOR Of your own making, then.

MISS LEVERING I had my guilty share in it—but the barrier (*her voice trembles*)—the barrier was your invention. 580

STONOR It was no 'invention'. If you had ever known my father—°

MISS LEVERING Oh, the echoes! The echoes! How often you used to say, if I 'knew your father!' But you said, too (*lower*)—you called the greatest barrier by another name.

STONOR What name? 585

MISS LEVERING (*very low*) The child that was to come.

STONOR (*hastily*) That was before my father died. While I still hoped to get his consent.

MISS LEVERING (*nods*) How the thought of that all-powerful personage used to terrorise me! What chance had a little unborn child against 590 'the last of the great feudal lords', as you called him.

STONOR You *know* the child would have stood between you and me!

MISS LEVERING I know the child *did* stand between you and me!

STONOR (*with vague uneasiness*) It *did* stand—

MISS LEVERING Happy mothers teach their children. Mine had to 595 teach me.

STONOR You talk as if—

MISS LEVERING —teach me that a woman may do a thing for love's sake that shall kill love.

    A silence

STONOR (*fearing and putting from him fuller comprehension, rises with an air of finality*) You certainly made it plain you had no love left for me. 600

MISS LEVERING I had need of it all for the child.

STONOR (*stares—comes closer, speaks hurriedly and very low*) Do you mean then that, after all—it lived?

MISS LEVERING No; I mean that it was sacrificed. But it showed me no barrier is so impassable as the one a little child can raise. 605

STONOR (*a light dawning*) Was that why you . . . was *that* why?

MISS LEVERING (*nods, speechless a moment*) Day and night there it was!—between my thought of you and me. (*He sits again, staring at her*) When I was most unhappy I would wake, thinking I heard it cry. It was my own crying I heard, but I seemed to have it in my arms. I 610 suppose I was mad. I used to lie there in that lonely farmhouse pretending to hush it. It was so I hushed myself.

STONOR I never knew—

MISS LEVERING I didn't blame you. You couldn't risk being with me.

STONOR You agreed that for both our sakes— 615

MISS LEVERING Yes, you had to be very circumspect. You were so well known. Your autocratic father—your brilliant political future—

STONOR Be fair. *Our* future—as I saw it then.

MISS LEVERING Yes, it all hung on concealment. It must have looked quite simple to you. You didn't know that the ghost of a child that had 620 never seen the light, the frail thing you meant to sweep aside and forget—*have* swept aside and forgotten—you didn't know it was strong enough to push you out of my life. (*Lower, with an added intensity*) It can do more. (*Leans over him and whispers*) It can push that girl out. (*Stonor's face changes*) It can do more still. 625

STONOR Are you threatening me?

MISS LEVERING No, I am preparing you.°

STONOR For what?

MISS LEVERING For the work that must be done. Either with *your* help—or *that girl's*. 630

    Stonor lifts his eyes a moment

MISS LEVERING One of two things. Either her life, and all she has, given to this new service—or a Ransom, if I give her up to you.

STONOR I see. A price. Well—?

MISS LEVERING (*looks searchingly in his face, hesitates and shakes her*

head) Even if I could trust you to pay—no, it would be a poor bargain
to give her up for anything you could do.   635

STONOR (*rising*) In spite of your assumption—she may not be your tool.

MISS LEVERING You are horribly afraid she is! But you are wrong.
Don't think it's merely I that have got hold of Jean Dunbarton.

STONOR (*angrily*) Who else?

MISS LEVERING The New Spirit that's abroad.   640

> *Stonor turns away with an exclamation and begins to pace,
> sentinel-like, up and down before Jean's door*

MISS LEVERING How else should that inexperienced girl have felt the
new loyalty and responded as she did?

STONOR (*under his breath*) 'New' indeed—however little loyal.

MISS LEVERING Loyal above all. But no newer than electricity was
when it first lit up the world. It had been there since the world   645
began—waiting to do away with the dark. *So has the thing you're
fighting*.

STONOR (*his voice held down to its lowest register*) The thing I'm fighting
is nothing more than one person's hold on a highly sensitive imagination. I consented to this interview with the hope—(*A gesture of*   650
impotence) It only remains for me to show her your true motive is
revenge.

MISS LEVERING Once say that to her and you are lost!

> *Stonor motionless; his look is the look of a man who sees happiness
> slipping away*

MISS LEVERING I know what it is that men fear. It even seems as if it
must be through fear that your enlightenment will come. That is why   655
I see a value in Jean Dunbarton far beyond her fortune.

> *Stonor lifts his eyes dully and fixes them on Vida's face*

MISS LEVERING More than any girl I know—if I keep her from you—
that gentle, inflexible creature could rouse in men the old half-
superstitious fear—

STONOR 'Fear'? I believe you are mad.   660

MISS LEVERING 'Mad.' 'Unsexed.' These are the words today. In the
Middle Ages men cried out 'Witch!' and burnt her—the woman who
served no man's bed or board.

STONOR You want to make that poor child believe—

MISS LEVERING She sees for herself we've come to a place where we   665
find there's a value in women apart from the value men see in them.
You teach us not to look to you for some of the things we need most.
If women must be freed by women, we have need of such as—(*her
eyes go to Jean's door*)—who knows? She may be the new Joan of Arc.

STONOR (*aghast*) That *she* should be the sacrifice!

MISS LEVERING You have taught us to look very calmly on the sacrifice of women. Men tell us in every tongue it's 'a necessary evil'.

   Stonor stands rooted, staring at the ground

MISS LEVERING One girl's happiness—against a thing nobler than happiness for thousands—who can hesitate?—*Not Jean.*

STONOR Good God! Can't you see that this crazed campaign you'd start her on—even if it's successful, it can only be so through the help of men? What excuse shall you make your own soul for not going straight to the goal?

MISS LEVERING You think we wouldn't be glad to go straight to the goal?

STONOR I do. I see you'd much rather punish me and see her revel in a morbid self-sacrifice.

MISS LEVERING You say I want to punish you only because, like most men, you won't take the trouble to understand what we do want—or how determined we are to have it. You can't kill this new spirit among women. (*Going nearer*) And you couldn't make a greater mistake than to think it finds a home only in the exceptional, or the unhappy. It's so strange, Geoffrey, to see a man like you as much deluded as the Hyde Park loafers who say to Ernestine Blunt, 'Who's hurt *your* feelings?' Why not realise (*going quite close to him*) this is a thing that goes deeper than personal experience? And yet (*lowering her voice and glancing at the door*), if you take only the narrowest personal view, a good deal depends on what you and I agree upon in the next five minutes.

STONOR (*bringing her farther away from the door*) You recommend my realising the larger issues. But in your ambition to attach that girl to the chariot wheels of 'Progress', you quite ignore the fact that people fitter for such work—the men you look to enlist in the end—are ready waiting to give the thing a chance.

MISS LEVERING Men are ready! What men?

STONOR (*avoiding her eyes, picking his words*) Women have themselves to blame that the question has grown so delicate that responsible people shrink—for the moment—from being implicated in it.

MISS LEVERING We have seen the 'shrinking'.

STONOR Without quoting any one else, I might point out that the New Antagonism seems to have blinded you to the small fact that I, for one, am not an opponent.

MISS LEVERING The phrase *has* a familiar ring. We have heard it from four hundred and twenty others.°

STONOR I spoke, if I may say so, of some one who would count. Some one   710
who can carry his party along with him—or risk a seat in the Cabinet.

MISS LEVERING (*quickly*) Did you mean you are ready to do that?

STONOR An hour ago I was.

MISS LEVERING Ah! . . . an hour ago.

STONOR Exactly. You don't understand men. They can be led. They   715
can't be driven. Ten minutes before you came into the room I was
ready to say I would throw in my political lot with this Reform.

MISS LEVERING And now . . .?

STONOR Now you block my way by an attempt at coercion. By forcing
my hand you give my adherence an air of bargain-driving for a per-   720
sonal end. Exactly the mistake of the ignorant agitators of your
'Union', as you call it. You have a great deal to learn. This movement
will go forward, not because of the agitation, but in spite of it. There
are men in Parliament who would have been actively serving the
Reform today . . . as actively as so vast a constitutional change—   725

MISS LEVERING (*smiles faintly*) And they haven't done it because—

STONOR Because it would have put a premium on breaches of decent
behaviour. (*He takes a crumpled piece of paper out of his pocket*) Look here!

MISS LEVERING (*flushes with excitement as she reads the telegram*) This is
very good. I see only one objection.   730

STONOR Objection!

MISS LEVERING You haven't sent it.

STONOR *That* is your fault.

MISS LEVERING When did you write this?

STONOR Just before you came in—when—(*He glances at the door*)   735

MISS LEVERING Ah! It must have pleased Jean—that message. (*Offers
him back the paper. Stonor astonished at her yielding it up so lightly, and
remembering Jean had not so much as read it. He throws himself heavily
into a chair and drops his head in his hands*)

MISS LEVERING I could drive a hard-and-fast bargain with you, but I
think I won't. If *both* love and ambition urge you on, perhaps—(*She
gazes at the slack, hopeless figure with its sudden look of age—goes over
silently and stands by his side*) After all, life hasn't been quite fair to
you—(*He raises his heavy eyes*) You fall out of one ardent woman's   740
dreams into another's.

STONOR You may as well tell me—do you mean to—?

MISS LEVERING To keep you and her apart? No.

STONOR (*for the first time tears come into his eyes. After a moment he holds
out his hand*) What can I do for you?

   Miss Levering shakes her head—speechless

STONOR For the real you. Not the Reformer, or the would-be polit-   745
ician—for the woman I so unwillingly hurt. (*As she turns away, struggling with her feeling, he lays a detaining hand on her arm*) You may not
believe it, but now that I understand, there is almost nothing I
wouldn't do to right that old wrong.

MISS LEVERING There's nothing to be done. You can never give me   750
back my child.

STONOR (*at the anguish in Vida's face his own has changed*) Will that
ghost give you no rest?

MISS LEVERING Yes, oh, yes. I see life is nobler than I knew. There is
work to do.   755

STONOR (*stopping her as she goes towards the folding doors*) Why should
you think that it's only you, these ten years have taught something to?
Why not give even a man credit for a willingness to learn something
of life, and for being sorry—profoundly sorry—for the pain his
instruction has cost others? You seem to think I've taken it all quite   760
lightly. That's not fair. All my life, ever since you disappeared, the
thought of you has hurt. I would give anything I possess to know
you—were happy again.

MISS LEVERING Oh happiness!

STONOR (*significantly*) Why shouldn't you find it still.   765

MISS LEVERING (*stares an instant*) I see! She couldn't help telling about
Allen Trent—Lady John couldn't.

STONOR You're one of the people the years have not taken from, but
given more to. You are more than ever . . . You haven't lost your
beauty.   770

MISS LEVERING The gods saw it was so little effectual, it wasn't worth
taking away. (*She stands looking out into the void*) One woman's
mishap?—what is that? A thing as trivial to the great world as it's sordid in most eyes. But the time has come when a woman may look
about her, and say, 'What general significance has my secret pain?   775
Does it "join on" to anything?' And I find it does. I'm no longer
merely a woman who has stumbled on the way. I'm one (*she controls
with difficulty the shake in her voice*) who has got up bruised and bleeding, wiped the dust from her hands and the tears from her face, and
said to herself not merely, 'Here's one luckless woman! but—here is   780
a stone of stumbling to many. Let's see if it can't be moved out of
other women's way'. And she calls people to come and help. No mortal man, let alone a woman, *by herself*, can move that rock of offence.
But (*with a sudden sombre flame of enthusiasm*) if many help, Geoffrey,
the thing can be done.   785

STONOR (*looks at her with wondering pity*) Lord! how you care!

MISS LEVERING (*touched by his moved face*) Don't be so sad. Shall I tell
you a secret? Jean's ardent dreams needn't frighten you, if she has a
child. *That*—from the beginning, it was not the strong arm—it was
the weakest—the little, little arms that subdued the fiercest of us.   790
(*Stonor puts out a pitying hand uncertainly towards her. She does not
take it, but speaks with great gentleness*) You will have other children,
Geoffrey—for me there was to be only one. Well, well—(*she brushes
her tears away*)—since men alone have tried and failed to make a
decent world for the little children to live in—it's as well some of us
are childless. (*Quietly taking up her hat and cloak*) Yes, *we* are the ones   795
who have no excuse for standing aloof from the fight.

STONOR Vida!

MISS LEVERING What?

STONOR You've forgotten something. (*As she looks back he is signing the
message*) This.   800

　　　She goes out silently with the 'political dynamite' in her hand

CURTAIN

Appendix

Original ending of *Votes for Women!*
(*This version of the ending, submitted to the Lord Chamberlain
and performed at the Court Theatre in April 1907, takes up from
3.626*)

MISS LEVERING No, I am preparing you. (*She walks away a few paces. He drops
his face in his hands. She turns, takes in his attitude of hopelessness, comes back
and stands beside him looking down on the bowed head*) After all, life hasn't been
quite fair to you—(*He raises his heavy eyes*) You fall out of one ardent
woman's dreams into another's.

STONOR You may as well tell me—do you mean to—? 5

MISS LEVERING To keep you and her apart? No. But I like that girl. I wonder
what your two lives will be like? Shall I tell you a secret? Her dreams needn't
frighten you, if she has a child. *That*—from the beginning, it was not the
strong arm—it was the weakest—the little, little arms that subdued the
fiercest of us. (*Stonor puts out a pitying hand uncertainly towards her. She does 10
not take it, but speaks with great gentleness*) You will have other children, Geoffrey—for me there was to be only one. Well (*she brushes her tears away*)—
since men alone have tried and failed to make a decent world for the little
children to live in—it's as well some of us are childless. (*Looking into
vacancy*) Yes, *we* are the ones who have no excuse for standing aloof from the 15
fight.

STONOR (*stopping her as she goes towards the folding doors*) Why should you think
that it's only you, these ten years have taught something to? Why not give
even a man credit for a willingness to learn something of life, and for being
sorry—profoundly sorry—for the pain his instruction has cost others? You 20
seem to think I've taken it all quite lightly. That's not fair. All my life, ever
since you disappeared, the thought of you has hurt. I would give anything I
possess to know you—were happy again. (*Significantly*) And why shouldn't
you—

MISS LEVERING (*with a flash of scorn*) Ah. She couldn't help telling about Allen 25
Trent—Lady John couldn't.

STONOR You're one of the people the years have not taken from, but given more
to. You are more than ever . . . You haven't lost your beauty.

MISS LEVERING The gods saw it was so little effectual, it wasn't worth taking
away. 30

STONOR (*he draws nearer and speaks with genuine feeling*) You've shown me how
little I gave and how much I took away. But I wish you'd give me something
more. Let me hear when the day comes that brings happiness your way again.
I begin to feel my own happiness won't mean much to me till then.

MISS LEVERING (*brushes her handkerchief across her eyes*) One woman's 35
mishap?—what is that? A thing as trivial to the great world as it's sordid in
most eyes. But the time has come when a woman may look about her, and say,
'What general significance has my secret pain? Does it "join on" to anything?' And I find it does. I'm no longer merely a woman who has stumbled
on the way. I'm one (*she controls with difficulty the shake in her voice*) who has 40
got up bruised and bleeding, wiped the dust from her hands and the tears
from her face, and said to herself not merely, 'Here's one luckless woman!
but—here is a stone of stumbling to many. Let's see if it can't be moved out
of other women's way'. And she calls people to come and help. No mortal
man, let alone a woman, *by herself*, can move that rock of offence. But (*with a* 45
sudden sombre flame of enthusiasm) if many help, Geoffrey, the thing can be
done.

STONOR I begin to see my own future leading me that way.

MISS LEVERING Ah! (*Rises*)

STONOR The women need a friend. 50

MISS LEVERING We have four hundred and twenty already. (*Goes to chair up
left centre by the door where her hat and cloak are lying*)

STONOR (*standing centre, hands in pockets, looking down at the floor*) Ah, but I
mean a fighter—a fighter, a leader—one who can pull his party along after
him.

MISS LEVERING Ah, if you could do that. 55

STONOR Why shouldn't I?

MISS LEVERING There's every reason you should—except one.

STONOR What is that?

MISS LEVERING Goodbye. We won't meet again but I shall be watching you.
(*Ironically*) I shall follow your career with an interest I take in no other man's. 60
And when I've seen your Resolution and heard how you support it—then
I shall know whether woman has found,—at last!—a Friend who doesn't
betray her.

STONOR I shall support the cause not because you or anyone else is watching,
but because I believe in it. 65

MISS LEVERING We shall see.

> *Exit Vida. Geoffrey stands motionless an instant, turns and walks across
> the room—stops, raises his eyes, goes quickly to the table, C, draws the
> telegraph form to him and writes as the curtain falls*

THE LAST OF THE
DE MULLINS
A Play without a Preface°

BY

ST JOHN HANKIN

βέλτωθ ύγιαίνειν°

THE LAST OF THE DE MULLINS

Cast of the original Production before the Stage Society°
at the Haymarket Theatre, London, on
6 and 7 December 1908

Hester De Mullin	*Miss Amy Lamborn*
Mr Brown	*Mr Nigel Playfair°*
Jane De Mullin	*Miss Adela Meason*
Mrs Clouston	*Miss McAimée Murray*
Dr Rolt	*Mr Ernest Young*
Hugo De Mullin	*Mr H. A. Saintsbury*
Ellen	*Miss Jean Bloomfield*
Janet De Mullin	*Miss Lillah McCarthy°*
Johnny Seagrave	*Master Bobbie Andrews*
Miss Deanes	*Miss Clare Greet*
Monty Bulstead	*Mr Vernon Steel*
Bertha Aldenham	*Miss Jean Harkness*

The play produced by Mr W. Graham Browne

1

HESTER Come in, Mr Brown. I'll tell mother you're here. I expect she's
upstairs with father. (*Going towards door*)

BROWN Don't disturb Mrs De Mullin, please. I didn't mean to come
in.

HESTER You'll sit down now you *are* here?   5

BROWN Thank you. (*Does so awkwardly*) I'm so glad to hear Mr De
Mullin is better. The Vicar will be glad too.

HESTER Yes. Dr Rolt thinks he will do all right now.

BROWN You must have been very anxious when he was first taken ill.

HESTER We were terribly anxious. (*Hester takes off her hat and cape and*   10
puts them down on the window seat)

BROWN I suppose there's no doubt it was some sort of stroke?

213

HESTER Dr Rolt says no doubt.

BROWN How did it happen?

HESTER We don't know. He had just gone out of the room when we heard a fall. Mother ran out into the hall and found him lying by the door quite unconscious. She was dreadfully frightened. So were we all.

BROWN Had he been complaining of feeling unwell?

HESTER Not specially. He complained of the heat a little. And he had a headache. But father's not strong, you know. None of the De Mullins are, Aunt Harriet says.°

BROWN Mrs Clouston is with you now, isn't she?

HESTER Yes. For a month. She generally stays with us for a month in the summer.

BROWN I suppose she's very fond of Brendon?

HESTER All the De Mullins are fond of Brendon, Mr Brown.

BROWN Naturally. You have been here so long.

HESTER Since the time of King Stephen.°

BROWN Not in this house?

HESTER (*smiling*) Not in this house, of course. It's not old enough for that.

BROWN Still, it must be very old. The oldest house in the Village, isn't it?

HESTER Only about four hundred years. The date is 1603.° The mill is older, of course.

BROWN You still own the mill, don't you?

HESTER Yes. Father would never part with it. He thinks everything of the mill. We get our name from it, you know. De Mullin. Du Moulin. 'Of the Mill'.

BROWN Were the original De Mullins millers then?

HESTER (*rather shocked at such a suggestion*) Oh no!

BROWN I thought they couldn't have been.

HESTER No De Mullin has ever been in trade of *any* kind!° But in the old days to own a mill was a feudal privilege. Only lords of manors and the great abbeys had them. The farmers had to bring all their corn to them to be ground.

BROWN I see.

HESTER There were constant disputes about it all through the Middle Ages.

BROWN Why was that?

HESTER The farmers would rather have ground their corn for themselves, I suppose.

BROWN Why? If the De Mullins were willing to do it for them?

HESTER They had to pay for having it ground, of course.

BROWN (*venturing on a small joke*) Then the De Mullins *were* millers,   55
after all, in a sense.

HESTER You mustn't let father hear you say so!

BROWN The mill is never used now, is it?

HESTER No. When people gave up growing corn round here and all the
land was turned into pasture it fell into decay, and now it's almost   60
ruinous.

BROWN What a pity!

HESTER Yes. Father says England has never been the same since the
repeal of the Corn laws.° (*Enter Mrs De Mullin and Mrs Clouston by
the door on the left, followed by Dr Rolt*) Here is mother—and Aunt   65
Harriet.

> *Mrs De Mullin, poor lady, is a crushed, timid creature of fifty-*
> *eight or so, entirely dominated by the De Mullin fetish° and quite*
> *unable to hold her own against either her husband or her sister-in-*
> *law, a hard-mouthed, resolute woman of sixty. Even Hester she*
> *finds almost too much for her. For the rest a gentle, kindly lady,*
> *rather charming in her extreme helplessness. Rolt is the average*
> *country doctor, brisk, sensible, neither a fool nor a genius°*

ROLT (*as they enter the room*) He's better. Distinctly better. A little weak
and depressed, of course. That's only to be expected. Good morning.
(*Shakes hands with Hester. Nods to Brown*)

MRS DE MULLIN Mr De Mullin is always nervous about himself.

ROLT Yes. Constitutional, no doubt. But he'll pick up in a few days.   70
Keep him as quiet as you can. That's really all he needs now.

MRS DE MULLIN You don't think he ought to stay in his room? . . .
Good morning, Mr Brown. Are you waiting to see me?

> *Brown shakes hands with both ladies°*

BROWN (*awkwardly*) Not specially. I walked over from the church with
Miss De Mullin.   75

HESTER Is father coming downstairs, mother?

MRS DE MULLIN Yes, Hester. He insisted on getting up. You know he
always hates staying in his room.

HESTER Oh, Dr Rolt, do you think he *should*?

ROLT I don't think it will do him any harm. He can rest quietly in a chair   80
or on the sofa . . . Well, I must be off. Good-bye, Mrs De Mullin.
(*Shakes hands briskly with every one*)

BROWN (*rising ponderously*) I must be going too. (*Shakes hands with Mrs
De Mullin*) You'll tell Mr De Mullin I inquired after him? Good-bye,

Mrs Clouston. (*Shakes hands*) And you're coming to help with the Harvest Decorations° on Saturday, aren't you, Miss De Mullin? 85

HESTER (*shaking hands*) Of course.

Brown and Rolt go out

MRS CLOUSTON (*seating herself [comfortably] and beginning to knit resolutely*) What singularly unattractive curates the Vicar seems to get hold of, Jane!

MRS DE MULLIN (*meekly*) Do you think so, Harriet?

MRS CLOUSTON Quite remarkably. This Mr Brown, for instance. He 90 has the most enormous *feet*! And his boots! I've never seen such boots!

HESTER (*flushing*) We needn't sneer if Mr Brown doesn't wear fine clothes, Aunt Harriet.

MRS CLOUSTON Of course not Hester. Still, I think he goes to the 95 opposite extreme. And he really is quite abnormally plain. Then there was that Mr Snood, who was curate when I was down last year. The man with the very red hands. (*These acid comments are too much for Hester, who flounces out angrily. Mrs Clouston looks up for a moment, wondering what is the meaning of this sudden disappearance. Then continues unmoved*) I'm afraid the clergy aren't what they were in *our* young days, Jane. 100

MRS DE MULLIN I don't think I've noticed any falling off.

MRS CLOUSTON It is there all the same. I'm sure Hugo would agree with me. Of course, curates are paid next to nothing. Still, I think the Vicar might be more happy in his choice.

MRS DE MULLIN I believe the poor like him. 105

MRS CLOUSTON (*to whom this seems of small importance compared with his shocking social disabilities*) Very likely. . . . Do please keep still, Jane, and don't fidget with that book. What *is* the matter with you?

MRS DE MULLIN I'm a little nervous this morning. Hugo's illness . . .

MRS CLOUSTON Hugo's almost well now.

MRS DE MULLIN Still the anxiety . . . 110

MRS CLOUSTON Nonsense, Jane. Anxiety is not at all a thing to give way to, especially when there's no longer anything to be anxious about. Hugo's practically well now. Dr Rolt seems to have frightened us all quite unnecessarily.

MRS DE MULLIN I suppose it's difficult to tell. 115

MRS CLOUSTON Of course, it's difficult. Otherwise no one would send for a doctor. What are doctors for if they can't tell when a case is serious and when it is not?

MRS DE MULLIN But if he didn't know?

MRS CLOUSTON Then he *ought* to have known. Next time Hugo is ill   120
you'd better send to Bridport.° (*Mrs De Mullin drops book on table
with a clatter*) Really, Jane, what *are* you doing? Throwing books
about like that!

MRS DE MULLIN It slipped out of my hand. (*Rises and goes up to window
restlessly*)

MRS CLOUSTON Is anything wrong?   125

MRS DE MULLIN (*hesitating*) Well, the truth is I've done something,
Harriet, and now I'm not sure whether I ought to have done it.

MRS CLOUSTON Done what?

MRS DE MULLIN (*dolorously*) I'm afraid you won't approve.

MRS CLOUSTON Perhaps you'd better tell me what it is. Then we shall   130
know.

MRS DE MULLIN The fact is some one is coming here this morning,
Harriet—to see Hugo.

MRS CLOUSTON To see Hugo? Who is it?

MRS DE MULLIN Janet.   135

MRS CLOUSTON (*with horror*) Janet?

MRS DE MULLIN Yes.

MRS CLOUSTON Janet! She wouldn't *dare*!

MRS DE MULLIN (*dolorously*) I sent for her, Harriet.

MRS CLOUSTON You *sent* for her?   140

MRS DE MULLIN Yes. When Hugo was first taken ill and Dr Rolt
seemed to think the attack was so serious . . .

MRS CLOUSTON Dr Rolt was a fool.

MRS DE MULLIN Very likely, Harriet. But he said Hugo might die. And
he said if there was any one Hugo would wish to see . . .   145

MRS CLOUSTON But would Hugo wish to see Janet?

MRS DE MULLIN I thought he might. After all Janet *is* his daughter.

MRS CLOUSTON I thought he said he would never see her again?

MRS DE MULLIN He did *say* that, of course. But that was eight years
ago. And, of course, he wasn't ill then.   150

MRS CLOUSTON When did you send for her?

MRS DE MULLIN Three days ago.

MRS CLOUSTON Why didn't she come *then*, if she was coming at all?

MRS DE MULLIN She was away from home. That was so unfortunate. If
she had come when Hugo was ill in bed it might have been all right.   155
But now that he's almost well again . . .

MRS CLOUSTON When did you hear she was coming?

MRS DE MULLIN Only this morning. Here is what she says. (*Produces
telegram from pocket*)

MRS CLOUSTON (*reads*) 'Telegram delayed. Arrive mid-day. Seagrave.' 160
Seagrave?

MRS DE MULLIN   Yes. She calls herself Mrs Seagrave now.

MRS CLOUSTON (*nods*) On account of the child, I suppose.

MRS DE MULLIN   I suppose so.

MRS CLOUSTON   I never could understand how Janet came to go so
wrong. (*Mrs De Mullin sighs*) None of the *De Mullins* have ever done 165
such a thing before.

MRS DE MULLIN (*plaintively*) I'm sure she doesn't get it from *my*
family.

MRS CLOUSTON   Well, she must have got it from *somewhere*. She's not
in the least like a De Mullin. 170

MRS DE MULLIN (*lamentably*) I believe it was all through bicycling.°

MRS CLOUSTON   Bicycling?

MRS DE MULLIN   Yes. When girls usen't to scour about the country as
they do now these things didn't happen.

MRS CLOUSTON (*severely*) *I* never approved of Janet's bicycling you 175
remember, Jane.

MRS DE MULLIN   Nor did I, Harriet. But it was no use. Janet only
laughed. Janet never would do what she was told about things even
when she was quite a child. She was so very obstinate. She was always
getting some idea or other into her head. And when she did nothing 180
would prevent her from carrying it out. At one time she wanted to
teach.

MRS CLOUSTON   I remember.

MRS DE MULLIN   She said girls ought to go out and earn their own
living like boys. 185

MRS CLOUSTON   What nonsense!

MRS DE MULLIN   So Hugo said. But Janet wouldn't listen. Finally we
had to let her go over and teach the Aldenham girls French three
times a week, just to keep her amused.

MRS CLOUSTON (*thoughtfully*) It was strange you never could find out 190
who the father was.

MRS DE MULLIN (*sighs*) Yes. She wouldn't tell us.

MRS CLOUSTON   You should have made her tell you. Hugo should have
insisted on it.

MRS DE MULLIN   Hugo did insist. He was terribly angry with her. He 195
sent her to her room and said she was not to come down till she told
us. But it was no use. Janet just stayed in her room till we had all gone
to bed and then took the train to London.

MRS CLOUSTON   You should have locked her door.

MRS DE MULLIN We did. She got out of the window.°   200

MRS CLOUSTON Got out of the window! The girl might have been killed.

MRS DE MULLIN Yes. But Janet was always fond of climbing. And she was never afraid of anything.

MRS CLOUSTON But there's no late train to London.   205

MRS DE MULLIN She caught the mail° at Weymouth, I suppose.

MRS CLOUSTON Do you mean to say she *walked* all the way to Weymouth in the middle of the night? Why, it's twelve miles.

MRS DE MULLIN She had her bicycle as I said.

MRS CLOUSTON Tck! . . . How did you know she went to London?   210

MRS DE MULLIN She wrote from there, for her things.

MRS CLOUSTON I wonder she wasn't ashamed.

MRS DE MULLIN So Hugo said. However, he said I might send them. But he made me send a letter with the things to say that he would have nothing more to do with her and that she was not to write again. For   215
a time she didn't write. Nearly five months. Then, when her baby was born, she wrote to tell me. That was how I knew she had taken the name of Seagrave. She mentioned it.

MRS CLOUSTON Did you show the letter to Hugo?

MRS DE MULLIN Yes   220

MRS CLOUSTON What did he say?

MRS DE MULLIN Nothing. He just read it and gave it back to me without a word.

MRS CLOUSTON That's the last you've heard of her, I suppose?

MRS DE MULLIN Oh no, Harriet.   225

MRS CLOUSTON Do you mean to say she goes *on* writing? And you allow her? When Hugo said she was not to?

MRS DE MULLIN (*meekly*) Yes. Not often, Harriet. Only occasionally.

MRS CLOUSTON She has no business to write at all.

MRS DE MULLIN Her letters are quite short. Sometimes I wish they   230
were longer. They really tell one nothing about herself, though I often ask her.

MRS CLOUSTON You *ask* her! Then *you* write too!

MRS DE MULLIN I answer her letters, of course. Otherwise she wouldn't go on writing.°   235

MRS CLOUSTON Really, Jane, I'm surprised at you. So you've actually been corresponding with Janet all these years—and never told *me*! I think you've behaved very badly.

MRS DE MULLIN I didn't like to, Harriet.

MRS CLOUSTON Didn't like to!   240

MRS DE MULLIN And as you don't think I *ought* to hear from her . . .

MRS CLOUSTON I don't think you ought to hear from her, of course. But as you do hear naturally I should like to have seen the letters.

MRS DE MULLIN I didn't know that, Harriet. In fact, I thought you would rather not. When a dreadful thing like this happens in a family 245 it seems best not to write about it or to speak of it either, doesn't it? Hugo and I never speak of it.°

MRS CLOUSTON Does Hugo know you hear from her?

MRS DE MULLIN I think not. I have never told him. Nor Hester. I'm sure Hester would disapprove. 250

MRS CLOUSTON My dear Jane, what *can* it matter whether Hester approves or not? Hester knows nothing about such things. At *her* age!

MRS DE MULLIN Hester is twenty-eight.

MRS CLOUSTON Exactly. A girl like that.

MRS DE MULLIN (*sighs*) Girls have such very strong opinions now- 255 adays.

MRS CLOUSTON What does Janet live on? Teaching?°

MRS DE MULLIN I suppose so. She had her Aunt Miriam's legacy, of course.

MRS CLOUSTON Only four hundred pounds. 260

MRS DE MULLIN Yes.

MRS CLOUSTON I never approved of that legacy, Jane. Girls oughtn't to have money left them. It makes them too independent.

MRS DE MULLIN Aunt Miriam was always so fond of Janet.

MRS CLOUSTON Then she should have left the money to Hugo. 265 Fathers are the proper people to leave money to.

MRS DE MULLIN Hugo did have the *management* of the money—till Janet was twenty-one.

MRS CLOUSTON Why only till she was twenty-one?

MRS DE MULLIN It was so in Aunt Miriam's will. Of course, Hugo 270 would have gone on managing it for her. It was very little trouble as it was all in Consols.° But Janet said she would rather look after it for herself.

MRS CLOUSTON Ridiculous! As if girls could possibly manage money!

MRS DE MULLIN So Hugo said. But Janet insisted. So she got her way. 275

MRS CLOUSTON What did she do with it? Spend it?

MRS DE MULLIN No. Put it into a Railway,° she said.

MRS CLOUSTON A Railway! How dangerous!

MRS DE MULLIN She said she would prefer it. She said Railways some-times went up. Consols never. 280

MRS CLOUSTON She lost it all, of course?

MRS DE MULLIN I don't know, Harriet.

MRS CLOUSTON You don't *know*?

MRS DE MULLIN No. I never liked to ask. Hugo was rather hurt about the whole thing, so the subject was never referred to.   285

MRS CLOUSTON Let me see. The child must be eight years old by now.

MRS DE MULLIN Just eight. It will be nine years next March since Janet went away.

MRS CLOUSTON What did she call him?

MRS DE MULLIN Johnny.   290

MRS CLOUSTON Johnny! None of the De Mullins have ever been called *Johnny*.

MRS DE MULLIN Perhaps it was his father's name.

MRS CLOUSTON Perhaps so. (*Pause*)

MRS DE MULLIN Do you think I ought to tell Hugo about Janet's coming?   295

MRS CLOUSTON Certainly.

MRS DE MULLIN I thought perhaps . . . .

MRS CLOUSTON Nonsense, Jane. Of course, he must be told. You ought to have told him from the very beginning?

MRS DE MULLIN Do you mean when I sent the telegram? But Hugo   300 was unconscious.

MRS CLOUSTON As soon as he recovered consciousness then.

MRS DE MULLIN I did mean to. But he seemed so weak, and Dr Rolt said any excitement . . . .

MRS CLOUSTON Dr Rolt!   305

MRS DE MULLIN (*goaded*) Well, I couldn't tell that Dr Rolt knew so little about Hugo's illness, could I? And I was afraid of the shock.

MRS CLOUSTON Still, he should have been told at once. It was the only chance.

MRS DE MULLIN Yes. I see that now. But I was afraid of the shock, as I   310 said. So I put it off. And then, when I didn't hear from Janet, I thought I would wait.

MRS CLOUSTON Why?

MRS DE MULLIN You see I didn't know whether she was coming. And if she didn't come, of course there was no necessity for telling Hugo   315 anything about it. I'm afraid he'll be very angry.

MRS CLOUSTON At any rate, you must tell him now. The sooner the better.

MRS DE MULLIN (*meekly*) Very well, Harriet. If you think so.

MRS CLOUSTON You had better go up to him at once.   320

> *Mrs De Mullin goes to the door on the left, opens it, then draws back hastily*

MRS DE MULLIN Here *is* Hugo. He's just coming across the hall. With Hester. How unlucky.

MRS CLOUSTON I don't see that it matters.

MRS DE MULLIN I'd rather not have told him before Hester.

> *Mrs Clouston shrugs her shoulders. A moment later Hugo enters. He leans on a stick and Hester's arm. He looks weak and pale and altogether extremely sorry for himself, obviously a nervous and a very tiresome patient*

HESTER Carefully, father. That's right. Will you lie on the sofa? 325

DE MULLIN (*fretfully*) No. Put me in the armchair. I'm tired of lying down.

HESTER Very well. Let me help you. There. Wait a moment. I'll fetch you some pillows. (*Props him up on pillows in an armchair*)

DE MULLIN Thank you. (*Lies back exhausted and closes his eyes*) 330

MRS DE MULLIN (*going to him*) How are you feeling now, Hugo?

DE MULLIN Very weak.°

MRS DE MULLIN I wonder if you ought to have come down?

DE MULLIN It won't make any difference. Nothing will make any difference any more, Jane. I shan't last much longer. I'm worn out. 335

HESTER Father!

DE MULLIN Yes, Hester. Worn out. (*With a sort of melancholy pride*) None of the De Mullins have been strong. I'm the last of them. The last of the De Mullins.

MRS CLOUSTON Come, Hugo, you mustn't talk in that morbid way. 340

DE MULLIN I'm not morbid, Harriet. But I feel tired, tired.

MRS DE MULLIN You'll be better in a day or two.

DE MULLIN No, Jane. I shall never be better. Never in *this* world. (*Pause*)

MRS DE MULLIN (*nervously*) Hugo . . . there's something . . . something I have to tell you . . . 345

DE MULLIN What is it, Jane? (*Fretfully*) What have you been keeping from me?

MRS DE MULLIN I ought to have told you before. Only I didn't like . . .

DE MULLIN Is it something about my illness?

MRS DE MULLIN Oh no, Hugo. 350

DE MULLIN (*relieved*) I thought Dr Rolt might have said something.

MRS DE MULLIN It's nothing of that kind.

DE MULLIN (*peevishly*) Well, well, what is it?

MRS DE MULLIN Hugo, some one is coming here today, to see *you*.

DE MULLIN To see *me*? Who? 355

MRS DE MULLIN You won't be angry, Hugo?

222

DE MULLIN (*testily*) How can I possibly say that, Jane, when I don't know who it is?

MRS DE MULLIN Hugo, it's . . . (*Bell rings loudly*)° Harriet, there's the bell! I wonder if it's she? Do you think it is?   360

> *All look towards the door on the right, expectantly*

DE MULLIN (*querulously*) Well, Jane? *Am* I to hear who this visitor is or am I not?

ELLEN (*showing in a lady leading a little boy by the hand*) Mrs Seagrave.

> *Enter Janet and Johnny L. Janet is a very handsome woman of six-and-thirty. She is admirably dressed,° but her clothes are quiet and in excellent taste, dark in colour and plain in cut but expensive. Her hat is particularly tasteful, but also quiet. Her clothes are in marked contrast to those of her mother and sister which are of the homeliest description and were probably made in the village. Johnny is a well-grown youngster of eight in a sailor suit°*

HESTER (*shocked*) Mother!

DE MULLIN Janet, my dear! (*Cry of welcome*)   365

JANET Father! (*Drops Johnny's hand, comes rapidly to him, falls on one knee and kisses him impulsively, patting his left hand with her right*) How are you? Better? (*Holding out her left hand to her mother but still kneeling*) How do you do, mother dear? (*Mrs De Mullin takes it. Puts her other hand on Janet's shoulder*) I should have come before, father, directly you sent for me. But your telegram was delayed. I was away   370 from home.

DE MULLIN (*nods*) I see.

JANET Have you been very ill, father? And did you frighten them all dreadfully? How naughty of you!

DE MULLIN Silly Janet! Let me look at you, my dear. (*Looks at her face   375 as she holds it up*) You're not much changed, Janet.

JANET Nor are you, father.

DE MULLIN A little greyer, perhaps.

JANET No! Not a hair!

DE MULLIN Well, my dear, I'm glad you've come. We parted in anger,   380 but that's all over now. Forgotten and forgiven. Eh?

JANET Yes. Forgotten and forgiven. (*Rises*) How are *you*, Aunt Harriet? I didn't see you. (*Eagerly*) Hester! (*Goes to her impulsively, holding out her hand. Hester takes it coldly. Janet tries to draw her towards her. Hester resists. She drops her hand and Hester turns away*)°

DE MULLIN Who is that? (*Pointing to Johnny*)

JANET (*turning to him*) That is Johnny. My son.   385

223

DE MULLIN My grandson?

JANET Yes. I *had* to bring him, father. We were away from home and there was no one to leave him with.

DE MULLIN I'm glad you brought him. Come here, Johnny. Don't be afraid.   390

JOHNNY (*in his confident treble*) I'm not afraid. Why should I be afraid? (*Goes to him*)

DE MULLIN (*taking his hand*) Say 'How do you do, grandfather'.

JOHNNY How do you do, grandfather?

DE MULLIN Will you give me a kiss, Johnny?

JOHNNY If you like, grandfather. (*Kisses him*)   395

DE MULLIN That's a good boy.

JANET Kiss your grandmother too, Johnny.

> *Mrs De Mullin snatches him up and kisses him passionately. Then holds him a little way off and looks at him admiringly*

MRS DE MULLIN What a fine little fellow, Janet!

JANET (*proudly*) Isn't he, mother? And *so* strong and healthy! He's hardly had a day's illness since he was born.°   400

JOHNNY (*who has been staring at the pictures on the walls, holding his grandmother by one hand*) Who are all these old men, grandfather?

DE MULLIN Your ancestors, my boy.

JOHNNY What's ancestors?

DE MULLIN Your forefathers. Your mother's forefathers.

JOHNNY Is that old man in the wig an ancestor?   405

DE MULLIN Yes. That is Anthony De Mullin, your great-great-grandfather.

JOHNNY What was *he*?

DE MULLIN (*puzzled*) *What* was he? I don't know that he was anything in particular. He was just a gentleman.   410

JOHNNY (*disappointed*) Is that all?

DE MULLIN Don't make any mistake, my boy. It's a great thing to be descended from gentle-people, a thing to be proud of and to be thankful for.°

JOHNNY Mother says the great thing is for every one to be of some use   415
in the world. Are gentle-people of more use in the world than other people, grandfather?

DE MULLIN Certainly.

JOHNNY And were all these old men gentle-people?

DE MULLIN All of them. And you must grow up like them.   420

JOHNNY They're very *ugly*, grandfather. (*Pause*) What did they *do*?

DE MULLIN They lived down here at Brendon.

JOHNNY Nothing else?

DE MULLIN They looked after their land.

JOHNNY Had they much land?   425

DE MULLIN A great deal. At one time the De Mullins owned all the land about here.

JOHNNY How much do they own now?

DE MULLIN (*sighs*) Not very much, I'm afraid.

JOHNNY Then they can't have looked after it very well, can they,   430
grandfather?°

MRS DE MULLIN (*feeling the strain of this conversation*) Now, Hugo, do you think you ought to talk any more? Why not go upstairs for a little and lie down?

DE MULLIN Perhaps I will, Jane. I *am* a little tired.   435

HESTER Shall I go with father?

MRS DE MULLIN No. I will. Come, Hugo. (*Helps him up*)

DE MULLIN Will you come, with me, Johnny?

MRS DE MULLIN (*hastily*) No, Hugo. He will only disturb you. Stay down here, Johnny, with your mother. Now then. Carefully. (*Leads*   440
De Mullin off by the door on the left)

> *There is a pause, during which the remaining occupants of the*
> *room obviously have nothing in particular to say to each other. At*
> *last Mrs Clouston speaks*

MRS CLOUSTON Well, Janet, how have you been all these years?

JANET (*nonchalantly*) All right, Aunt Harriet. And you?

MRS CLOUSTON Pretty well, thanks.

JANET Are you still living down at Bath?

MRS CLOUSTON Yes. You live in London, Jane tells me.   445

JANET Yes.

MRS CLOUSTON What do you do there? Teach?

JANET Oh no. Why should I be teaching?

MRS CLOUSTON Jane said you wanted to teach at one time.

JANET That was years ago. Before I left Brendon. I soon gave up that   450
idea. No. I keep a shop.

MRS CLOUSTON A shop!°

JANET Yes. A hat-shop.

MRS CLOUSTON Good heavens! A De Mullin in a hat-shop!

JANET (*a little maliciously*) Not a De Mullin, Aunt Harriet. A Seagrave.   455

MRS CLOUSTON Did Mr Seagrave keep a hat-shop?

JANET Mr Seagrave? . . . oh, I see. No. It's not a man's hat shop. It's a lady's°. (*Takes off hat*) This is one of ours. What do you think of it, Hester?

HESTER (*frostily*) It looks very expensive.   460

JANET (*looking at it critically*) Yes, I own I'm rather pleased with it.

MRS CLOUSTON (*acidly*) You seem to be able to *dress* very well altogether, in spite of the shop.

JANET (*correcting her*) Because of it, Aunt Harriet. That's the advantage
of being what is called 'in trade'. If I were a school teacher or a gov-   465
erness or something genteel of that kind I could only afford to dress
like a pauper. But as I keep a shop I can dress like a lady. Clothes are
a question of money, after all, aren't they?

MRS CLOUSTON (*contemptuously*) If one is in a shop it doesn't matter
how one dresses.   470

JANET On the contrary if one is in a shop it matters a great deal. A girl
in a shop *must* dress well. The business demands it. If you ever start a
hat-shop, Aunt Harriet, you'll have to dress very differently. Otherwise nobody will buy your hats.

MRS CLOUSTON Indeed? Fortunately I've no intention of starting a   475
shop of any kind.

JANET (*blandly*) No? Well, I expect you're wise. I doubt if you'd make a
success of it.°

Loud ring heard off

MRS CLOUSTON (*rather flustered—gasps*) Hester! I hope that's not a
visitor. (*Janet stares. Then laughs good-humouredly. Aunt Harriet's*   480
nervous desire to keep her out of the way of visitors strikes her as amusing)
What *are* you laughing at, Janet?

JANET (*shrugs*) Nothing, Aunt Harriet.

ELLEN (*showing in*) Miss Deanes. Mr Brown.

Miss Deanes is a bulky, red-faced, short-sighted woman of forty-
two, very fussy and absurd in manner, who talks very fast. Brown
carries a book

MISS DEANES How do you do, Mrs Clouston. *Such* a piece of news! I
felt I *must* tell you. I brought Mr Brown with me. He was just leaving   485
a book for you, Hester, so I made him come in. (*Shakes hands with*
Hester)

BROWN Here it is, Miss De Mullin. It's the one you wanted to borrow.
Blore on the Creeds.

HESTER Thank you. [(*Brown and Hester go upstage and converse in dumb-*
show)]

MISS DEANES (*seeing Janet for first time*) Janet! Is that you?

JANET Yes, Miss Deanes. How are you? (*Shakes hands*)   490

MISS DEANES Good gracious, child, when did you come? Why, you've
not been down to Brendon for years.

JANET It is a long time, isn't it?

MISS DEANES And who is this young gentleman? (*Noticing Johnny who is holding Janet's hand and staring at Miss Deanes*)

JANET (*calmly*) That is my son. Shake hands with Miss Deanes,   495
Johnny.

MISS DEANES (*astonished*) Your Son! There now! And I never knew you were even married!

JANET (*quite at her ease*) Didn't you?

MISS DEANES No.   500

MRS CLOUSTON (*nervously*) I forgot. I haven't introduced you. Mr Brown—Mrs Seagrave.

BROWN (*bows*) How do you do.

MRS CLOUSTON (*turning to Miss Deanes again*) And now what *is* your piece of news, Miss Deanes?   505

MISS DEANES (*volubly*) Oh yes, I *must* tell you. You'd never guess. Somebody *else* is engaged to be married. (*To Janet*) *Who* do you think?

JANET I've no idea.

MISS DEANES Bertha Aldenham—to Mr Bulstead.   510

JANET (*starts*) Mr Bulstead?

MISS DEANES Yes. But I forgot. *You* wouldn't know *them*. They didn't come here till long after you went way. They bought Brendon Park from the Malcolms three years ago. You remember the Malcolms, Janet?   515

JANET (*whose attention has wandered*) Eh! Oh yes, of course.

MRS CLOUSTON Which Mr Bulstead is it? The eldest?

MISS DEANES Yes. Montague.

JANET (*under her breath*) Monty Bulstead! Engaged!°

MRS CLOUSTON Are the Aldenhams pleased?   520

MISS DEANES Very, I expect. The Bulsteads are so rich, you see.

JANET Does he live down here; this Mr Montague Bulstead, I mean?

MISS DEANES Oh no. He's here on leave. He's in the army. He only got back three months ago. (*With a little giggle*) He and Bertha haven't taken long to settle things, have they?   525

JANET No, they haven't taken long.

MISS DEANES But I dare say he *will* live here when he's married. As the Bulsteads are so rich. The father makes frilling and lace and so on. All those things people used to make so much better by hand. And Bertha may not care about army life. I know *I* shouldn't. (*Janet smiles   530 discreetly*) It's not always very *nice*, is it?

BROWN (*to Johnny who has been staring at him round-eyed across the room,*

227

with heavy geniality) Well, young man. Who are you staring at, eh? Do *you* want to talk to *me*?

JOHNNY (*quite simply in his high piping treble*) No, thank you.

JANET Sh! Johnny! You don't mean that. Go to Mr Brown when he   535
speaks to you.

JOHNNY Very well, Mummie. (*Does so slowly*)

BROWN (*taking his hands*) Now then what shall *we* talk about, you and I?

JOHNNY I don't know.

BROWN Don't you? Suppose we see if you can say your catechism°   540
then? Would you like *that*?

JOHNNY What's catechism?

BROWN Come, Johnny, I'm sure your mother has taught you your
catechism. Can you repeat your 'Duty towards your Neighbour'?
(*Johnny shakes his head emphatically*) Try 'My duty towards my   545
neighbour . . .'

JOHNNY Mother says it's everyone's duty to be healthy and to be
happy. Is that what you mean?

BROWN (*scandalized*) No! No!

JOHNNY Well, that's what mother taught me.   550

JANET (*coming to the rescue*) I'm afraid he doesn't know his catechism
yet, Mr Brown. You see he's only eight. (*Brown bows stiffly*) Run
away, Johnny, and play in the garden for a little. (*Leads him to the door
in the bay*)

JOHNNY All right, Mummie. (*Johnny runs out into the garden. A certain
relief is perceptible on his departure. It is felt that his interview with Mr
Brown has not been a success*)

MISS DEANES (*who feels that a change of subject will be only tactful*) There   555
now, Hester! I do believe you've never asked after Dicky! He'll be *so*
offended!

HESTER (*smiling*) Has Dicky been ill again? I thought you said he was
better yesterday.

MISS DEANES He was. But he had a relapse, poor *darling*. I had to sit up   560
all last night with him!

JANET What has been the matter with him?

MISS DEANES Some sort of chill, Dr Rolt said. I was *dreadfully* anxious.

JANET What a pity! Colds are such troublesome things for children.

MISS DEANES (*puzzled*) Children?   565

JANET Yes. You were speaking of a child, weren't you?

MISS DEANES Oh no. Dicky is my *cockatoo*. He's the *sweetest* bird. Talks
quite like a human being. And never a coarse expression. That's so
unusual with cockatoos.

JANET Indeed?   570

MISS DEANES Yes. The voyage, you see. They come all the way from
  South America and generally they pick up the most dreadful language, poor lambs—from the sailors. But Dicky didn't. He has such
  a pure mind. (*Rising*) And now I really must be going. I have all kinds
  of people I want to tell about Mr Bulstead's engagement. (*Shaking*   575
  hands with Mrs Clouston and Janet)

BROWN I must be off too. Wait one moment, Miss Deanes. Good-bye,
  Mrs Clouston. (*Shakes hands with Mrs Clouston and bows stiffly to*
  Janet. He has not yet forgiven Johnny for not knowing his catechism. To
  Hester) Good-bye, Miss De Mullin. Shall I see you at Evensong?
  (*Shakes hands with Hester*)

HESTER I expect so.

> *Brown and Miss Deanes go out*

JANET Poof!°   580

MRS CLOUSTON Janet!

JANET What a fool Miss Deanes is!

MRS CLOUSTON (*indifferently*) She always was, wasn't she?

JANET I suppose so. Going on in that way about her ridiculous cockatoo! And that *hideous* little curate!   585

HESTER I don't see why you should sneer at all my friends.

JANET Are they your friends, Hester? Then I won't sneer at them. But
  you can't call Mr Brown *handsome*, can you?

HESTER Mr Brown is a very good man and works very hard among the
  poor. That's better than being handsome.   590

JANET Yes. But less agreeable, isn't it? However, if *you* like him there's
  an end of it. But he needn't have begun asking Johnny his catechism
  the very first time he met him. *I* don't call it good manners.

HESTER How was he to know the poor child was being brought up to be
  a little heathen? (*Takes up her hat and cape and begins putting them on*)   595

JANET (*shrugs*) How, indeed!

MRS CLOUSTON Are you going out, Hester? Lunch will be ready in half
  an hour.

HESTER Only to take Mrs Wason her soup,° Aunt Harriet.

JANET (*looking curiously at Hester*). Do you want to marry Mr Brown,   600
  Hester?

MRS CLOUSTON My dear Janet!

JANET Well, Aunt Harriet, there's nothing to be ashamed of if she does.
  Do you, Hester?

HESTER Why do you ask such a question?   605

JANET Never mind. Only answer it. (*Pause*) You do like him, don't you?

HESTER I've a great respect for Mr Brown.

JANET Don't blush, my dear. I dare say that's much the same thing.

HESTER I won't talk to you about it. You only sneer.

JANET I wasn't sneering. Come, Hester, don't be cross. Why shouldn't 610
we be friends? I might help you.

HESTER How could *you* help me?

JANET (*looking quizzically at poor Hester's headgear*) I might make you a
hat, my dear.

HESTER Mr Brown doesn't notice those things. 615

JANET All men notice those things, Hester.

HESTER (*with a sneer*) I suppose that's why *you* wear such fine clothes.

JANET (*quite good-humoured*) That's it. Fine feathers make fine birds.

HESTER Well, *I* call it shameless.

JANET My dear Hester, you're always being ashamed of things. You 620
always were, I remember. What is there to be ashamed of in that?
What on earth were women given pretty faces and pretty figures for
if not to make men admire them and want to marry them?

HESTER (*acidly*) Well, *your* plan hasn't been very successful so far, anyhow! 625

JANET (*quietly*) Nor has yours, Hester.

> *Hester makes exclamation of impatience and seems about to reply
> angrily. Then thinks better of it and goes out without a word.
> Janet follows her retreat with her eyes and smiles half cynically,
> half compassionately*

THE CURTAIN FALLS

2

SCENE° *On the edge of Brendon Forest. Time: three days later.*
A road runs along the back of the stage from which it is separated
by a fence and high hedge. In this but somewhat to the right is a
stile and also a gate. Round the trunk of a large tree to the left is a
rough wooden seat.

The stage is empty when the curtain rises. Then enter Mrs De
Mullin, Janet, and Johnny. They approach stile from the left and
come through gate. There is an exit on the right of the stage
through the Forest

JANET   I don't think I'll come any farther, mother.

MRS DE MULLIN   You won't come up to the house?

JANET   No, thanks. (*Rather grimly*) I don't want to see Mrs Bulstead.
And I'm sure Mrs Bulstead doesn't want to see me.

MRS DE MULLIN   I wish Hester could have come.   5

JANET   Why couldn't she?

MRS DE MULLIN   She's at the church putting up the decorations. It's
the Harvest Thanksgiving tomorrow.

JANET (*laughing*)   Mr Brown!

MRS DE MULLIN   Janet, I told you you weren't to laugh at Hester about   10
Mr Brown. It's not kind.

JANET (*lightly*)   It's all right mother. Hester's not here.

MRS DE MULLIN   Still, I don't like it, dear. It's not quite . . .

JANET (*soothing her*)   Not quite *nice*. I know, mother. Not the way really
refined and ladylike young women talk. But I'm only quite a common   15
person who sells hats. You can't expect all these refinements from *me*!
Mrs De Mullin sighs

MRS DE MULLIN   Are you going to turn back?

JANET   Not at once. I'll wait for you here a little with Johnny in case
they're out. Why, they've put a seat here. (*She sits on the side farthest*
from the road)

MRS DE MULLIN   Usen't there to be one?   20

JANET   No. Nor a gate in my time. Only a stile.

MRS DE MULLIN   Very likely, dear. I don't remember. I don't often
come this way.

JANET (*nods*)   I often used to come along it in the old days.

MRS DE MULLIN   I dare say. Well, I must be getting on to my call or I   25
shall be late. You're sure you won't come?

231

JANET Quite, mother. Good-bye.
> *Mrs De Mullin goes off through the forest*

JOHNNY Where's grandmother going, Mummie?

JANET Up to the big house.

JOHNNY What big house?   30

JANET Brendon Park.

JOHNNY Mayn't I go up to the big house too?

JANET No, dear. You're to stay with mother.

JOHNNY Who lives at the big house?

JANET Nobody you know, dear.   35

JOHNNY That's why I asked, Mummie.

JANET Well, don't ask any more, sonny. Mother's rather tired.° Run away and play, there's a good boy. (*Kisses him*)

JOHNNY Very well, Mummie. (*Johnny disappears into the wood*)
> *Janet falls into a brown study.° Presently a footstep is heard coming along the road, but she seems to notice nothing. Then a young man climbs over the stile. He starts as he sees her and draws back, then advances eagerly, holding out his hand*

JANET Monty!°   40

MONTY Janet, is that *you!*

JANET (*smiling*) Yes, Monty.

MONTY (*astonished*) Janet! Here!

JANET Yes, Monty.

MONTY (*nodding over his shoulder*) *Our* stile, Janet!   45

JANET Our stile.

MONTY (*nods*) The stile where you and I first met.

JANET (*relapsing for a moment into something like sentiment*) Yes. I thought I must see it again—for the sake of old times.

MONTY How long ago it all seems!   50

JANET (*matter of fact*) It *is* a longish time, you know.

MONTY (*thoughtfully*) I believe that was the happiest month of my life, Janet.

JANET Was it, Monty?

MONTY Yes. (*Pause*) I say, when did you come down? You don't *live* at   55
home any longer, do you?

JANET No. I only came down three days ago.

MONTY By Jove it *is* good to see you again. Why, it's eight years since we used to be together, you and I.

JANET Nearly nine.   60

MONTY Yes . . . You're not coming to live down here again, are you?

JANET No: why?

MONTY I thought perhaps . . .

JANET (*cynically*) Would you dislike it very much if I did, Monty?

MONTY Of course not.   65

JANET Confess. You *did* feel it would be rather awkward?

MONTY Well, of course . . .

JANET However you can set your mind at rest. I'm not.
      His relief at this intelligence enables him to realize the pleasure he
      is getting from seeing her again

MONTY I say, Janet, how well you're looking! I believe you're hand-
    somer than ever.   70

JANET (*smiling*) Am I?

MONTY You know you are.
      Pause. He looks at her admiringly. She turns away with a little
      smile

JANET (*feeling that they are getting on to dangerous ground*) Well, Monty.
    Where have you been these eight years?

MONTY Abroad with my regiment. We've been ordered all over the   75
    place.° I've been home on leave, of course. But not for the last three
    years. Not since father bought the Park. I've never been at Brendon
    since . . . (*Pause*)

JANET Since *we* were here? Don't blush, Monty. (*He nods shamefacedly*)
    How did he come to buy the place?   80

MONTY It was just a chance. He saw it advertised, came and looked at it
    and bought it. He's no idea I was ever at Brendon before. (*Rather bit-*
    ter laugh) None of them have. I have to pretend not to know my way
    about.

JANET Why?   85

MONTY It seems safer. (*Janet nods*) Sometimes I almost forget to keep
    it up. I'm such a duffer about things. But I've managed hitherto. And
    now, of course, it's all right as I've been here three months. I may be
    supposed to know the beastly place by this time.

JANET Beastly? You're not very polite.   90
    Monty laughs shamefacedly

MONTY You got my note, didn't you?

JANET What note? . . . Oh, eight years ago, you mean? Yes.

MONTY I left it with the woman at the lodgings. As you were coming
    over that afternoon, I thought it safer than sending a message. And of
    course I daren't telegraph. (*Janet nods*) I was awfully sick at having to 95
    go away like that. All in a moment. Without even saying good–bye.
    But I had to.

JANET Of course. Was your mother badly hurt?

MONTY   No. Only stunned. That was such rot. If people get chucked
out of a carriage they must expect to get stunned. But of course they   100
couldn't know. The telegram just said 'Mother hurt. Carriage accident. Come at once'. It got to me at the lodgings a couple of hours
before you were coming. I had just time to chuck my things into a bag
and catch the train. I wanted to come back after the mater° was all
right again. But I couldn't very well, could I?   105

JANET   Why not?

MONTY   Well, the regiment was to sail in less than three weeks and the
mater would have thought it rather rough if I'd gone away again. I'd
been away six weeks as it was.

JANET   Oh yes. Of course.   110

MONTY   (*with half a sigh*) To think if I hadn't happened to be riding
along that road and seen you at the stile and asked my way, you and I
might never have met. What a chance life is!

JANET   (*nods*) Just a chance. (*Pause*)

MONTY   Why did you go away, Janet? You weren't going the last time I   115
saw you.

JANET   Wasn't I?

MONTY   No. At least you said nothing about it.

JANET   I didn't know I was going then. Not for certain.

MONTY   Why *did* you go?   120

JANET   (*quietly*) I had to, Monty.

MONTY   (*puzzled*) You had to? (*Janet nods*) But why?

JANET   Mother found out.

MONTY   About us?

JANET   Yes. And she told father.   125

MONTY   (*genuinely distressed*) Oh, Janet! I'm so sorry.

JANET   (*shrugs*) It couldn't be helped.

MONTY   Does he know who it was?

JANET   Who *you* were? No.

MONTY   You didn't tell him?   130

JANET   Monty! As if I should.

MONTY   I don't know. Girls generally do.

JANET   *I* didn't.

MONTY   No. I suppose you wouldn't. But you're different from most
girls. Do you know there was always something rather splendid about   135
you, Janet?

JANET   (*curtseys*) Thank you.

MONTY   I wonder he didn't *make* you tell.

JANET   He did try of course. That was why I ran away.

MONTY I see. Where did you go to? 140

JANET London.

MONTY To London? All alone? (*Janet nods*) Why did you do that? And why didn't you let me know?

JANET (*shrugs*) You were out of England by that time.

MONTY But why London? 145

JANET I had to go somewhere. And it seemed better to go where I shouldn't be known. Besides it's easier to be lost sight of in a crowd.

MONTY But what did you do when you got there?

JANET (*calmly*) I got a place in a shop, Monty.

MONTY A shop? You! 150

JANET Yes, a hat-shop, in Regent Street.° My dear Monty, don't gape like that. Hat-shops are perfectly respectable places. Almost too respectable to judge by the fuss two of them made about employing *me*.

MONTY What do you mean?

JANET Well, when I applied to them for work they naturally asked if I 155
had ever worked in a hat-shop before. And when I said 'No' they naturally asked why I wanted to begin. In the innocence of my heart I told them. Whereupon they at once refused to employ me—not in the politest terms.

MONTY Poor Janet, What beastly luck! Still . . . (*Hesitates*) 160

JANET Yes, Monty?

MONTY I mean naturally they couldn't be expected . . .

JANET Monty!

MONTY (*flustered*) At least I don't mean that exactly. Only . . . (*Stops*)

JANET My dear Monty, I quite understand what you mean. You 165
needn't trouble to be explicit. Naturally they couldn't be expected to employ an abandoned person like me to trim hats. That was exactly their view.

MONTY But I thought you said you *did* get a place in a shop?

JANET Yes. But not at either of *those* shops. They were *far* too virtuous. 170

MONTY How did you do it?

JANET Told lies, Monty. I believe that's how most women get employment.

MONTY Told lies?

JANET Yes. I invented a husband, recently deceased, bought several 175
yards of crêpe° and a wedding ring. This is the ring (*Takes off glove*)

MONTY Oh, Janet, how beastly for you! (*Janet shrugs*)

JANET (*laughing*) Everything seems to be 'Beastly' to you, Monty. Brendon and telling lies and lots of other things. Luckily I'm less superfine. 180

MONTY Didn't they find out?

JANET No. That was why I decided to be a widow. It made inquiries more difficult.

MONTY I should have thought it made them easier.

JANET On the contrary. You can't cross-question a widow about a   185
recent bereavement. If you do she cries. I always used to look tearful directly my husband's name was even mentioned. So they gave up mentioning it. Women are so boring when they will cry.

MONTY They might have inquired from other people.

JANET Why should they? Besides there was no one to inquire from. I   190
called him Seagrave—and drowned him at sea. You can't ask questions of the sharks.

MONTY Oh, Janet, how can you joke about it?

JANET I couldn't—then. I wanted work too badly. But I can now—with your kind permission, I mean.   195

MONTY And you've been at the shop ever since?

JANET Not *that* shop. I was only there about six months—till baby was born, in fact . . .

MONTY (*horrified*) Janet, there was a baby!

JANET Of course there was a baby.   200

MONTY Oh, Janet! And you never wrote! Why didn't you write?

JANET I did think of it. But on the whole I thought I wouldn't. It would have been no good.

MONTY No good?

JANET Not then. You were in India.° I was in England.   205

MONTY You ought to have written at once—directly your mother found out.

JANET One week after you sailed, Monty. (*Defiantly*) Besides why should I write?

MONTY Why? I could have married you, of course.   210

JANET If I'd asked you, you mean? Thank you, my dear Monty.

MONTY No, I don't. Of course I should have married you. I *must* have married you.

JANET (*looking at him thoughtfully*) I wonder if you would.

MONTY Certainly I should. I should have been bound in honour.   215

JANET I see. Then I'm glad I never wrote.

MONTY You're *glad*? Now?

JANET Yes. I've done some foolish things in my life, Monty, but none quite so foolish as that. To marry a schoolboy, not because he loves you or wants to marry you but because he thinks he's 'bound in honour'. No, thank you.°   220

236

MONTY I don't mean that. You know I don't, Janet. I loved you, of
course. That goes without saying. I'd have married you like a shot
before, only the Governor° would have made such a fuss. The Governor was so awfully straitlaced about this sort of thing. When I was   225
sent away from Eton he made the most ghastly fuss.°

JANET Were you sent away from Eton for 'this sort of thing'?

MONTY Yes—at least I don't mean that either. But it was about a girl
there. He was frightfully wild. He threatened to cut me off if I ever
did such a thing again. Such rot! As if no one had ever been sent away   230
from school before!

JANET (*reflectively*) I didn't know you'd been sent away from Eton.

MONTY Didn't you? I suppose I didn't like to tell you—for fear of what
you'd think. (*Bitterly*) I seem to have been afraid of everything in
those days.   235

JANET Not *everything*, Monty.

MONTY Oh, you know what I mean. I was awfully afraid of the Govern-
or, I remember. I suppose all boys are if their parents rag° them too
much. But I would have married you, Janet, if I'd known. I would
honestly.   240

JANET (*blandly*) What is the pay of a British subaltern,° Monty?

MONTY The Governor would have had to stump up, of course.

JANET Poor Mr Bulstead! He'd have *liked* that, I suppose? And what
about your poor unhappy colonel? And all the other little subalterns?

MONTY (*obstinately*) Still, you ought to have written.   245

JANET (*quietly*) *You* never wrote.

MONTY I couldn't. You know that. You never would let me. That was
why I couldn't send that note to you to tell you I was going away. You
said my letters would be noticed.

JANET Yes. I forgot that. That's the result of having a father who is   250
what is called old-fashioned.

MONTY What do you mean?

JANET All letters to the Manor House are delivered locked in a bag.
They always have been since the Flood, I believe, or at least since the
invention of the postal service.° And, of course, father won't have it   255
altered. So every morning there's the ritual of unlocking this absurd
bag. No one is allowed to do that but father—unless he is ill. Then
mother has the privilege. And of course he scrutinizes the outside of
every letter and directly it's opened asks who it's from and what's
inside it. Your letters would have been noticed at once.°   260

MONTY How beastly!

JANET The penalty of having nothing to do, Monty.

MONTY I know. What a mess the whole thing is!

JANET Just so. No. There was no way out of it except the hat-shop.

MONTY (*remorsefully*) It's awfully rough on you, Janet.   265

JANET Never mind. I dare say I wasn't cut out for the wife of a subaltern, Monty; whereas I make excellent hats.

MONTY (*savagely*) You're still making the d——d° things?

JANET Yes. Only at another shop. The Regent Street place had no room
for me when I was well enough to go back to work. But the woman   270
who kept it gave me a recommendation to a friend who was starting
in Hanover Street.° A most superior quarter for a hat-shop, Monty.
In fact *the* superior quarter. Claude et Cie° was the name.

MONTY (*rather shocked*) A *French* shop?°

JANET No more French than you are, Monty. It was kept by a Miss   275
Hicks, one of the most thoroughly British people you can possibly
imagine. But we called ourselves Claude et Cie in order to be able
to charge people more for their hats. You can always charge fashionable women more for their clothes if you pretend to be French.
It's one of the imbecilities of commerce. So poor dear Miss Hicks   280
became Madame Claude and none of our hats cost less than seven
guineas.

MONTY Do people buy hats at such a price?

JANET Oh yes. Everybody in Society bought them. Claude et Cie was
quite the rage that season. Nobody who was anybody went anywhere   285
else.

MONTY She must have made a great deal of money.

JANET On the contrary. She made nothing at all and narrowly escaped
bankruptcy.

MONTY But I don't understand. If her hats were so dear and everybody   290
bought them?

JANET Everybody *bought* them but nobody *paid* for them. In the highest social circles I believe people never do pay for anything—certainly not for their clothes. At least, nobody paid Miss Hicks, and at
the end of six months she was owed £1,200 and hadn't a penny to   295
pay her rent.

MONTY Why didn't she *make* them pay?

JANET She did dun° them, of course, but they only ordered more hats
to keep her quiet which didn't help Miss Hicks much. And when she
went on dunning them they said they should withdraw their custom.   300

[MONTY That must have been awkward for Miss Hicks.

JANET It was. You see by that time it was the end of the season and
they'd got all the hats they wanted.] In fact, she was in a dilemma. If

she let the bills run on she couldn't pay her rent. And if she asked her customers to pay their bills they ceased to be customers.   305

MONTY How beastly!

JANET Not again, Monty!

MONTY What *did* she do?

JANET She didn't do anything. She was too depressed. She used to sit in the back room where the hats were trimmed and weep over the   310 materials, regardless of expense. Finally things came to a crisis. The landlord threatened to distrain° for his rent [and one or two other creditors were equally pressing]. But just as it looked as if it was all over with Claude et Cie a capitalist came to the rescue. *I* was the capitalist.   315

MONTY You?

JANET Yes. I'd an old Aunt once who was fond of me and left me a legacy when I was seventeen. Four hundred pounds.

MONTY That wouldn't go very far.

JANET Four hundred pounds goes a longish way towards setting up a   320 shop. Besides, it was nearly five hundred by that time. My shares had gone up.° Well, I and my five hundred pounds came to the rescue. I paid the rent and the most clamorous of the creditors, and Miss Hicks and I became partners.

MONTY But what was the good of that if the business was worth   325 nothing?

JANET It was worth several hundred pounds to any one, who had the pluck to sue half the British aristocracy. I sued them [or rather the firm did at my instigation.] It was tremendous fun. They were simply furious. They talked as if they'd never been sued before! As for Miss   330 Hicks she wept more than ever and said I'd ruined the business.

MONTY Hadn't you?

JANET That business. Yes. But with the £1,200—or as much of it as we could recover—we started a new one. A cheap hat-shop. Relatively cheap that is—for Hanover Street. We charged two guineas a   335 hat instead of seven, 100 per cent. profit instead of . . . You can work it out for yourself. But then our terms were strictly cash, so we made no bad debts. That was my idea.

MONTY But you said nobody ever paid for their hats.

JANET Not in the highest social circles. But we drew our customers   340 from the middle classes who live in South Kensington and Bayswater,° and are not too haughty to pay for a hat if they see a cheap one.

MONTY But wasn't it a frightful risk?

JANET (*cheerfully*) It was a risk, of course. But everything in life is a risk,

isn't it? And it succeeded, as I felt sure it would. We're quite a pros-   345
perous concern now-a-days, and I go over to Paris four times a year°
to see the latest fashions. That, my dear Monty, is the history of
Claude et Cie.
    Pause

MONTY And you've never married, Janet?

JANET No.   350

MONTY (*hesitates*) Janet . . . is it because . . . ?

JANET Because?

MONTY Because you still care for *me*?

JANET Monty, don't be vain.

MONTY (*repelled*) I didn't mean it like that. Janet, don't laugh. Of   355
course, I'm glad if you don't care any more. At least, I suppose I
ought to be glad. It would have been dreadful if you had gone on car-
ing all these years and I not known. But did you?

JANET No, Monty. You may set your mind at rest. I didn't.

MONTY You're sure?   360

JANET Quite. I had too many other things to think of.

MONTY Do you mean that beastly shop?

JANET (*quietly*) I meant my baby.

MONTY *Our* baby. Is it alive?

JANET Of course. What do you mean, Monty?   365

MONTY I thought, as you didn't say . . . (*Thoughtfully*) Poor little beast!
(*Janet makes gesture of protest*) Well, it's rough luck on the little beggar, isn't it? What's become of him, Janet?

JANET What's *become* of him! My dear Monty, what should have
become of him? He's quite alive as I said and particularly thriving.   370

MONTY Do you mean he's *living* with you! . . . But, of course, I forgot,
you're supposed to be married.

JANET (*correcting him*) A widow, Monty. An inconsolable widow!

MONTY Where is he? In London?

JANET No. As a matter of fact he's probably not fifty yards away. Over   375
there. (*Points towards the wood*)

MONTY (*jumping up*) Janet! (*Nervously looking round*)

JANET (*rallying° him*) Frightened, Monty?

MONTY Of course not. (*Shamefacedly*)

JANET [Confess!] Just a little?   380

MONTY (*regaining courage*) Janet, let me see him.

JANET (*amused*) Would you like to?

MONTY Of course I should. He's *my* baby as well as yours if it comes to
that. Do call him, Janet.

240

JANET All right. (*Calls*) Johnny! (*Pause*) John . . . ny! (*To Monty*) You 385
mustn't tell him, you know.

MONTY Of course not.

JOHNNY (*off R*) Yes, Mummie.

JANET Come here for a minute. Mother wants to speak to you.

JOHNNY (*off*) Very well, Mummie. (*Enters R*) Oh, Mummie, I've 390
found such a lot of rabbits. You must come and see them. (*Seeing
Monty for the first time, stares at him*) Oh!

MONTY Come here, youngster. Come and let me look at you. (*Johnny
goes to him slowly. Monty, grasping both hands, draws him to him, looking at him long and keenly*) He's like you, Janet.

JANET Is he? 395

MONTY Yes. He has your eyes. So your name's Johnny, young man?

JOHNNY Yes.

MONTY Well, Johnny, will you give me a kiss? (*Monty leans forward. He
does so*)That's right.

JOHNNY And now, Mummie, come and look at my rabbits. 400

JANET Not yet, dear. Mother's busy just now.

JOHNNY May I go back to them then?

JANET Yes.

MONTY Suppose I won't let you go?

JOHNNY I'll make you—and so will Mummie. 405

MONTY Plucky little chap. Off with you. (*Kisses him again, then releases
his hands. Johnny trots off R again. Monty follows him with his eyes.
Pause*)

JANET Well, Monty, what do you think of him?

MONTY (*enthusiastic*) I think he's *splendid*.

JANET (*proudly*) Isn't he? And such a sturdy little boy. He weighed ten
pounds before he was a month old. 410

MONTY (*shyly*) I say, Janet.

JANET Yes?

MONTY (*hesitates*) You'll let me kiss you once more, won't you? For the
last time? . . . (*She hesitates*) You don't mind?

JANET (*heartily*) Of course not, Monty. You're not *married* yet, you know. 415

MONTY Janet! My dear, dear Janet! (*Seizes her and kisses her fiercely*)

JANET (*releasing herself gently*) That's enough, Monty.

MONTY (*remorsefully*) I'm afraid I behaved like an awful brute to you,
Janet.

JANET (*lightly*) Oh no. 420

MONTY Yes, I did. I ought to have married you. I ought to marry you
still. On account of the boy.

JANET (*quite matter of fact*) Oh well, you can't do that now in any case, can you—as you're engaged to Bertha Aldenham.

MONTY You've heard about that? Who told you?   425

JANET A worthy lady called Miss Deanes.

MONTY I know. A regular sickener.

JANET My dear Monty!

MONTY Sorry.

JANET She brought the good news. The very day I arrived as it hap-   430
pened. We've hardly talked of anything else at the Manor House
since—except father's illness, of course.

MONTY Why?

JANET What else is there to talk about—in Brendon!

MONTY That's true. Isn't it . . . (*Stops himself, looks at watch. Whistles*)   435
Whew! (*Rises*)

JANET What is it, Monty?

MONTY I say, Janet, I wonder if you'd mind going now?

JANET Why? (*She rises too*)

MONTY (*awkwardly*) Well, the fact is I'm expecting some one here   440
directly. I . . .

JANET Bertha?

MONTY Yes. I was to meet her here at the stile at six.

JANET *Our* stile, Monty.

MONTY Yes, . . . You don't mind, do you—about my asking you to go,   445
I mean?

JANET (*sitting again*) Not in the least.

MONTY But you're not going?

JANET Why should I go?

MONTY Oh, well, I thought . . .   450

JANET That it wouldn't be quite suitable for us to meet?

MONTY I didn't mean that, of course. But I thought you mightn't
like—I mean it might be painful . . . (*Sits again*)

JANET For me to see her? On the contrary, I'm dying to see her.

MONTY Janet, sometimes I think you're not quite human.   455

JANET My dear boy, I'm extremely human—and therefore curious.
(*Pause*) What's she like, Monty? Now, I mean. She promised to be
pretty.

MONTY She is pretty, I suppose. (*Pause*) I wonder if Bertha and I will
ever have a son like Johnny!   460

JANET Let's hope so, Monty. For Bertha's sake.

MONTY Isn't that some one coming? (*Pause, listens*) I expect it's she.
(*Rising hastily and advancing towards stile*) Is that you, Bertha?

BERTHA (*at stile*) Oh! There you are. Yes. Isn't it hot? (*Entering by gate which he opens for her*) Am I punctual? (*With a cry*) Janet! When did you come home? (*Goes to her eagerly*) 465

JANET (*shaking hands*) Only three days ago.

       Bertha kisses her

BERTHA *Only* three days! And you've never been up to see us.

JANET I know. But with father ill . . .

BERTHA Of course. I understand. I was only joking. How is Mr De Mullin? 470

JANET Much better. Not well yet, of course. But he gets stronger every day.

BERTHA I'm so glad. I say, Janet, do you remember when you used to teach us French? 475

JANET Yes.

BERTHA I was awfully troublesome, I remember.

MONTY I expect you were an awful duffer at it too, Bertha.

BERTHA What cheek!

MONTY Wasn't she, Ja—(*pulls himself up*) Miss De Mullin? (*Janet smiles nervously*) 480

BERTHA I didn't know you'd met Janet, Monty?

MONTY Oh, yes.

BERTHA Why didn't you tell us? (*Quite unsuspicious of anything wrong. Merely curious*)

MONTY It was some time ago.

BERTHA (*surprised*) Not at Brendon? You've never been at Brendon before. 485

MONTY No. It was at Weymouth. I was there getting over typhoid years ago.

BERTHA I remember, you told me. Eight or nine years ago, wasn't it?

MONTY Yes. (*Looks at watch*) I say, Bertha, we must be off if we're not to be late. 490

BERTHA Give me two minutes to rest. The weather's simply stifling.

MONTY Rot! It's quite cool.

BERTHA Then you must have been sitting here a long time. *I've* been walking along a dusty road and I'm not going to start yet. Besides I want to know all about you two meeting. Were you staying at Weymouth, Janet? 495

JANET Oh no. I just bicycled over. Mr Bulstead ran into me.

MONTY I like that. She ran into *me*.

JANET Anyhow my front wheel buckled and he had to help me to put it right. 500

BERTHA   What gallantry!

MONTY   It was. The beastly thing took about half an hour. By the time
it was over we seemed to have known each other for a lifetime. (*Looks
at watch*) Two minutes is up. Time to start, Bertha.   505

BERTHA   It isn't.

MONTY   It is. You'll be late for dressing° to a certainty if you don't go.

BERTHA   I like that. I can dress as quickly as you if it comes to that.

MONTY   Oh no. I can dress in ten minutes. I'll give you a quarter of an
hour's start and be down in the drawing-room five minutes before   510
you're ready. Is it a bet?

BERTHA   Done. In sixpences.° (*To Janet*) I'm staying at the Park for a
few days longer, Janet. Come up and see me, won't you?

JANET   (*uncomfortably*) I'm afraid I can't promise. On account of
father.°   515

BERTHA   Well, after I've gone home then. Mother will want to see you.
And so will Helen. And now I suppose I really must go. Come along,
Monty.

MONTY   Not I. I needn't go for a quarter of an hour. You have a quarter
of an hour's start.   520

BERTHA   All right. Good-bye, Janet. (*Kisses her*) You won't forget about
coming as soon as you can? I go back home on Thursday.

JANET   I won't forget. Good-bye. (*Bertha goes off through the wood. Janet
watches her go and there is a pause*) Yes, she *is* pretty, Monty. Very
pretty.   525

MONTY   (*nods*) You don't mind?

JANET   Her being pretty? Of course not. It's a justification.

MONTY   A justification?

JANET   For forgetting me.

MONTY   (*impulsively, seizing her hands*) Janet, I've never done that. You   530
know I haven't.

JANET   (*drawing back*) No, Monty. Not again. (*Pause*)

MONTY   I say, I as nearly as possible called you Janet right out before
Bertha.

JANET   So I saw. You *did* call me Miss De Mullin, by the way,—which   535
wasn't very clever of you.

MONTY   Did I? What an ass I am! But I don't suppose she noticed.

JANET   I dare say not.

>   *A shrill cry comes from the wood on the right. Then silence, Janet*
>   *starts up*

JANET   What was that?

MONTY   I don't know.   540

244

JANET It sounded like a child. Where did it come from? Over here, didn't it?

MONTY I think so.

JANET (*alarmed*) I hope Johnny . . . I must go and see . . . (*A moment later Johnny runs in R, sobbing, followed by Mrs De Mullin and Bertha*) Johnny! What is it, my sweetheart? (*Runs to him*)   545

JOHNNY Oh, Mummie, Mummie, I was running after the rabbits and I tripped over some nettles and they stung me.

MRS DE MULLIN He put his foot in a hole, Janet. He fell just as I met Bertha. (*Shakes hands with Monty*) How do you do Mr Bulstead.

JANET There! There! my pet. Did it hurt very much? Mother shall kiss   550 it and make it well. (*Does so*)

JOHNNY (*sobs*) Oh-h-h—

BERTHA Is he your son?

JANET Yes. Don't cry any more, dear. Brave boys don't cry, you know.

JOHNNY (*gasps*) It h-hurts so.   555

JANET I know. But crying won't make it hurt less, will it? So you must dry your eyes. Come now.

JOHNNY All right, Mummie. (*Still sobs gradually*)

BERTHA (*astonished*) I'd no idea you were married, Janet.

JANET Hadn't you?   560

BERTHA No. When was it?

JANET Eight years ago. Nearly nine. To Mr Seagrave.

BERTHA Is he down here with you?

JANET No. My husband died soon after our marriage.

BERTHA Poor Janet. I'm so sorry. (*Pause*) And it was before your mar-   565 riage that Monty met you?

JANET How do you know?

BERTHA (*quite unsuspicious*) He called you Miss De Mullin.

JANET Of course.

MRS DE MULLIN (*pricking up her ears suspiciously at this*) I didn't know   570 you had met my daughter before, Mr Bulstead.

BERTHA Nor did I. They met down at Weymouth quite by chance eight or nine years ago.

MRS DE MULLIN (*gravely*) Indeed?

MONTY Yes . . . I say, Bertha, excuse my interrupting you, but we really   575 must be off now if we're not to be late.

BERTHA You want to win that bet!

MONTY The bet's off. There's no time to give you any start. I must come too or I shan't be in time myself and the Governor will simply curse.   580

245

BERTHA Is Mr Bulstead *very* fierce if people are late for dinner?

MONTY Simply beastly.

BERTHA How very unpleasant! I wonder if I'm wise to marry into the family? (*Shaking hands merrily with Mrs De Mullin and Janet. Then goes off R, laughing merrily*)

MONTY (*sardonically*) I wonder. (*Shakes hands with Mrs De Mullin and Janet. To Johnny*) Will you give me a kiss, old chap?   585

JOHNNY That's three times. (*Monty nods*)

> *Monty follows Bertha off R. A long pause. Mrs De Mullin looks fixedly at Janet. Janet looks at the ground*

MRS DE MULLIN (*slowly*) Mr Montague Bulstead seems unusually fond of children, Janet.

JANET Does he, mother? (*She does not look up*)   590

MRS DE MULLIN Yes. Johnny is rather old to be kissed by strangers.

JANET I supposed he kissed him because he was brave about being stung.

MRS DE MULLIN He seems to have kissed him before. Twice.

JANET I dare say. I didn't notice.   595

MRS DE MULLIN Johnny did, apparently.

JANET Well, it doesn't matter anyway, does it? (*Looks up defiantly. Meets her mother's eyes full on her*) Why do you look at me like that, mother?

MRS DE MULLIN Send Johnny away for a little, Janet. I want to speak to you.   600

JANET I'd rather not, mother. He might hurt himself again.

MRS DE MULLIN He will be quite safe. Run away, Johnny. But don't go too far.

JOHNNY All right, grandmother. (*Johnny trots off into the wood. Pause*)   605

JANET (*defiantly*) Well, mother?

MRS DE MULLIN Janet, why did you never tell us you had met Mr Bulstead before?

JANET When?

MRS DE MULLIN Any time during the last three days, when we were speaking of his engagement.   610

JANET I'd forgotten all about it, mother.

MRS DE MULLIN Indeed? And why didn't you tell us eight years ago, when you met him at Weymouth, when you were still 'Miss De Mullin'?   615

JANET Mother, don't badger me like this. If you want to ask me anything ask it.

MRS DE MULLIN Janet, Mr Bulstead is Johnny's father.

JANET Mr Bulstead? Absurd!

MRS DE MULLIN Then why did you pretend not to have met him? Why   620
did you conceal the fact of your meeting him from us eight years ago?
And why has he concealed the fact from Bertha and the Bulsteads?
      Pause

JANET (*resignedly*) Very well, mother, if you're determined to know you
must know. Yes. he's Johnny's father.

MRS DE MULLIN Oh, Janet!   625

JANET (*irritably*) Well, mother, if you didn't want to know you
shouldn't have asked. I told you not to worry me. (*Mrs de Mullin
begins to cry. Remorsefully*) There, there, mother! Don't cry. I'm sorry
I was cross to you. Don't let's talk any more about it.

MRS DE MULLIN (*snuffling*) No, Janet, we *must* talk about it. There's no   630
use trying to hide things any longer. You must tell me the truth.

JANET Much better not, mother. It won't give you any pleasure to hear.

MRS DE MULLIN Still, I'd rather know, Janet.

JANET (*shrugs*) As you please. What do you want me to tell you?

MRS DE MULLIN Everything. How did you come to be at Weymouth?   635
I don't remember your staying at Weymouth eight years ago.

JANET I wasn't staying there. But Monty was.

MRS DE MULLIN (*shocked*) Monty!

JANET Mr Bulstead. Oh, what *does* it matter now? He'd had typhoid
and was there to recruit.° I'd ridden over on my bicycle . . .   640

MRS DE MULLIN (*lamentably*) Bicycle! I always said it was all through
bicycling.

JANET (*another shrug*) He ran into me, or I ran into him. I was rather
shaken, and he asked me to come in and rest. It happened close to the
house where he was lodging.   645

MRS DE MULLIN You went in! To his lodgings! A man you had never
met before!

JANET My dear mother, when you have been thrown off a bicycle,
ordinary conventions cease to apply. Besides, as a matter of fact, we
had met once before—the day before, in fact.   650

MRS DE MULLIN Where?

JANET Here. By this very stile. Monty was riding past and he asked me
the way to somewhere—Thoresby, I think. I was standing by the
stile. Next day I happened to ride into Weymouth. We collided—and
the rest you know.   655

MRS DE MULLIN (*sternly*) Were those the *only* times you met him,
Janet?

JANET Of course not, mother. After the Weymouth collision we met

247

constantly, nearly every day. We used to meet out riding and I had tea
with him lots of times in his rooms.   660

MRS DE MULLIN (*horrified*) How long did this go on?

JANET More than a month—till he left Weymouth, in fact. Now
mother, is that all you want to know? Because if so we'll drop the
subject.

MRS DE MULLIN Oh, Janet, what *will* your father say!   665

JANET Father? He won't know.

MRS DE MULLIN Won't know? But I must tell him.

JANET Good heavens, why?

MRS DE MULLIN In order that Mr Bulstead may marry you, of course.
Your father will insist on his marrying you.   670

JANET If father attempts to do that, mother, I shall deny the whole
story. And Monty will back me up.

MRS DE MULLIN He would never be so wicked.

JANET He would have to if I ask him. It's the least he could do.

MRS DE MULLIN Johnny is there to prove it.   675

JANET There's nothing to prove that Monty is Johnny's father. Nothing whatever.

MRS DE MULLIN But, Janet, *why* won't you marry him?

JANET (*impatiently*) My dear mother, because I don't want to, of
course.   680

MRS DE MULLIN You don't *want* to?

JANET Great heavens, no. Why should I? Monty Bulstead isn't at all the
sort of man I should care to *marry*.

MRS DE MULLIN Why not?

JANET Frankly, mother, because he's not interesting enough. Monty's   685
a very nice fellow and I like him very much, but I don't want to pass
the remainder of my life with him. If I'm to marry anybody—and I
don't think I shall—it will have to be a rather more remarkable person than Monty Bulstead.°

MRS DE MULLIN Yet you *did* love him, Janet. You must have loved him   690
. . . then.

JANET Oh yes. Then. But that was ages ago, before Johnny was born.
After that I didn't care for anybody any more except Johnny.

MRS DE MULLIN But, Janet, you *ought* to marry him, for Johnny's sake.

JANET Too late, mother. That should have been eight years ago to be   695
any use.

MRS DE MULLIN Better too late than not at all.

JANET Better not at all than too late.

MRS DE MULLIN He seduced you, Janet.

JANET (*thoughtfully*) Did he? I was twenty-seven.° He was twenty. If 700
either of us was to blame, wasn't it I?

MRS DE MULLIN Janet, you're trying to screen him.

JANET Dearest mother, you talk like a sentimental novel.

MRS DE MULLIN (*indignantly*) And he's to be allowed to marry Bertha
Aldenham, just as if this had never happened? 705

JANET Why not? It's not *her* fault,° is it? And girls find it difficult
enough to get married nowadays, goodness knows.

MRS DE MULLIN Still, she *ought* to be told, Janet. I think *she must* be told.

JANET My dear mother, if *she* knows everybody will know, and the
scandal will make all the dead and gone De Mullins turn in their 710
graves. As for father it would simply kill him out of hand.

MRS DE MULLIN (*sadly*) Poor father.

JANET (*briskly*) So, on the whole, I don't think we'll tell any one. Come,
mother, it's time we started. (*More kindly*) Poor mother. Don't fret.
Perhaps Hester will have some news to cheer you when we get home. 715

MRS DE MULLIN Hester?

JANET (*rallying her*) An engagement, mother. Hester's engagement.
Hester and Mr Brown have been decorating the church for the last
four hours. What an opportunity for a declaration! Or don't people
propose in church? 720

MRS DE MULLIN Janet, how can you laugh after what has happened?

JANET Laugh? Of course I can laugh. What else is there to do? Let's go
home. Johnny! Johnny! (*Calls*)

> *By this time twilight is falling. A full moon has begun to rise,
> lighting up the scene*

JOHNNY (*off R*) Yes, Mummie.

JANET Come along, dear. Mother's going to start. 725

JOHNNY (*off R*) All right, Mummie. (*Entering R*) Oh, Mummie, you've
not seen my rabbits yet!

JANET No. It's too dark tonight. Mother must come and see them
another time.

JOHNNY You won't forget, will you, Mummie? (*Looking at Mrs De* 730
Mullin) Grandmother, you've been crying. Is that because I stung
myself with a nettle?

JANET Little egoist! Of course it is. Give your grandmother a kiss and
we'll all walk home together.

> *Mrs De Mullin stoops and kisses Johnny passionately. They go off
> through the gate and*

THE CURTAIN FALLS

3

Five days have passed since Act 2

SCENE *As in Act 1. Time: Late afternoon.*

*When the curtain rises Mrs Clouston, Mrs De Mullin, and Janet
are on the stage. The nervous tension of the last few days has
clearly told on Janet, who looks feverish and irritable*

MRS DE MULLIN (*speaking off into the hall on the right*) Good-bye.
Good-bye.

JANET (*who is standing about C, scornfully*) Good-bye! Good-bye!

MRS CLOUSTON (*shocked*) Janet!

JANET (*fiercely*) How many times a week does that Bulstead woman   5
think it necessary to call on us?

MRS CLOUSTON (*sitting*) She doesn't call very often.

JANET She's been three times this week.

MRS DE MULLIN (*closing door R*) Naturally she wants to hear how your
father is, dear.   10

JANET (*irritably*) My dear mother, what *can* it matter to Mrs Bulstead
whether father lives or dies?

MRS DE MULLIN Janet!

JANET (*exasperated*) Well, mother, do you seriously believe she cares?
Or Miss Deanes? Or Miss Rolt? Or any of these people? They only   15
call because they've nothing better to do. It's sheer mental vacuity on
their part. Besides, father's perfectly well now. They know that. But
they go on *calling, calling!* I wonder Miss Deanes doesn't bring her
cockatoo to inquire. (*Tramps to and fro impatiently*)

MRS CLOUSTON Really, Janet, I can't think what's the matter with you.   20
Do sit down and try and exercise some self-control.

JANET I've no self-control where these Brendon people are concerned.
They get on my nerves, every one of them . . . Where's Johnny?

MRS DE MULLIN In the garden, I think.

JANET Sensible boy! He's had enough of visitors for one day, I'll be   25
bound. I'll go out and join him. (*Goes out angrily*)

MRS CLOUSTON I can't think what's come to Janet the last day or two.
Her temper gets worse and worse.

MRS DE MULLIN Perhaps it's only the hot weather. No De Mullin—

MRS CLOUSTON Nonsense, Jane, don't be foolish. We can't have *Janet*   30
giving way to that sort of thing at her age.

250

MRS DE MULLIN I'm afraid she is rather irritable just now. She flew out quite savagely at Hester today just after luncheon.

MRS CLOUSTON Why was that?

MRS DE MULLIN Because of something she had been teaching Johnny. 35
The Athanasian Creed° I think it was. Yes, it must have been that because Johnny asked Janet what was meant by three Incomprehensibles.° Janet asked him where he had heard all that and Johnny said Aunt Hester had taught it to him. Janet was very angry and forbade Hester ever to teach him anything again. Hester was quite hurt about 40 it.

MRS CLOUSTON Naturally. Still, I do think Hester might have chosen something else to teach him.

MRS DE MULLIN That was what Janet said.

MRS CLOUSTON But that's no reason why she shouldn't behave herself 45
when visitors are here. She was quite rude to Mrs Bulstead. What they think of her in London when she goes on like this I can't imagine.

MRS DE MULLIN Perhaps she isn't like this in London.

MRS CLOUSTON Of course she is, Jane. Worse. Here she has the restraining influences of home life. Whereas in London, living alone 50
as she does . . .

MRS DE MULLIN She has Johnny.

MRS CLOUSTON She has Johnny, of course. But that's not enough. She ought to have a husband to look after her.

MRS DE MULLIN (*sighs*) Yes. (*Seats herself slowly beside her sister*) 55

MRS CLOUSTON Where's Hester?

MRS DE MULLIN At church, I expect.

MRS CLOUSTON Church! Why the girl's always at church.

MRS DE MULLIN It's a Wednesday. And it does no harm, I think.

MRS CLOUSTON Let us hope not, Jane. 60

> *De Mullin enters by the door on the left. He has evidently got over his recent attack and looks comparatively hale and vigorous*

MRS DE MULLIN Have you had your nap, Hugo?

DE MULLIN Yes. The sunset woke me, I suppose. It was shining full on my face.

MRS DE MULLIN What a pity it woke you.

DE MULLIN It didn't matter. I've slept enough . . . (*Wanders towards* 65
sofa, C) Where's Johnny?

MRS DE MULLIN In the garden, I think, with Janet.

DE MULLIN (*wanders to window, C, and looks out*) Yes. There he is. He's playing hide and seek with Ellen . . . Now she's caught him. No, he's got away. Bravo, Johnny! (*Stands watching intently for a while. Then* 70 *turns and comes down* C) What a fine little fellow it is! A true De Mullin!

MRS DE MULLIN   Do you think so, Hugo?

DE MULLIN   Every inch of him! (*Pause, sits C, half to himself*) If only Janet had been married!   75

MRS DE MULLIN (*sighs*) Yes.

DE MULLIN (*musing*) I wonder who the father really was. (*Looking up*) She has never told you, Jane, I suppose?

MRS DE MULLIN (*steadily, without looking up*) No, Hugo.

MRS CLOUSTON   And never will. Nobody was ever so obstinate as Janet.   80

DE MULLIN (*nods sadly*) Janet always had plenty of will.

MRS CLOUSTON   Far too much! (*Pause*)

MRS DE MULLIN   You'll quite miss Johnny when he goes away from us, won't you, Hugo.

DE MULLIN   Yes. I never thought I could grow so fond of a child. The   85
house will seem empty without him.

MRS DE MULLIN   I shall miss him too.

DE MULLIN   We shall all miss him. (*Pause, thoughtfully*) I wonder if Janet would° leave him with us when she goes back to London?

MRS DE MULLIN   Leave him with us? Altogether, you mean?   90

DE MULLIN   Yes.

MRS DE MULLIN   I'm afraid not, Hugo. In fact, I'm quite sure she would not. She's so fond of Johnny.

DE MULLIN   I suppose she wouldn't. (*Pause*) I was greatly shocked at what you told me about her the other day, Harriet.   95

MRS CLOUSTON   About her keeping a shop, you mean?

DE MULLIN   Yes. And going into partnership with a Miss Higgs or Hicks. It all sounds most discreditable.

MRS CLOUSTON   Deplorable.

MRS DE MULLIN (*meekly*) She had to do something to keep herself,   100
Hugo.

DE MULLIN   No doubt. Still, it can't be considered a proper sort of position for my daughter. I think she must give it up at once.

MRS DE MULLIN   She would only have to take to something else.

DE MULLIN   Not necessarily. She might come back here to live with us   105
... with Johnny, of course.

MRS DE MULLIN (*astonished*) *Live* with us?

DE MULLIN   Why not, Jane?

MRS DE MULLIN   Well, of course if *you* think so, Hugo.

MRS CLOUSTON   Are you sure you will like to have Janet living at home   110
again, Hugo?

DE MULLIN I think it might be the best arrangement. And I shall like to have Johnny here. He's our only descendant, Harriet, the last of the De Mullins. If you or Jane had had a son it would be different.

MRS CLOUSTON (*sighs*) Yes.   115

DE MULLIN As it is I don't see how we can do anything better than have them both down here—as Jane doesn't think Janet would part with Johnny. It would be better for Janet too. It would take her away from her present unsatisfactory surroundings. It would give her a position and independence—everything she now lacks.   120

MRS DE MULLIN I should have thought she was *independent* now, Hugo.

DE MULLIN (*irritably*) My dear Jane, how can a woman possibly be independent whose income comes out of selling hats? The only form of independence that is possible or desirable for a woman is that she   125
shall be dependent upon her husband or, if she is unmarried, on her nearest male relative. I am sure *you* agree with me, Harriet?

MRS CLOUSTON Quite, Hugo.

DE MULLIN Very well. I will speak to her about it at once.

MRS DE MULLIN (*nervously*) I hardly think I would say anything about   130
it today, Hugo.

DE MULLIN Why not, Jane?

MRS DE MULLIN Well, she seems nervous and irritable today. I think I should put it off for a day or two.

DE MULLIN (*testily*) My dear Jane, you are always procrastinating. If   135
such an arrangement is to be made the sooner it is made the better. (*Goes to window, C, calls*) Janet my dear. Janet.

> Pause. Then Janet appears at window, C

JANET Did you call me, father?

DE MULLIN Yes. Come to me for a moment. I want to speak to you. (*De Mullin wanders undecidedly to the fireplace. A moment later Janet enters from the garden*) Is Johnny with you?   140

JANET No. He's having tea with Ellen. I said he might. (*Pause. Janet comes down*)

DE MULLIN Janet, your mother and I have been talking over your future.

JANET Have you, father? (*With a quick glance at her mother. Mrs De Mullin, however, makes no sign*)

DE MULLIN Yes. We have come to the conclusion that it would be   145
better for you to come back here to live.

> Janet faces round towards her father

JANET But what would become of the business?

DE MULLIN You will have to give up the business, of course. So much
the better. You never ought to have gone into it. It was not at all a suitable occupation for you.   150

JANET But I like it, father.

MRS CLOUSTON *Like* it! A De Mullin *like* keeping a shop! Impossible.

JANET (*firmly*) Yes, Aunt Harriet, I like it. And I'm proud of it.

DE MULLIN (*sharply*) Nonsense, Janet. Nobody can possibly be proud
of keeping a shop.   155

JANET *I* am. I made it, you see. It's my child, like Johnny.

DE MULLIN (*amazed*) Janet! Do you understand what you're doing? I
offer you the chance of returning to Brendon to live as my daughter.

JANET (*indifferently*) I quite understand, father. And I'm much obliged
for the offer. Only I decline it. That's all.   160

MRS CLOUSTON Really!

DE MULLIN (*with dignity*) The question is, are you to be·allowed to
decline it, in Johnny's interests if not your own?

JANET Johnny's?

DE MULLIN Yes. Johnny's. As long as he was a child it made little dif-   165
ference where he was brought up. Relatively little that is. Now he is
getting to an age when early associations are all-important. Living
here at Brendon in the home of his ancestors he will grow up worthy
of the race from which he is descended. He will be a true De Mullin.

JANET (*quietly*) Perhaps I don't want him to be a true De Mullin, father. 170

DE MULLIN What do you mean?

JANET My dear father, you're infatuated about your De Mullins. Who
are the De Mullins, after all? Mere country squires who lived on here
down at Brendon generation after generation. What have they ever
done that I should want Johnny to be like them? Nothing. There's   175
not one of them who has ever distinguished himself in the smallest
degree or made his name known outside his native village. The De
Mullins are, and have always been, nobodies. Look at their portraits.
Is there a single one of them that is worth a second glance? Why they
never even had the brains to be painted by a decent artist. With the   180
result that they aren't worth the canvas they're painted on. Or is it
board? I'd make a bonfire of them if they were mine.

MRS DE MULLIN Janet!

JANET (*impatiently*) I would. You seem to think there's some peculiar
virtue about always living in the same place. I believe in people   185
uprooting themselves and doing something with their lives. What
was the good of the De Mullins going on living down here century
after century, always a little poorer and a little poorer, selling a farm

here, mortgaging another there, instead of going out into the world to
seek their fortunes? We've stayed too long in one place, we De   190
Mullins. We shall never be worth anything sleeping away our lives
down at Brendon.

DE MULLIN (*sharply*) Janet, you are talking foolishly. What you say
only makes it clearer to me that you cannot be allowed to live by yourself in London any longer. Such a life is demoralizing to you. You   195
must come back to Brendon.

JANET I shall not come back to Brendon, father. On that I am quite
determined.

DE MULLIN (*with dignity*) My dear, this is not a matter that rests with
you. My mind is made up. Hitherto I have only asked you to return.   200
Do not force me to command you.

JANET (*fiercely*) Command? By what right do you command?

DE MULLIN By the right of a father, Janet. By that right I insist on your
obedience.

JANET (*losing her temper*) Obedience! Obedience! I owe no one obedi-   205
ence.° I am of full age and can order my life as I please. Is a woman
never to be considered old enough to manage her own affairs? Is she
to go down to her grave everlastingly under tutelage? Is she always to
be obeying a father when she's not obeying a husband? Well, I, for
one, will not submit to such nonsense. I'm sick of this everlasting   210
obedience.

DE MULLIN (*fiercely*) Janet . . .!

> *Door opens L. Ellen enters with the lamp. There is a considerable
> pause, during which Ellen puts down the lamp, turns it up, pulls
> down the blind and begins to draw the curtains. In the middle of
> the last process De Mullin intervenes*

DE MULLIN (*irritably*) You can leave the curtains, Ellen.

ELLEN Very well, sir. (*Exit Ellen L with maddening deliberation. Pause*)

JANET Father, I'm sorry if what I said vexed you. Perhaps I spoke too   215
strongly.

DE MULLIN (*with great dignity*) Very well, Janet. You will remain with
us.

JANET No, father, that's not possible. For Johnny's sake, as well as my
own, it would be madness for us to live down here.   220

DE MULLIN For Johnny's sake?

JANET Yes, Johnny's. In London we're not known, he and I. There he's
simply Johnny Seagrave, the son of a respectable widow who keeps a
hat-shop. Here he is the son of Janet De Mullin who ran away
from home one night eight years ago and whose name was never   225

mentioned again by her parents until one fine day she turned up with an eight-year-old boy and said she was married. How long would they take to see through *that* story down here, do you think?

MRS CLOUSTON (*tartly*) Whose fault is that?

JANET Never mind whose fault it is, Aunt Harriet. The question is, will they see through it or will they not? Of course, they *know* nothing so far, but I've no doubt they suspect. What else have people to do down here but suspect other people? Miss Deanes murmurs her doubts to Mrs Bulstead and Mrs Bulstead shakes her head to Miss Deanes. Mrs Bulstead! What right has *she* to look down that huge nose of hers at *me!* She's had *ten* children!

MRS DE MULLIN Janet! She's married.

JANET To Mr Bulstead! That vulgar animal! You don't ask me to consider that *a merit*, do you? No, Mrs Bulstead shan't have the chance of sneering at Johnny if *I* can help it. Or at me either.

MRS DE MULLIN Janet, listen to me. You don't understand how your father feels about this or how much it means to him. Johnny is his only grandchild—our only descendant. He would adopt him and call him De Mullin, and then the name would not die out. You know how much your father thinks of that and how sorry he has always been that I never had a son.°

JANET (*more gently*) I know, mother. But when Hester marries . . .

DE MULLIN Hester?

JANET Yes.

DE MULLIN (*turning angrily to his wife*) But whom is Hester going to marry? *Is* she going to marry? I have heard nothing about this. What's this, Jane? Has something been kept from me?

MRS DE MULLIN No, no, Hugo. Nothing has been kept from you. It's only some fancy of Janet's. She thinks Mr Brown is going to propose to Hester. There's nothing in it, really.

DE MULLIN Mr Brown! Impossible!

MRS CLOUSTON Quite impossible!

JANET (*calmly*) Why impossible, father?

DE MULLIN He would never dare to do such a thing. *Mr Brown* to have the audacity to propose to *my* daughter!°

JANET (*quietly*) Why not, father?

DE MULLIN (*bubbling with rage*) Because he is not of a suitable position. Because the *De Mullins* cannot be expected to marry people of *that* class. Because . . .

JANET (*shrugs*) I dare say Mr Brown won't think of all that. Anyhow, I hope he won't. I hope he'll propose to Hester and she'll accept him and then when they've a whole herd of little Browns you can select one of them and make a De Mullin of him, poor little wretch.

At this moment Hester enters from the garden. An uncomfortable silence falls

MRS DE MULLIN Hush, hush, Janet. Here is Hester. Is that you, Hester? Have you come from church? 270

HESTER Yes, mother. (*She comes down, her face looking pale and drawn, and stands by her mother*)

MRS DE MULLIN You're very late, dear.

HESTER A little. I stayed on after service was over.

MRS CLOUSTON How very eccentric of you!

HESTER (*quietly*) I suppose saying one's prayers does seem eccentric to 275
you, Aunt Harriet?

MRS CLOUSTON My dear Hester, considering you'd only just finished *one* service . . .

JANET (*who has not noticed the look on her sister's face*) Well, Aunt Harriet, who was right? 280

MRS DE MULLIN Hush, Janet!

JANET (*gaily*) My dear mother, what on earth is there to 'hush' about? And what on earth is there to keep Hester in church half an hour after service is over, if it's not what I told you?

HESTER What do you mean? 285

JANET Nothing, dear. Come and give me a kiss. (*Pulling her towards her*)

HESTER (*repulsing her roughly*) I won't. Leave me alone, Janet. What has she been saying about me, mother? I insist on knowing.

MRS DE MULLIN Nothing, dear. Only some nonsense about you and Mr Brown. Janet is always talking nonsense. 290

JANET Yes, Hester. About you and Mr Brown. *Your* Mr Brown. Confess he has asked you to marry him as I said?

HESTER (*slowly*) Mr Brown is engaged to be married to Agatha Bulstead. He told me so this evening after service.

JANET He told you! 295

HESTER Yes. He asked me to congratulate him.

JANET The little wretch!

MRS DE MULLIN To Agatha Bulstead?° That's the plain one, isn't it?

HESTER The third one. Yes.

JANET The plain one! Good heavens, it oughtn't to be allowed. The 300
children will be little monsters.

MRS CLOUSTON So that's why you were so long at church?

HESTER Yes. I was praying that they might be happy.

JANET Poor Hester!

MRS DE MULLIN Are you disappointed, dear?   305

HESTER I'd rather not talk about it if you don't mind, mother.

MRS DE MULLIN Your father would never have given his consent.

HESTER So Mr Brown said.

JANET The little *worm*.

MRS DE MULLIN My dear!   310

JANET Well, mother, isn't it too contemptible?

DE MULLIN I'm bound to say Mr Brown seems to have behaved in a very fitting manner.

JANET You think so, father?

DE MULLIN Certainly. He saw what my objections would be and   315 recognized that they were reasonable. Nothing could be more proper.

JANET Well, father. I don't know what you do want. Ten minutes ago you were supposed to be wanting a grandson to adopt. Here's Hester going the right way to provide one, and you don't like that either.   320

HESTER What is all this about, father? What have you all been discussing while I've been out?

MRS DE MULLIN It was nothing about you, Hester.

HESTER I'm not sure of that, mother. Anyhow I should like to hear what it was.   325

MRS CLOUSTON Hester, that is not at all a proper tone to use in speaking to your mother.

HESTER (*fiercely*) Please don't interfere, Aunt Harriet. I suppose I can be trusted to speak to my mother properly by this time.

MRS CLOUSTON You certainly ought to, my dear. You are quite old   330 enough.

HESTER Very well then. Perhaps you will be good enough not to dictate to me in future. What was it you were discussing, father?

JANET I'll tell you, Hester. Father wanted to adopt Johnny. He wanted me to come down here to live altogether.   335

HESTER Indeed? Well, father, understand, please, that if Janet comes down here to live *I go!*

MRS DE MULLIN Hester!

HESTER I will not live in the same house with Janet. Nothing shall induce me. I would rather beg my bread.   340

JANET That settles it then. Thanks, Hester. I'm glad you had the pluck to say that. You are right. Quite right.

HESTER I can do without *your* approval, Janet.

JANET (*recklessly*) Of course you can. But you can have it all the same. You never wanted me down here. You always disapproved of my   345

258

being sent for. I ought never to have come. I wish I hadn't come. My coming has only done harm to Hester, as she knew it would.

DE MULLIN How harm?

JANET Mr Brown would have asked Hester to marry him if I hadn't come. He meant to; I'm sure of it.   350

MRS DE MULLIN But he said . . .

JANET I know. But that was only an excuse. Young men aren't so considerate of their future fathers-in-law as all that nowadays. No. Mr Brown heard some story about me from Miss Deanes. Or perhaps the Vicar put him on his guard. Isn't it so, Hester? (*Hester nods*)   355

MRS DE MULLIN But as your father would never have consented, dear . . .

HESTER (*slowly*) Still, I'd rather he had asked me, mother.

JANET Quite right, Hester! I'm glad you've got some wholesome feminine vanity left in your composition. And you'd have said 'yes', like a   360 sensible woman.

HESTER Oh, you're always sneering!

JANET Yes. But I'm *going*, Hester, *going! That's* the great thing! Keep your eyes fixed steadily on that and you'll be able to bear anything else. That reminds me. (*Goes to door, L, and calls loudly into the hall*)   365 Johnny! Johnny!

MRS CLOUSTON Really, Janet!

JANET Oh, I forgot. It's not genteel to call into the passage, is it? I ought to have rung. I apologise, Aunt Harriet. (*Calls again*) Johnny!

MRS DE MULLIN Why are you calling Johnny?   370

JANET To tell him to put on his hat and coat, mother dear. I'm going to the station.

DE MULLIN You're going tonight?

JANET Yes, father, tonight. I've done harm enough down here. I'm going away.   375

JOHNNY (*entering L*) Do you want me, Mummie?

JANET Yes. Run and put on your things and say goodbye to Cook and Ellen and tell Robert to put in the pony.° Mother's going back to London.

JOHNNY Are we going now, Mummie?   380

JANET (*nods*) As fast as the train can carry us. And tell Ellen to lock my trunk for me and give you the key. Run along. (*Exit Johnny, L*)

DE MULLIN Lock your trunk! But you've not *packed*!

JANET Oh yes, I have. Everything's packed, down to my last shoelace. I don't know how often I haven't packed and unpacked during the   385 last five days.

MRS DE MULLIN (*astonished and hurt*) You meant to leave us then, Janet? You've been *wanting* to leave us all the time?

JANET Yes, mother. I've been wanting to leave you. I can't stay here any longer. Brendon stifles me. It has too many ghosts. I suppose it's your ridiculous De Mullins. 390

DE MULLIN Janet!

JANET I know, father. That's blasphemy, isn't it? But I can't help it. I must go. I've been meaning to tell you every day for the last four days, but somehow I always put it off. 395

DE MULLIN Understand me, Janet. If you leave this house tonight you leave it for ever.

JANET (*cheerfully*) All right, father.

DE MULLIN (*growing angrier*) Understand, too, that if you leave it you are never to hold any communication either with me or with any one 400 in it henceforward. You are cut off from the family. I will never see you or recognize you in any way, or speak to you again as long as I live.

JANET (*astonished*) My dear father, why are you so angry? Is there anything so dreadful in my wanting to live in London instead of in the country? 405

DE MULLIN (*getting more and more excited*) Why am I angry! Why am I...!

MRS DE MULLIN Sh! Hugo! You mustn't excite yourself. You know the doctor said ...

DE MULLIN Be quiet, Jane! (*Turning furiously to Janet*) Why am I angry! 410 You disgrace the family. You have a child, that poor fatherless boy ...

JANET (*quietly*) Oh come, I could have got along quite well without a father if it comes to that. And so could Hester.

MRS DE MULLIN Janet!

JANET Well, mother, what has father ever done for Hester or me except 415 try and prevent us from doing something we wanted to do? Hester wanted to marry Mr Brown. Father wouldn't have allowed her. He's not genteel enough to marry a De Mullin. I want to go back to my shop. Father objects to that. That's not genteel enough for a De Mullin either. Well, hang all the De Mullins, say I. 420

DE MULLIN (*furious*) I forbid you to speak of your family in that way—of *my* family! I forbid it! It is an outrage. Your ancestors were honourable men and pure women. They did their duty in the position in which they were born, and handed on their name untarnished to their children. Hitherto our honour has been unsullied. You have sullied 425 it. You have brought shame upon your parents and shame upon your son, and that shame you can never wipe out. If you had in you a spark of human feeling, if you were not worthless and heartless you would blush to look me in the face or your child in the face. But you are utterly hardened. I ought never to have offered to receive you back 430 into this house. I ought never to have consented to see you again. I was wrong. I regret it. You are unfit for the society of decent people. Go back to London. Take up the wretched trade you practise there. It is what you are fit for.

JANET That's exactly what I think, father. As we agree about it why 435 make such a fuss?

DE MULLIN (*furious*) Janet . . .

HESTER Father, don't argue with her. It's no use. (*Solemnly*) Leave her to God.

JANET Hester, Hester, don't deceive yourself. In your heart you envy 440 me my baby, and you know it.

HESTER (*indignant*) I do not.

JANET You do. Time is running on with you, my dear. You're twenty-eight. Just the age that I was when I met my lover. Yes, my lover. In a few years you will be too old for love, too old to have children. So soon 445 it passeth away and we are gone. Your best years are slipping by and you are growing faded and cross and peevish. Already the lines are hardening about your mouth and the hollows coming under your eyes. You will be an old woman before your time unless you marry and have children. And what will you do then? Keep a lap–dog, I sup- 450 pose, or sit up at night with a sick cockatoo like Miss Deanes. Miss Deanes! Even she has a heart somewhere about her. Do you imagine she wouldn't rather give it to her babies than snivel over *poultry*? No, Hester, make good use of your youth, my dear. It won't last always. And once gone it is gone for ever. (*Hester bursts into tears*) There, 455 there, Hester! I'm sorry. I oughtn't to have spoken like that. It wasn't kind. Forgive me. (*Hester weeps more and more violently*) Hester, don't cry like that. I can't bear to hear you. I was angry and said more than I should. I didn't mean to vex you. Come, dear, you mustn't give way like that or you'll make yourself ill. Dry your eyes and let me see you 460 smile. (*Caressing her. Hester, who has begun by resisting her feebly, grad-ually allows herself to be soothed*) That's better! My dear, what a sight you've made of yourself! But all women are hideous when they've been crying. It makes their noses red and that's dreadfully unbecom-ing. (*Hester sobs out a laugh*) No. You mustn't begin to cry again or I 465 shall scold you. I shall, really.

HESTER (*half laughing, half crying hysterically*) You seem to think every woman ought to behave as shamefully as you did.

261

JANET (*grimly*) No, Hester. I don't think that. To do as I did needs pluck and brains—and five hundred pounds. Everything most 470 women haven't got, poor things. So they must marry or remain childless. You must marry—the next curate. I suppose the Bulsteads will buy Mr Brown a living° as he's marrying the plainest of the daughters. It's the least they can do. But that's no reason why *I* should marry unless I choose. 475

MRS CLOUSTON Well, I've never heard of anything so disgraceful. I thought Janet at least had the grace to be ashamed of what she did!

JANET (*genuinely astonished*) Ashamed? Ashamed of wanting to have a child? What on earth were women created for, Aunt Harriet, if not to have children? 480

MRS CLOUSTON To *marry* and have children.

JANET (*with relentless logic*) My dear Aunt Harriet, women had children thousands of years before marriage was invented. I dare say they will go on doing so thousands of years after it has ceased to exist.

MRS DE MULLIN Janet! 485

JANET Well, mother, that's how I feel. And I believe it's how all wholesome women feel if they would only acknowledge it. I *wanted* to have a child.° I always did from the time when I got too old to play with dolls. Not an adopted child or a child of some one else's, but a baby of my very own. Of course I wanted to marry. That's the ordinary way 490 a woman wants to be a mother nowadays, I suppose. But time went on and nobody came forward, and I saw myself getting old and my chance slipping away. Then I met—never mind. And I fell in love with him. Or perhaps I only fell in love with love. I don't know. It was so splendid to find some one at last who really cared for me as women 495 should be cared for! Not to talk to because I was clever or to play tennis with because I was strong, but to kiss me and to make love to me! Yes! To make love to me!

DE MULLIN (*solemnly*) Listen to me, my girl. You say that now, and I dare say you believe it. But when you are older, when Johnny is 500 grown up, you will bitterly repent having brought into the world a child who can call no man father.

JANET (*passionately*) Never! Never! That I'm sure of. Whatever happens, even if Johnny should come to hate me for what I did, I shall always be glad to have been his mother. At least I shall have lived. 505 These poor women who go through life listless and dull, who have never felt the joys and the pains a mother feels, how they would envy me if they knew! If they knew! To know that a child is your very own, is a part of you. That you have faced sickness and pain and death itself

for it. That it is yours and nothing can take it from you because no one   510
can understand its wants as you do. To feel its soft breath on your
cheek, to soothe it when it is fretful and still it when it cries, that is
motherhood and that is glorious!

> *Johnny runs in by the door on the left. He is obviously in the high-*
> *est spirits at the thought of going home*

JOHNNY The trap is round, Mummie, and the luggage is in.

JANET That's right. Good-bye, father. (*He does not move*) Say good-bye   515
to your grandfather, Johnny. You won't see him again.

> *De Mullin kisses Johnny*

MRS DE MULLIN Janet!

JANET No, mother. It's best not. (*Kisses her*) It would only be painful for
father. Good-bye, Aunt Harriet. Good-bye, Hester. (*Looks at Hester*
doubtfully. Hester rises, goes to her slowly and kisses her)

HESTER Good-bye.   520

> *Exeunt Johnny and Janet by the door on the right*

DE MULLIN (*his grey head bowed on his chest as Mrs De Mullin timidly lays*
her hand on his shoulder) The last of the De Mullins! The last of the
De Mullins!°

THE CURTAIN FALLS

EXPLANATORY NOTES

The New Woman

Cast Page

Comedy Theatre: this theatre, in Panton Street, Haymarket, was under the management of Comyns Carr, whose great success in 1893 had been Grundy's *Sowing the Wind* with Cyril Maude, Winifred Emery, and Brandon Thomas.

Fred Terry: played Gerald Arbuthnot, the young male lead, in Oscar Wilde's *A Woman of No Importance* at the Haymarket in 1893. His sister, the actress Ellen Terry, was Henry Irving's leading lady. William Archer found both Terry and J. G. Grahame (Sylvester) 'unduly declamatory' in *The New Woman* (*The Theatrical World of 1894* (1895), 226).

Cyril Maude: premièred the role of another *raisonneur*, Cayley Drummle, in Pinero's *The Second Mrs Tanqueray* in 1893. Manager of the Haymarket, 1896–1905, he was married to Winifred Emery.

Winifred Emery: born 1862, so already 32 when she played this ingenue. She took the title role in Wilde's *Lady Windermere's Fan* (1892) and the female lead in Grundy's *Sowing the Wind* (1893). A drawing of her by Beardsley appeared in *The Yellow Book* (1894). The leading lady of Maude's Haymarket company, she became an active feminist and a member of the Actresses' Franchise League.

Rose Leclerq: played Lady Hunstanton, another dowager, in *A Woman of No Importance*; Grundy's character develops the type which comes to full flower in Lady Bracknell, a role she premièred, in Wilde's *The Importance of Being Earnest* (1895).

Alma Murray: an experienced actress who, as a long-time member of Irving's Lyceum company, had played opposite Pinero in the première of his early comedietta, *Daisy's Escape* (1879). Although cast here in the central role satirizing the new woman, she was much associated with *avant garde* initiatives, including playing Beatrice in the closed-house production of Shelley's *The Cenci* in 1886 and Raina in Florence Farr's Avenue Theatre production of Bernard Shaw's *Arms and the Man* earlier in 1894.

Gertrude Warden: played Mrs Linden in the Achurch–Charrington production of Ibsen's *A Doll's House* (1889).

Walter Johnstone, Walter Hann: it was not unusual for scene designers to be prominently acknowledged in nineteenth-century theatre publicity and programmes, nor for different designers to work, as here, on successive scenes.

1 S.D. *boudoir . . . flowers*: the properties and decorative elements here are immediate indicators of the feminization of Gerald.

flat: the back wall (timber frame covered by stretched canvas) of the box set. The original practice of creating the scene from two flats slid along grooves from either wing to meet in the centre had been replaced in the second half of the century by flown scenery but the old terminology was often still used. The doors in this realistic setting were built to be practicable.

4 *stench of flowers!*: the impression of effeminacy given by the set is endorsed in Cazenove's dialogue here and in his subsequent denunciations of the furniture and antimacassars.

17–18 *distinction at Oxford*: just as was famously achieved by Oscar Wilde with his double first. Intellectual brilliance was a recurrent target for Grundy's as for *Punch*'s humour.

41 *rusticated*: sent down from university for bad work or behaviour. Both Sylvester and Cazenove boast their philistinism. (The literal meaning of the term is 'sent to the countryside', in which sense it is used at lines 202–3.)

45 *real woman*: like 'womanly woman' this was a common phrase in 1890s writing. This is the first of many distinctions in the play between 'true' or 'real' feminine women or masculine men and the corrupted gender attributed to emancipated women and aesthetes.

62 *ethereal*: an adjective which evokes the memory of the sexually compromised heroine of *The Second Mrs Tanqueray*. Mrs Patrick Campbell, who played Paula, was notoriously thin, as observed in Beardsley's illustrations for *The Yellow Book* (Apr. 1894). Agnes Sylvester's skinniness denotes the neurosis of emancipation.

68–9 *cut the leaves*: he is pretending that he has read the book. Four or eight pages of a book were printed on a single sheet which was folded and then bound. The reader of a new book had to cut along the folds to separate the pages.

80 *Frankenstein*: the hero of Mary Shelley's novel *Frankenstein* (1818), who created a monster. In a common error, Cazenove—or probably Grundy—mistakes the maker for the monster.

93 *latchkeys*: since they enabled the possessor to come and go at will, doorkeys were instantly recognizable signifiers of female independence. They are much discussed in this play.

106 *one of them!*: the somewhat heavy-footed humour of the previous dialogue gives way to didactic statement. That Grundy offers little to subvert Cazenove's viewpoint marks him as the equivalent of the *raisonneur* figure of Society Drama, offering the common-sense viewpoint, as Cazenove's actor, Maude, had done as Cayley Drummle, the previous year.

129 *the nights I had!*: the *raisonneur* in Society Drama invariably admits to a wild past, an indicator of red-blooded manliness. The casual ease of the

discussion of women's physical attributes is also characteristic although its expression is cruder here than in the work of Henry Arthur Jones or Pinero.

163 *Percy Pettigrew*: aesthetes, as much the object of ridicule and innuendo about corrupted gender as emancipated women and often associated with them, were denoted in Society Drama and magazines such as *Punch* by lengthy affected names. Fergusson Pybus is the equivalent figure in Jones's 1894 play, *The Case of Rebellious Susan*. Wilde utilizes the convention for his own ends in *The Importance of Being Earnest* where Algernon Moncrieff is both a red-blooded male and well-informed aesthetically.

175 S.D. *(A little nervously)*: her social position, her relationship to the hero, and his anticipatory nervousness all signal that Lady Wargrave will be that recognizable type figure, the formidable dowager.

192 *dea ex machinâ*: the goddess (or god—*deus*) who appeared suddenly with the aid of ingenious stage machinery at the end of Greek drama to resolve problems.

198 *Mapledurham*: a picturesque village on the Thames in Oxfordshire with much-painted lock, water mill, and manor house. John Galsworthy's Soames Forsyte chooses to build his country house there in *The Man of Property* (1906).

216 *sculls!*: the sculling oar is lighter weight and shorter than the usual rowing oar and the sculler uses two blades.

220 *feathers*: a rowing term for turning the blade from vertical to horizontal as the oar leaves the water.

S.D. *Pantomime*: Gerald and Cazenove mime the actions described. The use of mime and gesture to emphasize points in the dialogue or to draw out their humorous potential was a feature of the older comedy.

232 *bachelor!*: again, conforms to the type of the *raisonneur* who retains an eye for the women but remains unfettered, although, often, he gives his heart at the end of the play.

249 *Horse Guards*: the military headquarters on Whitehall. Originally the guard house for Whitehall Palace.

253 *The same mutton?*: the emancipated woman was assumed to neglect cooking and other domestic duties, so one day's meat would be served up again cold the next.

257 *the club*: men-about-town could take dinner at one or another of the London clubs of which they were members. Since both Sylvester and Cazenove are members, this is presumably their regimental club. Women, as is still the case in a few such today, were not admitted.

264 *the Empire*: a Music Hall in Leicester Square (subsequently a cinema). Its promenade, notorious as a haunt of prostitutes, was in the news in 1894 because it had recently been attacked by Mrs Ormiston Chant as part of her Purity Campaign.

287 *Oh*: 'On' (Licensing Copy and published text). Editor's suggested emendation.

348 *union of souls*: since the new woman was believed to want relationships devoid of sexuality she was often portrayed as unnatural, neurotic, or frigid. In Society Drama this is frequently shown to mask predatory sexuality, as in the case of Mrs Sylvester, or self-deception, as in the case of Agnes Ebbsmith in Pinero's play.

356 *mésalliance?*: mismatch on social grounds (French). The play is more liberal in matters of class than in matters of gender. Mrs Sylvester's narrow-mindedness is exposed here.

363 S.D. *retires up*: goes up stage; to the part of the stage furthest from the audience.

376 *at ease! Dismiss!*: Cazenove's use of military idiom is one of many indications in this play of Grundy's roots in light comedy and melodrama. Following the huge success of Douglas Jerrold's *Black-Eyed Susan* (1829), whose hero used a nautical idiom, such linguistic identifiers became a familiar comic device.

378 *Peccavi!*: I have sinned! (Latin).

388 *Newdigate*: a prize awarded at Oxford University for the best poem on a set subject. It was famously won by Oscar Wilde in 1878.

427 S.D. *Sotto voce*: in an undertone (Latin).

436 *Stroke*: a rowing term for the oarsman who sets the pace; the erotic overtone is doubtless intentional.

439–40 *caught a crab*: been vanquished; as when, the oar having failed to strike deep enough in the water, the rower loses balance and may slip from the seat.

460 *Decalogue*: Ten Commandments.

479 *tête montée?*: worked up, over-excited (French); *tête exaltée*—head in the clouds—was probably the phrase meant.

487 S.D. *without*: off-stage.

489 S.D. *They take opposite . . . notice of anybody*: they clearly have no social grace. Their positioning on stage means their argument takes over the action and becomes a comic turn. The debate, a parodic version of one that continues still, grows increasingly farcical, culminating in Victoria's absurd assertion that the woman 'ought to reek with infamy as well' as the man.

498 *come home with the milk*: stay out very late—the milk being delivered early in the morning, in time for breakfast.

516 *Dr Mary Bevan*: medicine was one of the few professions in which women had, despite much opposition and ridicule, made some advance at this time. The London School of Medicine for Women was founded in 1874. In 1891 there were 101 woman doctors in London.

526–7 *prefer to be alone*: Lady Wargrave identifies the culture clash. In her code, medical matters are no subject for the drawing room; Dr Bevan insists that frankness should supplant notions of what is polite or taboo, hence her book, *Naked and Unashamed*.

547 *Everything's New nowadays!*: an article in volume 182 of *The Quarterly Review* in 1895 began, 'Novelty is the keynote of the dying century. With the "New Woman" and the "New Humour" we also have the "New Drama".' Bernard Shaw in the preface to *Plays Unpleasant* (1898) wrote, 'We called everything advanced "the New" at that time', while William Archer, reviewing the play, declared, 'It is a pity that the word "new" cannot be temporarily banished from the English language—It has become an unmitigated nuisance, a mere darkener of counsel' (*Theatrical World, 1894*, 224).

568 *They want a husband*: Cazenove voices the 'common sense' view.

571 S.D. *a babel*: a confusion of tongues, evoking that caused by God as punishment for the building of the Tower of Babel (Genesis 11).

S.D. *'Peter Robinson's', 'Swan and Edgar's', 'Stagg and Mantle's'*: London drapery stores. The first two survived into the post-Second World War period, Peter Robinson at Oxford Circus, Swan and Edgar at Piccadilly Circus.

593 S.D. *still*: Grundy provides no direction as to when Gerald first holds her. It may be as early as his 'Not yet' at l. 577. Her recoil would, however, probably be more effective if Gerald seized her for the *first* time at 'Be my wife'.

596 *Mr Gerald!*: use of the title indicates her consciousness of class difference. Forms of address are important markers of degrees of intimacy and respect in each of the plays in this edition.

602 *made love to me?*: the phrase, then, meant simply 'paid amorous attention to me?'.

666 *Form square!*: military order to infantry to adopt a four-sided formation as defence against a hostile charge.

681 *'Obey', forsooth!*: Dr Bevan indicates her disgust at the vow women took in the marriage service to 'obey, serve, love and honour' their spouse whereas the man vowed to 'love, comfort and honour' his wife. The argument foregrounds the curtain line of this Act, where Margery, the real woman, willingly offers to obey.

687 S.D. *works down stage*: moves gradually to the front of the stage.

2.48–9 *Never call . . . it's vulgar!*: the astuteness of Margery's perceptions about the social code here and subsequently in the scene sit uneasily with her pranks, naïveté, and silly laughter. As Clement Scott put it in his review, 'few men who live would not have been aggravated to death with such an irritating puss as the "Mapledurham maiden" is made to be after marriage' (*Illustrated London News*, 8 Sept. 1894).

50 *an olive-branch*: a token of peace.

63 S.D. *Aside*: direct statement to the audience is a convention imported by

Grundy into the well-made play of Society Drama from the melodrama. In this act, the fourth wall is frequently broken to point audience response to the comic action.

73 *I shan't spell it wrong!*: she may be ignorant of social decorum; but, like other humble nineteenth-century heroines, she is not illiterate. As Phyllis, the Arcadian Shepherdess in Gilbert's *Iolanthe* (1882), says, 'I can spell all the words that I use, | And my grammar's as good as my neighbour's'.

85–6 *Somehow . . . Mapledurham*: comic parallelism, with Margery's aside, uttered from the opposite side of the stage to Gerald's at ll. 63–4, directly echoing his.

156 S.D. *business*: like the discussion of 'obey' in Act 1, Margery's light-hearted rehearsal of the action here is a structural device, foregrounding the sad climax of this Act.

197 *tobacco?*: like the latchkey, smoking, regarded as a male habit, was an immediate signifier of female emancipation. Indeed, the custom of ladies leaving the dinner table before gentlemen arose to prevent their delicate nostrils being offended by the smoke. (A third signifier, cycling, is not on view in this play.)

203 S.D. *Lights up . . . gold-tipped cigarette*: Victoria's farcical ignorance about how to smoke emphasizes her affectation. The gold tip signals decadence but also enables the audience to see the error more clearly.

219 *Bradshaw*: travel guide to all of Europe, including complete railway and steamer timetables.

251 *told you everything?*: Enid's presumption that Gerald will have confessed and been forgiven previous *amours* is a comic reference to contemporary interest in the sexual double standard. In Hardy's *Tess of the d'Urbervilles* (1891), Angel Clare, having been forgiven the erotic past he has confessed, is horrified to learn that Tess, too, has experience to confess.

256–7 *It's such women . . . (Turns off)*: the patterned action compliments the patterned dialogue. The theatricality is emphasized by Margery's grimace at the audience which serves as a prelude to a further farce sequence centring on women smoking.

285 *I do wish she wouldn't!*: endorsing Cazenove's earlier opinion that what they really want is a husband, and foregrounding Enid's eventual capture of his heart.

286 *ordering my gown!*: the first stages of flirtation are signalled here. *He* has arranged for Enid to be invited, *she* is as eager as the most unemancipated to dress up for the occasion. Victoria, clearly jealous, departs leaving the stage clear for the subsequent extended duologue. This includes Cazenove's increasingly suggestive asides and culminates in the erotic farce of the blind-man's-buff game.

299 *succès d'estime!*: a limited success, based on the sympathy of friends (French).

326 *Vigilance Committee*: a reference to pressure groups, very active in the

1880s and 1890s, concerned with identifying and reporting indecency in the arts, particularly in music-hall acts. The National Vigilance Association had been much in the news in August 1894 when it denounced the suggestiveness of an act at the Palace Variety Theatre.

361–2 *Zola's novels*: a by-word for all that was shocking in foreign, and particularly French, culture. In 1889, Vizetelly had been sentenced to three months' imprisonment for publishing translations of French naturalism, notably Zola's *Rougon-Macquart* novels.

436 *neglected you too long*: Lady Wargrave implies that these—especially Sylvester—are inappropriate companions for her nephew's wife and that she must intervene.

453 *story*: story-teller; fibber.

482 *As far as you have gone*: Lady Wargrave's repetition of the phrase makes clear that she refers to the liaison she suspects rather than to the book. The double entendre is continued through her next few speeches.

485 *collaborateur?*: collaborator; Lady Wargrave's use of the older, French, form of the word is, no doubt, wry.

501 S.D. *(avoids her eyes)*: making clear, as the previous two lines have suggested, that both have picked up Lady Wargrave's insinuation, as the audience will have done.

3 S.D. *A buzz of general conversation; and a band is heard*: the implication is that the conversation and music are heard before the curtain rises.

S.D. *after the picture is discovered*: once the tableau is revealed. The impression of reality, of the audience coming upon a reception in full swing, that the presence of characters on-stage at the rise of the curtain conveys, is intensified if music and conversation have already been heard.

1 *Miss Vivash*: William Archer claimed that the presence of the feminist set in the drawing room of such an opponent as Lady Wargrave was one of the least credible sights in the play. It is a fair point, although Cazenove has boasted of getting Enid, at least, an invitation. Elizabeth Robins is careful to suit the costume and manner of the feminist Vida Levering to the country-house setting of Act 1 of *Votes for Women!*

8 *unfamiliar*: Pettigrew shares his first names with the poet Percy Bysshe Shelley. The banning of a centenary production of Shelley's play *The Cenci* in 1886 had established a link in public imagination between the poet and all things avant-garde.

14 *The Corset*: a ribald reference to Oscar Wilde's editorship, from 1887–9, of the magazine, *Woman's World*.

17 *rattle!*: (i) infant's toy and (ii) a stream of idle chatter: both meanings suggest noise and inconsequentiality.

18 S.D. *[Enter Dr Bevan]*: stage direction supplied by editor.

23 *The best of 'em!*: figures in popular comedy were commonly given a catch-phrase and the audience would quickly recognize this as Cazenove's. Although here addressed to Sylvester, it is subsequently nodded directly to the audience who would understand it as a pointer to an eventual pairing off.

30 S.D. *(All shiver)*: choric echoing of Percy's gesture follows the practice of comic opera and leads in to what is, in effect, a metatheatrical sequence, featuring the topics subject to humorous treatment in this play. Such artifice is repeatedly evident in Grundy's use of the comic chorus in this act.

33–4 *signs of repentence?*: a metatheatrical nod to the spate of plays, including *The New Woman*, which, subsequent on the 1889 production of *A Doll's House*, addressed 'the sexual problem'.

39 *Dixi!*: I have spoken! (Latin).

77–8 *a woman is entitled . . . a man's past?*: a recurrence of the Act 2 discussion of the double standard (cf. Act 2, l. 250).

92 *Molière*: the reference is to the comic treatment of bluestockings and female education in *Les Femmes savantes* by the seventeenth-century French dramatist, Molière, author of such classic comedies as *Le Misanthrope* and *Tartuffe*.

97 *Or the Music Halls . . . Trixy Blinko?*: Grundy is here mocking the pretension of intellectuals who made a cult of popular entertainment and its stars.

159–76 *Ever since I saw . . . above a love like hers?*: in this, the first long speech of the play, Grundy slips into the conventional language of melodrama, in which he was well versed. The speech signals the turning point in Gerald's attitude to feminism as well as to love and Margery. From here on he thinks and acts as a 'true man'.

202–3 *my life . . . mine to bestow*: although necessary to the plot, as a means of keeping him from declaring himself to Margery again, Gerald's scruple about his responsibility to Mrs Sylvester is hardly convincing since marriage gives Margery the prior claim, legally and morally. Any declaration having been private, Mrs Sylvester only has public shame to live down if she herself declares it publicly. As is clear in the exchange between Sylvester and Margery which follows, even Mrs Sylvester's husband is unaware of the reasons for the change in Margery's demeanour at this point in the plot.

415 *Yes*: the only significant changes between the Licensing Copy and the copy published in 1895, following the run of the play, occur between this point and the end of the Act. In the Licensing Copy, and presumably in performance, Margery enters here followed gradually by the other characters and, until the last three lines, her speeches are addressed to the company generally. The alteration, which makes for a more direct confrontation between Margery and Mrs Sylvester, may well have been a response to William Archer's criticism that an opportunity for a strong confrontation between the two women had been missed.

429 S.D. *omnes*: all (Latin, and common nineteenth-century stage usage).

436 *calm too long!*: the Licensing Copy includes '*addressing the company*' as a stage direction here.

438 *That's what I do remember!*: Margery's curtain speech is shortened in the published version. The cuts are restored in square brackets.

445 *yourself a New Woman*: 'yourselves New Women' (Licensing Copy).

451 *If you*: in the Licensing Copy, Margery addresses Mrs Sylvester directly for the first time here.

4.5 *screw*: decrepit horse.

12 *splint*: bony lumps which develop in a pony's cannon bone, on the foreleg, below the knee, a result of minute fractures caused by repeated jarring.

33 *old customer*: gentlemen down for the fishing would pay local residents for riverside board and lodging.

96 *cast a stone at her?*: popular idiom implying hypocrisy, deriving from Christ's declaration to accusers demanding the punishment of stoning for a woman taken in adultery: 'He that is without sin among you, let him first cast a stone at her' (John 8: 7).

126 *He'll go back . . . her fault*: even at a time of strong stage conventions of reunion, this seemed unlikely to some. Clement Scott commented that 'the reunion that is absolutely impossible in this play is that between Mrs Sylvester with the strong intellect and the concealed passion and her absolutely unintellectual and unsensitive husband'.

135 *ordnance*: military term for artillery; Cazenove, meaning 'ordinance', is referring to the institution of marriage.

139 *ordinances*: prescribed religious observances or ceremonies, usually, as here, indicating those through which the church impacts on social life, as baptism, confirmation, marriage, and burial.

191 *the Mutiny*: the Indian Mutiny of 1857; a massive uprising in India, quelled by British troops.

Rotten Row!: running through Hyde Park, from Apsley Gate to Kensington Gardens, this road was a fashionable place to ride in carriages and exercise horses. The adjutant was presumably run over or thrown ignominiously from his horse.

201 s.d. *(Quite forgetting himself)*: his gesture and confidence would seem over-familiar, given that Armstrong is a social inferior.

202 *My lady's very welcome*: Armstrong takes Cazenove to mean that Lady Wargrave enjoys a glass of ale too.

274 *a lady*: the difference in the terms here is indicative of social class differences. (Margery has, of course, been shown to be a natural lady.)

277 s.d. *fan half spread . . . face*: she averts Cazenove's gaze—a musical and

light–comedy convention, marking discretion in the presence of the intimate behaviour of others.

The Notorious Mrs Ebbsmith

Cast Page

Garrick Theatre: this theatre on Charing Cross Road was built by W. S. Gilbert. Its actor-manager was John Hare who opened the theatre in 1889 with Pinero's first play of ideas, *The Profligate*.

Mrs Patrick Campbell: named Stella, she invariably used her husband's name on the stage and was popularly known as 'Mrs Pat'. Following her London debut in 1890, she gained overnight fame with *The Second Mrs Tanqueray* (1893) and was drawn by Beardsley for *The Yellow Book*. She played the Rat Wife and then Rita in Henrik Ibsen's *Little Eyolf* (1896). Shaw wrote the part of Eliza in *Pygmalion* for her (1914). Her intimate correspondence with Shaw was subsequently published.

Johnston Forbes-Robertson: acted with the Bancrofts and Irving. Pinero wrote the part of Aubrey Tanqueray for him. He became manager of the Lyceum later in 1895 where, among other roles, he played Romeo to Mrs Pat's Juliet. He became famous as a Shakespearean actor and was the Hamlet of his age. Knighted, 1913.

John Hare: a friend of the dramatist. Having nervously rejected *The Second Mrs Tanqueray*, he sought to remedy his error by commissioning this play. His most famous role was Benjamin Goldfinch in Grundy's farce, *A Pair of Spectacles* (1890). Knighted, 1907.

C. Aubrey Smith: Stonor in *Votes for Women!*

Gerald du Maurier: subsequently a famous actor-manager, he began acting in Hare's company in 1894, joining Beerbohm Tree later in 1895 for a small role in *Trilby*, adapted from the novel by his father, George du Maurier. Acted Ferdinand Gadd in Pinero's *Trelawny of the 'Wells'* (1898) and was the first Captain Hook in J. M. Barrie's *Peter Pan* (1904). Knighted 1922.

1 s.d. *The Scene*: the Palazzo Arconati is fictional. Although the furnishings are tawdry, its style and its location on the Grand Canal suggest a degree of smartness as compared with the lodgings of Gertrude and her brother in the humbler Campo San Bartolomeo area. The Licensing Copy contains much fuller directions which note the positions of specific pieces of furniture and give details of the fittings, bell pulls, old pictures on the walls, books and papers, and a note of the location of props which will be used later in the scene: a tray with cut flowers, a jug of water, a vase of flowers, a man's hat, a workbasket with plain needlework.

1 *Ascolta!* *[Listen!]*: the exchange in Italian between the picturesquely attired servants helps set the scene. The translations are Pinero's and were included in both the Licensing and the published version.

2 *Una gondola allo scalo*: more local colour. This being Venice, guests arrive by gondola.

17 S.D. *boot-trees*: leg-shaped blocks inserted into boots to keep them in shape.

32 *ze Pâque*: Easter; Pinero takes this early opportunity to make clear that, unlike the house servants who are local, the personal servant is French.

36 *constitution*: bodily health. Gertrude corrects Fortuné's manners as much as his English. A polite Victorian did not go into physical details. Cf. Lady Wargrave's horror at the brash talk of Dr Bevan and the feminists in *The New Woman*.

46 *win the race*: Kirke acknowledges his lack of worldly success by comparison with Sir George, who is doctor to the aristocracy in London. Venice was at the time a cheap place for Englishmen to live, and here, as in other foreign cities, they would expect to be treated by a British doctor.

61 *Hotel d'Italie*: a smart hotel on Lungarno Amerigo Vespucci, overlooking the Arno. Pinero uses well-known Society locations in this play. It is rather unlikely that Agnes, then a poor nurse, would have moved Lucas there, or that the north-country vicar would have put up there.

80–3 *Mrs Cleeve's opinions . . . glide through life—!*: from the outset, Pinero distinguishes Agnes's 'views' from her essential character which is 'gentle', 'sweet', 'patient'. The 'devotion' and 'beautiful stillness' of this veritable angel in the house are curiously at odds with the neurosis Pinero will later attribute to her.

101–2 *his—his associate*: Sir George cannot bring himself to name the shocking relationship. The audience is gradually enlightened as to its true nature, Amos and his sister are wholly deceived.

111 *Roman fever*: a form of malaria, prominent in Rome. The heroine of Henry James's novella, *Daisy Miller* (1878), dies of it.

117 *A highly-strung, emotional creature?*: the first of many references to Lucas's neurosis and an immediate signifier of the gender distortion thought characteristic of aesthetes and those who associated with emancipated women.

121 *quinine*: a bark extract introduced in 1820 as a febrifuge and a tonic—its evident use here.

123 *Merceria*: the principal business and shopping street of Venice, it runs from the Rialto to the Piazza San Marco.

126 *Danieli*: the leading Venetian Hotel, situated then as now on the Riva degli Schiavoni, it was patronized by Henry James among others.

127 *Duke of St Olpherts*: an imaginary dukedom. Like Wilde and Jones, Pinero

in his 1890s plays introduces the glamour of aristocracy, which gives Society Drama its name.

137 *The woman*: the epithet and the conspiratorial undertone prepare Agnes's entry.

S.D. *Agnes enters*: while the 'sweet low voice' confirms Gertrude's account of Agnes, the insistence on the plainness of dress signals the presence of a New Woman, as it did with Elaine Shrimpton in Jones's *Case of Rebellious Susan* the previous season, but, since this is not a minor comic character but the heroine who would have been expected to wear the most glamorous clothes, the distortion implied is more extreme here, the ugliness more surprising and, probably, disappointing. The original audience, moreover, would have recognized, and many would have come specifically to see, Mrs Pat, famously well-dressed in *The Second Mrs Tanqueray*. The shock here foregrounds the moment of transformation in Act 3, when, fired by passion, the plain woman is revealed as a beauty (a cliché subsequently much used by cinema).

169 *hipped*: low-spirited, depressed.

174 *Great Cumberland Place?*: running off the north-west corner of Hyde Park, this is a fashionable London address, which, Sir George's response makes clear, is that of Lucas's mother. Lucas's taking Sir George aside to make his enquiry is, despite his protestations to the contrary, the first of several indications of his uncertainty about his present position.

187 *foul Roman hotel*: what Lucas was doing in a foul hotel in Rome is unclear, since the funds to move up-market in Florence and Venice were clearly his, Agnes being poverty-stricken. It does, however, have sentimental value, as does Lucas's insistence here on her having saved him from certain death.

192 *Qu'y a-t-il*: What is it? (French).

201 *Mettez . . . la gondole*: put the cushions in the gondola (French). Agnes's solicitude is emphasized.

202 *Bien, madame*: Very well, Madam (French).

211 S.D. *Sir George simply bows*: although he acknowledges the quality of her nursing, Sir George will not shake the hand of a woman living in sin. Kirke's ostentatious shaking of her hand shortly afterwards makes the earlier rebuttal more marked.

243 *Come molto meglio voi state!*: how very much better you're looking! (Italian)

248 *'God's in His heaven'*: Gertrude quotes Robert Browning's poem 'Morning' from *Pippa Passes* (1841). The audience would be expected to supply the next line: 'All's right with the world'.

264 *Caffè Quadri*: fashionable café on the north side of the Piazza San Marco.

267 *home from India*: service (military or civil) in India was a common occupation of members of upper-class families in the days of Empire. Following

the opening of the Suez Canal, the route home would go through the canal and either by boat through the Straits of Gibraltar or up the Adriatic and on by train from Venice, thus avoiding the turbulence of the Bay of Biscay.

268 *quizzing*: observing and commenting on; the word is used by characters promenading in fashionable haunts in the novels of Jane Austen and Fanny Burney.

275–6 *after I went out*: '. . . to India' is understood.

293 *Ebbsmith*: as the audience must have recognized well before this, Agnes now reveals that she is the 'notorious Mrs Ebbsmith' of the title.

303 *almost certain you would not*: the convention was that any woman who offended against the sexual code must be ostracized by polite society: women in particular would be tarnished by association. One of the more famous examples of such treatment was George Eliot, socially ostracized after she began living with G. H. Lewes.

315 *the Park*: Hyde Park.

310–23 *Jack Thorold . . . quite so irrational today!*: as was pointed out by both William Archer and Bernard Shaw, Agnes's language here, that of a conservative outsider, is hardly convincing as the utterance of someone brought up a revolutionary socialist, even one attempting to explain revolutionary ideas to an outsider. Both idiom and attitudes are inappropriate.

332–3 *Most of our married friends were cursed in a like way*: although he seems to endorse the institution of marriage, unhappy marriage is a constant in Pinero's Society Drama.

336–7 *St Andrew's Church in Holborn*: a Wren church, erected 1686; incidentally the place where Disraeli was christened.

341–2 *any girl in a parsonage*: Shaw points out the absurdity of Agnes having recourse to such a comparison (*Saturday Review*, 16 Mar. 1895). Pinero adopts a similarly sentimental position in *The Second Mrs Tanqueray* when he has Paula sigh 'a few years ago' as she recalls her innocent girlhood.

349 *in a harem*: she means that he used her for his sexual pleasure as, it emerges later, Gertrude's husband did her. This element of male lust is one of Pinero's recurrent themes—its introduction here prepares for Agnes's recognition of and brief response to it in Lucas later in the play.

376–7 *Starvation . . . nursing for a living*: Shaw labelled this 'a piece of fiction which shews that Mr Pinero has not the faintest idea of what such a woman's career is in reality' (*Saturday Review*, 16 Mar. 1895).

385 *Less than three years ago*: one of many indications that Lucas is shallower than Agnes. She endured her terrible marriage until death ended it. He left his very quickly.

433 *Oh!*: Gertrude's gasp marks her recognition that social convention will prevent her continuing friendship with Agnes.

445 *On his back in a gondola*: gondolas, the normal form of transport in Venice, could be hired, with gondolier, by the day, or the week by tourists.

447 *Palazzo Sforza*: presumably the Cà del Duca Sforza which is a little beyond the Accademia Bridge and immediately adjacent to the fifteenth-century Palazzo Falier, for some time occupied by the American critic and novelist W. D. Howells. This situates the apartment of Lucas and Agnes on the first bend in from the Lagoon, possibly in Howells's Palazzo.

467 *A propos?*: With regard to? What's the implication of that?

506–7 S.D. *(Slipping the letter . . . opening another)*: this signals that Lucas prefers that Agnes should not see the letter and that he is less frank than she.

517 *the House*: the chamber of the elected Members of Parliament, the House of Commons.

520 *the Party*: i.e. the Conservative Party.

535–48 *I couldn't foresee . . . instead of to—! Ah!*: Lucas reveals his weakness and his conventionality in this speech which makes his neurosis, his selfishness and his need for the support of a self-sacrificing woman all too clear.

570–1 *if passion had no share in it*: where Lucas has just shown himself hot-blooded, Agnes, cold in response to his kiss, conforms here to the idea of the emancipated woman as frigid or asexual but, whereas the higher love was a ploy for Grundy's Agnes Sylvester, Pinero's Agnes Ebbsmith speaks in recoil from sexual intimacy, like Sue Bridehead in Hardy's 1895 novel, *Jude the Obscure*.

599 *Qu'avez-vous là?*: What have you there? (French).

603 *Est-il parti?*: Has he gone? (French).

607 *improving the shining hour*: making good use of the time—from Isaac Watts's poem, 'How doth the little busy bee | Improve each shining hour', which was given further currency by its parody 'How doth the little crocodile' in chapter 2 of Lewis Carroll's *Alice in Wonderland* (1865).

610 *musical glasses*: a set of glass tubes or bowls from whose rim musical tones could be sounded; the invention of Benjamin Franklin in 1762.

623 S.D. *flings the bouquet*: for all her seeming calmness and tendency to sit patiently sewing, Agnes is given to dramatic gestures as this flinging away of St Olpherts's bouquet makes evident. It also provides a piquant surge of emotion for the close of Act I.

627 *laugh at me!*: Lucas's self-centredness is reiterated.

2 S.D. *Through the windows . . . seen in the distance*: the distant sails and mast-heads provide pleasing local colour. They also help locate the apartment at the first bend in the Grand Canal looking down to the Lagoon.

8 *Via Rondinelli*: the real street in which Pinero's fictional dressmaker is situated runs off the Via Tornabuoni, at the time Florence's smartest shopping street.

16 *Mettez-la n'importe où*: Put it wherever you like (French). It is not clear to me why Agnes, an Englishwoman who seems to understand their Italian, speaks to the servants in French.

21 *Laissez-moi!*: Leave me! (French).

48 *décolletée*: low-necked.

56 *hang this on my bones?*: an appropriately metatheatrical image, the actress, Mrs Pat, being notoriously thin, even to anorexia.

71 *slovenliness*: although Lucas modifies the statement to 'shabbiness', neglect of appearance was a common indicator of feminists and intellectuals.

96 *the Grünwald?*: a restaurant on the Via Ventidue Marzo, much patronized by German tourists (and given a star for the quality of its food in the 1894 Baedeker *Guide to Venice*).

98 *Montefiascone?*: a sweet white wine made from Muscat grapes from the area south-west of Orvieto.

99 *chocolate*: cioccolata—a hot chocolate drink fashionable in Italian cafés.

110 *the Piazza*: presumably the Piazza San Marco, the big café-lined square in front of St Mark's Cathedral.

120–1 *the Campo*: a small Venetian square, presumably the one closest to the palazzo. It was usual to go on to the balcony, into the garden or otherwise outside to smoke.

124 S.D. *[Gertrude rises quickly]*: a comedy of embarrassment is enacted in the Licensing Copy's stage directions. Gertrude's reluctance to meet the sinful Lucas is emphasized when, having just seated herself, she gets up again quickly at the prospect of meeting him.

146 *ammonia*: ammonium valerate, used as a sedative, is probably intended here; of the many ammonium salts used in medicine, *sal volatile* (smelling salts) is the best known.

203–4 *a time when I may cease to be—necessary to Mr Cleeve*: this is a recurrent fear of women in plays of the time. It is shared by Nora in Act 1 of *A Doll's House* and dominates Paula's thinking in the later part of *The Second Mrs Tanqueray*.

235 *Vous savez, n'est-ce pas?*: You know what to do, don't you? (French).

239–40 *Les ordres que je vous ai donnés, répétez-les*: The orders that I gave you, repeat them (French).

242 *Non, non—tout haut*: No, no—out loud (French). Agnes has no wish to hide her plans from Gertrude; Fortuné whispers, thinking Agnes has a secret assignation.

248 *Dépêchez-vous*: Hurry up (French).

253 *Florian's*: a fashionable café on the south side of Piazza San Marco.

270–1 *Portez ce carton dans ma chambre*: Take this box into my room (French).

277 *Duke of St Olpherts?*: title, dress, polished manners, and what has already

been learned about his life-style would inform the audience that this is the play's *raisonneur*, as would his being acted by Hare. Like Cayley Drummle and Sir Richard Kato in *Rebellious Susan* he is perceptive about the characters of those he observes and, for all his worldly wisdom, more honourable than his supposedly upright family. He is also, as suggested in the tendency of his conversation, his limp, and the use of such words as 'wreck' and 'weary' in the stage direction, more evidently decadent and failing in moral courage, more sinisterly predatory, than was usual in the type.

284 *directly he returns*: Pinero makes the point here and throughout the scene that Agnes's behaviour towards the opposite sex is completely decorous. He also makes her interestingly well able to hold her own against what proves to be the most acute male character in the play, free from the pettishness and irritability of Paula Tanqueray. She is, indeed, shown to be a 'serious woman', as St Olpherts observes.

325 *ballet-girl*: members of the ballet, like chorus girls, were assumed to be of easy virtue and out to entrap rich young men. Cf. 'The consequence was he was lost *totally*, | And married a girl in the *corps de bally*', W. S. Gilbert, *Patience* (1881).

344 *I challenge you*: Pinero provides opportunity for exposition.

348 *which was minus a host*: the implication here is that either the husband was often away, creating opportunities for adultery, or a woman was living alone—possibly set up there by St Olpherts—and so was available for his pleasures.

372 *the kennel*: the gutter.

366–77 *The sufferers, the toilers . . . as surely as yours is going!*: Agnes voices her socialistic views, cast in notably general and abstract terms, with the harsh voice and violent gestures of the fanatic. That her manner is so changed suggests dislocation, a mode alien to her true nature.

396 *Carter Street*: in the Shoreditch area of East London where Agnes would find a working-class audience. The group from the men's club in St James's were 'slumming' or experiencing the thrill of venturing into the dark places of the city.

405 *sanguinary*: bloodthirsty.

416 *saccharine?*: artificial sweetener, used as a sugar substitute by sufferers from diabetes and certain other diseases rather than, as often now, as a slimming aid. It is, like his gout, a further suggestion of St Olpherts's decrepit state.

418 *rip*: roué or rake.

436 *designing danseuse of commerce*: *see* note on *ballet-girl* at l. 325.

458 *pernicious pipe*: opium pipe. St Olpherts elaborates his metaphor for Lucas's craving of adulation.

466 *an epicure*: a sybarite, one giving himself up to sensual pleasure; deriving from the Greek philosopher, Epicurus.

470 S.D. *The light in the room*: a picturesque lighting effect outside the windows is introduced to complement Agnes's emotion. Subsequent lighting cues, as the scene progresses, flood the stage with rich evening light and introduce lengthening shadows.

544–5 *she doesn't appear to spend much time in dressing her hair*: a stock characteristic of the satirized New Woman. From this point onwards, any admiration Agnes's emancipated stance might have drawn is undermined.

551 *Trafalgar Squared me*: launched into a proselytizing attack. Open political meetings were held, then as now, in Trafalgar Square in Central London.

552 *red rag*: provoker of her fury. Since the colour, reputedly, enraged bulls, red cloths were brandished before a bullfight, hence the saying, abbreviated here, 'like a red rag to a bull'.

552–5 *This spirit of revolt . . . cared for*: Lucas's words show that he does indeed, as St Olpherts has claimed, share the conventional male attitude to gender relationships.

569 *her junior?*: Mrs Sylvester is similarly older than Gerald in *The New Woman*; Vida Levering than Alan Trent in *Votes for Women!* and Janet than Monty in *The Last of the De Mullins*. Only the woman dramatist shows the woman uninterested in the charms of the admiring younger man.

573–4 *[That's it; if women are to get stout . . . her time of life.]*: dropped from the published text, this comment would have had particular resonance in the first production in view of Mrs Pat's notorious thinness.

583 *Dr Jaeger*: inventor of knitted jersey wool suits, famously worn by Bernard Shaw in preference to the stiff formality of conventional male clothing. This reference, too, which would have created a stir of recognition in performance, was dropped from the published version.

604 *Free Union*: a couple choosing to live together but not to be bound by marriage. Eleanor Marx and Edward Aveling were a famous contemporary example. Barfoot proposes that Rhoda live with him in a free union in Gissing's *The Odd Women* (1893).

634 S.D. *a beautiful woman*: Agnes's startling transformation is the turning point of the play. Hereafter she takes on the characteristics of a fallen woman, self-sacrificing, loving too much. As Shaw's review teasingly put it Mrs Campbell entered 'with her plain and very becoming dress changed for a horrifying confection apparently made of Japanese bronze wallpaper' (*Saturday Review*, 16 Mar. 1895).

635 *Un petit châle noir tricoté—cherchez-le*: a little black knitted shawl—find it (French).

663 *how sweet you look!*: Lucas is shown to be wholly insensitive to Agnes's mood.

666 *fifty new gowns!*: the man is willing to reward the biddable woman.

Rebellious Susan ends with the gratified husband offering to buy his now-submissive wife the biggest jewel they can find.

696–7 *as simple, tender women are content to love?*: cf. Margery's declaration about 'we who love with our hearts' at the end of Act 3 of *The New Woman*.

3.15 *pier-glasses*: mirrors (literally, those placed in the space between windows).

29 *those things*: cigarettes, as Agnes herself suggests, are a lingering emblem of her emancipated self.

34 *bouillon*: broth; nutritious but easily digested, so particularly suitable for invalids.

56 *Naya's, the photographer's*: although other traders are given fictional names, Naya, famous for scenic photographs, did exist, at 78 Piazza San Marco.

90 *this change coming over me!*: Agnes's repressed femininity asserting itself. She will shortly admit that she is not unhappy.

129–30 S.D. *As he paces the room, she walks slowly to and fro*: Pinero's awareness of use of the stage space is demonstrated more clearly in the Licensing Copy's direction that *he* paces the upper, *she* the lower part of the stage.

130–1 *I'll work. My new career!*: Lucas's egocentricity, already apparent, is here directly expressed. Previously, it had been their shared work that was centred.

147–8 *my marriage—all over again!*: the aside—more common in Grundy's than Pinero's drama—lets the audience see Agnes's horror. Her recognition of the past repeating itself echoes Mrs Alving when she overhears Oswald and Regina in Act 1 of Ibsen's *Ghosts*.

186 *Capello Nero*: Albergo Orientale e Capello Nero, a good second-class hotel with trattoria open to non-residents located behind Piazza San Marco and entered from the Merceria.

215 *Priez Monsieur le Duc d'entrer*: Ask the Duke to come in, please (French).

240 *Zabajone*: or zabaglione, a frothy dessert made from beaten egg yolks, sugar, and marsala.

256 *Very nice*: at a time when even children knew, like Lewis Carroll's Alice, that 'it is rude to make personal remarks', St Olpherts does so unabashed, as do Cazenove and Sylvester in *The New Woman*.

273 *[Shall we lay this little white cloth, you and I?]*: the Licensing Copy provides stage business to bring St Olpherts close to Gertrude.

287 *Campo San Bartolomeo*: the area abutting the Rialto on the Right Bank of the river. Furnished rooms or apartments advertised with white window placards and to be paid fortnightly in advance, were commonly available for tourists.

291 S.D. *writing upon his shirt-cuff*: starched and white, the cuff made a good temporary note pad; Algernon Moncrieff similarly notes the address of a lady on his cuff in Act 1 of *The Importance of Being Earnest*.

298–9 *leave early tomorrow morning*: Gertrude, the good woman, gets the better of the bad man. Her strength and wit in this scene off-set Agnes's weakness and self-betrayal.

365–7 *'Bell' amore . . . parte dal cuore—'*: 'Beautiful love, lend an ear, | To a song that comes from the heart'.

389 S.D. *slipping his cloak off*: 'coat' in published version. I have restored 'cloak' from the Licensing Copy since, at l. 528, the stage direction again has 'cloak'.

403 *dooced*: deuced. A modish intensifier given an affected pronunciation by St Olpherts.

422 *nitric and sulphuric acid, with glycerine*: ingredients for home-made explosives, as famously used in contemporary anarchist bomb-throwing incidents.

439 *This is my hour*: a reiteration of the view expressed by Paula Tanqueray, and denounced in Shaw's review of *Mrs Ebbsmith* as 'detestable', that woman's moment of intense life is inevitably brief. Agnes, who once had other ambitions, now accepts that hers is dependent on looks and sexual allure.

485 *à la mode*: in the fashion, with a cynical suggestion here that what is proposed would give a mere appearance of propriety.

492–3 *in vogue at my end of the town*: continuing the cynical implication that such arrangements were a commonplace of upper-class 'respectability'.

584 *whited sepulchre*: hypocrisy, as in: 'Woe unto you, scribes and Pharisees, hypocrites! for ye are like unto whited sepulchres, which indeed appear beautiful outward, but are within full of dead men's bones and of all uncleanness' (Matthew 23: 27).

668–9 *saved by the blessed mercy of Heaven!*: by killing off the man she loved, Heaven removed the temptation to run away with him. Amos's comment a few lines later that Gertrude was saved by the mercy of Heaven, suggests that Pinero is not being ironic here.

684 *Once—!*: in *The Second Mrs Tanqueray* Paula, reminded of her former innocence, cries 'Oh God, a few years ago!' before going off to commit suicide. In *Theatre and Friendship* (1932), Robins recalled telling Henry James, 'When I write my great play there are three words I won't have in it . . . "Twenty years ago" . . . and he agreed solemnly that they should be cut out of *any*body's "great play" ' (p. 147).

702 S.D. *leather-bound book*: so described since Hare was indignant at the idea that a Bible be put to this use; but the subsequent dialogue, and the fact that the parson carries a well-thumbed copy, make clear that a Bible is intended.

732 S.D. *hurl the book into the fire*: Having ended Act 2 with the theatrical coup of Agnes's physical transformation, Pinero ends Act 3 with another highly charged theatrical effect. Shaw described the response to Agnes's thrusting of the Bible into the stove: 'a thrill of horror runs through the audience as

they see, in imagination, the whole Christian Church tottering before their eyes. Suddenly, with a wild scream, she plunges her hand into the glowing stove and pulls out the Bible again. The Church is saved; and the curtain descends amid thunders of applause' (*Saturday Review*, 16 Mar. 1895). The sequence was much commented on in reviews. Edmund Gosse told Mrs Pat that 'it jarred upon me as an incoherent and stagy and, therefore, disturbing element in an otherwise splendid and interior drama' (Mrs Patrick Campbell, *My Life and Some Letters* (1922), 100).

4 S.D. *moonlight*: Pinero's theatrical craftsmanship is in evidence in the temporal rhythm and lighting cues of the play. Although a week passes between Acts 1 and 2, the action moves as if through a day into night. Breakfast things were being cleared at the opening of the play, Act 2 was set in late afternoon, Act 3 in the evening, and Act 4 in moonlight.

4 *A'reet*: All right. Heppy's Yorkshire accent and occasional dialect words continue the varied local-colour effects the servants bring to the play.

11 *nobbut*: nothing but. Affection between mistress and servant is reflected in the shared register when Gertrude, in her response in the next line, repeats Heppy's word.

24 *Jo*: sweetheart.

38 *(... significantly) Reading?*: the shared recognition makes clear that she is reading the Bible.

72 *a Home for—*: 'Fallen Women' is understood here.

121–2 *an inversion of the picturesque ... not a pathetic figure*: the *woman* betrayed or abandoned was a common image of sentimental fiction and painting.

192–200 *One word ... For God's sake!*: Pinero, now in wholly melodramatic mode, introduces the notion of a crisis point with a succession of stock phrases, 'impossible to drag her', 'sacrifice herself utterly', 'falling to the lowest depths a woman can attain'.

231 S.D. *stuff dress*: dress made of woven woollen material, presumably plain.

258 *Cannot we be left alone?*: a scene between two women contending for a man, as in the close of Act 3 of *The New Woman*, traditionally offers the opportunity for a 'strong scene'. The version which follows here is both titillating, since the wife appeals to the mistress to stay with the husband, and disconcerting, since Sybil increasingly figures as wronged by both Lucas and his family.

321 *A character*: a reference.

334 *Tears—tears—*: the confrontation appears to end quasi-sentimentally with one woman responding to the other's emotional appeal; but, in contradiction of all the conventions of sentimental literature, the outcome is hurtful and repugnant to both. Archer, suggesting the confusion members of the audience may have experienced, wrote that 'Agnes's acquiescence in Sybil's proposal simply takes my breath away. I can trace it only to a

queer survival of the heroic-self-sacrifice superstitions that inspired so many of the French sentimental dramas of twenty years ago' (*World*, 27 Mar. 1895).

357–9 *Mrs Cleeve . . . You have utterly destroyed her*: the intervention of the wholly upright woman allows the more recognizably sentimental ending, the fallen woman's retreat into solitary penitence, which so distressed the actress playing the role.

411 *laws made and laws that are natural*: man-made laws and biologically determined laws. Agnes here accepts the common contemporary assumption that gender roles are fixed and incontrovertible.

430 *Pray! . . . you! . . .*: evidence of the final capitulation of the New Woman. Mrs Pat wrote of the ending, 'the last act broke my heart. I knew that such an Agnes in life could not have drifted into the Bible-reading inertia of the woman she became in the last act. I felt she would have risen a phoenix from the ashes. That rounding off of plays to make the audience feel comfortable is a regrettable weakness' (*My Life and Some Letters*, 98–9).

Votes for Women!

Title
Votes for Women!, the slogan on the banner in Act 2, was suggested by Granville Barker in place of Robins's original title 'The Friend of Women'. It appeared, as did the subtitle, 'A Dramatic Tract in Three Acts', on the Court Theatre Playbills and on publicity for the production. I have thought fit to retain these indicators of the excitement and polemic of the early performances of the play although the subtitle of the first published version was modified to 'A Play in Three Acts' and the exclamation mark was dropped from the title.

Cast Page
Royal Court Theatre: this theatre, in Sloane Square, London, was the base, between 1904 and 1907, of an independent theatre company led by Granville Barker, in association with J. E. Vedrenne. Its programme of new plays established Bernard Shaw as a major dramatist, gave scope to Barker's innovative directing talents, and a stage to the New Drama, the mainly realist writing of John Galsworthy, St John Hankin, and Barker himself. The 'Court Seasons' were the inspiration, in the years up to the First World War, of numerous independent companies and productions of new plays in London and the provinces. In 1956 the theatre was again the nursery of new drama when it became the base for the English Stage Company.

Athol Forde: took the role of Brovik in the Robins–Archer production of Ibsen's *The Master Builder* (1893).

Aubrey Smith: played Amos Winterfield in *The Notorious Mrs Ebbsmith* (1895).

Lewis Casson: a leading actor in Barker's productions at the Court, 1904–7, and the Duke of York's, 1910, he also acted with William Poel and directed the Manchester Repertory Company, 1911–14. He was married to the actress Sybil Thorndike and was knighted in 1945.

Mr Walker: the character's name-change to Pilcher was possibly effected to dispel association with thuggish Bill Walker in Shaw's *Major Barbara* (1905). Max Beerbohm praised the 'humour and vitality' of Edmund Gwenn's masterly performance in the role (*Saturday Review*, 13 Apr. 1907). Gwenn was also a member of Barker's Duke of York's Company.

Lady John Wynnstay: the character is a political hostess, like Robins's friend Florence, Lady Hugh Bell, she is also, like Lady Bell, sceptical about women's suffrage.

Frances Ivor: joined Lena Ashwell's independent company at the Kingsway Theatre (1908).

Miss Vida Levering: the character was originally to be called Christian. Robins's biographer, Angela V. John, notes that the name was changed at the request of Mrs Pankhurst who, fearing identification of the character and her past with Christabel Pankhurst, wrote to Robins in November 1906, that 'we should not like this to happen, should we?' (*Elizabeth Robins: Staging a Life* (1995), 145). Edith Wynne-Matthison, who was Robins's own choice for the role, became a founder member with Robins of the Actresses' Franchise League (AFL), the association founded in 1908 to promote women's suffrage.

Miss Beatrice Dunbarton: called Beatrice in the first production and the Licensing Copy, Jean in the published version. She was named first for the Renaissance patroness, Beatrice d'Este, then for Jeanne d'Arc (Robins, *Way Stations* (New York, 1913), 245–6).

Miss Ernestine Blunt: the character is identified by Angela V. John (p. 145) with the suffragette Theresa Billington. Dorothy Minto 'caught exactly the spirit of her part—the blithe spirit of the budding platformist', according to Max Beerbohm. Minto became a member of the AFL and acted with Barker's Duke of York's company and Edy Craig's Pioneer Players.

A Working Woman: the only speaker not given a name, she is identified by Sheila Stowell in *A Theatre of their Own: Feminist Playwrights of the Suffrage Era* (Manchester, 1992) with Hannah Mitchell, whose book *The Hard Way Up* was published in 1968. Agnes Thomas, who took the role, became a member of the AFL and played Aunt Ann in Githa Sowerby's *Rutherford and Son* (1912).

1 S.D. SCENE: 'July 1906' (Licensing Copy); the change to 'the end of June' in the published text makes the events less time-bound and sits more

comfortably with the suggestion in the text of a forthcoming General Election—there were General Elections in *January* 1906 and January 1910. The location was also changed from Herefordshire to Hertfordshire in the published version. The country-house scene is based in experience, Robins being a frequent guest at Rounton Grange, the Northallerton country house of Lady Florence Bell. Having originally set Act I outside, Robins pencilled 'Yes!' next to Henry James's suggestion in his notes on the play that she move the action to the 'big free accessible workable hall' of the house, it 'lending itself much more to certain verisimilitudes of movement, natural determinations of coming and going . . . rather than the open air scene where all this has the air of a perpetual and rather rotary or revolutionary walk' (13 Nov. 1906, Robins Collection, Fales Library, New York University). Stage plans for Acts 1 and 3 were included with the published text.

18–19 *no authority on motoring*—: the car still being something of a novelty, a wealthy but old-fashioned man like Sir John might well have disdained it.

30 *I've come to ask you to help me*: a line suggested by James in his notes and taken into the dialogue by Robins.

34 *Such rot!*: 'Such nonsense!' (Licensing Copy). In the manner of the well-made play, Robins alerts the audience to Miss Levering's attractiveness and the fact that she is thought unreachable, well before her first appearance.

46–7 *I wanted to see you about the Secretaryship*: Robins suggests the power wielded by a political wife such as the fictional Lady John, or the actual Lady Bell.

62 *Geoffrey Stonor's re-election*: Robins introduces a fictional forthcoming General Election. This is clearly not a by-election. Since Geoffrey's result is always 'a foregone conclusion' he could not be taken for one of the many Tories who lost their seats in the 1906 election.

66–7 *the Liberals swept the country the last time*—: a reference to the landslide Liberal victory in the General Election of January 1906, which was still 'last time' when Robins came to publish the play.

92 *for the week-end*—: the uncompleted sentences and cutting in, here and in successive speeches, speed the opening expository exchange between Farnborough and Lady John.

103 *[my niece]?*: the suggestion in the Licensing Copy is dropped from the copy-text.

111 *Jean*: 'Bea', throughout the Licensing Copy.

149 *promised to keep me posted*: the Licensing Copy followed this with an explanation, no longer necessary by the time of the published version, of the fictional General Election: 'The immense unexpected pressure of work you know—now that we've forced the Liberals to appeal to the country'.

158 *Church Brigade*: those house guests and family members who have attended Sunday morning church.

180 *so beautifully much*: a notably Jamesian use of the adverb.

189–90 *approve of us on more intimate acquaintance*: altered in manuscript in the Licensing Copy, and therefore probably in rehearsal, from 'like us'. The alteration gives Lord John a more old-fashioned, formal register.

194 *Dissenters*: those who decline to conform to the rites and ceremonies of the Established Church, the reference here being to Scots Presbyterians, who dissociated themselves from the ruling Anglican ascendancy.

198–9 *that Old Covenanter . . . an abhorred motor-car*: the Solemn League and Covenant, to defend their religious beliefs and practices, was signed by Scots Presbyterians in 1643. They observed the sabbath strictly and were known for their objection to dancing and light pursuits and, Lady John suggests, the new-fangled motor-car.

205–6 S.D. *[Pressing her cheek against Lady John's shoulder]*: manuscript addition to the Licensing Copy, presumably reflecting performance practice.

209 *dreffly*: dreadfully (modish affectation).

219 *Beginning to 'think in parties'!*: Jean, prospective wife of a Tory MP, is already embracing the factionalism of the British party political system.

226–7 *Well, if I do think with my husband . . . as, of course, I shall*: Jean, more modern than her uncle, changes the submissiveness of his 'think like' to the more mutual 'think with'. There is dramatic irony here, since one of the play's themes is Jean's discovery that she has a mind and opinions of her own.

229 *at Dutfield*: 'the other night at the Queen's Hall' (Licensing Copy). The shift from a London to a regional location for the speech suggests that Jean has joined Stonor in his constituency campaigning.

266 *a balance wheel*: a counterpoise, as in mechanics, to keep her steady—here, meaning a man.

277 S.D. *an attractive, essentially feminine . . . Why doesn't she marry?'*: in a notable shift from 1890s representations, the emancipated woman of this play looks smart and comports herself well, as Mrs Pankhurst, the suffragette leader, famously did.

300 *smells of indiarubber*: Greatorex, on the other hand, holds to the old stereotype of the active political woman. A rubber mackintosh, although practical, would have been unshapely.

318–19 *about Women's Trade Unions*: the women in this play are all notably active in public works: Lady John and Mrs Heriot are philanthropists of an older generation set on improving the lot of the poor, whereas Mrs Freddy is clearly set on women helping themselves at a time when male Trade Unionism was largely closed to women. Although she speaks in public, it emerges that her feminism is gradualist and that she must accommodate her husband's prejudices about female activism.

337 *that rowdy scene in the House of Commons?*: a reference to an actual event on 25 April 1906. As members engaged in talking out a suffrage resolution introduced by Keir Hardie, one of the few MPs in any party who genuinely supported suffrage, Irene Miller and Theresa Billington (the model for Ernestine Blunt in Act 2) led a noisy protest from the Visitors' Gallery.

359–60 *among the mill operatives . . . the papers said so, didn't they?*: mindful of her status as a guest, Vida avoids seeming too knowledgeable.

385 *a week-ender*: one of the right class and manner to join a week-end house party. This exchange reworks an actual conversation, recorded in her diary for 1905, that Robins had with the Radical MP Henry Labouchere, who, like Greatorex, had refused to meet a suffragette delegation: ' "I couldn't have done it for worlds", he said with a comic look of terror, "but I sent another fellow. He came back and, says he, 'you're quite right my dear fellow . . . don't you go, its appalling to look at 'em. There isn't a week-ender among 'em' " '; and to Robins's objections, he said 'You don't mean to say you—You don't look that sort' (quoted Angela V. John, *Elizabeth Robins*, 143).

401 *pace*: with deference to, or, forgive me for saying so (Latin; literally, 'peace').

403 *JEAN*: 'BEA' (Licensing Copy). Dropped from the published version, the extended exchange here, which is handwritten into the Licensing Copy, makes a more waspish Vida sting the younger woman.

411–12 *Mr Soper's*: Mr Soddy's (Licensing Copy).

415 *FREDDY*: editor's suggestion, replacing the copy-text's 'MRS FREDDY', which cannot be correct since the speech is a response to her question. It could appropriately bring Freddy back into the conversation or function as a feed-line from Farnborough.

418 *Bah-ee Jove!*: By Jove!

421 *All she needs is—*: Lord John figures as a throw-back to another generation and helps mark the difference between this play and those of the 1890s. His attitudes are those of Cazenove and other 1890s *raisonneurs*, but they are consistently side-lined in this play. His refrain that Vida, being an attractive woman, needs a husband becomes ridiculous by virtue of its increasingly inappropriate repetition.

432 *Soper didn't ask that*: she makes it clear that she is rebuffing Greatorex's propositioning of her.

471–2 *Rowton Houses*: founded by Lord Rowton, formerly Private Secretary to Disraeli, these hostels provided homeless men with clean sheets, hot water, tiled wash-rooms, and lodgers' kitchens for sixpence a night. The first, opened in Vauxhall in 1892, let 140,105 beds in its first year. Others were established at King's Cross (1894), Hammersmith and Newington Butts

(1897), and Whitechapel (1902). Arlington House, the largest, had been founded in Camden Town as recently as 1905.

478   *Tramp Ward*: room in a hospital for the accommodation of sick vagrants.

486–7   *The wrong person found her crying on the platform*: She was taken up by one who seemed to offer her protection but put her into prostitution. Domestic servants had few rights and employers could be very harsh in treatment of any infringements, hence her fear.

488   *Friendly Societies*: associations that would provide financial help in times of sickness or unemployment, usually to those who had subscribed small sums over some years, but they would also give charitable hand-outs.

490   *Rescue Leagues*: voluntary groups concerned to help women leave prostitution.

515   *Into the Underworld*: Robins, who would herself later go in disguise in the poorest areas of London for research, here draws on Mary Higgs's recently published account, *Three Nights in Women's Lodging Houses* (1905). Robins's novel, *Where Are You Going To?* (1912) takes prostitution and the white slave trade as its subject.

523   *Jean!*—: Mrs Heriot rises to take the young unmarried woman away lest her innocence is disturbed by talk about female sexuality and its abuses. Jean, however, is fascinated. The stage directions show that Lady John and Vida are also protective of the younger woman's innocence.

553   *I turned my back on my father's house*—: many employers notoriously took sexual liberties with their domestic servants. Such may have been the ugly goings-on Vida observed, but she was not prepared to reveal what she knew to her relations nor in the presence of Jean—or of the audience.

622   *Well, so she is*: Mrs Heriot's hints make clear that Vida has something to hide.

630   *Eaton Square*: Jean's London address—an elegant square in Belgravia. The address had originally been 'Queen Anne's Gate'. 'Eaton Square' is hand-written in on the Licensing Copy.

647   *They were for turning the girl out*: this, and the reference to the 'shady-looking doctor', make it clear that an illegal abortion is being discussed. It is surprising that the Examiner of Plays, who was notoriously fierce with the blue pencil, let these references stand.

669   *I'm not sure I understand*: it is possible that the Examiner of Plays also failed to understand or that he considered that the delicacy and opacity of the account made it harmless.

701   S.D. *Motor horn louder*: manuscript addition to Licensing Copy, retained in published version. Cars, only in production for a decade and still quite rare, brought instant excitement to the stage. Henry James, in his notes on the play, pronounced Stonor's arrival by car 'absolutely characteristic of the moment'. Shaw had startled the audience of *Man and Superman* (1905) by

not only placing a car on stage for the beginning of Act 2 but having it driven off at the end of the act.

711 S.D. *a dustcoat*: Motoring gear was needed to protect motorists from the dust raised by open cars and the often un-made-up roads on which they ran.

752–3 *As to the seat . . . a good talk after luncheon*: (Licensing Copy); a further indication of the power of the political wife.

771 *You know one another?*: the evident recognition, hastily denied, is a conventional device of the well-made play.

794–5 *dog whips and spitting in policemen's faces*: a dog whip was used in self-defence by Theresa Billington when ejected from a meeting in June 1905. Christabel Pankhurst was famously accused of spitting at the police in the first militant demonstration in 1905.

811 *the little group of*: 'two or three' (Licensing Copy).

859 *Sh! Sunday*: the views, he suggests, are too horrible to be discussed on the sabbath.

872 *'Paradiso'*: third section, following 'L'Inferno' and 'Il Purgatorio', of Dante's *Divine Comedy*, evidently the book Greatorex had earlier carried for her and the subject of their discussion of Italian Literature.

873 *The thing itself!*: suggesting that if not talking they would be doing; he, in making love to her, would be in Paradise.

892 *'Church Times'*: the house journal of the Church of England, founded in 1863 and still current.

902–3 *when he sees my name among the speakers on the placards*: 'seeing me plac-arded' (Licensing Copy).

913 *a handful of*: 'two or three' (Licensing Copy).

916 *sackcloth?*: the traditional dress of the penitent.

920–1 *from Land's End to John o'Groats?*: the length and breadth of Britain, the one being the most south-westerly point, the other the most north-easterly.

942 *The Bill*: 'A Suffrage Bill' (Licensing Copy). A petition for female suffrage was presented to Parliament in 1866. Private Members' Bills to enfranchise women passed their second readings in 1897 and 1904 but were taken no further.

999–1000 *for centuries*: 'since the creation' (Licensing Copy).

1001 *Piccadilly at midnight*: a notorious place for men to pick up prostitutes; so any woman alone there would be vulnerable to assault.

1006 *Nine Elms*: a working-class area in South Lambeth by Vauxhall Bridge. The Licensing Copy has 'Soho' handwritten in.

1054 *Guelf or Ghibelline?*: the two factions that struggled for power in medieval Italy and particularly Florence. Very roughly, the Guelfs wanted constitutional government and looked to the Papacy for support, the Ghibellines, the aristocratic party, supported the authority of the Emperor.

1053–60 *the Vigliacchi . . . the pangs of partisanship*: Vida talks allegorically to Jean, challenging her to commit herself. In Canto 3 of 'The Inferno', Dante puts at the outer edge of Hell the nay-sayers, those too selfish or too apathetic to commit themselves, including the angels who stood aside at the Fall. Despised both by God and Satan, forgotten by the world, they rush about pointlessly for eternity, goaded by a swarm of hornets. Of them the narrator says 'ch'i' non averei creduto | che morte tanta n'avesse disfatta', quoted by T. S. Eliot in *The Waste Land* (1922) as 'I had not thought death had undone so many'.

1061 *the abortions*: having avoided using the term earlier when evoking the procurement of a miscarriage, Robins uses it metaphorically here.

1100 *I didn't know her name was Vida; how did you?*: for all her subversive tactics, Robins retains the structure of the well-made play, and particularly its use of strong curtain lines. Max Beerbohm, who could 'hardly suppress a yawn' when Stonor stood momentarily transfixed at the sight of Vida, claimed to have 'yawned outright' when the ancient device of a dropped handkerchief was used at curtain-fall to confirm his past acquaintance with her (*Saturday Review*, 13 Apr. 1907).

2 S.D. SCENE: Robins's brilliant stroke in shifting the action from the conventional well-made play setting of Act 1 to the notably unconventional public meeting in Trafalgar Square of Act 2 was widely praised even by the otherwise dismissive Max Beerbohm. The ensemble acting was particularly praised: *The Sketch*, publishing a photograph of the scene that had 'caused the greatest interest in theatrical circles', reported it 'generally accepted as the finest stage crowd that has been seen for years' (15 May 1907), and *The Observer* found it 'a marvel of verisimilitude akin to that which might be achieved by a joint use of megaphone and cinematograph' (quoted Dennis Kennedy, *Granville Barker and the Dream of Theatre* (Cambridge, 1985), 61). Robins, who described her own conversion to the suffrage cause in *Way Stations* as happening in Trafalgar Square on a 'Sunday afternoon, in front of Nelson's Monument', drew on press reports and detailed notes of eight suffrage meetings between July and October 1906 in constructing the scene and the speeches. The crowd activity was largely shaped by Barker who used some forty actors, many of them experienced members of his company, and staged the action with the crowd facing upstage to the steps and raised pedestal of the Column from which the speakers, flanked by two huge 'Votes for Women!' banners, addressed both the crowd and the audience directly. Behind the pedestal a painted backcloth re-created the Square and its surroundings.

momentarily: moment by moment.

3 *be'yve as you're doin' tod'y*: 'behave as you're doing today'. Colloquial

pronunciation was commonly represented, as here, through orthography. J. M. Synge demonstrated in his plays from 1903 onwards that it was possible to represent Irish dialect through syntax and idiom alone, leaving actors (and readers) to supply pronunciation. Shaw followed suit, jettisoning orthographical representation of Cockney dialect after the opening sequence of *Pygmalion* (1914). The vividness of the scene is enhanced by its opening mid-speech.

6 *Poor Law Guardian*: a member of the Board responsible for administering the laws relating to the support of paupers at public expense. The holding of such a post marks her as a particularly respected member of the working class.

7 *Think of that, now—gracious me!*: This and several other interjections not in the Licensing Copy may well have accumulated during performance or very late rehearsals. Robins had accepted Barker's suggestion that he write in a 'good deal of patter' for the crowd.

12 *clean yer own doorstep!*: stone doorsteps, given a cream or white finish with a chalk stone, were soon marked by footprints. Keeping a clean doorstep was a matter of pride for respectable working-class women.

39 *women 'oo go to prison*: over 1,000 women were imprisoned for suffrage activities between 1906 and 1914.

s.d. *distinct phrases*: much of the repartee here and in other bursts of crowd noise in this Act are added in manuscript to the Licensing Copy.

'*They get their 'air cut free*': a sardonic reference to the cropping of prisoners' hair.

61–2 *Canning Town!—come with me to Bromley—come to Poplar and to Bow!*: adjacent East End slum areas, between West Ham Marshes and the London Docks.

80 *black-leggin' the men!*: taking men's jobs because willing to do them for less. The term is usually applied to those who fill the places of men on strike.

110 *John Stuart Mill*: English philosopher and economist (1806–73). Mill's essay *The Subjection of Women*, published in 1869, following his attempt to extend the franchise, became an important feminist text. As each of the speeches demonstrates, franchise reform, as Mill himself argued, was seen not as an end in itself but as a readily-identifiable step towards more general emancipation and equality.

s.d. *Voice: 'Mill? Who is he when he's at home?'*: not in the Licensing Copy.

113 *towards the close of the year 1905*: 'at the opening of this year' (Licensing Copy).

115 *in this generation*: the Licensing Copy has the more specific 'in 1906'.

120–2 *VOICES 'Not by scratching . . . 'Chartist riots, she's thinkin' of!'*: the suggested phrases are added in manuscript in the Licensing Copy. Benjamin Disraeli, nicknamed Dizzy, was Prime Minister in Conservative administrations in 1868 and 1874–80. County Council Scholarships enabled poorer people to continue their education. The People's Charter, demanding electoral reform, was published in 1838 after which the Chartist movement grew culminating in demonstrations and a huge petition to Parliament in 1848.

127 *month 'ard*: month's hard labour in prison.

148 POETIC YOUNG MAN: *I admit that*: not in Licensing Copy.

192 *Better 'urry up. Case of early closin'*: a sardonic reference to the long-rumbling discussion of the need to reform—or abolish—the House of Lords.

195–6 *'oo killed cock robin?*: the first line of the nursery rhyme is used inconsequentially by a heckler.

204 *lorgnon*: eyeglass with a handle.

225 *The Boer women did*: how much actual fighting the Boer women did is debatable, but they certainly helped defend their own homesteads and supplied what was essentially a citizen and guerrilla Boer army in the war against the British in South Africa (1899–1902). In 1901 the British developed a policy of imprisoning women in concentration camps to cut supplies from the farms and demoralize the Boer army.

225–6 *The Russian women face . . . can show*: peasants, who made up more than three-quarters of the population of Russia, lived in extreme poverty, many hardly above starvation level for most of the year. Landowners had lost the right to beat them only in 1904. The General Strike of September 1905, followed by a revolutionary uprising and fierce civil strife in Moscow in December, had drawn attention to the plight of the Russian people.

272 *Pilcher*: 'Walker' (Licensing Copy). Beerbohm said the actor, Gwenn, 'magnetised the whole audience' as he paced about, hands in pockets, chin thrust forward, good humour shining from him. The long well-paced speeches give each actor an opportunity for the minutely observed character acting for which the Court was famous.

274 *Tatcho*: trade name, presumably of a hair oil.

283 *munch your tommy*: eat your daily provisions. A colloquial expression deriving from the daily ration of bread issued to 'Tommies' (English soldiers).

290 *Labour Party?*: twenty-nine members of the Labour Representative Committee were elected in the 1906 General Election, whereupon the Committee adopted the name of Labour Party.

294 *bottom o' the street*: the Houses of Parliament are at the opposite end of Whitehall from Trafalgar Square.

297 *on your own shoulders*: i.e. the cost of their victory, bought with your votes,

is your continued oppression. The literal carrying of the triumphant candidate on his supporters' shoulders is suggested by the image.

301–4 *because 'e thinks . . . and 'appy, while you see*: 'because 'e's got you to go swellin' his majority again and to keep quiet, while you see' (Licensing Copy).

342 *maybe my grammar would have been better*: in making Pilcher and the Working Woman both verbally acute and evidently of the people, Robins is ahead of her time. The advanced drama from George Moore's *The Strike at Arlingford* (1893) to Galsworthy's *Strife* (1909) tended to represent working-class leaders as of a higher social class than their followers.

343–5 *Wait a bit . . . Lucky for me!*: this exchange is not in the Licensing Copy.

392–7 *Now, I ask you to listen . . . if you'll behave yourselves, her impressions*: this introduction of Vida and the heckler's joke replace the Licensing Copy's more sober 'A lady will now speak to you who can tell you something of her impressions'.

427 *[say]!*: (Licensing Copy). The published text has the more unlikely 'do!'.

435 *Marlborough Police Court instead of to Marylebone*: diversionary tactics: the one being in south-east, the other in north-west London.

436 *'Olloway*: Holloway, the main London women's prison; still in use.

492–3 *London County Council*: the unitary authority for the City of London and the 27 surrounding metropolitan boroughs which was brought into being by the Local Government Act of 1888. The Greater London Council, which superseded the LCC in 1965, was abolished in 1986, making London the only major European city without a strategic authority for its whole area.

528 *Strangeways Gaol*: Manchester's prison; still in use.

540 *so long ago*: 'as long ago as—' in the Licensing Copy, presumably changed when it was realized that, although known to exist in the thirteenth century, the origin of jury trial is obscure.

576 *the Union*: the Women's Social and Political Union, of which Robins was a member.

582 *shoulder to shoulder*: together, side-by-side. The phrase was used as a suffragette slogan.

589 *This is the way I must go*: this classic announcement of conversion to a cause yields another dramatic curtain.

3.30 *Abolition of the Upper House—*: conflict between the two Houses of Parliament reached a crisis point late in 1906 with the Lords' defeat of Liberal Government Bills that had passed the Commons with huge majorities. Much discussion of schemes for reform or abolition of the hereditary right to a seat in the Upper House followed.

55 *Lord Windlesham*: the Licensing Copy has 'his Lordship' and a pencilled note, 'Can he speak him so? I want to avoid a new name.' She presumably decided he couldn't. Either mode identifies Stonor as the younger brother of a peer.

55–6 *the Carlton*: the leading Conservative Club, located at 94 Pall Mall.

87 *women are much more conservative than men—aren't they?*: Stonor's observations here, as Beerbohm suggests, bring 'a tinge of opportunism' to Stonor's eventual conversion. The rest of this speech, a quasi-soliloquy which develops this line of thinking, is the first of several additions to the published version which sharpen and harden the attitudes of both Stonor and Vida.

104 *isn't there, little girl?*: this patronizing mode of address, markedly inappropriate given the rethinking in which Jean is engaged, concludes the addition to the published version.

216–17 *[as far as Tarsus is from Damascus and seen a sign in the heavens]*: the comparison, which is in the Licensing Copy but not the published version, is with the conversion of Saul of Tarsus, which happened with a blinding light on the road to Damascus (Acts 9: 3–9).

294 *You would be impertinent*: the sentimental idea is undercut by the realistic statement.

330 *Nemesis*: Greek goddess of retribution.

371–2 *sweated girls*: women engaged in sweated labour, i.e. working very long hours for very low pay.

403 *fishes!*: cold-blooded or frigid.

427 *I don't understand you . . . I'm free to say what I think. They aren't*: not in the Licensing Copy.

491–4 *(looking at her from immeasurable distance) I am not sure I understand . . . what I believe is called 'amends'*: in the Licensing Copy, Stoner, much less combatively, says merely, 'I have come to offer you amends'.

531–41 *. . . and the Past are one . . . The eyes of both go to Jean's door*: '. . . and the Past are one. How else would you be here admitting a debt so old? | STONOR "Debt!" "Debt!" Let me tell you it was solely to avoid discussion that I did not contest what you called "my debt" | VIDA What?' (Licensing Copy).

581 *If you had ever known my father—*: struggle between the generations and the oppression of dominant fathers in particular is a recurrent theme of Edwardian New Drama.

627 *No, I am preparing you*: from this point onwards the ending of the published text, which is reproduced here, diverges considerably from that in the Licensing Copy which, much shorter and somewhat sweeter, with its suggestion that Geoffrey's is a whole-hearted conversion, is given in the appendix.

709 *four hundred and twenty others*: the Liberal Members of Parliament, elected in 1906, who then delayed and prevaricated over the introduction of a Suffrage Bill.

The Last of the De Mullins

Title-Page
A Play without a Preface: a teasing tribute to Bernard Shaw, who provided lengthy, argumentative prefaces to his plays. The subtitle for the Licensing Copy is 'A Tragedy of Gentility'.

βέλτωθ ὑγιαίνειν: 'to be healthy is best'. A slight misquotation of the Greek of the archaic poet Theognis (255) who ranks the human attributes, good health being the best of all.

Cast Page
Stage Society: founded in 1899 to give a West End hearing to new plays of merit which commercial managements were unwilling to stage. The actors were mainly professionals who performed without a fee in a West End theatre (in this instance, the Haymarket), hired for one or two matinée or Sunday evening performances. The Stage Society, the Court, and other avant-garde companies had many actors and audience members in common.

Nigel Playfair: a stalwart of Barker's Court company, he also made a mark as Bottom in Barker's production of *A Midsummer Night's Dream* in 1914. He ran the Lyric, Hammersmith from 1918 to 1932 and was knighted in 1928.

Lillah McCarthy: the leading lady in Barker's productions, she gained celebrity playing Ann Whitefield to Barker's Jack Tanner in Shaw's *Man and Superman* (1905) and was a much-praised Viola in Barker's *Twelfth Night* (1912). She married Barker in 1906. A member of the AFL, as manager of the Little Theatre she premièred Shaw's *Fanny's First Play* (1911).

1 S.D. SCENE: a stage plan, a note of the distribution of furniture on the stage, and fuller details of the presumed lay-out of the Manor House are included with the Licensing Copy. The Haymarket set, incorporating a usable space between the back-cloth with its painted garden scene and the back flat with practicable doors and windows (a common device in turn-of-the-century realist theatre), allows characters to be seen coming and going outside the room.

mostly Jacobean or older: 'quaint and spindly legged' (Licensing Copy).

rather unwholesome-looking curate: clergymen in advanced drama are invariably represented as spiritually or physically unprepossessing. From Ibsen's Pastor Manders in *Ghosts* onwards, they give demonstrably unreliable or inappropriate advice.

20–1 *None of the De Mullins are, Aunt Harriet says*: this is an upper-class family in decline, like the protagonist's family in Strindberg's play, *Miss Julie*, and very set in its ways as its reiterated self-references will show.

28 *the time of King Stephen*: the early Middle Ages. Stephen reigned 1135–54, which marks the family as a very ancient one.

34 *about four hundred years. The date is 1603*: Hester gives the year of the accession of James I, *three* hundred years earlier. Since nothing is made of it, the error may be Hankin's not hers.

43 *No De Mullin has ever been in trade of any kind!*: a classic piece of genteel snobbery which prepares the ground for Janet's reception later.

63 *since the repeal of the Corn laws*: i.e. since 1845. The complaint marks De Mullin as a Tory of the old school. The repeal, which removed the protection (the import tax imposed on competitive foreign goods) from English corn production and led to a freeing of English trade generally, although enacted by the Conservative, Sir Robert Peel, had been one of the great nineteenth-century Liberal causes.

66 S.D. *the De Mullin fetish*: the family obsession with its own history and position in society.

Mrs De Mullin . . . nor a genius: Hankin develops with great clarity a number of types that would become increasingly common in the New Drama. Hester's appearance has already revealed her to be a spinster daughter and her reporting of his opinions has suggested that De Mullin is a domineering *pater familias*, but now Mrs De Mullin appears as the crushed wife while her sister-in-law is evidently, like Mrs Heriot in *Votes for Women!*, a middle-class version of the formidable dowager of Society Drama. In the Licensing Copy, Mrs De Mullin is described as 'a stout, rather flabby lady'. The description there of Mrs Clouston as 'stringy, angular' is crossed out and 'more solid' written in—presumably a response to casting McAimée Murray in the role. Dr Rolt is described as a 'blue-eyed man of forty with a clever, pleasant face'.

73 S.D. *shakes hands with both ladies*: Hankin's insistence on the formalities of meeting and parting, early in this Act, suggest the old-fashioned routine of life in the village. Barker achieves a similar effect in the Huxtable household in Act 1 of *The Madras House* (1910).

85 *Harvest Decorations*: the church would be decorated with flowers and produce for the late September Harvest Festival, a service of thanksgiving for the safe gathering-in of the Harvest.

121 *Bridport*: on the Dorset coast between Weymouth and Lyme Regis, presumably the nearest town to the fictional Brendon-Underwood.

171 *all through bicycling*: the safety bicycle, invented in the late 1880s, figures, with latchkeys, messy hair, and smoking, as a prime signifier of female independence. Numerous contemporary works—H. G. Wells, *The*

History of Mr Polly (1910), for example—show it as giving new freedom to working-class men, too.

200 *She got out of the window*: the lightness of treatment of a seemingly serious subject is notable. The audience is offered not an abashed but an admirably spirited woman with whom they are invited to laugh.

206 *the mail*: the mail train for London left Weymouth Town station in the early hours of the morning.

235 *Otherwise she wouldn't go on writing*: Hankin introduces a different kind of female self-determination here, the avoidance tactics of the meek wife who goes her own way in secret. Other New Dramatists—Houghton in *The Younger Generation* (1910), for example—supply their tyrannical male characters with similarly subversive wives, but few have the breathtakingly logical mildness of Mrs De Mullin.

225–47 *Oh no, Harriet . . . Hugo and I never speak of it*: the exchange about the letters is a manuscript addition to the Licensing Copy.

257 *Teaching?*: one of the few openings for a reasonably well-educated girl that a conservative family might think respectable.

272 *Consols*: government stocks (Consolidated Annuities) at a fixed rate of interest which would give security but not a marked profit.

277 *Put it into a Railway*: in a period of free market for railways numerous companies set up. Speculators made good profit from those that flourished and lost their money on those that failed.

332 *Very weak*: although he has indeed been very ill, De Mullin's response shows him to be self-pitying. Like Shaw's, Hankin's 'strong men' tend to behave in an unheroic way in a crisis.

359 *Hugo, it's . . . (Bell rings loudly)*: a shameless use of dramatic coincidence.

362 S.D. *She is admirably dressed*: as with Vida Levering, Janet's dressing well is a rebuttal of the idea that emancipated women are dowdy. A handwritten comment on her clothes in the Licensing Copy reads, 'It is essential that they should be made by a first-rate dressmaker in contrast to those of her mother and sister which are cheap and shabby.'

S.D. *sailor suit*: smart wear for small boys, modelled on the uniform of the able-bodied sailor, its characteristic feature being a wide square collar.

383 S.D. *Hester turns away*: like the jealous sibling in the biblical parable of the Prodigal Son, Hester resents the return of the sinful sister (Luke 15: 11–32).

400 *He's hardly had a day's illness since he was born*: unlike the De Mullins. Like his name, his robust health, reiterating the play's epigraph, suggests he represents a new start.

409–14 *What was he? . . . and to be thankful for*: added in manuscript to the Licensing Copy, replacing the blander 'DE MULLIN It's a great thing to come of good stock. | JOHNNY What's good stock? | DE MULLIN Gentle-people'. The MS addition neatly emphasizes disparity of viewpoint: whereas Johnny asks 'What was he?', a question about occupation, De Mullin would clearly have asked 'Who was he?', a question about lineage.

430–1 *Then they can't . . . can they, grandfather?*: out of the mouths of babes and sucklings . . .

452 *A shop!*: after the manner of Lady Bracknell's 'A handbag!' in Oscar Wilde's *The Importance of Being Earnest*. A profession might be tolerable but not trade.

457–8 *It's a lady's*: she is, then, with characteristic Hankin humour, not a miller but a milliner.

477–8 *I expect you're wise. I doubt if you'd make a success of it*: Janet wins this jousting match and carries the audience with her by virtue of the bland good humour with which she parries each of her aunt's snobbish jibes.

519 *(under her breath) Monty Bulstead! Engaged!*: essentially an aside of a well-made play kind; if the audience missed Janet's start on hearing the name, they would not fail to pick up her use of the familiar form, a clue compar-able with Stonor's knowledge of Miss Levering's first name in Robins's play.

540 *catechism*: a series of questions and answers in the Book of Common Prayer rehearsing the principles of Anglicanism.

580 *Poof!*: a vocal imitation of blowing out a candle or puffing something away, so expressing scorn.

599 *her soup*: Hester, taking the duties of the manor house seriously, dispenses kindly charity to a villager.

2 S.D. SCENE: The built pieces of hedge and fence with their inset stile and gate allow characters to appear as if from some distance. The stage plan included with the Licensing Copy shows a plantation of trees at stage left between the rough wooden seat and the back of the stage. The artificial nature of the supposedly realistic set becomes more evident in outdoor scenes, especially when natural greenery—hedge, grass, and branches—is used.

37 *rather tired*: the first indication of the sapping effect of Brendon on Janet, this is also a convenient device for sending the child off-stage temporarily to enable the meeting of Janet and Monty.

39 S.D. *brown study*: state of mental abstraction.

40 *Monty!*: comic coincidence is a driving force of this play. Despite finding Monty too much of a stereotype, Shaw thought the scene between Monty and Janet 'the best thing Hankin has yet done' (quoted Jan Macdonald, *The 'New Drama'* (1986), 173).

75–6 *ordered all over the place*: in this heyday of British Empire, regiments had frequent and various foreign postings.

104 *mater*: mother (Latin), used in public-schoolboy slang. Monty's general register, peppered as it is with such expressions as 'rather rough', 'awfully sick', 'beastly', contrasts markedly with Janet's maturity of language and outlook.

151 *Regent Street*: the smarter of the two main Central London shopping streets, it bisects the other, Oxford Street.

176 *crêpe*: the black material used for widows' mourning clothes.

205 *India*: the prime colony of the British Empire; one of the most distant as well as most common army postings.

221 *No, thank you*: Hankin continues the trend begun by Robins in *Votes for Women!* of women rejecting a proposal of marriage from men 'bound in honour' to make it.

224 *the Governor*: adolescent slang for father.

226 *most ghastly fuss*: Hankin gives Monty a particularly heavy load of school-boy slang and attitudes in the aftermath of Janet's rejection of his honourable offer, which reinforces the soundness of her refusal although that runs counter to prevalent social morality.

238 *rag*: scold.

241 *subaltern*: a junior army rank, below captain.

254–5 *or at least since the invention of the postal service*: Janet self-corrects her use of the common reference to the Flood in the Book of Genesis to indicate time immemorial, with the more precise and self-deflationary reference to the postal service. It suggests both the precision of her mind and the dry sense of humour which led her to choose 'Mr Seagrave' as the name of her fictional drowned husband.

260 *letters would have been noticed at once*: this information serves the needs of the plot and contributes to the audience's sense of the minor tyrannies of De Mullin but is at variance with the Act 1 revelation that Mrs De Mullin has received Janet's letters unbeknown to her husband for the past eight years.

268 *d—d*: printed thus in both the Licensing and published version to avoid the swear word 'damned' which it signified. It is not marked by the Examiner's blue pencil, but possibly the euphemism 'dashed' was used in performance. The use of the phrase 'Not bloody likely' on stage in *Pygmalion* caused excitement in 1914. 'Damme it's too bad' in W. S. Gilbert's *HMS Pinafore* (1878) is immediately qualified by the chorus's 'Oh, the monster overbearing! | Don't go near him . . . he is swearing!'.

272 *Hanover Street*: running off Regent Street, a street of very smart clothes shops.

273 *Cie*: an abbreviation for Company.

274 *A French shop?*: All things French being considered *risqué* as well as

glamorous, country people would fear the one, city sophisticates value the other. This is explored further in Barker's *The Madras House* with its parade of French mannequins and its mocking discussion of selling garments designed for French courtesans to the respectable wives of wealthy Englishmen.

298 *dun*: press for repayment of debt.

312 *distrain*: seize goods to the value of the debt.

321–2 *My shares had gone up*: which vindicates her having taken responsibility for her own investments.

341–2 *South Kensington and Bayswater*: newly developing areas for the up-and-coming and newly rich, west and north-west of the smarter St James's, Mayfair, and Belgravia addresses.

346 *four times a year*: 'every year' (Licensing Copy).

378 S.D. *rallying*: teasing.

507 *late for dressing*: in many upper-class households the family would change into formal dress for the evening meal, dinner.

512 *Done. In sixpences*: Bertha's jolly acceptance of the bet and her general mode of expression show her to be a considerably more appropriate partner for Monty than Janet would be. There were forty sixpences, small silver coins, to the pound.

514–15 *On account of father*: Janet, honourable as well as emancipated, is conscious of the impropriety of socializing under false colours with her ex-lover's family or fiancée.

640 *to recruit*: to convalesce.

688–9 *it will have to be a rather more remarkable person than Monty Bulstead*: a sentiment echoed by Houghton's heroine in *Hindle Wakes* (1912): 'the chap Fanny Hawthorn weds has got to be made of different stuff from you, my lad'.

700 *Did he? I was twenty-seven*: the emancipated women in all the plays in this volume are older than their lovers—perhaps a remaining link with the dangerous courtesan of French melodrama. In Sowerby's *Rutherford and Son* (1912), too, the master's daughter says of the man, 'I went after him'.

706 *It's not her fault*: the betrayed women of New Drama, from Vida Levering to Fanny Hawthorn, are invariably protective of their innocent successors.

3.36 *The Athanasian Creed*: one of the three creeds, with the Apostles' and the Nicene, of the Christian church, it states the doctrine of the Trinity and the Incarnation.

37–8 *three Incomprehensibles*: the name given in the Athanasian Creed to that which cannot be known or contained within limits, namely, 'the Father incomprehensible, the Son incomprehensible and the Holy Ghost incomprehensible'.

67–89 *In the garden, I think . . . I wonder if Janet would*: these lines expand the exchange in the Licensing Copy which runs: 'MRS DE M. Playing in the garden, Hugo. | DE M. Is Janet with him? | MRS DE M. Yes. | DE M. Yes, it's pleasant to have children about one. It makes one feel young again. It doesn't do to get old before one's time, does it? | MRS DE M. No. | DE M. I wonder if Janet would . . .'. The expanded version introduces Mrs De Mullin's steady lie to her husband concerning her knowledge of Johnny's father. Throughout the scene, Mrs De Mullin accurately predicts her daughter's responses.

205–6 *I owe no one obedience*: Janet's fiery speech voices the main concern of the feminist movement: the assumption of responsibility for herself and her own affairs.

246 *I never had a son*: her use of 'I' rather than 'we' shows Mrs De Mullin accepting the belief that the gender of the child was the woman's responsibility.

260 *the audacity to propose to my daughter!*: his offence is being lower in the social order. De Mullin prefers that Hester stay single rather than shame him by marrying out of her class.

298 *Agatha Bulstead?*: since the Bulsteads are very rich, they can marry into the Aldenhams, who must be of higher class, since Janet was allowed to teach their daughters; but, since Bulstead's money comes, presumably, from trade or speculation, he would be unlikely to share De Mullin's objection to a curate as husband for one of his ten children.

378 *put in the pony*: i.e. into the trap for the drive to the station.

473 *buy Mr Brown a living*: until 1924 church livings—benefices or parishes—were transferable by gift or purchase.

487–8 *I wanted to have a child*: Janet speaks an updated version of what it is to be a real woman; impelled not by social but by biological laws.

521–3 *The last of the De Mullins!*: Hankin ends his play in a markedly nineteenth-century way, with a curtain line that repeats the title and an expressive tableau.

JANE AUSTEN	**Catharine and Other Writings**
	Emma
	Mansfield Park
	Northanger Abbey, Lady Susan, The Watsons, and Sanditon
	Persuasion
	Pride and Prejudice
	Sense and Sensibility
ANNE BRONTË	**Agnes Grey**
	The Tenant of Wildfell Hall
CHARLOTTE BRONTË	**Jane Eyre**
	The Professor
	Shirley
	Villette
EMILY BRONTË	**Wuthering Heights**
WILKIE COLLINS	**The Moonstone**
	No Name
	The Woman in White
CHARLES DARWIN	**The Origin of Species**
CHARLES DICKENS	**The Adventures of Oliver Twist**
	Bleak House
	David Copperfield
	Great Expectations
	Hard Times
	Little Dorrit
	Martin Chuzzlewit
	Nicholas Nickleby
	The Old Curiosity Shop
	Our Mutual Friend
	The Pickwick Papers
	A Tale of Two Cities

SHERWOOD ANDERSON	Winesburg, Ohio
WILLA CATHER	Alexander's Bridge
JAMES FENIMORE COOPER	The Last of the Mohicans
STEPHEN CRANE	The Red Badge of Courage
THEODORE DREISER	Sister Carrie
F. SCOTT FITZGERALD	The Great Gatsby The Beautiful and Damned
BENJAMIN FRANKLIN	Autobiography and Other Writings
CHARLOTTE PERKINS GILMAN	The Yellow Wall-Paper and Other Stories
BRET HARTE	Selected Stories and Sketches
NATHANIEL HAWTHORNE	The Scarlet Letter
HENRY JAMES	The Portrait of a Lady
JACK LONDON	The Call of the Wild White Fang and Other Stories
HERMAN MELVILLE	The Confidence-Man Moby-Dick
EDGAR ALLAN POE	Selected Tales
HARRIET BEECHER STOWE	Uncle Tom's Cabin
HENRY DAVID THOREAU	Walden
MARK TWAIN	The Adventures of Tom Sawyer
LEW WALLACE	Ben-Hur
EDITH WHARTON	Ethan Frome
WALT WHITMAN	Leaves of Grass
OWEN WISTER	The Virginian

American Literature

British and Irish Literature

Children's Literature

Classics and Ancient Literature

Colonial Literature

Eastern Literature

European Literature

History

Medieval Literature

Oxford English Drama

Poetry

Philosophy

Politics

Religion

The Oxford Shakespeare